LAWMEN,
OUTLAWS,
AND
S.O.Bs.

GUNFIGHTERS
OF THE OLD SOUTHWEST

LAWMEN,

OUTLAWS,

AND

S.O.Bs.

GUNFIGHTERS
OF THE OLD SOUTHWEST

BY BOB ALEXANDER

WITH AN INTRODUCTION BY CHUCK PARSONS

HIGH-LONESOME BOOKS
SILVER CITY, NEW MEXICO

ISBN #0-944383-66-1   softcover
ISBN #0-944383-65-3   hardcover

Library of Congress control Number 2004100801

First Edition May 2004
Hardcover Edition Limited to 400 copies

Front Cover: William D. "Keechi" Johnson, Grant County, New Mexico Territory, deputy sheriff and noted man-tracker. Courtesy, Roy B. Sinclair.

Back Cover: Renowned Texas/Mexican border lawman, Joe Sitter (left) and unknown cohort, hamming it up for an Old West photographer. The letter "s" at the end of the Sitter family name is an appellation of subsequent generations. Courtesy, Jake Sitters.

High-Lonesome Books
P.O. Box 878
Silver City, New Mexico 88062

TABLE OF CONTENTS

INTRODUCTION

Some say the "Western" is dead. The same will add that since the Western is dead there is no need to try and breathe life back into it because of a minimal importance in the overall picture of U.S. history. During the 1950s television screens featured numerous Western programs, some of real artistic value, many solely produced for entertaining the masses. Those who believe the Western is dead see no need expending energy bringing it back to what it once was. But others have differing views, and see studying the lives of Western personalities—the good and the bad, the famous and the forgotten—as worth the effort. It is not only important to preserve the record of lives of these men and women, but in presenting their stories to the public of today important moral lessons may be learned.

Those who read book introductions are familiar with such classics as Stuart N. Lake's writings on Wyatt Earp, Walter Noble Burn's *Saga of Billy the Kid*, or William E. Connelly's work on Quantrill and the bloody Border Wars. In their time these biographies were accepted as worthy histories, and they still rightfully deserve places in our libraries. But there has been a change in recent years, and thankfully so. For a special group of historians of the Old West accuracy matters most of all. The made-up conversation is no longer acceptable, in spite of the exciting atmosphere it may add to the narrative. "Artistic creativity" is also not acceptable. If something cannot be documented then, for the purposes of these writers, it simply didn't happen. These select few historians are focused on getting the facts, to determine what actually happened, without embellishment or fictionalized creativity. To do so they are going to the original records, wherever they may be, finding descendants and discovering new material. They read miles of microfilm, get their hands dusty in courthouses examining old documents which may crumble if not handled very carefully. Some have much better luck than others of course. Contemporary documents are vital, and sins of omission are as unacceptable as sins of commission among this elite group of Old West historians. Robert K. DeArment, Leon C. Metz, Joseph G. Rosa, and Frederick

Lawmen, Outlaws and S.O.Bs.

Nolan are among the leading examples of this new Old West historian. And now comes Bob Alexander.

Alexander has authored several biographies prior to this collection of brief studies of violent men. His first biography was *Dangerous Dan Tucker* of New Mexico (2001); this was followed by *John H. Behan: Sacrificed Sheriff* (2002), the first full-length objective biography of the "Johnny" Behan of Tombstone and elsewhere. In general John Behan is known thanks to such minor Hollywood masterpieces as Kurt Russell's *Tombstone* and Kevin Costner's *Wyatt Earp*. Then came Alexander's third book spotlighting another frontier lawman, the biography *Fearless Dave Allison* (2003). Tucker and Allison have yet to make the silver screen, either large or small. They remain among the many lesser known men who also played a part in building the West. Profiled in this volume are several additional Old West lawmen—and the others—those that forcefully slowed down the progress of establishing law and order.

Bob Alexander represents those authors, historians and researchers who are no longer satisfied with delving into the lives of the few personalities whose names are known the world over, their stories told time after time. Quite to the contrary. These authors are now digging deeply into lives of the *contemporaries* of Wild Bill, Wyatt Earp and Billy the Kid. They know full well that there is little need for yet another biography of Earp or Hickok or Jesse James. Those stalwarts were not alone in the developing West, and the many others who led equally exciting lives, who experienced equally deep tragedies and painful hurts, who agonized over lost loves and the too-early deaths of friends and family members are equally as valid.

The traditional Western shootists are still topics of research, but as well, others whose names are unknown are of intense interest, too. And some have a story more remarkable than those whose names are better known. Their stories need telling and are now being told, thanks to such writers as Bob Alexander.

This gathering of *Lawmen, Outlaws, and S. O. Bs.* represents fifteen violent characters who lived and fought on a wild frontier, who today are virtually unknown by all except the most astute Western historians, yet whose stories are just as compelling. As effective as the work of John B. Jones was in mastering command of the Frontier Battalion, Captain Frank Jones (no relation) and Joe Sitter provided valuable service in running down and shooting it out with train robbers who hit the westbound Galveston, Harrisburg and San Antonio Railroad during September 1891.

Introduction

Dan Coomer, a southwestern New Mexico rancher and designated as a "cow-thief's nightmare," refused to be pacified by Sheriff Harvey Whitehill's recommendation to just forget about his cattle being stolen. Instead he gathered up a prominent black rancher and together the amateur manhunters set out in pursuit. Coomer was certainly aware of the racial prejudice of the day, but that didn't matter for this manhunter; he needed with him a good man to track down the cattle thieves, and color was of no consequence. And they caught up with the rustlers, both of them, and "settled their hash" in the most approved Old West manner, killing them when they resisted Coomer's demand of "Hands Up!"

On the other side of the aisle of conscientious lawmen was Jimmy McDaniels. He played numerous roles, at times a manhunter, a *compadre* of rustler king John Kinney, a Texas Ranger during the fill-fated El Paso Salt war experience, and a member of the team battling the Tunstall/McSween faction during the Lincoln County War. McDaniel's origins have been obscure—up until now—but the intense research of Bob Alexander shows Nashville, Tennessee was where he first saw the light of day, sometime during 1852. By the early 1870s he was a cowboy working for cattleman John Chisum. Within a few years he was raiding Apache horse herds. His "moral code" did not prevent him and several companions from shooting through windows into a crowded dance hall to avenge a real or imagined insult. Violence came easier and easier to him, yet his demise is uncertain. Historian Alexander hopes that his efforts will inspire others to continue researching this dangerous figure.

McDaniels is not unique. Many Old West hardcases, those who gave great amounts of grief to sheriffs, constables, amateur manhunters and professional detectives, not to mention Texas Rangers, served periodically as lawmen—McDaniels swore an oath to serve the state of Texas "honestly and faithfully." To this historian, that is one thing which makes these characters so fascinating; that they could easily step across the line from lawlessness to join the group which enforced the law. And then perhaps become outlaws once again.

Jones, Coomer, McDaniels—these are but three of the tough characters whose lives are drawn across the pages of this work. Another dozen complete the study of late 19th century, and early 20th century, violence in the American Southwest. Some were characterized by worthy qualities, qualities we all admire and try to emulate. Others were inherently evil, with no discernible positive worth. These were the men who made up the Old West, at least who left enough of a paper trial for later historians to follow. Their

Lawmen, Outlaws and S.O.Bs.

stories are here told in detail, each chapter focusing on a significant incident in their lives, but also rounding out the man with background information, much of it—most of it— brand new.

Chuck Parsons, Editor
National Outlaw/Lawman History Association [NOLA] *Quarterly*

PREFACE AND ACKNOWLEDGMENTS

Many aficionados of Old West nonfiction literature may to some extent be familiar with a sampling of the names biographically sketched herein. Others will not be. Chances are, even ardent adherents of the topic will not be acquainted with *all* of the characters profiled. Optimistically two strangers may therefore be introduced, one evocatively looking backwards in time, the other stepping from the blameless abyss of historic anonymity. Unquestionably, there has been a lamentable overshadowing of the bona fide exploits of innumerable legitimate law enforcers, several downright despicable desperadoes, and a smattering of the early day ne'er-do-wells who could plainly be labeled as, well, just sons-of-bitches. That their breathtaking stories are true is indisputable; they are documented herein. The fact they have been shabbily neglected is unarguable. Payment of their just debt—recognition—is long in arrears. This then is an effort to, in a small way, rectify the shortfall and authenticate the sagas of several scoundrels and stalwarts.

The individual reader is tasked with giving his/her own weight to the actual historical significance of a particular story and passing their own brand of judgment, scoring so to speak, as to the real relevance of cited material. In the past, there has been a tendency for many scholars with hard-earned academic credentials to look down their collective noses at the worth of analyzing and retelling stories about drunken barroom brawls and scorching Western shoot-outs. And, in some cases, rightly so! As illustration, the nineteenth-century tragedy detonating near the O. K. Corral in the rip-roaring mining metropolis of Tombstone, Arizona Territory, has sometimes been dubbed America's classic gunfight, an assertion hotly debated today but, in actuality at the time, an untidiness that raised not too many eyebrows and was given short-shift and scant notice by a nationwide readership more engrossed in practical matters, earning a living and taking advantage of speedily encroaching technology. The gunplay happened, that is truthful. In the broadest gamut of historic overview, however, the deaths of three comparatively unknown cowboys and the subsequent flight of dubious feudists fearfully assuming false identities and under the shrewd blanket of duplicity and deception fleeing the territory ahead of lawfully drawn murder warrants is a damn good story, but inconsequential in the bigger picture. Twentieth-century efforts to dramatize the wastefully foolish scenario and then pirate the proceeds no doubt gave diligent and painstaking historians cause for heartburn. As righteous result, many educators began to look askew at Old West narratives revolving around a hub of lawmen and outlaws, and their shared penchant for violence. Certainly an accomplished professor could appropriately focus on much more expansive topics, answering philosophical questions of greater weightiness regarding the opening and development of America's western frontiers.

So the good writers wrote their novels, corralling rapt readers, informing them how life in the Wild West really was—or should have been. Others improvised, laminating their work with allusions to factuality, as long as it interdicted not with their agenda, manufacturing a hero. Competent penmen composed, adroit authors scribbled and scrawled and, sorrowfully, conspiracy theorists conspired. Tall frontier tales were the oysters to be gobbled up, choked down if necessary—and they were. Implausible and incredible stories were not the repast palatable to everyone though, and a new breed of writer chimed in with his two-cents worth; the grass-roots historian. Digging and burrowing amongst long forgotten courthouse records, interviewing willing old-timers, unearthing lost letters and daily journals, diligently unraveling the misnomers and misinformation inflicted on a whole generation, the grass-root researchers gradually began to make their mark. Usually, in the end, common sense and reasonableness triumphs. Over the last fifty years or so truthfulness is, although somewhat tardy, washing away a muddle of the falsehoods inadvertently or intentionally dealt upon the reading public.

Puzzlement as to whether or not there is twenty-first century appeal attached to Old West shootists is not fuzzy. The allure is authentic. Disappointedly though, there seems to have been a gratuitous overemphasis on righting the wrongs written about the Earps, or Wild Bill, or Billy the Kid, or in just which America Butch and Sundance took their fateful last gasp. The draw toward the more recognized Western personalities, the household names, has unfortunately depreciated writings about other persons equally as thrilling. With a bit of luck the reader of these legit Outlaw/Lawman stories and the no-nonsense realities they faced, will be awarded

Preface and Acknowledgments

fresh glimpses at characters they have heretofore overlooked. Perhaps there is a lesson about dogged determination to be learned from William D. "Keechi" Johnson as he tracks and trails reckless fugitives deep into Old Mexico or, later, into the mysterious and secret fastness of the Mogollons; or perchance the student of a fledgling frontier Criminal Justice System will wonder in amazement, examining the courtroom trials and scary tribulations of an authentic mankiller and thoroughly audacious Texas lawman, Horace Lorenzo Roberson; possibly readers for the very first time will ponder just how they missed hearing about the life and death of a real Southwest desperado, the wicked character Arizona, New Mexico, and Texas lawmen, as well as history, simply knew as Charley Small; maybe with regret a reviewer of these yarns will bemoan the fact he never figuratively shook hands with a bold babyfaced borderliner, Herff A. Carnes; or maybe the armchair buff will stand in awe before Jimmy McDaniels, a Lincoln County *mal hombre* who would cut you or shoot you—your choice; hopefully even the most serious student of borderland murder and mayhem will be able to uncover a new fact or two regarding that ever formidable river rider, Joe Sitter; and if all goes right, the researcher thumbing these pages will gather untapped material about the other nine resolute officers or odious owl-hoots.

There is no design to hoodwink the reader. Taken separately the intrepid actions of any early day law enforcers, in the much broader scheme of frontier development played but small and seemingly insignificant roles. Emphatically, when balanced against much larger historic topics, such as subjection of America's Indian population, railroad expansionism, widespread proliferation of an organized labor movement, the exploitation of mineral and other natural and animal resources, or an explosive extension of a viable coast to coast communications network, the solitary shooting down of individual badge wearers or good-for-nothings is pallid in comparison. Make no mistake though—when assessed in the aggregate the steadfast contributions of frontier peace keepers are worthy of especial commendation and consideration. For then, just as today, there were men who were good all of the time, men who were good part of the time, and men who were good none of the time. A few sported tin-stars, others robbed banks and trains and things. Some did both! Overall though, most frontier lawmen were hard-working and honest, playing well their assigned parts, furnishing a stabilizing presence to their jurisdictional sphere and, in turn, in the cumulative, to the whole American West.

Lawmen, Outlaws and S.O.Bs.

Reportedly John Wesley Hardin, the notorious Texas mankiller, remarked that "every tub should rest on its own bottom," conjecturing that a man's man must stand alone, unsupported, answering for his own missteps and foul-ups. Much the same approach has been taken in writing this volume, an assemblage of fifteen Old West stories highlighting the careers of policemen and prisoners, each story resting on its very own foundation, totally independent from the preceding or succeeding chapter. Admittedly there is a degree of understandable overlap, as the characters in one scenario may make a sketchy appearance in another. After all, each were traipsing about in the American Southwest and there was a common denominator for their tales—trouble! But for the most part, the reader may skip around freely and haphazardly, reading a chapter out of numerical order and not finding himself/herself critically handicapped. The journalistic thrust was to produce a readable volume for casual enjoyment, yet, truthful and respectably researched with precise attention to comprehensive endnotes. The secondary aim, as uncomplicated logic suggests, allows interested readers bibliographic knowledge to further their own inquires into matters of particular curiosity. There are yet still hundreds, perhaps thousands of compelling Outlaw/Lawman stories in want of telling.

Working within the framework that the bibliography and the chapter endnotes are reasonably wide-ranging, it is in that format that an individual's name is with specificity mentioned. The thorny part of penning acknowledgments is not then the act of surrendering a heartfelt "thank you," but the phantom of a creeping fear of forgetfulness, a gloomy failure to be all-inclusive. Should it have inadvertently and unjustifiably happened no excuse is sufficient, but the most humble forgiveness is sought.

Another category of contributors must be recognized, the nonprofessionals. Fortunate, indeed, for this journalistic try at recapturing a tad of legitimate Outlaw/Lawman history was the author's receipt of first-hand biographical data and delightful photographs affably furnished by actual descendants and relatives by marriage of certain frontier personalities silhouetted herein. The congenial conversations and pleasant face-to-face visits are truly treasures to be cherished. They too are listed, by name, in source citations.

Genuine thanks must be also extended to the widely and favorably well-known Old West historian Chuck Parsons of Luling, Texas. He is one of the genuine icons making up the subspecies commonly dubbed Outlaw/Lawmen history experts. Esteemed is his personal friendship, appreciated is his advice, valued is his

Preface and Acknowledgments

encouragement. And in particular, for this volume a special thanks is in order. Amiably, as Editor for the National Association For Outlaw And Lawman History, Inc., *Quarterly*, Chuck has granted permission for the reprinting of three articles that over time have graced the pages of his prestigious periodical. He too is of the mulish notion that several early day Outlaws/Lawmen have been needlessly overlooked, overshadowed, and their exciting life's stories underreported and undervalued. He is committed to correcting the deficit.

An especially warm thank you must be dished out to Jan Devereaux of Waxahachie, Texas. A fine writer in her own right, but in this instance Jan gladly subverted her self-interests and journalistic projects to make room for conspicuous contributions to this collection of Old West gunfighter stories. Not only were her suggestions unassailable, but so too were her perceptions pertaining to weaknesses in need of fixin' and segments suffering simple clarity deficiencies. Jan's sounding board attributes are exemplary. Supplementing her input regarding the actual writing was her steadfast support while gathering research data. Jan made much of the process not a cumbersome chore, but a productive pleasure. Her analytical skills complemented by intrinsic intuitiveness and inquisitiveness profited not only the concept but the finished work.

CHAPTER 1

"CIGAR STUMPS AND PEACH PEELS"

Captain Frank Jones and Texas Train Robbers

In that faraway West of the Pecos country, during March 1885, Val Verde County, Texas, was surveyed and by May had been officially organized, with Del Rio as county seat.[1] The western face of Val Verde County was Roy Bean country, that waggish scalawag Justice of the Peace who had taken up residence at Langtry, and then set to work administering his peculiar brand of much publicized justice. His escapades are legendary and, no doubt, some are even true.[2] Aside from Roy Bean, the landscape was habitat for rattlesnakes and rocks. Naturally there was a smattering of honest people, just not too many, law abiding or otherwise. It is inhospitable and stingy looking country. Haphazardly crafted, so it seems, for just passing through. Geography not meant for residing, but for resting, while on a trip to or coming back from—somewhere. Cutting through the broken, hilly and brushy country, and spanning the Devils and Pecos rivers were iron rails connecting east with west, west with east. The Galveston, Harrisburg and San Antonio Railroad tracks, later more commonly known as the Southern Pacific, marked the thoroughfare.[3] The last Val Verde County stop, heading west, was Pumpville. Earlier, before the 1887 drilling of a much needed water-well, the beguilingly lonesome and desolate wide spot was simply called Samuel's Siding, a designation not readily relinquished by old-timers or brainy newspapermen.[4]

During wee morning hours of Wednesday, September 2, 1891, around 4 o'clock, masked badmen robbed the westbound G. H. & S. A., Number 20, approximately a mile east of Samuels, at Horseshoe Bend.[5] Forced to apply air breaks, rather than collide with obstructions purposefully placed on the tracks, the train's engineer effectively brought the locomotive to a stop. A horrendous train

10

Cigar Stumps and Peach Peels

wreck was thwarted; the nefarious crime was not. Facing menacing Winchesters poked in their ribs, the engineer and fireman were marched back to the passenger coach. At the express car, J. Ernest Smith, Wells, Fargo and Company messenger, knowing something was awry, smartly and quickly "barred his doors."[6] J.E. Smith was not a man to discount flippantly. On October 14, 1887, four years earlier during an aborted holdup of a G. H. & S. A. train, the intrepid express messenger had killed Jack Smith and Dick Myers while they had foolishly attempted an act of railroad piracy.[7] This time, however, the wicked strategy was dynamic entry. Smith elaborates:

> My idea was to watch and get a dead shot at them, but they were no novices and remained down under the side of my car, and I'm glad now I did not get a shot for there was a regular army of them. Only six showed up, but others could be heard talking in the bushes. I was ordered to come out, but refused and heard the captain of the gang give orders to shoot into my car, and immediately they proceeded to pump lead in to my apartments. I started across the car to get behind my safe. The captain called to me: "Open up and come out of there or I will blow the blamed car up."[8]

Messenger Smith demurred from giving way, but did detect ominous and tell-tell sounds emanating from the other side of an express car's heavy and sturdily blockaded door—striking matches. Shortly thereafter he was "thrown off his feet" by an exploding charge of red-wrapped dynamite. After reassurance that he would not be summarily shot if he capitulated and granted access to the bandits, Smith reluctantly "opened the door and jumped out," and a robber relieved him of his six-shooter.[9] Staring into the foreboding depths of Winchesters' muzzles, Smith was compelled to open a company safe for the brigands and, too, they rifled the United States' canvas mail bags, a federal offense. Specifically remarking he was only attacking "corporations," the gang's leader ordered his coconspirators not to molest the property of trainmen or passengers, a move that everlastingly endeared him as a "jolly good fellow."[10] Such a nice outlaw was he, the proffer to share drinks was extended: "We will treat you boys, the first time we catch you in San Antonio."[11] Gathering up their rich plunder, $3600, the outlaws walked the terrified train crew about 100 yards from the railroad tracks and then bade them "a courteous good night and disappeared."[12] J.E. Smith was not amused. His reputation as the "Fighting Express Messenger" was sullied, at least in his own mind, and in disgust he pondered offering his resignation.[13]

Lawmen, Outlaws and S.O.Bs.

Immediately a reward amounting to $1,750 a head, dead or alive, was posted. For robbing the U.S. Mails, the federal government chipped in $1000 per hijacker; Wells, Fargo & Co. sweetened the kitty with $500 for each crook caught or killed; and the railroad kicked in $250 apiece for corralling and convicting the holdup artists.[14]

Company D, Texas Rangers. Seated, Captain Frank Jones. Standing, left to right, Ira Aten, Frank Schmid, Charles Fusselman, Ira Barton, John W. "Wood" Saunders, John R. Hughes, J. Walter Durbin, Baz Lamar Outlaw, Charles Barton, Ernest Rogers, and Gerry Jones. Courtesy, Old West historian and editor for the National Outlaw and Lawman History Association, Quarterly, *Chuck Parsons.*

Not surprisingly, straight away after the alarm had been sounded, posses took to the field. At Del Rio a squadron of about eight or ten men, under command of the Val Verde County Sheriff, August Kieffer, loaded their "horses and accouterments" on a westbound train and started for the scene.[15] At Alpine, Texas, Captain Frank Jones, Company D, Frontier Battalion (Texas Rangers), accompanied by five other rangers, departed on a "special car" eastbound and primed for an exhilarating chase after explosively charged robbers. By four o'clock in the afternoon, the rangers were on the ground and cutting for fresh and meaningful sign.[16] At Horseshoe Bend, the two law enforcement platoons merged into one unit, heading for the Rio Grande, hot on the trail, finding some "cigar stumps and peach peels" as they tracked.[17] At the river's soggy edge and with light fast fading, the dogged lawmen halted, "tying up their horses without any grass" and camped.[18] In the soft sand, after daybreak, readable tracks were revealed; five horses "shod all round," crossing into Mexico. International diplomacy be damned! The outlaws were trailed south, across the border, and then after an abrupt turn to the north, back across the muddy current, once more on Lone Star soil. It was cat and mouse, catch as catch can. Like furtive Apace raiders the pursued maneuvered back and forth across the river, splitting up, only to reunite temporarily and then kick off their tactics again, and again. Although unable to close with the elusive enemy, Frank Jones' haggard posse was unshakable. Investigation at one of the train robbers' camps disclosed they had "burned quite a lot of paper, as the ashes showed, and unshod their horses."[19] On the fifth day, the fugitives nailed horseshoes back on cracked and chipped hooves, and proceeded to camp in a dense canebrake. During day six, gaunt law dogs surrounded the outlaws' lair which was characterized as "too dense, and besides was very dangerous."[20] Texas Rangers, as Captain Frank Jones reveals, had a game plan of their own:

> I then surrounded the brake as well as I could and set fire to it in several places and closed in as it burned. We then located the camp and closed in on it but the men had mounted fresh horses and fled. I found a camp that has evidently been there for several months with quite a lot of plunder. There was 3 extra saddles in this camp of men who must have been murdered. This was the camp of a man named John Flynt who has some stock on this side of the river. The only way for the Mexican authorities to get at his camp would have been to cross to this side. We found a great many stolen cattle there and letters that prove they were regular in the business. After leaving their camp I trailed them to this side and then back into Mexico at a point a few miles higher up the river where they left their horses and again went into the cane. I spent 3 days beating and burning out the brakes on both sides but failed to ever catch them. Three of them are well known in this section. There is no Mexican settlements anywhere in that region and Flynt has murdered several on the other side and they don't dare come near him. If we had not found the robber camp we would have been without rations for several days. I demolished their roost entirely, and am satisfied hunger will drive them from the River...[21]

Supposing there could very well be "international trouble" spinning forth from incursions into Mexico, and because his horses were "completely broken down," Captain Jones, for the time being abandoned the chase.[22] Justifiably, Frank Jones, in his leadership position, could ill afford to personally stay in the field day after day. The search for the wily wrongdoers, however, was not forsaken. Company D Sergeant Bazzel Lamar "Baz" Outlaw led a ranger detachment on a nine day scout after the train robbers, covering an exhaustive 275 miles through what then were designated as Foley and Buchel counties, but since (1897) were dissolved, and legally adopted by West Texas' gargantuan Brewster County. Sergeant Outlaw "failed to find any trace of the train robbers" and returned to camp.[23]

Renowned Texas/Mexican border lawman, Joe Sitter and unknown cohort, hamming it up for an Old West photographer. The letter "s" at the end of the Sitter family name is an appellation of subsequent generations. Courtesy, Jake Sitters.

Limited, indeed, are the writings about this jaunt after the Samuel's Siding train robbers, and by most secondary renditions a redoubtable border country denizen is cast in the leading role of tracking desperadoes to their hideout in the impenetrable canebrakes. Joe Sitter was his name but, up until this point in the neat story, his actual participation is lacking, evidenced by his own words. After the posses had joined at Horseshoe Bend, Joe Sitter ambled into Comstock and was appraised of the train robbery by merchant George W. Ames, who added that there had been a reward posted for the thugs capture. Joe Sitter replied, "I laughed at him and said I'll get some of that" but, "I said this as a joke..."[24] And, clearly indicating he was not playing in the opening act chase after hard-sought fugitives was his remark, "The *pursuers* (emphasis added) lost the track and finally abandoned the chase altogether and returned home—the Sheriff, the posse and the Rangers."[25]

The sometimes irascible and pugnacious Judge Roy Bean at his Langtry, Texas headquarters. He, and others, chased after the Samuel's Siding train robbers, but turned back after Texas Rangers cut the owl-hoots trail near the Rio Grande River. Courtesy, Robert G. McCubbin.

Summoned as a witness in a "horse-stealing" case against Frank Haverley, about a month after the robbery, and carrying a deputy sheriff's commission, Joe Sitter managed a trip to Del Rio.[26] While in attendance at court, Sitter was approached by Ben Bendele who passed on hearsay intelligence garnered from his younger brother Joe that heavily armed men had gone into camp near Blue Hill, northwest of Del Rio. A few days later, as Sitter was told, these same men had made an impulsive appearance at Henry Stein's store at Juno, almost due north of Del Rio, and "bought clothing, undershirts and slickers." The items were paid for with $20 gold pieces "that looked like they had been in the fire." Joe Sitter, a savvy *hombre*, shrewdly deduced the quartet were the much sought after train robbers. Receiving permission from Judge Winchester Kelso to absent himself from the District Court proceedings, Joe Sitter departed by train for Comstock, the railhead nearest Juno, and by coincidence where he had parked his horse when boarding the train that had delivered him to Del Rio.[27]

Early the next day Joe Sitter looked up fifteen year-old Joe Bendele, and persuaded or ordered the boy to pilot him to the suspected train robbers' campsite, about fifteen miles west of Juno. Finding where the fugitives had butchered a calf and discarded their old clothes, Joe Sitter was, at last, thoroughly convinced he was trailing the right party. The lawman and the apprentice pressed on another fifteen miles or so, to Johnson's Run, where they noticed "fresh tracks of horses where the robbers had them hobbled." The inexperienced Joe Bendele not unwisely proposed, "Come on, let's go, and not run into them; they're camped here nearby." Joe Sitter consented to common sense, and they returned to Juno hopeful of enlisting reinforcements. There were none. Joe Bendele went home. Alone, Joe Sitter hightailed it for Comstock, and help.[28]

Upon arrival in town he wired the United States Marshal's Office at San Antonio, but got no response. He then frantically telegraphed Texas Ranger Captain Frank Jones at El Paso, who answered promptly, reassuringly promising to join Joe Sitter in double quick time with the crucial manpower. Reassured, but knowing reinforcements were still at least a day or two away, Joe Sitter demonstrated the type mettle he was made of. Paying strict attention to business, Joe Sitter mounted his horse and headed back to Juno to "look after my game," having left word for the rangers as to how his whereabouts could be ascertained, through another Bendele brother, Frank. Not daring to wait too long for the ranger contingent, and let his prey get away, Joe Sitter enlisted the help of Bob Stockman and the angst-ridden teenager Joe Bendele. Their plan was simple. At some point, during some time, stakeout the outlaws' horses, and then when they came to look after them, probably one at a time, make an arrest and then wait till the next one showed himself. The two grown men each had a rifle and a six-shooter, the boy, just a pistol.[29]

Again, triumphant with his trailing, the tenacious Joe Sitter found an abandoned camp, discovering the guts and hide of another slaughtered beef, and even the forked sticks used in broiling bloody meat over white-hot coals. Traveling north, the pursuit took the trio of man-hunters toward a celebrated landmark, Howard's Well, near old Fort Lancaster in Crockett County. Close at hand was "a big sheep ranch" where they found "Mr. Estelle, who was boss of the ranch, in the midst of his shearing." Estelle, upon learning Sitter's business in the area, proposed that he loan the lawman ten "Mexican sheep shearers" to help run the odious train thieves to ground. While scouting, making preparations for an all out assault on the morrow, Sitter determined the quarry had vamoosed from the vicinity of Howard's Well, headed toward the Pecos River. Next day, Captain Frank Jones and five rangers arrived at the sheep-shearing station. Mr. Estelle withdrew his offer of reinforcements, commenting there were now enough bona fide lawmen to handle the pursuit.[30]

Texas Ranger Joe Sitter on a "scout" in the Texas Big Bend country. Note camp meat in the foreground and his well-known spotted pack animal in the background. Courtesy, Jake Sitters.

Joe Sitter's small force and the Texas Rangers set forth. Sitter narrates, "We then took up to follow the trail to where they camped after leaving Howard's Well, about ten miles distant, where they had nooned. About ten miles further on they had camped for the night… From there we trailed them over to **77** Ranch on the head of Live Oak creek."[31]

The sign was fresh, horseshoe dints undisturbed, manure moist and soft. Surely, the outlaws were taking a break, refreshing themselves within comforting confines at the out-of-the-way ranch house. The place was surrounded. Frank Jones and his nephew, Gus Jones, entered the house. Inside, the only person was Mrs. Roy, wife of the ranch owner, sleeping in her bed. Awakening to strangers in her bedroom was terrifying, "scaring her very badly," so much so, "she could hardly talk."[32] Sympathetically she was soothed into telling a story. Four men, badly in need of fresh mounts had been there, just four hours before. A youthful **77** Ranch cowboy had horses for sale, and at the very moment was negotiating a trade at "the next pasture."[33] The hunt was pressed.

After a grueling eight mile ride, the posse halted for a dinner (lunch) break and to rest fatigued and footsore horses. It was noontime, October 16, 1891. During the unpacking of foodstuffs and the loosening of cinches, a rider "hallooed" the camp, and rode in. Stepping down, almost before his boot touched ground, he was questioned, aggressively. He proved to be, in fact, the **77** Ranch cowboy, and as luck would have it, had just had dinner with four men, about four miles further up the canyon.[34] After describing his previous luncheon partners, lawmen were sure of the identity of the murderous John Flynt, and one other, Jack Wellington. The young cowboy exclaimed, "My God, I'm sure glad you didn't run on them while I was there."[35] Without delay the decision was made to "run on them" no matter when or how they were found.[36]

And then, about one o'clock in the afternoon, there they were, leisurely riding ahead of the lawmen, four horsemen leading a packhorse, about a mile away, for the moment seemingly unconcerned. Frank Jones ordered his men into the "bed of a dry ravine," one paralleling their target's likely course. After a brisk trot, closing the distance to about one half mile, the officers erupted from the shielding arroyo, and charged![37]

Not until the outlaws' horses shied at the noises made by hard-riding peace officers did they comprehend their dire mess, a tight spot to be sure. Putting spurs to their horses the guttersnipes ran, pulling rifles from saddle scabbards. Captain Jones hollered an order to stop; they didn't. He then commanded his steadfast soldiers to open fire, to "kill their horses, and to arrest the men alive—if possible."[38] James "Jim" Lansford, wheeled about, and surrendered. Tom Fields (Tom Strouts) too, after a short chase, his blowing horse fagged, gave up. John Flynt and Jack Wellington raced the wind, full-well knowing if captured their freedom was forfeited. With two down and two to go, Captain Frank Jones, Joe Sitter and Bob Stockman feverishly galloped after Flynt and Wellington, who were "flying ahead." The shooting, at least according to Joe Sitter, was "promiscuous and lively."[39] Jack Wellington's horse lurched, shot, immobilized. Jumping from the saddle, rifle in hand, he scampered for nearby rocks. Frank Jones was worried:

> When he dismounted I was sure that Flynt would too and that they would fight to the death. I dismounted and shot at Wellington 3 times but it was at a long distance and I undershot him. He had a much better gun than mine, it being a large longrange rifle with cartridges as long as your finger. I knew that he was a famous shot and at long range had a decided advantage…I remounted my horse and ran up to about 100 yards of him where I felt pretty sure I could kill him the first shot. I then called out to him that I was an officer and did not wish to hurt him and he surrendered. In the meantime, Flynt ran on and the two men who were next to me (Sitter and Stockman) I sent on after him telling them to follow him until they ran him into some hole and that as soon as I captured or killed Wellington I would follow on…There had been so much talk about Wellington that I was anxious to try conclusions with him and I guess we would have had a regular Winchester duel only he saw some of the men coming on up the flat and knew that in case he killed me he could not get away with his life. He was not a particle unnerved.[40]

John Flynt was "riding like fury" about two miles ahead of Sitter and Stockman. After about a threemile chase, Joe Sitter had closed the shrinking gap sufficiently. He and Flynt "exchanged a few shots."[41] Bob Stockman, riding to Sitter's left, too, swapped shots with the fleeing Flynt. After starting the frantic chase, seven torturous miles had swept past before John Flynt went to ground. On foot, seeking concealment in a ravine, Flynt made ready to fight, so it seemed.[42] Just as Joe Sitter reined up in saddle gun range, Flynt popped from the ditch and made a mad dash for his winded horse, retrieved something from the saddle pocket, and feverishly scooted back to cover. Joe Sitter "hallooed at him, trying to get a talk out of him in order to get him to surrender. He paid no attention…"[43] Directing Bob Stockman to seal off the most likely escape route, Joe Sitter began a flanking movement in order to flush loose the last badman. Not precisely confident of Flynt's position, Sitter cautiously moved through "lots of shin-oak bushes" and was uneasy and befuddled when without warning a shot rang out. Joe Sitter thought Bob Stockman had fired. Bob Stockman thought Joe Sitter had fired. John Flynt never heard the ugly blast; he had "suicided." Logically, two possemen mistakenly deduced that Flynt had fired a pot-shot at one of them, and missed. Reinforcements came in the form of Texas Rangers, J.A. Wolfe, Jim Putman and Carl Kirchner.[44] Their numbers augmented, the lawmen vigilantly forced themselves into the deathly silent ravine, gingerly poking for one last gunplay with Flynt. They found him dead, lying on his back, pistol across his chest, rifle beside him, "choked with a cartridge in it," and a self-inflicted gunshot wound to the right side of the head; John Flynt was a train robber no more. Postmortem of the casual kind, by Joe Sitter and others, laid bare another bullet wound, "in the right nipple of his breast, evidently done by some of our men."[45] An inventory of Flynt's personal belongings revealed he had "$75.00 in gold in his cartridge-belt and four dollars, Mexican, in his pocket." In Flynt's bootleg was found a hastily scribbled note, which curtly instructed officers to turn his personal belongings over to his brother, J.M. Flynt.[46]

With three brigands in shackles, Flynt sprawled lifelessly, and a burdened packhorse, possemen began their mopping up chores. Lansford, "had $1525.00 in green backs in his vest pocket".[47] Wellington and Field's pockets were empty, but the former had a six-shooter in his possession with the serial number filed off, the one taken from Express Messenger Smith.[48] "On the packhorse was found four bundles of money, some in gold, but mostly in silver. The money on the packhorse and what the robbers had amounted to something over two thousand dollars."[49] Hurriedly, Flynt's body was covered. At dusk, the posse with prisoners in tow headed back for the **77** Ranch headquarters. At the ranch, Captain Jones purchased a "partition out of a house to get lumber to make a coffin" for Flynt.[50] While others were busily engaged constructing the crude pine box, the Captain and Joe Sitter, driving a hack, recovered Flynt's body and returned just as the clock struck 3:00 A. M.[51] Flynt was interred at the ranch, and after resting a day, the lawmen set out for Comstock, arriving five days later.[52] Captain Jones telegraphed his boss:

> With deputy sheriff (Sitter) and two citizens (Stockman and Bendele) of Val Verde County struck trail of train robbers 75 miles north of Del Rio & overtook them 50 miles above Howard's Well & killed John Flynt & captured Wellington, Lansford and Fields. Will give you full particulars by mail.[53]

Cigar Stumps and Peach Peels

Texas Ranger Captain Frank Jones. From Texas Ranger Sketches*, courtesy the author, Robert W. Stephens.*

Joe Sitter and Frank Jones, at Comstock, favorably parted company. While Deputy Sitter's efforts where lauded in the press, with remarks such as he "hunted this gang like a bloodhound and has hung on their trail with bulldog tenacity for more than a week," there was indeed a minor dispute brewing as to who should have rightful custody of the train robbers. "Sheriff Kieffer went up today with warrants for the men, but Captain Jones refused to deliver them to him."[54] Despite the protests, Captain Frank Jones and his complement of gutsy, but washed-out Texas Rangers transported their three prisoners to El Paso.[55] Upon arrival at El Paso, the accused train robbers were turned over to the deputy U.S. Marshal, federal charges were pending against the living.[56] Pithy notation about the dead was made in the *San Antonio Daily Light* of October 24, 1891:

> Flint, the suiciding express robber, was the right kind of a thief. If a man is going in for that kind of thing and proposes to defy law let him have the courage of his actions and not squeal when it comes to taking his gruel.

Little did authorities need the evidence, but John Lansford, a widower originally from La Salle County, Texas, and a full-fledged member of the "rough cowboy element," turned state's evidence:[57]

> He had been sent out from San Antonio to take charge of Mr. Wilson's horses. Flint (Flynt) was on the same ranch taking care

of the cattle. He told Lansford of a scheme to rob the train and asked him to rob the train and asked him to join in the work. Lansford was afraid to trust Wellington, but finally consented and the party Wellington, Flint (Flynt), Fields (Strouts), and Lansford set out for the railroad...They placed horseshoes on the track to jolt the engine so that the engineer would stop the train, and when it did stop Lansford himself covered the engineer and the fireman and held them prisoners while the others secured the booty. The robbers remained at a safe distance, eating fruit, until the train left. Then they crossed into Mexico, traveled down the river, took the shoes off their horses and re-crossed into the United States and played a long game of hide and seek until they were finally captured by Captain Jones and his rangers. Lansford says they secured $3600 from the express and mail. He saw Wellington with the pistol claimed by Express Messenger Smith, the day after the robbery and saw Wellington filing off the numbers.[58]

After positive identification by victimized trainmen, supplemented by declarations from Captain Frank Jones, and "very damaging" testimony from Sergeant Baz Outlaw, coupled with the eyewitness account of Texas Ranger private Gus Jones, the defendants stood little chance of coming clear on the criminal charges during an April 1892 trial.[59] And they didn't. After overnight deliberations a jury returned its verdict against Tom Fields (Strouts) and Jack Wellington—guilty.[60] Each now owed an unforgivable debt, ten years in the federal penitentiary. Jim Lansford, due to his "squealing," walked—a free man.[61]

Of course, after the Samuel's train robbery, a linking of legitimate facts and an intertwining of West Texas folklore was historically imprinted on rapt readers. Reliably it can be reported, Frank Jones, as a beloved Texas Ranger Captain, rode a spirited and honest horse to fame, while his Sergeant, Baz Outlaw, rode an ornery one to shame.[62] And of Joe Sitter, who had nonchalantly kidded about participating in the manhunt, "I laughed at him and said, I'll get some of that anyhow, and I did, but I said this as a joke, never expecting to have a hand in it." Well, later, he pocketed his cut of the reward, $750, and took an oath to defend the State of Texas, as a *Lone Star Ranger*.[63] Mythically, the rumors ran rampant there had been $50,000 stolen during the daring holdup, and somewhere along the way, the loot had been buried by owl-hoots, who even after their capture refused to reveal the location of the missing treasure.[64] Rationally, at this time far removed, it would seem to have made much more sense to have peeked under the "cigar stumps and peach peels."

ENDNOTES CHAPTER 1

"CIGAR STUMPS AND PEACH PEELS"

[1] Gournay, Luke, *Texas Boundaries—Evolution of the State's Counties*. P. 107. Val Verde County, Texas, was named after the Civil War battle fought at Val Verde, New Mexico Territory.

[2] For a refreshing look at Roy Bean and a fascinating glimpse at the country and people traipsing thereabouts, see, Skiles, Jack, *Judge Roy Bean Country*. For a biography of Bean see, Sonnichsen, C.L., *Roy Bean, Law West Of The Pecos*. Also see, McDaniel, Ruel, *Vinegarroon—The Saga of Judge Roy Bean, "Law West Of The Pecos"*

[3] Awbrey, Betty Dooley & Dooley, Claude, *Why Stop?—A Guide To Texas Historical Roadside Markers*. P. 107. The Southern Pacific building east and the Galveston, Harrisburg, and San Antonio Railroad building west, joined tracks on January 12, 1883, near the Pecos High Bridge in Val Verde County. The connection of the two railway systems called for celebration and a silver spike was driven to commemorate the occasion.

[4] *The New Handbook Of Texas*. At one time, there was a Post Office, a church, a school, and a store at Samuels (Pumpville).

[5] *El Paso Daily Times*, September 3, 1891. And, *Monthly Returns*, Frontier Battalion, Company D, September 1891. Courtesy, Texas State Library and Archives Commission (TSLAC), Austin. And, handwritten statement, "Joe Sitter's Account of the Trailing and Capture of the Train Robbers," statement of Joe Sitter as recorded by Harry Warren during an interview. Hereafter cited as Sitter to Warren. Courtesy, Sul Ross State University, Bryan Wildenthal Memorial Library, Archives of the Big Bend (ABB). Alpine, Texas. And, Burton, Jeff, *Dynamite And Six-Shooter*. P. 195-196.

[6] *Ibid.*

[7] *Ibid.* And, Burton. "But, Smith himself was held up for a second time, near Stein' Pass, in February 1888, and his express car efficiently plundered." P. 196.

[8] *Ibid.*

[9] *Ibid.* Author Burton advises the safe was breached by means of explosives, a "incident noteworthy in its own context as marking the very first instance where train robbers opened an express safe by blasting it with dynamite." P. 31. To an *El Paso Daily Times* reporter, Smith declared, "Winchesters were then leveled on me and I was compelled to open the safe or be shot." September 3, 1891. The use of explosives is not in doubt, as reported in the September 7, 1891, edition of the *San Antonio Daily Express*, "The car under which they exploded dynamite must have been badly shaken up, as all the dust, dirt and grease which usually collects on cars was shaken off." Evidence of the loss of Smith's revolver to the outlaws is highlighted in the April 21, 1892 edition of the *El Paso Daily Times*.

[10] *Ibid.*

[11] *Ibid.*

[12] *Ibid.* Although it is rumored the robbers made off with upwards of $50,000, officially it was said, "The loss of money sustained by the Wells-Fargo Express Company in the robbery has been more accurately placed at $3600, which is within about $20 of the correct amount." See, *San Antonio Daily Express*, September 10, 1891. And see, *El Paso Daily Times*, April 21, 1892, "Lansford says they secured $3600 from the express and mail."

Lawmen, Outlaws and S.O.Bs.

[13] *San Antonio Daily Express*, September 3, 1891. "…has lost his reputation, as he (Smith) failed to kill a single robber and talks of resigning…" And, Burton, "After the Samuels hold-up he offered his resignation." P. 196.

[14] *Ibid.* October 24, 1891.

[15] Sitter to Warren. According to Joe Sitter, two of the possemen besides the sheriff are identified, Del Duvies (?) and Tom Manto, "a one-armed man."

[16] Captain Frank Jones, Company D, Frontier Battalion, to W.H. Mabry, Adjutant General, Austin, Texas. September 11, 1891. (TSLAC) Frank Jones was born at Austin, Texas to Judge William E. and Kezziah Rector Jones on June 12, 1856. He first enlisted in the Texas Rangers on September 1, 1875. He was killed by Mexican bandits near El Paso on June 30, 1893. For a biographical profile of this interesting Southwest lawman, see, Stephens, Robert W., *Texas Ranger Sketches*. P. 65-69. And see, Utley, Robert M., *Lone Star Justice*, "In 1891 Jones headquartered his tiny company at Alpine, a cow-town on the Southern Pacific …." P. 229.

[17] Jones to Mabry, "…and with 4 citizens of Val Verde County and one of Brewster took up the trail which led in the direction of Mexico." Sitter to Warren, "Sheriff Kieffer took the trail of the robbers at Horse Shoe (sic) Bend and served with Capt. Frank Jones and his Co. D, Texas Rangers." And see, *San Antonio Daily Express*, September 7, 1891.

[18] *Ibid.* According to the newspaper edition cited above, at the Rio Grande, Judge Roy Bean who was leading local citizens in pursuit of the gang, met with the Texas Rangers before turning back and presumably heading for his headquarters at Langtry, the Jersey Lilly. Additionally, this newspaper account has the Texas Rangers and the Sheriff's posse joining forces at the Rio Grande rather than at Horseshoe Bend, as indicated by Joe Sitter. "Roy Bean followed three hours later and stopped at the river, as did the sheriff's posse, to await the Rangers' arrival."

[19] *Ibid.* And see, Webb, Walter Prescott, *The Texas Rangers, A Century of Frontier Defense.* P. 438-441.

[20] *Ibid.*

[21] *Ibid.* Outlaw John Flynt's name is sometimes spelled "Flint," and in certain primary source materials, even within a single report, the two spellings are used, jumping back and forth, from one to the other. For the purpose of this tale, the more commonly used "Flynt" is adopted. For another allegation that outlaw Flynt was a murderer, see, Casey, Robert J. *The Texas Border And Some Borderliners*, "Shortly before that time the Negro cook of the Flint (Flynt) gang of train robbers, who had been getting too friendly with the Rangers in Sanderson (Texas), was found dead." P. 266.

[22] *Ibid.* Captain Jones advised Adjutant General Mabry that Texas Governor Hogg might learn of the incursions into Mexico "through the papers" and should be forewarned.

[23] *Monthly Returns*, Company D, Frontier Battalion, October 1891. (TSLAC) And, Gournay. P. 108. Baz Lamar Outlaw, reportedly from Lee County, Georgia, first became a Texas Ranger on August 11, 1885, resigned May 16, 1889, and re-upped on September 1,1889. He was later promoted to Sergeant, Company D. He was killed by John Selman at El Paso on April 5, 1894. See, Stephens, *Texas Ranger Sketches*. P. 108-111. And see, Stephen's later work, *Bullets And Buckshot In Texas*, in which the author after extensive research rightfully determined that Outlaw's first name was Bazzell or Bazel, depending on the particular census enumerator's spelling. Also see, Rasch, Phillip J., "Bass Outlaw,

24

Myth And Man," *Real West*, July 1979. Frequently Outlaw's first name is popularly transformed into "Bass."
[24] Sitter to Warren. Often in print, Joe Sitter who would later serve as a Texas Ranger and afterward as a U.S. Mounted Customs Inspector, is referred to as Joe Sitters. During an interview on October 26, 2002, and later correspondence with his grandson, Jake Sitters, correctness was determined. The "s" was added to the family name by a subsequent generation. Records at St. Louis Church, Castroville, Texas, Joe Sitter's birthplace, clearly reveal that when he was Baptized on January 22, 1863 and when he married his first wife, Margretha (Maggie) on April 4, 1884, it was by last name "Sitter". His tombstone is marked, "Joe Sitter." And see, Application to Adjutant General for Commission as a Special Ranger, December 7, 1896, signed, "Joe Sitter." Courtesy, Texas Ranger Hall of Fame and Museum, Waco, Texas. (TRHFM) In most secondary accounts Sitter is injected into the story too early. Walker, Wayne T., "Joe Sitters: The Best Damn Tracker In Texas," *Oldtimers Wild West*, December 1978. "Finally, about 100 miles south of Marathon, Sitters (sic) spotted their (robbers) camp in a canebrake near the Rio Grande and the Rangers closed in on them." P. 30. And see, Michaels, Kevin, "Tracker," *Great West*, September 1974. "…Sitters spotted their camp hidden in a canebrake near the Rio Grande and the Rangers closed in on them." P. 22. Joe Sitter, himself, claimed to be elsewhere during initial phases of the chase after the train robbers. For additional biographical data and related story about this unique border country personality, see Chapter 10.
[25] *Ibid.*
[26] *San Antonio Daily Express*, October 23, 1891. "…Captain Jones and citizens under Deputy Sheriff Joe Sitter…Deputy Sheriff Joe Sitter has hunted this gang like a bloodhound…" And, Sitter to Warren.
[27] Sitter to Warren. Although Warren wrote the family name as Bentley rather than Bendele it is an understandable phonetic mistake. A later newspaper identifies them as the Bendeles. Also, it is logical to opt for the latter choice, as Joe Sitter's deceased wife's maiden name was Bendele, and more than likely these were her relatives.
[28] *Ibid.*
[29] *Ibid.* The *San Antonio Daily Express* of October 23, 1891 spells the last name of Sitter's civilian helpers as Bendele rather than Bentley, and does confirm that brother Frank remained at Juno to inform the Texas Rangers as to Sitter's direction and likely course of travel in trying to close with the train robbers. And see, Wilkins, Frederick, *The Law Comes To Texas*, "Jones was patient, kept his agents busy, and in time received word while in El Paso concerning a possible location for John Flint (Flynt) and his gang." P. 300.
[30] *Ibid.* And, *Monthly Returns*, Company D, Frontier Battalion, October 1891. (TSLAC) And see, Hunter, J. Marvin, "The Killing of Captain Frank Jones," *Frontier Times*, January 1929. The *Frontier Times* article contains a letter from Jones to Mrs. Pauline Baker, Uvalde, Texas, detailing the chase after the train robbers. Interestingly, Jones acknowledges he "came to a ranch at Howard's Well," but does not mention, at this time, Joe Sitter by name, merely remarking , "some parties had seen the men we were following and they were yet 3 days ahead of us."
[31] *Ibid.* Although Sitter is clear that it was the **77** Ranch, a newspaper account mentions it as **7 D** Ranch.

[32] *Ibid.* Joe Sitter identifies the startled lady as Mrs. Roy. Frank Jones simply makes reference to her as a "Northern woman," but does acknowledge she was "so frightened she could hardly talk." Jones to Baker.
[33] Jones to Baker. Joe Sitter says "they (outlaws) bought two horses there (77 Ranch) that very morning."
[34] *Ibid.* Jones uses the one mile figure, Sitter reports the desperadoes were camped four miles away. Sitter to Warren. And, *Monthly Returns*, Company D, Frontier Battalion, October 1891. (TSLAC)
[35] Sitter to Warren. Interestingly, Sitter remarks the lawmen had three pack animals with them, assuring the posse reasonable commissary and camp equipment—and extra cartridges.
[36] Jones to Baker. "I had fully made up my mind to go on them no matter when or how I found them."
[37] *Ibid.* "...I (Jones) ordered a charge at them and we went with our guns drawn." And see, Sitter to Warren, "When we got about even with them (outlaws) Capt. ordered us to come out of the low place, into the open where the robbers were...We proceeded till we got within 350 yards of them and then made a charge." Also see, *Monthly Returns*, Company D, Frontier Battalion, October 1891. (TSLAC)
[38] Sitter to Warren.
[39] *Ibid.* According to a mention in the *San Antonio Daily Express* of November 3, 1891, Tom Field's true name was revealed, "The right name of Fields is Tom Strouts. He is from Williamson county (Texas) and previous to the robbery is said to have had a reputation not to be proud of." And see, Tyler, Ronnie C., *The Big Bend, A History Of The Last Texas Frontier.* P. 158. "A shootout occurred as the Rangers closed in on the desperadoes."
[40] Jones to Baker.
[41] Sitter to Warren. And see, *San Antonio Daily Express*, October 23, 1891, "Flint (Flynt) ran at full speed a distance of ten miles, firing back upon his pursuers as he went. The fire was returned and he was mortally wounded, being shot in his left breast..." And see, *El Paso Daily Times*, October 23, 1891, "...John Flynt lead in the chase to get away and was run ten miles before a bullet from the rifle of a ranger went through him. Then he threw himself from his horse, wrote out his will and drawing his pistol shot off the top of his own head."
[42] *Ibid.* In his report to Adjutant General Mabry, on October 24, 1891, Captain Jones estimates that Sitter and Stockman chased Flynt eight miles, "The other (Flynt) ran about 8 miles and after being wounded blew his brains out." (TSLAC)
[43] *Ibid.* Bob Stockman, at this time joined Joe Sitter in the standoff with Flynt.
[44] *Ibid.* Texas Ranger private J.A. Wolfe was enlisted by Captain Jones on January 24, 1891, and discharged from Company D, March 27, 1892. James Mitchell "Jim" Putman was born May 12, 1859, to William and Addie Gibson Putman. He enlisted in the Texas Rangers on June 1, 1890, at Marfa, Texas, and served until, July 22, 1893. He gained West Texas fame when, during a horrific shoot-out, he killed a wanted killer, Fine Gilliland. Putman died on December 19, 1923. Carl Kirchner was born in Bee County, Texas, on November 19, 1867, to Christian and Martha Burditt Kirchner. He enlisted as a Texas Ranger on May 18, 1889, and served until the 24th day of July 1895. Considered by the majority of authorities to be an excellent lawman, Kirchner distinguished himself on several harrowing occasions, most notably when Captain Frank Jones was killed in 1893.

Carl Kirchner died on January 28, 1911, at El Paso, Texas. See, Stephens, *Texas Ranger Sketches*.

[45] *Ibid*. And, Jones to Baker. "Some time in the chase he (Flynt) had been shot through the body, but I do not think the wound was necessarily a fatal one…The ball entered just under the right shoulder blade making its exit through the right nipple." Logically, this account relating to Flynt's torso wound seems to be worded more accurately than Joe Sitter's remark, although historically the discrepancy is insignificant. A fleeing felon is, indeed, more likely to be shot in the back, but a man turning in the saddle and firing at his pursuers could catch a bullet in the chest. *Quien Sabe?*

[46] *Ibid*. J.M. Flynt, according to Joe Sitter, was brother to the deceased outlaw. As with almost any Old West gunplay, there are conspiracy theorists. See, Martin, Jack, *Border Boss, Captain John R. Hughes—Texas Ranger*. P. 117. "Gossip is still heard along the border to the effect that Flint (Flynt) did not kill himself; that in reality one of the possemen forced him to write a will and then murdered him, and escaped with the $50,000…Hughes had ample proof that this gossip was false and malicious; that the entire incident occurred exactly as Captain Jones detailed it in his report."

[47] *Ibid*.

[48] *El Paso Daily Times*, April 21, 1892.

[49] Sitter to Warren.

[50] Jones to Baker.

[51] Sitter to Warren.

[52] Captain Frank Jones, El Paso, Texas to Adjutant General Mabry, Austin, Texas. October 24, 1891. "We buried him (Flynt) as well as we could and then came back. Our horses are used up and will require a long rest." (TSLAC)

[53] *Western Union Telegram*, Frank Jones, Comstock, Texas, to Adjutant General Mabry, Austin, Texas. October 22, 1891. (TSLAC)

[54] *San Antonio Daily Express*, October 23, 1891.

[55] *Ibid*. The dispute as to who should have custody of the prisoners revolved around whether the criminal charges would be filed in state or federal court.

[56] *Ibid*., October 24, 1891. "The state authorities wanted the men turned over to them, but the ranger captain would hear of no such thing, and he took them to El Paso. It is stated by Assistant United States Attorney Terrell that all four (three) men captured were indicted at El Paso during this term of court. The men were indicted under section 5472 of the United States statutes for robbing a carrier of the United States mail."

[57] *San Antonio Daily Express*, November 3, 1891.

[58] *El Paso Daily Times*, April 21, 1892. Certainly, the rumor persisted that as much as $50,000 had been taken in the Samuel's train robbery, however, based on primary source materials, including the testimony of one of the culpable, the $3600 figure seems more apposite, more especially when factoring in negotiations for a *plea bargain*. Wilkins, however, opts for the $50,000 figure. P. 299.

[59] *Ibid*. April 22, 1892.

[60] *Ibid*. April 28, 1892.

[61] *Ibid*. "It is conjectured that Judge Maxey will give the prisoners ten years in the pen." And see, Sitter to Warren. "The prisoners were tried before the U.S. Court at El Paso. 'Jack' Evans, the celebrated U.S. District Attorney prosecuted. Maj. T. T. Teel defended. Lansford, since he had turned State's evidence, went free, the other two were each sent to U.S. prison for ten years."

Lawmen, Outlaws and S.O.Bs.

[62] Numerous are the mentions of Baz Outlaw's misbehavior and discharge from the Texas Rangers. As Stephens, *Texas Ranger Sketches* reports, many considered Baz Outlaw "dangerous and notorious" or as others characterized him "the worst and toughest man I had seen." Interesting indeed are the words of his Captain, Frank Jones, "His bravery was beyond question. He was considered to possess 'unusual courage and coolness' and 'in a close place he is worth two or three ordinary men." P. 108-109. Perhaps, through the lens of historical balance, a second look at Baz Outlaw's career would not be inappropriate.

[63] *Oath*, Frontier Battalion, September 6, 1894. Signed by Joseph Sitter, and others. (TRHFM)

[64] Reportedly, and most writers offer little, if any, primary source documentation, it is alleged that Baz Outlaw obsessively searched for the elusive $50,000 stolen in the train robbery at Samuels. See, Rosson, Mary'n, "The Day Bass Outlaw Tried To Drink Up The Town," *Frontier West*, December, 1974. "Although train officials reported only a small amount of silver was stolen, rumors persisted that over $50,000 was taken. The money, thought to have been hidden in some canebrakes, was the subject in every bar and cowboy gathering all over Texas. This was the object of Outlaw's secret journey, a fact known full well by Gillett." P. 63. And see, Majors, Frederick, "Bass Outlaw Was A Texas Riddle," *Golden West*, August, 1974. "Brooding and stewing, Bass spent some months all by his perverse self looking for gold said to have been buried by an expired long rider, John Flint (Flynt). The luckless Mr. Flint (Flynt) had committed suicide near the sheep town of Ozoma (Ozona) as a Ranger posse had been right up on him. For all the silly legends about such characters, he probably left no peso interred anywhere."

CHAPTER 2

"ADRENALINE, ALCOHOL, AND ATTITUDE"

Jimmy McDaniels, Lincoln County *Mal Hombre*

Almost fifty years ago a prominent authority on Old West literary histories, Ramon F. Adams, reported his personal library was the repository for "approximately two hundred books that deal with Sam Bass or devote some space to him."[1] Since Adams penned those illuminating words, a plethora of supplementary commentaries on the nefarious bandit's short-lived criminality and the final six-shooter sojourn at Round Rock have been offered to a rapt readership. James "Jim" McDaniels has not suffered the same journalistic notice. Conscientiously following McDaniel's historic footprints is much more problematic, despite the fact he undeniably was a legitimate, although collateral, player in such noteworthy Southwest epics as the El Paso Salt War and the Lincoln County War. The purpose of this narrative is not to suggest that it's time to close the book on Jim McDaniels, but more exactly to pique interest and hopefully serve as fascinating and captivating catalyst for others who might be attracted to unearthing biographical clues about this cryptic, hard-core outlaw.

From the best evidence thus far developed it seems Jim McDaniels first saw the light of day sometime during 1852, and somewhere within reasonable proximity to Nashville, Tennessee; at least that's what he declared.[2] Scavenging Jimmy's family tree might bear fruit, but realistically the allure is with the man, not the boy. Suffice to say, by the time he sprouted to maturity, Jim McDaniels, adorned with a fiery crown of auburn hair, measured in at 5', 8," and looked at the world with steel-blue eyes. Jim McDaniels was illiterate in the ways of reading and writing, but as we shall discover, was schooled in the use of a six-shooter and bowie knife. Plus, he was bilingual, English and Spanish.[3] Jim McDaniels was fashioned of grit and gristle. How he ended up in

Lawmen, Outlaws and S.O.Bs.

Texas is undetermined, but he did. Somewhere along the way he served an apprenticeship in the cow-business, and through the school of hard knocks honed the requisite skills of an efficient steer-tripper and a bronc-stomper. Jim McDaniels worked himself into a position of extraordinary trust with the illustriously renowned ranching tycoon, John Simpson "Cattle King of the Pecos" Chisum.[4]

"Cattle King of the Pecos" and Jimmy McDaniel's boss, John Simpson Chisum. Courtesy Nita Stewart Haley Memorial Library and J. Evetts Haley History Center.

Chisum's Home Creek Ranch, just east of the Concho, a refreshingly cool West Texas river bountifully supplied with fresh water oysters, was were Jim McDaniels at twenty-one came of age as a cowboy and foreman.[5] When Chisum migrated further west to

Adrenaline, Alcohol and Attitude

flat tableland of southeastern New Mexico Territory, so too did Jim McDaniels.[6]

John S. Chisum for a time during the 1870's was a powerhouse in the American livestock industry, ranging some seventy-thousand head of cattle over unoccupied federal lands, an empire stretching well over a hundred miles north to south along the Pecos River, seventy-five miles east to west, the colossal kingdom tended by several dozen armed herders.[7] Because Chisum's beeves were conspicuously earmarked, a cut flap hanging down like the clapper in a bell, the uniquely notched cattle were nicknamed jinglebobs, and the cowboys who watched over them were known as Jinglebob men.[8] Most of Chisum's cowboys were top-notch hands; others were those hard-edged swashbuckling souls who were innately haunted with the principles of a pirate.[9] Jim McDaniels was both.

Cowboy Ike Fridge worked on Chisum's New Mexico ranch, and thus his first-level bossman was Jim McDaniels. Fridge penned his remembrances in *History of the Chisum War; or, Life of Ike Fridge—Stirring Events of Cowboy Life on the Frontier.*[10] It's a footnote fact the Jinglebob cowpuncher knew Jim McDaniels, and according to Fridge's account he was personally on the bloody ground when McDaniels unflinchingly exhibited the mettle he was truly made of. Meticulous bibliophile Ramon Adams rightfully questions the validity of Ike Fridge's comments in his ambitious critique of Outlaw/Lawman literature, *Six-Guns and Saddle Leather.*[11] Upon closer examination of Adam's criticism, however, it is plainly revealed the author appropriately identifies only historic blunders made pertaining to the infamous "Billy the Kid" saga, unquestionably hearsay which Fridge was merely repeating. Ike Fridge is not challenged at all for factuality on matters he claimed to have witnessed or personally participated in. Perhaps then, what Fridge had to say about McDaniels is right on the money. And, researcher Philip J. Rasch in writing a succinct biographical sketch incorporated Ike Fridge's first-person narrative into his profile of McDaniels.[12] Likewise, modern-day journalists now integrate brief mentions of Jim McDaniels in their much-admired works with citations to Rasch. Herein is part of what Ike Fridge said about Jim McDaniels.

A cowboy named Tabb, and Fridge, opted to "cut" a herd of Pete Maxwell's cattle near Fort Sumner, looking for any stray Chisum cattle inadvertently mixed therein. Maxwell's unidentified range boss took offense. Forthrightly he jerked his six-shooter and killed Tabb. Skillfully spurring his horse in a nifty 180 degree arc, the Maxwell foreman skeedaddled, only to make it about a hundred yards before he too dropped from his saddle, the result of slapdash shots fired by Ike Fridge. Hearing the commotion, other Jinglebob cowhands came to the rescue, indiscriminately fired into Maxwell's crew of *vaqueros* and killed one. Both sides gathered up their casualties and retreated, but ill feelings between the Chisum men, who were predominately Anglos, and the Hispanic *vaqueros* of Maxwell, smoldered. Later, another *vaquero* was gunned down, and Jinglebob cowboys found themselves locked away in the calaboose at Las Vegas. Accordingly, foreman Jim McDaniels, who Fridge characterized as having lots of nerve, and "we were all willing to do as he said in any emergency," led a platoon of Chisum cowboys to Las Vegas and at gunpoint liberated their compadres.[13]

Shortly thereafter another Jinglebob cowboy, Charlie Rankins, was killed while he and Fridge fled another bunch of Maxwell's *vaqueros*. Rankins was killed outright and Ike Fridge reportedly smoked another foe before he managed to find Chisum reinforcements. At an adobe house on Macho Creek the Chisum ensemble encamped, only to be surrounded by their enemies deceitfully posing as a posse of lawmen demanding immediate and unconditional surrender. There was no way! McDaniels "took charge of the affair and directed the fight in his usual able manner," so said Fridge. During an ensuing standoff and shoot-out, a lad named Curtis on the Jinglebob team was killed, and McDaniels was wounded, although their opponents suffered a number of dead and were ultimately forced to forfeit the battlefield. Fridge remarked, "Several of us went out the next morning and picked up the dead rustlers and threw them into a canyon. We had no tools for grave digging, and we didn't care to scratch a grave in the hard ground with our hands. After all, this was a ruthless bunch of outlaws who had tried to put us out of the running just the night before."[14] The leader of the Chisum squad recovered from his gunshot wound. There was still a lot of fight left in Jim McDaniels. A case in point:

> There was a Negro in our bunch who was helping us brand the cattle. He and a White man—I think his name was Carnahan—had had some trouble, and before we finished the branding, the Negro saw a good chance to take advantage of the puncher.
> The Negro said, "I am ready for you now," and made a move to draw his gun. Jim McDaniel(s) heard him and whirled around, drawing his own pistol and firing as he turned, shooting the Black between the eyes before he could kill the cowboy, which is what he surely would have done, if McDaniel(s) had not interfered."[15]

Adrenaline, Alcohol and Attitude

Lone Star Cowboy Ike Fridge. Jimmy McDaniels was his foreman on the Chisum Ranch and, reportedly, he witnessed his boss in scorching action on more than one occasion. Courtesy, Robert G. McCubbin.

Jim McDaniels was a plucky sort of fellow, and too, during the tumultuous 1874-1875 time period fiercely loyal to his employer, John S. Chisum. When his boss rightly or wrongly opted to pilfer some Mescalero Apache horses in retribution for mounts stolen from his remuda, it was to Jim McDaniels he turned. In company with henchmen, some of whom would later earn disreputable reputations, men like Jessie J. Evans, Marion Turner, Tom Bostick, Frank Baker, and a few others, the squadron of accomplished operatives "systemically robbed the Indians of thousands of dollars worth of stock."[16] At least so claimed an investigator sent to look into the situation, E.C. Watkins.[17] The United States Indian Inspector made his inquiry and tersely proclaimed "...the evidence shows conclusively that in the matter of horse stealing, Mr. Chisum is far ahead of the Indians and that a balance should be struck in their favor..."[18] Practically speaking, and John S. Chisum was a methodically pragmatic man, he unabashedly owned the blame—and the horses. As Philip Rasch reiterated though, "When the shoe was on the other foot, however, it fit poorly."[19]

Notorious owl-hoots collectively known as the Mes gang, who in larger-than-life newspaper stories were reportedly responsible for every crime committed throughout the whole Southwest, all the way to the "...Gulf of California and the Pacific Ocean...," boldly misappropriated thirty head of Chisum horses, and the manhunt was on, Jim McDaniels at the forefront.[20] There is little doubt that Jim McDaniels had a predetermined plan for dealing with the bothersome Mes boys—once he got his hands around their throats. There was already bad blood between them, dating back (1873) to an earlier incident when after a search of their "fortified citadel" a *"placita* on the lower Hondo called *La Boquilla,"* McDaniels & Company came up empty-handed—the stolen beeves had already been barbecued.[21] And although it has been written that Jim McDaniels and Jessie Evans were deathly afraid of the Mes crowd, it is an assertion that seems somewhat dubious due to a simple fact; it was Jim McDaniels who was doing the chasing—not the other way around![22]

The risky pursuit is a grueling monument to tenacity. For six days McDaniels tracked the rustlers, subsisting only on "mesquite beans which he gathered from the bushes as he rode, and one young hawk he shot."[23] Whether McDaniels was assisted by four or by five cow-country cohorts is dependent on which newspaper account is cited, but in the end it matters little. The fugitives were trailed to San Ignacio, Chihuahua, Mexico, and somewhat surprisingly the hard-boiled possemen were successful in convincing Mexican authorities to forthwith arrest and deliver up the four horse thieves—on McDaniel's solemn pledge that he would escort the captives back to Lincoln County and into hands of justice.[24] On the way with the rustlers in tow, Jim McDaniels and crew managed a wearisome journey along the pockmarked eastern face of the Organ Mountains, and into secure sanctuary at the San Agustin ranch, a "welcoming haven for every horse and cattle thief" working southern New Mexico Territory and far western Texas.[25] A naïve tourist just passing through might have seen the beguiling landscape and sociable ranch as picturesque, a long-awaited and refreshing oasis. The traveler with a tad more sophistication, however, after taking note of the wicked whorehouse, whiskey-scented saloon, ribald dance-hall and the wanton conglomeration of shiftless sports who were lounging about, would no doubt make haste in getting his fanny on down the road. The owner of the sinful spot, Warren H. Shedd, wasn't running a church camp!

Jim McDaniels and boys recuperated at Shedd's safe haven awhile, and then resumed their return of the detainees to Lincoln County, aiming to pass close by the southern edge of the White Sands and across a dehydrated Tularosa Basin. Well, maybe they intended to. A scant seven miles into the trip, mysteriously, a drove of masked men appeared on the scene, "...forced McDaniel(s) and the one guard to one side, and shot the prisoners."[26] To the amazement of no one, Jim McDaniels couldn't offer a solitary clue to the murderous culprit's true identities. After all, their faces had been covered by sweaty bandannas, but a hard-nosed local newspaper editor didn't mask his satisfaction and pithily rationalized, "It is a blot upon our county, but those men won't run off any more stock."[27] And there the matter ended. Jimmy McDaniels, hands washed of the bloody affair, meandered back to turbulent Lincoln County, but in the overall scheme not for too long.[28]

Lily Klasner in *My Girlhood Among Outlaws* offers an anecdotal story in which John Chisum allegedly plays a practical joke, himself vying for amorous affections of Jim McDaniel's sixteen year old sweetheart, Flo Fredericks. Whether or not McDaniels appreciated the prickly humor goes unrecorded.[29] Women, of any age in that lonesome Jinglebob country were in such short supply Ike Fridge moaned, "...at one period I didn't see a woman of Anglo origin for four years."[30] Perhaps Jim McDaniels, nursing hurt feelings, impetuously moved on or maybe the reason was grounded in a bitter dispute with the boss over wages, as another writer mentions.[31] Regardless of the rationale, most believed he wanted to "get even" with Chisum, and for sure it's known Jim McDaniels bid *adios* to "old John."[32]

Lawmen, Outlaws and S.O.Bs.

For awhile anyway, Jim McDaniels teamed up with two who marvelously fit the bill, a cow thief extraordinaire, John Kinney, who the *Silver City Enterprise* caustically and candidly called "the chief mogul of the gang of rustlers," and the decadent Charles "Pony Diehl" Ray.[33]

John Kinney, "the chief mogul of the gang of rustlers" and a wicked six-shooter crony of Jimmy Daniels. Courtesy, Robert G. McCubbin.

Jim McDaniels rang in the new year, 1876, with a bang—literally! Near Las Cruces, he, along with John Kinney, Jessie Evans, and Charles Ray found themselves involved in a head-thumping battle of fisticuffs with Eighth Cavalry troopers stationed at Fort Selden, a military reservation acknowledged as home for some pretty tough customers in its own right, and in fact, more soldiers were killed during fracases with area civilians than in combat with wayward Apaches.[34] Jim McDaniels and chums, during the battle royal came out second best, but not for long! The "boys" surreptitiously returned to the *baile*. Poking their six-shooters barrels through open windows, the cowardly actors shot through the throng. The scorecard? Two blue-coated privates seriously wounded, two soldiers dead, one innocent civilian killed.[35] No criminal charges were ever filed due to the "supiness of the civil authorities" in the vicinity.[36]

Jim McDaniels would brook no insult, not from a soldier, or from a Mexican, or from a Negro, or most assuredly from one of those hardhearted hellions he was running with. Another of his stinging scenarios caught a frontier newspaperman's notice, matter-of-factly reported in the *Grant County Herald*:

> Mr. Taylor gave our reporter the particulars of what he was pleased to term a thrilling midnight duel in the wilderness, with knives, which occurred on the road, between a couple of stockmen well known in Lincoln county, named James McDaniels and Ben Rinehart (Reinhardt). They had all started together coming north and had traveled about 36 miles when a dispute arose between McDaniels and Rinehart (Reinhardt) as to the location of a trail which they had desired to take. Harsh words ensued, and at last they concluded to end the dispute by a contest with bowie knives. In the encounter both men received severe stabs in the breast which may prove fatal. The blows succeeded one another so quick that Mr. Taylor had not time to interfere. The wounded men were taken back to Dow's ranch, about 30 miles from the mines, where they were cared for, and Mr. Taylor came on to this city. He thinks that one, or perhaps both, of the men will die.[37]

Jim McDaniels didn't die. The ultimate fate of Ben Reinhardt is unknown, although one respected historian notes he was "patched up," but not soon enough; Jim McDaniels recovered quicker and slyly made off with his adversary's horse and six-shooter.[38] No doubt, if in the end Reinhardt did survive the stab wounds he would have been outright dumbfounded to learn of his bitter antagonist's next career move. Jim McDaniels became a Texas Ranger.[39] On November 17, 1877, owning a horse valued at $80 (Reinhardt's ?), Jim McDaniels and others, took an oath:

Lawmen, Outlaws and S.O.Bs.

We do solemnly swear that we with true faith and allegiance bear to the State of Texas, that we will serve her honestly and faithfully, that we will defend her against all her enemies and oppressors and that we will obey the orders of the Governor and the officers appointed over us according to an act of the Legislature for frontier defense approved April 10th, 1874 so help us God.[40]

At San Elizario, El Paso County, Texas, after swearing to the obligatory oath of office, Jim McDaniels stepped up and made his mark, an "X," as did several who could not write their names.[41] And with the quick stroke of an ink-pen, incredibly, quick-triggered Jim McDaniels was made a Lone Star lawman. Of the Texas Ranger class of 1877, one adroit Western writer recently said a sampling of the freshly christened privates were hard-bitten hooligans who had, "…wormed their way into the ranks and used their insider position…"[42] The highly revered historian C.L. Sonnichsen characterized some of the rangers as, "…hard faced and battle scarred…they nearly all had reputations."[43]

Beefing up Texas Ranger presence at El Paso County was deemed a quick fix for the predicament citizens found themselves suffering, one deeply rooted in an abyss of cultural misunderstandings, ruthless racial bigotry, inflated egos, ticklish political trickery, and too, pure greed. Historically the vehement dissension has been tagged the El Paso Salt War, but truthfully, the resultant murder and mayhem was much more complex than a dispute over the shallow saline lakes located about 90 miles east of town.[44]

The Salt War became a race war. Earlier, Judge Charles Howard had shotgunned to death Louis Cardis, an opinionated, but greatly appreciated voice for the Mexicans and Hispanics living in the flat-roofed adobe houses haphazardly scattered along both banks of the muddy international borderline, the Rio Grande. After the murder, Howard had maneuvered himself safely to Mesilla, New Mexico Territory, but thereafter in another act of irrationality had defiantly returned to El Paso County. At San Elizario, he along with Lt. J.B. Tay's company of Texas Rangers, Jim McDaniels included, found themselves surrounded by a horde of Spanish speaking protesters, some of whom were engaged in runaway raiding and rioting, allegedly being whipped into a merciless frenzy by a Catholic Priest, Father Antonio Borrajo, who was stridently proclaiming, "Shoot all the *gringos* and I will absolve you."[45]

Adrenaline, Alcohol and Attitude

The rangers all too soon grasped their untenable situation. Wholly cut off from the rest of the world, hopelessly outnumbered, and with nearby U.S. Army troopers hesitant to intervene, the lawmen's best calculated judgment indicated it was time to think in terms of a negotiated settlement. The dilemma was that their leader, Lieutenant J.B. Tays, couldn't speak the native language of the mob. Accordingly, Jim McDaniels and John G. Atkinson were burdened with the delicate chore of acting as interpreters during the life or death parley.[46]

The exacting truth as to what really transpired during the summit between those desperate rangers and an unmanageable mob, evidently will never be known due to later pains aimed at face-saving and scape-goating. What Jim McDaniels heard, precisely translated, or perhaps misinterpreted goes unrecorded. History's testimony is that the Texas Rangers capitulated, surrendering their arms, and Judge Howard, John Aitkinson, and John McBride were hastily executed by a rag-tag firing squad, their deaths put on the fatality list with two others, El Paso merchant Charles Ellis and Texas Ranger C.E. Mortimer, who had been murdered earlier.[47] The remaining Texas Rangers, sans six-shooters and Winchesters, scampered back toward El Paso (Franklin) thankful to be alive. El Paso County Sheriff Charles Kerber wired Texas Governor R.B. Hubbard requesting permission to raise a contingent of mercenaries from nearby New Mexico Territory. The governor replied, "...Raise 100 men at once, to resist invasion, put down insurrection, and re-enforce State troops..."[48]

And indeed, reinforcements from New Mexico arrived on the scene, "primed with adrenaline, alcohol, and attitude."[49] Captained by an intrepid Grant County deputy sheriff and proven man-killer, Dan Tucker, with bloodlust in their eyes the volunteers, including an ill-famed John Kinney, demanded an unregulated dogfight—tooth and nail![50] The Texas Rangers now reinforced, set out on a course of retribution and revenge. There were several episodes of prisoners killed while *escaping*, women suffering humiliating sexual assaults, private property callously appropriated, and in general, unrestrained behavior and felonies, not to mention lesser offenses such as pot-shooting chickens and indiscriminately intimidating laboring peons, many who were innocent of any wrongdoing whatsoever. One historian wryly theorized, "Sheriff Kerber had been promised the aid of fifty men from Silver City...thirty men from Silver City arrived; judging by their performance it is well that fifty did not come."[51]

Mostly, Jim McDaniel's particular behavior during the "spree," like so many of his reckless cohorts, cannot with certainty be identified, but there are a couple of logical clues. Interestingly, one witness testified that a ranger called "Jim" stole a rifle. Another, George Zwitzers, under oath swore that McDaniels, through him, had sent a threatening message to J. Boyle Leahy who had "spoken very hard of him" and that Leahy had better leave the country as he (McDaniels) did not want at first sight to "kill an American."[52] However the most telling hint as to the excesses credited to McDanies may be found in the pages of a New Mexico newspaper which reported that the agitating and corrupt priest, Antonio Borrajo, was publicly offering $1000 for the severed head of Jim McDaniels.[53]

Shortly after their reprisals, the unapologetic New Mexico gang of mercenaries disbanded.[54] Dan Tucker went home to accept a position as marshal at Silver City and John Kinney remained at El Paso, opening the Exchange Saloon, for awhile.[55] Jim McDaniels, dependent on which Texas Ranger *Muster Roll* is scrutinized, on the 2nd day of February, 1878, was discharged or by other archival reports, deserted.[56] Either way, Jim McDaniels was a Texas Ranger no more.

He jumped from the Lone Star state, landed in Mesilla, New Mexico Territory, and one more time, found himself embroiled in another bloody scrap. Although the details are sketchy, it seems that during the course of a frenzied altercation over an undisclosed wrangle of some type, he once again resorted to six-shooter justice to resolve a dispute with an alleged cow-thief, H. Martin, wounding him in the neck. For whatever the reason, maybe fear of a punishing payback, the injured owl-hoot chose not to follow through at the Doña Ana County courthouse with the filing of formal charges, and after spending the week-end in jail as the guest of Sheriff Mariano Barela, Jim McDaniels was released.[57]

Understandably the precise date cannot be documented, but circa 1878 Jim McDaniels established what has been commonly referred to as a ranch, or more specifically a "cattle hideaway" about five miles northwest of San Nicolas Spring in the San Andres Mountains, not too far north of Shedd's villainous hangout.[58] One of the preeminent specialists on the topsy-turvy Lincoln County hubbub submits that Jim McDaniel's canyon retreat was, "...one of the toughest places in New Mexico."[59] That he maintained a contemptible reputation can be extracted from several sources. Philip Rasch highlights one anecdotal story told by George R. Bowman in which an unidentified traveler near Tularosa, on the western slope of the Sacramento Mountains, commented, "...that he hoped they did not meet McDaniels because he was not on friendly terms with him, and finally hid himself in the back of the wagon." He legitimately feared McDaniels would try to rob him of the $1,200 in Mexican silver he was clandestinely carrying in a scruffy leather trunk.[60] Unequivocally, it was not just in unruly New Mexico Territory that Jim McDaniels preserved status as a sure enough stinker. Old-timer Joe Waide, way back at the tiny hamlet of Bolivar, just north of Denton, Texas, said, "Sometimes they'd mention names of outlaws like Billy the Kid, Jesse Evans, Jim McDaniels, them guys—all bad fellows. We'd heard 'bout them guys—all the way down here in Texas. We knew what they was!"[61]

That the subject of this narrative was personally acquainted with William Henry Harrison Antrim's most famous stepson there is not in doubt; in fact, Pat Garrett (and/or Ash Upson) wrote in *The Authentic Life of Billy, The Kid*, "It was here, at Mesilla, and by Jim McDaniels, that Billy was dubbed 'The Kid' on account of his youthful appearance…"[62] An esteemed expert disputes the assertion, commenting that the first time the "immortal sobriquet" was used, was when it was printed in an editorial for the December 3, 1878 edition of the *Las Vegas Gazette*.[63] Incontestably determining just when Billy was labeled as being the "Kid" would seem a rather elusive project. It's not beyond reason to suppose that maybe rambunctious free-wheeling frontier spirits chided the youthful Billy, playfully or otherwise, tagging him with a dramatically simplistic nickname, perhaps even prior to some newspaperman picking up on the brainy idea. What is significant for this story is not whether or not McDaniels was or was not the first person to ever call Billy, "Kid," but rather that Pat Garrett already knew of his wretched standing and mentioned Jim as one of the "cowboys" who were "…well known from the Rio Grande to the Rio Pecos."[64] Jim McDaniels was better known then, than now.

As with the turbulence at Tombstone, the troubles at lively Lincoln County have been skillfully revisited, reviewed, researched, recorded, and at times resentfully rehashed. There will be no effort here spent stepping into the quagmire of historic minutia. In the big picture Jim McDaniels was but a trooper, not a general. Commonly, it is written that Jim McDaniels smartly "forted up" in the *torreon* for a portion of the time exhausted during the legendary five-day battle and sweltering siege of lawyer Alexander McSween's home.[65] Retracing McDaniel's exacting footprints is not possible. Undeniably he was there; arguably he shouldn't have been. Frank Warner Angel, a Justice Department special investigator sent to snoop around about the squalid and sordid mess, casually characterized Jim McDaniels with but one word, "desperado."[66]

Lawmen, Outlaws and S.O.Bs.

The "desperado" headed for the Silver City area for an as yet undisclosed reason, and while prowling around on the lower Gila made a grizzly discovery. Jim McDaniels after leaving the scenic Charlie Ennis ranch on an agreeable June (1879) evening, just about sundown, managed to make it to the Murrian and Galbraith place by dusk. There he found the lifeless bodies of Con Murrian and Dick May, both shot to pieces. Suspecting it to be the work of reservation jumping Apache renegades Jim McDaniels "followed the trail" of five suspected raiders until it merged with the trail of ten more.[67] That's what he said anyhow. Whether or not his story was believed is ambiguous. The two deceased cowmen had been robbed of their weapons, horses, and too, of money they were known to have had just hours earlier. Sardonically a newspaperman penned, "...that the killing was supposed to be have been the work of Indians..." and noted that "opinions differ as to whether this outrage was or was not the work of Indians."[68] If the sometimes shadowy actions of Jim McDaniels were suspect, in this instance, it was not so noted in the local press reports.

Of another somewhat mysterious man-killer and viciously inclined character, Sam R. Perry, the dogged sleuth (actually a New York lawyer) sent by Washington, D. C., Frank Angel, descriptively said, "...I think reliable—But of no standing."[69] He was, however, on strong footing with Jim McDaniels. The depth of his regional esteem can be correctly calculated from comments gleaned out of an edition of the local newspaper, *Thirty-Four*, after Perry had gunned down Frank Wheeler. "Now if Perry would die of remorse the honest people of this county would sleep more soundly."[70] Presumably Jim McDaniels was similarly well-liked. From the best evidence, although admittedly sketchy, it looks as if Jim McDaniels and Sam Perry after the Lincoln County untidiness had teamed up for a little sideline business of their very own—stealing and/or *recovering* horses, the pair cunningly working the vicinity of Las Cruces and the "Monte Carlo of the West," old El Paso.[71] Allegedly the independently minded equine entrepreneurs made off with livestock belonging to William Jerroll, but according to data exposed by the ever steadfast Philip J. Rasch, Perry was later found "not guilty," whereas McDaniel's case on a change of venue was moved to Silver City, a fact furthermore confirmed in aged and crumpled pages of *The Daily Southwest.*[72] While free on a $500 bail bond in the first instance, Jim McDaniels was forced to ante up the other half of the thousand dollar bill for a second case of larceny.[73] Whether his bondsmen, who ever they might have been, got their money back remains uncertain.

Adrenaline, Alcohol and Attitude

Of Jim McDaniel's legally mandated rendezvous with some black-robed, District Judge, one noted writer simply says, "He beat the rap the hard way—by dying at Las Cruces on March 2, 1881."[74] An alternative scenario is proffered by a different writer held in high regard who says that Jim McDaniels was killed sometime during July, 1885, at San Geronimo, Texas.[75] At one place or the other he was declared dead. And although Ike Fridge may have been right most of the time, if he now could, assuredly he would recant from saying Jim McDaniels, his onetime Jinglebob bossman, "...was a peaceful man and never rushed into trouble..."[76] "Trouble" had been Jim McDaniel's middle name!

Lawmen, Outlaws and S.O.Bs.

ENDNOTES CHAPTER 2

"ADRENALINE, ALCOHOL, AND ATTITUDE"

[1] Martin, Charles, *A Sketch of Sam Bass, the Bandit*. Introduction by Ramon F. Adams. P. xv.

[2] *Muster Roll* of Company C, Frontier Battalion, Texas Rangers. Texas State Library and Archives Commission. Austin. Ingmire, Frances, in *Texas Ranger Service Records, 1847-1900*, Vol. IV, P. 41, reports McDaniel's place of birth as El Paso County, which is assuredly, in light of other information, not correct. Likewise in conflict with the *Muster Roll* is a comment in the Robert N. Mullin Collection at the Nita Stewart Haley Memorial Library & J. Evetts Haley History Center, Midland. Clearly Mullin, referencing a letter from (Walter Noble) Burns was given information that McDaniels was born in Nashville, Texas, but in fact, careful inspection of the *Muster Roll* indicates it was instead Nashville, Tennessee. Naturally, if indeed McDaniels lied, establishing his place of birth is problematic, but a renowned historian asserts that such was not the case, see endnote 39. All other physical description features of McDaniels found in Mullin's notes match with the *Muster Roll*.

[3] *Ibid.* Physical description from *Muster Roll*. The fact McDaniels was illiterate is obvious from an inspection of his Texas Ranger *oath*. His signature is recorded as "his X mark". Texas Ranger Hall of Fame and Museum. Waco. That McDaniels could speak fluent Spanish is mentioned in the December 22, 1877, edition of the *Grant County Herald*.

[4] McDaniel's employment with John Chisum is well documented throughout Klasner, Lily, *My Girlhood Among Outlaws* (Ball, Eve, editor) and in Ike Fridge's account repeated in *Riders of the Pecos and The Seven Rivers Outlaws*, by Clarence S. & Joan N. Adams. P. 94-120. Fridge knew and worked with McDaniels. For this narrative, references made to Fridge will be cited from *Riders of the Pecos*, rather than the rare edition he authored, *History of the Chisum War: or Life of Ike Fridge, Stirring Events of Cowboy Life on the Frontier*. Also see, Rasch, Phillip J., *Warriors of Lincoln County*, (DeArment, Robert K., editor) P. 17-20.

[5] Rasch, *Warriors*, "...he was foreman of John S. Chisum's Home Creek Ranch in Texas..." P. 17. And see, Fridge, "...with instruction for him to take the money to the foreman, Jim McDaniel(s) at the ranch." P. 99. And, "Jim McDaniel(s), our faithful foreman,..." P. 109.

[6] *Ibid.*

[7] Hinton, Jr., Harwood P., "John Simpson Chisum, 1877-84," *New Mexico Historical Review*, Vol. XXI, No. 3 (July 1956). P. 177. And see, Sinclair, John L., "On the Hoof," *New Mexico Magazine*, October, 1939. P. 27. "For a hundred miles in all directions Jinglebob cattle grew fat on the grassy ranges."

[8] Clarke, Mary Whatley, *John Chisum, Jinglebob King of the Pecos*. P. 1. For exacting information on how the legendary earmarking was actually performed see, Potter, Jack, "The Jingle-Bob Herd," *New Mexico Magazine*, (July 1945) P. 21.

[9] Hinton, "John Simpson Chisum," P. 182. "Many, (Jinglebob cowboys) over a period of time, were transients; others were law-dodgers. Chisum, however, asked no questions about a man's past; he was concerned only with his ability to handle stock and obey orders."

[10] Adams, Ramon F., *Six-Guns and Saddle Leather.* P. 235.

[11] *Ibid.*

[12] Rasch, *Warriors,* P. 17-20.

[13] Fridge, *Riders of the Pecos*, P. 101-104.

[14] *Ibid.,* P. 107-111.

[15] *Ibid.,* P. 118-119.

[16] Rasch, *Warriors,* P. 18. Also see Klasner, *My Girlhood*, P. 249. In speaking of the raid to steal Mescalero Apache horses she says, "They came past our place, and it was upon this occasion that I first saw Jesse Evans and Jimmie McDaniels." And see, Nolan, Frederick, *The Lincoln County War, A Documentary History*, P. 298. "The names of Frank Baker, Tom Hill, Frank Rivers {John Long}, Jim McDaniels, and Marion Turner were prominent among those said to have been hired by Chisum to rustle horses." Dependent on the source cited Evans first name is spelled "Jessie," or sometimes "Jesse". His biographers opted for the former in their historical excavation of his wicked six-shooter career. Understandably, an absolute listing of those so engaged is elusive—there was no roster.

[17] *Ibid.* And see, Nolan, Frederick, "The Horse Thief War," *Old West*, Summer, 1994. P. 16. "...to steal back as many horses as they could and kill without compunction any Apache who got in their way."

[18] Rasch, Philip J. *Gunsmoke in Lincoln County*, (DeArment, Robert K., editor) P. 138. And see, McCright, Grady E. & Powell, James H., *Jessie Evans: Lincoln County Badman.* P. 20.

[19] Rasch, *Warriors,* P. 18.

[20] *Ibid.* Rash quoting the *Mesilla News*, 08-14-1875. In the *Grant County Herald* of 08-22-1875, the number of stolen horses is generalized, "a large number of horses and mules..." Interestingly in her account, Lily Klasner is not hesitant in saying the subject of this narrative was afraid of the outlaws, "The Mes brothers resented the search and openly made threats about waylaying and killing Jesse Evans and Jimmie McDaniels as well as any Chisums they might happened to find. News of the threats reached Evans and McDaniels, and being footloose they decided to leave the Chisums and go elsewhere...They told us they were headed for Arizona but expected to return when the Mes brothers quieted down." See, Klasner, *My Girlhood*, P. 155.

[21] Nolan, "Horse Thief War," P. 16.

[22] *Ibid.* Apparently utilizing Lily Klasner's allegation, Nolan says, "Still, the gang resented the search and made threats strong enough to convince Evans and McDaniels that an Arizona vacation might be advisable."

[23] *Grant County Herald*, 08-22-1875. "James McDaniels tells us that for six days..." Part of the story in the *Herald* was picked up from the Las Cruces *Borderer*.

[24] *Ibid.* "McDaniels promised that he would turn the thieves over to the officers of Lincoln County." And see, Nolan, "Horse Thief War," P. 17, quoting the *Mesilla News*, "...The Mexican authorities arrested the men and horses and turned them over to McDaniel upon his word of honor that he would return them to Lincoln." Indeed there is variance in naming the possemen, depending on which source is cited. Jessie Evans, Tom Bostick, Charles Woolsely, Frank Freeman, John Mosely, and one or two others, are the most frequently mentioned. It must be noted, however, that Jim McDaniels is the only posseman identified by name in

the contemporary newspaper accounts, and is undeniably credited with being the leader of the infamous squadron.

[25] Nolan, Frederick, "The Saga of the San Augustine Ranch," *True West.* June 1999. P. 43-52. Also see, *Grant County Herald*, 08-22-1875 & *Mesilla News*, 08-14-1875. Both newspapers offer the spelling as "San Agustin." Price, Paxton P., *Pioneers of the Mesilla Valley*, offers "San Augustin Ranch," P. 334. Regardless of the spelling, as Nolan so rightfully declares, it was "...one of the toughest places in New Mexico." P. 44.

[26] *Ibid.* Nolan quoting the *Mesilla Valley Independent* identifies the prisoners as Jesus Mes, Pas Mes, Thomas Madrid and Jermin Aguirre. However, in "Horse Thief War" he allows for the possibility that the executed prisoners were instead, Pancho, Gruz and Roman Mes, as well as Thomas Gurule. Rash, *Warriors*, P. 18, opts for the first four mentioned. Klasner, *My Girlhood*, P. 156, says, "...killed all of them while they were asleep, and succeeded in getting back the horses." Either way, McDaniel's detainees were issued summary judgment, and never reached Lincoln and their date with the Blind Mistress of Justice.

[27] *Grant County Herald*, 08-22-1875.

[28] Klasner, *My Girlhood*, P. 138-140. A letter from Abneth McCabe to Mrs. Eveline E. Casey, dated October 7, 1875 (three months after the San Agustin executions) mentioning Jim McDaniels seems to indicate he was for a short while back on the Chisum range, "Mr. Clark is riding a horse of Jimmie McDaniels. Jimmie says you can take the horse and use him just as your own and as long as you wish for nothing; but if you and Clark cannot agree you must let Clark ride the horse back to Bosque, and he will send him to you."

[29] *Ibid.*, P. 324-326.

[30] Fridge, P. 109.

[31] Fulton, Maurice G., *History of the Lincoln County War*, (Mullin, Robert N., editor). P. 67

[32] *Ibid.* And see, Clarke, *John Chisum.* P. 65.

[33] *Silver City Enterprise*, 02-22-1883. And, Nolan, Fredrick, "'Boss Rustler', The Life and Crimes of John Kinney," *True West*, September 1996. P. 15. Also see, McCright & Powell, *Jessie Evans:* P. 21. And see, *Frontier Times*, Vol. 14, No. 1. (October 1936) P. 11, repeating a story appearing in the Santa Fe *New Mexican*, "Kinney is a sort of major-general, having command over all the rustlers."

[34] Mullin, Robert N., "Here Lies John Kinney," *The Journal Of Arizona History.* No. 14. (Autumn 1973), P. 226. And see, Cohrs, Timothy & Caperton, Thomas J., *Fort Selden*, P. 16. "In the entire history of the post, at least three soldiers committed suicide and an additional five troopers died violently at the hands of their fellow soldiers or the nearby civilians." Price, *Pioneers*, P. 158. "Indeed six soldiers died in Leasburg due to lawlessness, twice the number lost in the fort's combat history."

[35] Nolan, "Boss Rustler," P. 16. The author lists Private John Reovir as dead, Privates Benedict Alig, Hugh McBride and Samuel Spence, seriously wounded. The civilian remains unnamed. Apparently one of the wounded soldiers later expired, see the *Rio Grande Republican*, 06-20-1883, as quoted by McCright & Powell, P. 24. "The notorious Charles Ray, otherwise known as Pony Diehl, together with Jessie Evans, Jim McDaniels, and two other desperadoes, it may be remembered, about eight years ago, killed three soldiers of the 8th Cavalry, at a dance hall in this city."

Adrenaline, Alcohol and Attitude

[36] *Ibid.* And see, DeMattos, Jack, "John Kinney," *Real West*, February 1984. P. 22. DeMattos reports one of the players to be Jim McMasters rather than Jim McDaniels as contemporary newspapers clearly identify, but does confirm, "As far as is known, no warrants were ever issued for this affray."

[37] *Grant County Herald*, 06-30-1877.

[38] Nolan, *The Lincoln County War*, P. 473. And see, Rash, *Warriors*, P. 157.

[39] *Muster Roll*, Company C, Frontier Battalion, Texas Rangers. Texas State Library and Archives Commission. And see, Cool, Paul, "El Paso's First Real Lawman, Texas Ranger, Mark Ludwick," National Association for Outlaw and Lawman History, Inc., (NOLA) *Quarterly*, Vol. XXV, No. 3 (July-September 2001). P. 45. At the Nita Stewart & J. Evetts Haley History Center, in the Robert N. Mullin Collection there is a notation, "McDaniels was one of the few who enrolled under his own name."

[40] *Oath*, Enlistment Roll, Recruits for Co. C, Frontier Battalion. Texas Ranger Hall of Fame and Museum. The value of McDaniel's horse is taken from the *Muster Roll*, Company C, Frontier Battalion.

[41] *Ibid.*

[42] Cool, Paul, "El Paso's First Real Lawman,…". And see, Brand, Peter, "Sherman W. McMaster(s), The El Paso Salt War, Texas Rangers & Tombstone," Western Outlaw-Lawman History Association (WOLA), *Journal*, Winter 1999, P. 3-7.

[43] Sonnichsen, C.L., *The El Paso Salt War*. P. 58.

[44] *Galveston Daily News*, 12-26-1877. "The blood shed by the Mexican butchers at San Elizario will hardly be suffered to go unavenged for the flimsy technical reason that it was purely local squabble over a salt pond."

[45] Sonnichsen, *The El Paso Salt War*. P. 49-58. And for a comprehensive examination refer to, *United States House of Representatives, Executive Document No. 93. 45th Congress, 2d Session. 1878.* Interestingly, Jim McDaniels is mentioned by name several times in the sworn testimony taken by the Military Board charged with investigating the "El Paso Troubles."

[46] *Grant County Herald*, 12-22-1877. "…agreed to meet the agents of the mob, which he (Tays) did and proceeded to the headquarters of the mob with John G. Atkinson and James McDaniels as interpreters, the lieutenant not understanding Spanish."

[47] Sonnichsen, *Salt War*, 49-58.

[48] *Executive Document No. 93, 45th Congress, 2nd Session, 1878.* Kerber to Hubbard, 12-14-1878 and Hubbard to Kerber, 12-15-1878.

[49] Alexander, Bob, *Dangerous Dan Tucker, New Mexico's Deadly Lawman.* P. 37. Confirming Tucker's command of the Silver City "Rangers" can also be noted in John Kinney's discharge from the squadron where it refers to him being a *private* in Lt. Tucker's company of state volunteers. See, Nolan, Frederick, "Boss Rustler—The Life and Crimes of John Kinney," *True West.* September and October, 1996.

[50] *Ibid.* Tucker's leadership role is further evidenced by the *Grant County Herald* edition of 01-05-1878, "D. Tucker has been chosen captain of the Silver City Company now in El Paso county." And also by numerous citations in *Executive Document No. 93.* And refer to, Webb, Walter Prescott, *The Texas Rangers—A Century of Frontier Defense*, P. 363. "In the meantime the Silver City men led by Kinney and Tucker, had arrived, some on foot and some without arms…There can be little doubt that the men, whether of the Rangers or posse, conceived it to be

their duty to avenge in blood the death of Howard, Atkinson, and McBride." And see, Gillett, James B., *Six Years With the Texas Rangers*, "...swept into the Rio Grande Valley with a band of New Mexico cowboys to relieve the besieged rangers...the rescue party raided up and down the valley from San Elizario to El Paso..." P. 140.

[51] Ward, Charles Francis, "The Salt War of San Elizaro (1877)," *Master of Arts Thesis*, 1932., P. 10-12. University of Texas. Austin. And see, Wilkins, Frederick, *The Law Comes to Texas, The Texas Rangers, 1870-1901*. "...and a group of Americans arrived from Silver City. The revenging expedition was not a glorious one;..." P. 142.

[52] *Executive Document No. 93, 45th Congress, 2nd Session, 1878*. {Statement of George Zwitzers}

[53] *Grant County Herald*, 01-12-1878.

[54] *Ibid.*, 01-26-1878, "A considerable number of the Silver City contingent to the El Paso army of occupation returned to town last Saturday. The expressed themselves as well satisfied with their lark. No expense, plenty of fun, and a measure of experience which may be turned to advantage in future campaigns."

[55] Naegle, Conrad Keeler, "The History of Silver City, New Mexikco, 1870-1886," *Master of Arts Thesis*, University of New Mexico, 1943. P. 180. And see, Alexander, *Dangerous Dan Tucker*, P. 47. Also see, Mullin, "Here Lies John Kinney," P. 228.

[56] *Muster Rolls*, Company C, Frontier Battalion, Texas Rangers. Texas State Library and Archives Commission.

[57] Notes. Robert N. Mullin Collection. Nita Stewart Haley Memorial Library & J. Evetts Haley History Center. And see, Rash, *Warriors*, P. 19. Nolan, *The Lincoln County War*, P. 510, says McDaniels killed Martin, which would certainly explain why he failed to follow through with the filing of formal charges. Or, *perhaps* Martin was in fact, Bob Martin, a sure enough Southwestern badman. For an excellent and long overdue biographical sketch of Martin, see; Cool, Paul, "Bob Martin: A Rustler in Paradise," Western Outlaw-Lawman History Association, *Journal*. Vol. XI No. 4. (Winter 2003) Also see, Ball, Larry D., *Desert Lawmen, The High Sheriffs of New Mexico and Arizona, 1846-1912.*, P. 357, for Barela's tenure as Dona Ana County Sheriff.

[58] *Ibid.* And see, Julyan, Robert, *The Place Names of New Mexico*. P. 319.

[59] Nolan, "Saga of the San Augustine Ranch," P. 44. The author also includes Shedd's ranch and Beckweth's Seven Rivers ranch as being notoriously tough New Mexico hot-spots for horse and cattle thieves. For Seven Rivers, see, Cramer, T. Dudley, *The Pecos Ranchers in the Lincoln County War*.

[60] Rasch, *Warriors*, P. 157.

[61] Adams, *Riders of the Pecos*, P. 32.

[62] Garrett, Pat, *The Authentic Life of Billy, The Kid*. Annotated by Frederick Nolan. P. 29. And for thumbnail sketches of some of the early "Billy the Kid" materials, including Garrett's volume, see, Metz, Leon, "Nobody Calls Him Henry," *The Roundup*, Vol. XXXII, No. 9. (October 1984) P. 4-8. Also see, Cline, Don, "Secret Life of Billy the Kid," *True West*, April 1984. The author cites a telegram written in 1877 regarding the killing of Frank Cahill. "His murderer, Antrim, alias "Kid," was allowed to escape and I believe is still at large." P. 16. As mentioned in this text, identifying the *very* first time the youthful Billy was tagged as being the "Kid" is an exercise in pointlessness.

[63] *Ibid.*, P. 30.

[64] *Ibid.*, P. 29. Garrett also named William Morton and Frank Baker.

[65] Rasch, Philip J., *Gunsmoke*, P. 118. Fulton, *History of Lincoln County War*, P. 249. McCright & Powell, *Jessie Evans:*, P. 144. Nolan, Frederick, *Lincoln County War*, P. 312. And see, Hertzog, Peter, *Outlaws of New Mexico*, P. 28.

[66] Theisen, Lee Scott, (editor) "Frank Warner Angel's Notes On New Mexico Territory, 1878," *Arizona and the West.*, Vol. 18. No. 4. (Winter 1976), P. 359. Nolan, *Lincoln County War*, P. 345 suggests that after the siege at Lincoln and the death of McSween, that Jim McDaniels and other "hard-core toughs," men like, John Kinney, Jessie Evans, Bob Speaks, John and Tom Selman, "Rustling Bob" Bryant, and others, blatantly went on a rampage of rustling and robbery. Unquestionably the author is right, but exactingly following McDaniel's mischievously malicious footprints on a day by day basis with a paper trial is imperceptibly possible.

[67] *Grant County Herald*, 06-21-1879 & 06-28-1879.

[68] *Ibid.*

[69] Theisen, "Frank Warner Angel's Notes...," P. 361.

[70] Rasch, *Warriors*, P. 162. Quoting the 07-16-1879 edition of Las Cruces *Thirty-Four.*

[71] *Ibid.*, P. 19. And see, Rasch, *Gunsmoke*, P. 229. Perry later killed Frank Wheeler.

[72] *Ibid.* And see, *The Daily Southwest*, 07-28-1880. "Territory vs. Jas. McDaniels—Larceny. Continued." In the Robert N. Mullin collection there is a notation indicating McDaniels and Perry were charged "...in June 1878, with stealing horses." Nita Stewart & J. Evetts Haley History Center.

[73] *Ibid.*

[74] *Ibid.*, Quoting the Las Cruces *Thirty-Four*, March 10, 1881. P. 20. Another unidentified news clip (Lundwall collection) dated 03-12-1881 simply says, "Jas. McDaniels died in Las Cruces, last week."

[75] Nolan, *Lincoln County War*, P. 473. "One version has it that he (McDaniels) died at Las Cruces March 2, 1881; another, that he was killed by police officers near San Geronimo, Tex., in July 1885." In a more recent comment, the author in annotated remarks for *The Authentic Life of Billy, The Kid*, says, "He (McDaniels) was killed at San Geronimo, Tex. in July 1885," but does not elaborate. P. 47. Undeniably, it was reported that a Texas desperado named Jim McDaniels, a member of the Robbers' Cave Gang, was killed in a horrendous gunbattle with lawmen near New Braunfels, Texas during the fall of 1884. And for sure, the hellion died game showing plenty of "grit and gristle," wounding two officers before his bullet riddled body collapsed in death's unmerciful grip. Whether or not this Jim McDaniels and the Jim McDaniels of New Mexico fame, the subject of this particular story, can be *conclusively* and ironclad linked as being one in the same person has proved indeterminate, as of yet, at least to this author's imperfect knowledge. Perhaps, there is in truth another captivating chapter to the Jim McDaniel's saga. Historic conundrums are indeed intriguing, it's what makes it all worthwhile. See, Hunter, Sr., J. Marvin, "Early Day Stage Robbers," *Frontier Times*, January, 1947. P. 293, picking up a story from the *San Antonio Express*.

[76] Fridge, *Riders of the Pecos*, P. 109.

CHAPTER 3

"WE WANT TO GET AWAY BEFORE WE GO DEFUNCT"

George Stevenson, New Mexico Incorrigible

John M. Storz didn't have any time to waste; the sun was up. There wasn't time to fiddle around, not on this bustling Thursday morning, May 19, 1899. Keeping his end of the contractual business deal, nearby Silver City, New Mexico Territory builder Richard W. Grabe had supervised the driving of the very last square-headed nail. The commodious new saloon, at last, was finished. At this point it was up to the owner, that free-wheeling Santa Rita entrepreneur Storz, to have the opulent mahogany bar waxed, the shot-glasses polished, enticing games of chance ready, the amber current flowing, and a clamorous band primed—ready—to pound out a few ribald classics at the opening night gala.[1] Beyond doubt, Storz knew it was going to be a bona fide shindig, a humdinger! Surely he was genuinely happy, yet, a very busy man. Rumors were running rampant; a crowd of thirsty guests were anticipated from budding communities scattered throughout the area, not just a smattering of scruffy Santa Rita miners.

Of the celebration there is not anyway of knowing just how well John Storz did that night and, likewise, totaling the amount of cash raked in by monte dealer William "Billy" Woods, is undetermined. Woods was remarkably well-liked, and by most accounts was measured as a straightforward frontier gambler—amicable and honest. And too, it can be reported with candor, the merriment was "attended by all the boys for miles around."[2] Into wee morning hours the band did play, the boys did imbibe, and the underpinnings for woozy hangovers were fermented. Although many stayed late, by dawn, most had staggered or wobbled or puked their way out of the taproom and were off for home, or somewhere. Billy Woods too, called it a night, tallied his earnings, and sleepily ambled toward the inviting bed at a nearby house.[3] George Stevenson, a hardscrabble miner from the nearby village of Central, however, was not quite ready to call it a night.[4]

G.L. Turner store, Santa Rita, New Mexico Territory. The street in front is where George Stevenson was standing when he "let loose" and killed Billy Woods. Courtesy, Don Turner.

Around six o'clock in the morning, outside, standing in the all but deserted street, Stevenson was "drunk and wild in his language," as he stridently conversed with Ed Dalrymple and Pat Welch.[5] Suddenly during a slurred and slobbery harangue, senselessly, George Stevenson jerked a six-shooter from his pant's pocket and let go with three madly misdirected shots. Pointy splinters flew, as zinging "blue whistlers" haphazardly drilled through whitewashed pine boards, and beyond. Involuntarily and instantaneously, snoozing Billy Wood's right arm shot straight up in a grotesque shudder, whilst the pistol ball went into the crown of his head, plowed through his brain, then tore a gaping hole in his whiskered chin before the projectile thudded into the cabin's grimy plank floor.[6] The other two shots did no damage, but Billy Woods knew not—he was doornail dead.[7] Immediately two men with vastly differing missions raced to the bloody crime scene, Dr. Guthrie who got there too late, and Grant County Constable J.H. Hankins who didn't. George Stevenson was forthrightly arrested.[8]

Lawmen, Outlaws and S.O.Bs.

Another view of Santa Rita, circa 1900. Courtesy, Terry Humble.

Justice of the Peace Cornelius McCarthy impaneled a coroner's jury and officiated at the inquest.[9] Incredibly, for someone in Stevenson's unsmiling legal predicament, he "...displayed considerable nonchalance, apparently not fully realizing the condition in which he was placed. He assumed to instruct the court in its duties and his actions were the occasion of much comment among the on-lookers, who marveled greatly at the patience of the court."[10] And, in a separate account, "He laughed and joked after the verdict had been rendered, and he evidently is not worrying much over the outcome."[11] In the end, George Stevenson's case was bound over for action by the Grand Jury. He was to be held in jail until he could come up with the requisite $2000 bail bond. Later in the morning, Sheriff James K. Blair, who was described as a "model officer," made the scenic sixteen mile trip from Silver City, took physical custody of Stevenson and delivered him to the county jail.[12] Bleak reality was slowly beginning to creep into George Stevenson's befuddled brain.

Apparently, George Stevenson's buddies, if he had any, were reluctant or not capable of standing his cash bond. The prisoner languished in jail for almost a year. During the March 1900 term of District Court, after a jury trial, and just thirty effortless minutes of deliberation, George Stevenson was convicted of murder in the third degree.[13] The convicted felon, a few days later, stood before the court to take his medicine, five years confinement in the territorial penitentiary at Santa Fe. Straight away his attorney, Edward Baker, announced intentions of filing an appeal to the Supreme Court thus forestalling Stevenson's delivery to the prison.[14] Seven other prisoners, having exhausted all other recourse, were made ready for the trip to prison and departed by train, guarded by Sheriff Blair and his number one deputy, forty-three year old, W.D. "Keechi" Johnson.[15]

While the sheriff was gone, a flock of the remaining jailbirds were making plans.

The Grant County Jail, Silver City, New Mexico Territory, from which the ever incorrigible George Stevenson and ratty James Brooks (and many others) made their reckless but futile escape. Courtesy, Silver City Museum.

After making a repetitive, but necessary headcount on March 28th, W.H. Rose, a guard for the Grant County lockup, came up short. Six prisoners had flown the coop, and not unexpectedly, George Stevenson was among them.[16] Initial investigation revealed, one of the inmates had fashioned a workable key from a pewter spoon.[17] The half dozen prisoners marched through the iron-barred cell door and set in motion their plans. A hastily shaped posse was put in the field.[18]

Left: George Stevenson, #1402, as he appeared entering New Mexico Territorial Penitentiary at Santa Fe. Courtesy, New Mexico Commission of Public Records, State Records Center and Archives.

Right: James Brooks, #1362, as he appeared entering New Mexico Territorial Penitentiary at Santa Fe. Courtesy, New Mexico Commission of Public Records, State Records Center and Archives.

Upon their return from the territorial capitol at Santa Fe, Sheriff Blair and "Keechi" Johnson grabbed their Winchesters, saddled up, and started in pursuit of the fugitives.[19] The first to be bagged was the suspected cow-thief, Delbert O'Neal, who was promptly captured south of Silver City, near Cow Springs on the old Santa Rita-Janos Road, by one of the intrepid range detectives working for George Scarborough and the Grant County Cattlemen's Association.[20] Shortly thereafter, a proven escapee and accused burglar, Robert Bisbee, was literally run to ground on the Frost Ranch by "Keechi" Johnson and deputy Miles Marshall, meekly surrendering after dancing to a few rifle balls, delicately fired into his getaway path. Two of the other fleeing prisoners, Frank Harvey and George Brown had been in jail for minor misdemeanors, and as a newspaperman rightly deduced, they "...are short term men and their absence is really more of an advantage to the county than their presence in the jail, at the expense of the taxpayers."[21] A different correspondent wrote, "The remaining two were tramps, whose absence was more desired than their presence."[22] Good riddance may have been awarded to two prisoners, but for two more, George Stevenson and James Brooks the hunt was pressed. Both were considered threatening men, Stevenson already having been convicted of the thoughtless murder of an inoffensive gambler, and Brooks, who earlier had "figured prominently" in the murder of a school teacher at Cook's Peak, Professor Simmons, and was implicated in a Las Cruces bank holdup, but at this juncture in life he was only charged with stealing a stock-saddle from J. T. Rabb.[23]

Grant County Sheriff James K. Blair. He ordered his redoubtable deputies William D. "Keechi" Johnson and Miles Marshall not to abandon the trail of escapees Stevenson and Brooks. Courtesy, Frank Blair.

Grant County Sheriff Blair was not a happy man, and justifiably so. Just the month before, on Wednesday, February 21, 1900, five

55

incarcerated thieves finally finished their shifty plot, sawing through and enlarging a wooden window sill, and then crawling out into fresh air.[24] In the matter at hand, from his fuming internal investigation it was determined that jailer William Rose had negligently left the heavy brass key-ring on an unattended desk. Blair made a "clean sweep" of his jail employees, appointing James W. Gill and J.W. Dickerson to manage the Grant County lockup.[25] Otherwise, he was thoroughly sickened by news he received from Deming regarding a fellow Southwest lawman with an earned man-killing reputation, George A. Scarborough. Sorrowfully, it was reported that Scarborough had been wounded during a southeastern Arizona mountain pursuit and the resultant lopsided shoot-out. Efforts directed at saving his life were futile. Sadly, the doughty peace officer died on April 5, 1900.[26] For a short while some few surmised George Stevenson and James Brooks could have been participants in the ghastly ambush of Scarborough but, in truth, they weren't. Nevertheless, they were still very much wanted renegades, and deputies "Keechi" Johnson and Miles Marshall were doggedly hounding after the desperate duo. They had been spotted crossing the tracks near Separ, headed south, Mexico bound.[27]

By April 20th the *Silver City Enterprise* reported the desperados had made it across the boundary line.[28] A week later, after a grueling manhunt over torturous topography, and by playing an analytical hunch, deputies Johnson and Marshall latched on to George Stevenson and James Brooks "in Pilares, Montezuma county, state of Sonora, old Mexico."[29] Surprisingly, largely due to the proficiency of the two lawmen involved, there was no spectacular gunfight; there was, however, a predictable skirmish shaping up—an international battle over extradition.[30]

Various local lawyers were proclaiming to the world, or anyone else that would listen, their theories regarding the intricacies of an international extradition. A short time earlier a new agreement over the subject had been made between the United States and Mexico. It was now time for a genuine test. Attorneys were asserting that on the American side of the line, unquestionably, the paperwork would have to be officially approved by the territorial governor, and several precisely suggested. Even President McKinley's signature would be necessary. Who knew what machinations were requisite on the other side of the sometimes bothersome border? A majority seemed to concur and were predicting it would result in an "extremely difficult matter." A long and drawn out affair, at best.[31]

While waiting for the legal niceties to be worked out at a level above his pay grade, and acknowledging that as far as the prisoners were concerned it was "getting very monotonous," the obliging "Keechi" Johnson dutifully wrote an informative letter to his anxious bossman, Sheriff Blair, which herein is cited, in part:

Deputy Sheriff, William D. "Keechi" Johnson, a member of the resolute duo that successfully tracked Stevenson and Brooks deep into Mexico. Courtesy, Roy B. Sinclair.

...We had them (Stevenson and Brooks) in a tunnel for several days, but moved them into an adobe house, and we occupy the next room to them; have leg irons on them all the time, and guard them day and night. We have a Mexican police on one watch, and pay him $3.00 per day Mexican money. Marshall and I are baching, and have a frying pan and two three pound lard buckets in stock; eat twice a day and think it good, in fact it beats the restaurants at $1.00 a day for "frijoles y menudo."

Deputy Sheriff Miles Marshall, the other half of the team responsible for the capture and return of wily fugitives Stevenson and Brooks. Courtesy, Everett Marshall.

We are about eighty-five or ninety miles from San Barardino (sic), and have no communication except to go there, and our horses would not justify the trip. We have mail once a week from Naco. I am looking every mail for an order to take them out, and hope it will come on next mail.

Stevenson don't think he can be touched. Brooks would have gone through without papers if Stevenson had not influenced him to stay. These officers here are anxious for us to take these fellows away from here, and they say that the Governor will give them up without a doubt.

I will telegraph you from San Barnardino when I arrive there and will want you to meet us at Lordsburg for prisoners. I will have to get conveyances from Slaughters to San Simon ranch and send horses back to Slaughter's, then to Lordsburg, and get my horses at Duncan and hope it will be soon…

Our financial standing is: Liabilities $30.00 Mexican money. Assets $70 gold and $10 Mexican money. So you see we are pretty well fixed for several days to come yet, but want to get away before we go defunct or have to go to San Barnardino for more money. We are here to stay until we get the fellows out…[32]

The red tape was finally rolled up tight, and sheriff's deputies were handed lawfully drawn extradition documents and allowed to proceed north with their prisoners, and to legally cross the international line.[33] It was a punishing three hundred mile trail, but the officers in time meandered into town and deposited their manacled prisoners in the Grant County jail.[34] Johnson and Marshall had been tracking or guarding the brigands for just shy of three months, a fact not missed by a local reporter, who remarked it was "…one of the longest pursuits every made by a local officer."[35] Of the capture, another news-bird declared that "no greater task has ever been undertaken by any officer of the County and none was ever more faithfully performed."[36] It, for sure, had been a wearisome adventure and tenacious test, but an incorrigible George Stevenson's abrasive tilting with New Mexico Territory's criminal justice system was far from over.

Exactly how Sheriff Blair developed the criminal intelligence is indeterminate. On Wednesday morning, September 12, 1900, most likely by talking with a confidential source, an informant, Blair learned that another "jail delivery" was in the works, and the identity of one of the schemers should not come as a startling surprise. The sheriff straight away spotted George Stevenson and one of "Uncle Sam's" prisoners, Duke White, in jail for stealing goods from nearby Fort Bayard, as the inmates responsible for concocting a liberating plan. While the pair of connivers uneasily stood by, a methodical search of their austere cells was executed.

The upshot—two hacksaws. Just how illicit tools materialized, deep in the bowels of the Grant County jail, is mysterious yet.[37] James K. Blair must have hung his head in disbelief and thrown up his hands in dismay. That damn jail and George Stevenson were causing both real problems for the sheriff. One he had to suffer, the other he didn't. It was time to get shed of a vexing George Stevenson.

Long overdue, George Stevenson was delivered to the territorial prison at Santa Fe. Straightforwardly the new inmate was issued three things; a drab, but nonetheless distinct suit of horizontal-striped prison clothes; a compulsory close-cropped haircut; and a number—1402.[38]

Whether or not George Stevenson and the politically polished prison superintendent, Holm Olaf "H.O." Bursum, had a face to face consultation, reviewing institutional rules, is vague. Certainly though, there would be, at a later date, a meaningful clash between one man sworn to maintain peace and another who had adopted a life's work of willfully ignoring the law.[39]

H.O. Bursum, a long-term New Mexican, had cut his law enforcement teeth in one of the toughest bailiwicks in the territory, Socorro County. In 1894 he was elected sheriff and, at the time, his jurisdictional reach stretched from central New Mexico west one hundred and seventy miles to the Arizona Territorial line, and from north to south, eighty-five miles—an area of 15,386 square miles.[40] Amplifying Bursum's constabulary nightmare, one author wrote, "…since the Southwest was one of the last havens for the reckless breed, Bursum was familiar with the gangs…" of two different Black Jacks, "Kid" Johnson, Bronco Bill Walters, "Kid" Swingle, the wide-ranging Butch Cassidy, and many of the disreputable lesser lights.[41]

As history has recorded, when it was crucial, H.O. Bursum could spend hours in the saddle chasing after *mal hombres* and, if need be, he was deathly adept at taking decisive action. There, however, was another side to the sheriff. H.O. Bursum was attuned to the fact he was functioning on a frontier in transition. During one high-profile homicide investigation the sheriff judiciously made use of developing forensic technology. Allegedly, the criminal defendant in a killing, Frank Williams, mysteriously disappeared, leaving behind a camp in "disarray" and copious amounts of blood-splatter evidence on his saddle and bed roll—clear proof of foul play. William's scheming pals brashly guided Bursum to what was a conclusive crime scene. Plainly, Williams had been disgustingly massacred, his missing body, well, buried someplace in the dark mountains. Unmistakably, there couldn't be sound logic in charging a dead man with a murder, therefore the criminal case should be dismissed, or so William's pals recommended. H.O. Bursum wasn't so sure. Meticulously, the skeptical sheriff collected blood samples, cautiously avoiding any external contamination. Upon his return to Socorro the evidence was submitted to the Zoology Department at the University of New Mexico. At the laboratory, competent analysis revealed the blood was from a horse, not a human. Apparently the indicted suspect hadn't been murdered, after all! Later, Frank Williams was arrested, in spite of his botched trickery.[42] The Socorro County Sheriff was lauded for his clever detective work and devotion to duty.

Holm Olaf "H.O." Bursum, an ex-Socorro County Sheriff and innovative forensic investigator, and a future New Mexico U.S. Senator. As Warden at the New Mexico Territorial Penitentiary he decisively thwarted a vicious prison break, stopping George Stevenson cold in his tracks, two bullets to the heart, one through an eye. Courtesy, New Mexico Commission of Public Records, State Records Center and Archives.

Lawmen, Outlaws and S.O.Bs.

By the time (1899) New Mexico Governor Miguel Otero appointed H.O. Bursum to the patronage job as Prison Superintendent, the ex-sheriff was well-known throughout the territory and a powerhouse player in Republican politics.[43] With his ascendancy to the leadership position at the prison, Bursum brought new ideas to what many considered a draconian institution, such as an honor system, and a program for the common good of both the public and the prisoner, "free-world" road work.[44]

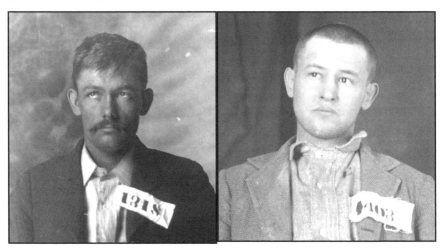

Left: William Simmons, #1318, a Chaves County horse-thief, as he appeared entering New Mexico Territorial Penitentiary at Santa Fe. Foolishly he bought his way into a vicious but, failed, prison break, and ended up paying for the tomfoolery by forfeiting his life. Courtesy, New Mexico Commission of Public Records, State Records Center and Archives.

Right: Frank Carper, #1403, as he appeared entering New Mexico Territorial Penitentiary at Santa Fe. He was a pitiable Chaves County livestock thief and a pathetically inept escape artist. Courtesy, New Mexico Commission of Public Records, State Records Center and Archives.

Convict #1402 was unrepentant. From the top of his shaven head to the very bottom of his prison issued footwear, George Stevenson was fed-up. On the morning of April 17, 1901, after having been in prison for less than a year, he made his move. Accompanied by two fellow disgruntled inmates, William Simmons from Colfax County and Frank Carper from Chaves County, both convicted of "cattle stealing," George Stevenson made a fierce break from the work-detail at the prison's bakery where he was assigned for the day. His shameful pals were each armed with a "solid iron rod two feet long and an inch thick," and Stevenson had in his possession, somehow, a .38 caliber Smith & Wesson revolver and fifty cartridges stuffed in a pant's pocket.[45]

Convict George Stevenson sprinted to a lower-level dining room where unarmed guards were casually assembled, taking a break. With the hammer on his handgun cocked, Stevenson commanded the bewildered employees to throw up their trembling hands. George Stevenson was not in the least ready for Captain of the Guard Felipe Armijo's cool-headed reaction. Armijo grabbed a sturdy wooden chair, flung it at Stevenson, and made a mad-dash from the cramped quarters, not running away, but racing for a gun. George Stevenson shot prison guard Pedro Sandoval in the head. The bullet only creased his skull, but it knocked him to the floor and put him out of the action.[46]

After negotiating an interior walk-way to the "first" watchtower, Armijo grabbed a loaded shotgun and zipped back toward the chaotic battleground, focused on aiding his trapped comrades. George Stevenson lurked at the tight doorway, weighing his diminishing options. Felipe Armijo forced his hand. Rushing headlong into harm's way, Armijo may or may not have heard the three gunshots, but he did stagger, nearly lurching to the floor as one of Stevenson's bullets found its mark, piercing his cheek and shattering his jawbone. Armijo fired back with the scattergun, a few of the pelting buckshot connecting with Stevenson, but not inflicting serious wounds. George Stevenson hobbled away, seeking an advantage. Armijo, spitting teeth and suffering terribly, gutted up and, once again, charged! Finding one of the scurrilous convicts, William Simmons, holding the prison doctor, David Knapp, and a guard, Carlos Dominguez, hostage, Armijo shot through a glass-paned window and sledgehammered Simmons to the floor, inflicting serious wounds to his groin, arms, and back. Frank Carper, the third villain, lost his nerve during the bedlam and gave it up. Another prisoner, Jose Monica Sena, somehow interjected himself into the fractious mêlée, was misidentified as a blundering escapee, and was shot, but luckily, not critically wounded.[47]

Hearing the sound of multiple gunshots, Warden H.O. Bursum, from a second floor observation platform, thirty feet above, stared down on the pandemonium. Instinctively he darted for a storage cabinet and snatched a Winchester from within, rapidly levering a round into the rifle's chamber.[48]

Lawmen, Outlaws and S.O.Bs.

New Mexico Territorial Penitentiary at Santa Fe. The scene of the abortive prison break during which the Warden, H.O. Bursum killed inmate George Stevenson, and Captain of the Guard Felipe Armijo mortally gunned down prisoner William Simmons. Courtesy, New Mexico Commission of Public Records, State Records Center and Archives.

Whether or not George Stevenson ever looked up goes unmentioned, as too, does any warning proffered by H.O. Bursum. George Stevenson had made his play, he had a .38 revolver; but now Bursum shot Stevenson twice in the heart and once in the right eye and knocked him to the ground.[49]

George Stevenson was dead. William Simmons was mortally wounded, suffering acute pain from Captain Felipe Armijo's horrific shotgun blast. Prisoner Frank Carper was standing in a puddle of his own making, hypnotically dazed. Immediately, now that it was reckoned a safe maneuver, wary entry into the prison yard was accomplished, and the injured were speedily transported to St. Vincent's Hospital for medical treatment. Two days after the shoot-out, at 4 o'clock in the morning, prison inmate Simmons, "who had been shot in the loins and the liver," died.[50] Employees Felipe Armijo and Pedro Sandoval fortunately recovered, as did the inmate wounded by mistake, Jose Sena.[51]

Prison Superintendent H.O. Burusm's clear-thinking and gutsy action was acclaimed by newspapermen and the general public alike. He and Armijo were credited with fearlessly saving the day and preventing "the success of the plot of the three convicts to escape and perhaps a general mutiny."[52] The Santa Fe community, in fact, the whole of New Mexico Territory had been enthralled with the story, and not just a few pondered how a convict could get a six-shooter, but interest in an inquiry of that type faded rather quickly, as did any degree of sympathy for the dead prisoners.

Meanwhile, in southwestern New Mexico, at Santa Rita, as she did everyday, a new morning sun was cracking first light. And too, businessman John M. Storz was hustling about, running to and fro, making everything right—polishing and waxing—getting ready for another hell-to-pop night on the town.

ENDNOTES CHAPTER 3

"WE WANT TO GET AWAY BEFORE WE GO DEFUNCT"

[1]   Humble, Terrence M., "The Pinder-Slip Mining Claim Dispute of Santa Rita, New Mexico, 1881-1912" *Mining History Journal.* 1996. P. 94. And, for more information on prominent Silver City builder Richard W. Grabe, see, Berry, Susan and Russell, Sharman Apt, *Built to Last, An Architectural History of Silver City New Mexico.* P. 42. "Ornamental brickwork, particularly in segmental arches over windows and door openings, often characterized buildings which Richard Grabe constructed." Citations for Grabe throughout the volume. For Santa Rita, see, Sherman James E. and Barbara H., *Ghost Towns and Mining Camps of New Mexico.* P. 188-191.

[2]   *Silver City Enterprise*, May 26, 1899. "Woods seems to have been known as a quite inoffensive man, much liked by all who met him." And see, *Silver City Independent*, May 23, 1899. "…quite a number came from surrounding towns to enjoy the festivities."

[3]   *Ibid.*

[4]   *Ibid.* "…when George Stevenson, excited by drink…"

[5]   *Silver City Independent*, May 23, 1899.

[6]   *Ibid.* Other reports list the time of death as 5 A. M. The *Enterprise* story reveals, "…He (Stevenson) returned it (six-shooter) to his pocket, but pulled it out again."

[7]   *Silver City Enterprise*, May 26, 1899.

[8]   *Ibid.* And see, Humble, P. 94.

[9]   Humble, P. 94. The author characterizes Woods as a bartender rather than a "monte dealer."

[10]   *Silver City Independent*, May 23, 1899.

[11]   *Ibid.* In the same story it is reported, "He (Stevenson) and the deceased were always good friends."

[12]   Humble, P. 94. And see, Ball, Larry. *Desert Lawmen, The High Sheriffs of New Mexico and Arizona, 1846-1912.* P. 52. "Siringo applauded Sheriffs Arthur Goodell and James K. Blair of Grant County. They were 'model officers.'"

[13]   *Silver City Enterprise*, March 23, 1900 & *Silver City Independent*, March 20, 1900.

[14]   *Ibid.* The attorney's name is found in the March 30th edition of the *Enterprise*.

[15]   Santa Fe *New Mexican*, April 30, 1900.

[16]   *Silver City Enterprise*, March 30, 1900 & *Silver City Independent*, April 3, 1900. Also see, DeArment, Robert K., *George Scarborough, The Life and Death Of A Lawman On The Closing Frontier.* P. 227.

[17]   *Ibid.* "…a roughly made key was found, almost a perfect reproduction of the key in the possession of the guard…A pewter spoon was also found, the handle of which was broken off…"

[18]   *Ibid.*, March 30, 1900. The posse consisted of Deputy Sheriffs Burnside, Durnan, and Marshall, as well as Constable Perfecto Rodriquez. "Keechi" Johnson's son, Don, also accompanied the squadron.

[19]   Santa Fe *New Mexican*, April 30, 1900. "Upon their (Blair and Johnson) return immediate steps were taken to recapture the prisoners."

[20]   *Silver City Enterprise*, April 6, 1900. Interestingly, O'Neal's father was also in jail for "unlawful defacing of brands and larceny of neat cattle," but refused to

participate in the jailbreak. And see, DeArment, P. 227. Also see, Julyan, Robert, *The Place Names of New Mexico*. P. 99.

[21]   *Silver City Independent*, April, 3, 1900. And, DeArment, P. 227. "Two of the six had been jailed for minor offenses, so little effort was made to apprehend them." Also see, Santa Fe *New Mexican*, April 30,1900. "…a short distance from Cow Springs…"

[22]   *Ibid.* May 29, 1900.

[23]   *Silver City Enterprise*, March 30, 1900. And see, Rasch, Philip, "The Las Cruces Bank Robbery," *Frontier Times*, January 1981. P. 48-50. Brook's alleged role in the crime is yet to be clarified adequately. For an excellent reappraisal of the bank holdup at Las Cruces, see, Edwards, Harold, "Sheriff Pat Garrett's Puzzle: A Blow-by-Blow Account of Solving a New Mexico Bank Robbery," *The National Tombstone Epitaph*. January 2003.

[24]   *Ibid.* February 23, 1900. Almost unbelievably it is reported, "The escaped prisoners have evidently been working some length of time with their pocket knives in cutting the window sill, which cutting they concealed by covering it up with dirt."

[25]   *Ibid.* April 6, 1900. "It appears now that guard Rose left his bunch of keys lying on his desk and they simply extracted the key belonging to the lock of the south door and walked out."

[26]   DeArment, P. 229.

[27]   *Ibid.* P. 227. And see, Santa Fe *New Mexican*, April 30, 1900. "…he supposing that Stevenson and Brooks had endcavored to cross the border into Mexico." Separ was a Southern Pacific Railroad settlement between Deming and Lordsburg. See, Julyan, P. 331. "With the coming of the RR Separ became a cattle-loading station for nearby ranches."

[28]   *Silver City Enterprise*, April 20, 1900.

[29]   *Ibid.* April 27, 1900. Also see, Thrapp, Dan. *Encyclopedia of Frontier Biography.* Vol. III, P. 1272-1273. Certainly Thrapp is accurate in reporting that Stevenson and Brooks were arrested by Johnson and Marshall, but he does inadvertently criss-cross the chronology placing the Silver City jailbreak after, rather than before the apprehension in Mexico. Additionally, he characterizes Stevenson as a "purported cattle rustler," an assertion which seems to be in conflict with primary source material.

[30]   *Ibid.* "It will be an extremely difficult matter to extradite the captured criminals from old Mexico. It was so under the old treaty and will be equally as difficult under the recent treaty made between the United States and Mexico."

[31]   *Ibid.* April, 27, 1900.

[32]   *Ibid.* May 25, 1900.

[33]   *Ibid.* June 15, 1900.

[34]   *Ibid.* June 22, 1900. And see, *Silver City Independent*, June 19, 1900.

[35]   *Silver City Independent*, April 23, 1901.

[36]   *Silver City Enterprise*, August 31, 1900.

[37]   *Ibid.* September 14, 1900.

[38]   Correspondence to author from Felicia Lujan, Archivist, State of New Mexico, Commission of Public Records, Santa Fe. April 25, 2002.

[39]   *The National Cyclopedia of American Biography.* P. 524. "…superintendent of the territorial penitentiary, 1899-1906." And see, Owen, Gordon R., *The Two Alberts—Fountain and Fall.* P. 360.

[40]   Moorman, Donald R. "Holm O. Bursum, Sheriff 1894," *New Mexico Historical Review*. No. 36 (1964) P. 334. And see, Bryan, Howard. *Robbers, Rogues and Ruffians*. P. 187-188. "Fresh horses were obtained for two men of the posse, while Bursum and Cipriano Baca headed back to Socorro to obtain fresh horses and more men, intending to transport them from Socorro west to Magdalena, a distance of about twenty-five miles, and from there travel north toward the Alamo Navajo community by horseback in an effort to intercept the two train robbers."

[41]   *Ibid.* P. 335. And see, Edwards, Harold L., "The Shooting of Bronco Bill," *Quarterly* for the National Association For Outlaw and Lawman History, Inc., (NOLA) Vol. XXI. No. 2. (April-June 1997) P. 26-31.

[42]   Moorman, P. 338. And see, Ball, for this, and other examples of frontier forensics. P. 296. Also see, Tanner, Karen & John, *Last Of The Old-Time Outlaws, The George West Musgrave Story*. The authors report a similar blood on the saddle story, which in fact may relate to the same crime scene, but the suspect is identified as D. C. Kyle, rather than Frank Williams. Their breakdown of the murderous offense is related to the killing of a "Mexican herder," and the subsequent flight of Kyle to Montana, in efforts designed for dodging Socorro County prosecution before an all Mexican jury. P118-119.

[43]   Curry, George. *George Curry 1861-1947, An Autobiography*. P. 194. "During my eight years in the Philippines, Holm O. Bursum of Socorro had become one of the dominant Republican leaders of New Mexico. He had been appointed superintendent of the Territorial penitentiary by Otero." And see, Fernlund, Kevin J. "Senator Holm O. Bursum and the Mexican Ring, 1921-1924," *New Mexico Historical Review*. October 1991. "Bursum's appointment to the U.S. Senate marked the apex of a long and eventful career in politics." P. 435. For additional comments on Bursum's political activities, see, Keleher, William A., *The Fabulous Frontier, Twelve New Mexico Items*. Citations to Bursum throughout. And see, French, William. *Recollections of a Western Ranchman*. P. 270. "Mr. Bursum, of Socorro, was warden of the penitentiary at the time, and Mr. Gilian Otero was governor."

[44]   Santa Fe *New Mexican*, August 6, 1953.

[45]   *Ibid.* April 17, 1901. Also see, *Silver City Enterprise*, April 19, 1901. And see, *Silver City Independent*, April 23, 1901.

[46]   *Ibid.*

[47]   *Ibid.* Convict Jose Monica Sena was shot in the arm and back with buckshot.

[48]   *Ibid.*

[49]   *Ibid.* And see, DeArment, P. 236.

[50]   *Ibid.*, April 19, 1901. Of Simmons the newspaper reported, "Had he lived after his release, he would have been taken to Colfax county, where an indictment of highway robbery, for robbing a store at Springer has been pending against him."

[51]   *Ibid.*

[52]   *Ibid.* Of the other guards it was said that "...they did their duty although being unarmed they were somewhat helpless."

CHAPTER 4

"DON'T GIVE UP THE FIGHT"

Roy Woofter, Roswell's Temperance Tiger

Roy Woofter as a young boy in Alum Bridge, West Virginia. Courtesy Carol Marlin.

The son of blue-coated Civil War veteran George Marion Woofter, Roy Woofter was born on February 3, 1880, not in the wild and woolly West, but in the mountains of West Virginia, at Alum Bridge.[1] Little is known regarding the migration, but Woofter family genealogical notations and early newspaper reports clearly reveal Roy, seeking a more healthful climate, joined his older brother Homer at Albia, Monroe County, Iowa, not too far north of the Missouri boundary, about 1903.[2] Homer Woofter was a respected policeman and a deputy constable in the pleasant farming community.[3] Somewhere along the way, at least according to one archival report, from time to time Roy Woofter assisted his brother in constabulary duties.[4] Whether his sweetheart, Margaret Forsyth, favorably accepted her beau's predilection for law enforcement work goes unrecorded, but alas, for a time, twenty-seven year old Roy Woofter had to bid her farewell; his health was steadily deteriorating and a drier and warmer clime was prescribed.[5]

Roy Woofter headed for what would later be known as the Land of Enchantment, but at the time it was simply designated New Mexico Territory.[6] He opted for exploring the possibilities at Roswell, Chaves County, in the southeastern portion of the Territory. Just a few years earlier there had been but nine houses in the area, and the population was so small it wasn't even listed in the U.S. Census of 1880.[7] However, with the creation of Chaves County in 1889, and development of "the nation's most important artesian basin," augmented by adroit newspapermen cranking out public relations editions of the *Pecos Valley Register* and the *Roswell Daily Record*, the area was experiencing a flourishing boom.[8] The climate, free from excessive humidity and hard winters, was attractive. By the time Roy Woofter came to the area, Roswell, so he was being told, was an enlightened community, proudly boasting of a U.S. Land Office, first-class mercantile storehouses, eateries, hotels, fraternal lodges, churches, and a few offices inhabited by scalawag lawyers, and there was even a cadre of policemen serving under a lethargic, if not corrupt, City Marshall named J.C. Champion.[9] Roswell town was divided, as far as the Hispanic population was concerned, into five subdivisions: "*Barrio de los Ricos*, 'neighborhood of the rich folks', where the Anglos lived; *Chihuahita*, 'little Chihuahua'; *El Alto*, 'the height', on a hill on the west side; *La Gara*, 'the rag,' because the poor people hung their ragged laundry outdoors; and *Zaragosa*, the name of a city either in Mexico or Spain."[10] Not too far outside village limits it was still as it had always been, ranch country; level land giving way to distant foothills, then to ominous looking Sacramento and Capitan Mountains on the west. To the east, Chaves County's precisely surveyed line, well past the zigzagging Pecos River, disappeared, merging with the horizon's haze, seemingly lost somewhere on that forlorn and mysterious flatland table, the *Llano Estacado*. Once it had been cattleman John Chisum's kingdom, but he was gone. Yet still, it was undeniably cow country, big ranch country, transit home for practiced buckaroos and proficient *vaqueros*. Roy Woofter, unlike much of the literary material fashioned for Old West dime-novels, was no cowboy—he wanted a "town job" but, for the short go, was forced to accept work as a stockman on the Schwartz-Galloway Ranch, a local Pecos Valley farming and livestock operation.[11]

Roy (left) and brother Homer Woofter. Both dedicated lawmen. Roy as City Marshal (Chief of Police) at Roswell, New Mexico Territory, and Homer at Albia, Iowa. Courtesy, Sarah Hindman.

With gainful employment and better health, Roy Woofter returned to Albia, scooped up his beloved fiancée, and brought her to Roswell. On May 10, 1908, at Roswell, he and Margaret were married.[12] The newlyweds set up housekeeping.[13] A reasonably short time later, November 7, 1908, the couple joined the First Methodist Church, aspiring to maintain their ideals of living a "devoted and Christian life."[14] During July 1909, Roy Woofter pinned on a city officer's badge and holstered a revolver.[15] He was now one of Roswell's finest.

Roy and Margaret Forsyth Woofter. A wedding photograph. Courtesy, Sarah Hindman.

Don't Give Up The Fight

And a fine example the city could well use. Old-timers, depending on partisan loyalties, could recall days gone by when misfits like Jimmy McDaniels, Jessie Evans, the Horrells, John Selman, and a buck-toothed hellion, "Billy the Kid" Antrim," galloped hither and yon across the masking landscape, ducking into and out of enticing and secretive hideouts, murdering as they went. Many citizens well remembered a later time when public officials absconded with county or city coffers: "In early 1893 Frank Lesnet, receiver of the Federal Land Office, disappeared; his accounts were missing $8,933.48. In the late spring of 1896, Sheriff Charles C. Perry vanished; a deficit was found amounting to $7,639.02."[16] The passage of just a few years had not assuaged citizen's skepticism with certain politicos and policemen. Roy Woofter was living right; apparently one of his associates, the City Marshal (Police Chief), J.C. Champion, wasn't.

Roswell City Marshal Roy Woofter, standing next to wagon driver, and unidentified lawman after a successful "Whiskey War" raid. Courtesy, Sarah Hindman.

Lawmen, Outlaws and S.O.Bs.

During a verbal mêlée Roswell City Attorney Bowers resigned. Reportedly he abandoned the municipal ship because he could not "get the cooperation of the police department in enforcing the anti-gambling and the anti-bawdy house ordinances."[17] Slyly, while the hullabaloo was in full tilt, the Roswell Mayor ordered Patrolman Roy Woofter, without "tipping off" anyone to "raid a room at the Central Hotel," the nerve center for an alleged gambling operation, an order the Chief of Police had defiantly and inexplicably neglected to carry out. While City Marshal Champion was at the fractious City Council meeting completely unawares, Roy Woofter, assisted by Patrolman Tobe Stewart "swooped down on the suspected room" and not surprisingly interdicted an illicit game of chance. Caught with their Aces around their ankles were: "One of the leading physicians of the city, who was for many years a member of the city governing body. Another physician who is now an official of the city and also a member of the board of education. A prominent real estate man. A well known cattleman. And one of Sheriff Ballard's deputies."[18] A former city police officer was "sweating" the game.[19] Needles to mention, the "whole incident was the topic of conversation" and Roswell's mayor vocally affirmed:

> The officers have been instructed from the first to strictly enforce the law in regard to gambling and the bawdy houses, and I have done everything in my power to see that the whole official staff did their duty. The law is very plain in both lines, and it has been my policy to see that the officers enforced it. I ordered Marshal Champion to pull this same room Tuesday evening, but for some reason my orders were not complied with. I do not, and I do not believe the council does, stand for the infraction of the existing laws, and this particular case will be vigorously prosecuted.[20]

City Marshal Champion resigned. Roy Woofter was promoted in his place and it was predicted in one editorial that "unless the job spoils him" he would make a good and faithful police chief, "especially if his supporting force" was well chosen.[21] Roswell's Aldermen Bell, however, vigorously championed for installing an ex-Town Marshal to fill the vacancy, "Uncle" Jesse J. Rascoe.[22] The aging one-armed Rascoe was a legend in his own time. A native born Texan and a man-killer with legitimate cuts on his notch-stick, J. J. Rascoe was not to be trifled with, even in old age.[23] At the time when a hubbub about selection of the new Chief of Police was in full tilt, many, young and old, could well-remember just a short time earlier, when Jesse Rascoe, riding his big sorrel gelding, a Winchester in one saddle scabbard, a sawed-off double-barreled shotgun in another, and a Colt's six-shooter, .45 caliber, on his left hip, rode about keeping Roswell's peace and taming troublemakers.[24] Messing with Jesse was foolishness, as everyone knew, but times were changing and a fresh face was the municipal powebrokers' answer. The citizenry righteously demanded enlightened change, as extrapolated from the following chide:

> A majority of the council had declared that they will support any and all changes that he (Mayor) may see fit to make in the police force. That being the case, it is simply a matter of getting the right men, of using the same principle as is used in every private business. If the appointees are not wholly satisfactory, fire them every Saturday night until a bunch is gotten that is worthwhile, that will see that the law is enforced, that will not protect the law breakers, that do not break the law themselves, and that are right all around. It is all poppy-cock to say that such a force cannot be gotten. The salaries are sufficient to get them. They are here. The administration can get them easy enough if it really wants to. It will get them if it will promptly bounce every weak brother, and keep on bouncing until the proper timber is secured...[25]

Roy Woofter was made of the right timber, tough as a bois d'arc knot. He would have to be, the brouhaha over fluid temperance was bubbling, and during the April, 1910 municipal elections the political pot boiled over, a new and reform minded administration picked up the reins of city government. Roswell went dry! No liquor! No excuses! No apology![26] Gambling too, was to be a shelved pastime. And public boxing too![27] Christian soldiers were in lockstep, marching to stomp out the evils of sin. Chief of Police Roy Woofter at the forefront.

Plunging forward with no nonsense methodology Roy Woofter led a contingent of officers and forthrightly arrested six bootleggers, an act the local newspaper characterized as a "Big Batch of Arrests."[28] On another occasion, Chief Woofter arrested Jim McNiece, "a negro," who was nabbed for selling a quart of whiskey to J.E. Rowe, a Roswell barber.[29] At the depot, an inebriate stepped off the train and boldly proclaimed "he was looking for Jesus." Promptly, loafing chaps sardonically made him aware that he "had got off at the wrong place." Chief Woofter was summoned and placed the befuddled traveler in jail.[30] When a drunken denizen (Frank Meyerscough) tried to purchase a flask of whiskey from D.R. Patrick, Chief Woofter "butted into the little game" and made one more arrest.[31] The religiously devout lawman's efforts were not absent danger. During one apprehension mission he was stabbed during a "hard fight" with a besotted badguy before caging him behind steel bars. Luckily, Chief Woofter's wounds were not life threatening.[32] No doubt Roy Woofter was convinced right was on his side when he publicly commented about celebrating the Christmas Holidays in Roswell, "If your people don't want you at home with booze in you, we certainly don't want you on the streets."[33] For the most part Woofter's efforts were lauded, confirmed by remarks of a hometown editor praising a Chief of Police for keeping the city free from "high feelers."[34] Not everyone, however, was enthralled with Roy Woofter's uncompromising performance.

City Marshal Roy Woofter, standing on the left, and other Roswell City officials in front of the firehouse. Courtesy, Sarah Hindman.

Not just a few eyebrows were raised when Chief Woofter filed a *complaint* against the Eastern Railway Company of New Mexico for "knowingly bringing into the city from another town within the territory a certain quantity of intoxicating liquors."[35] To many, the Chief's outlook toward temperance was simply pigheaded and mulish—impracticably stubborn. And almost implausibly, Roy Woofter's opposition, the "Wets," were successful in having the Chief of Police and Roswell's newly-elected Mayor, Dr. George T. Veal, the son-in-law of prominent Texas cattle baron C.C. Slaughter, arrested.[36] After once again apprehending the aforementioned D.R. Patrick at his confectionery store and confiscating the stock of illicit liquor stashed therein, the Chief and the Mayor were taken into custody for not releasing the wet goods to Doug Wilson, a former saloonkeeper who had "replevined the liquor seized, alleging it belonged to him." Chaves County Constable Fred Behringer arrested the city officials, and then after Woofter and Veal made bond, Behringer himself was taken into retaliatory custody for "interfering with an officer in discharge of his duty." Then, almost comically, Chief Woofter was again arrested, charged with "malicious prosecution." To a casual observer the tumult was laughable. An out of town newspaper heralded, "Pious Roswell In Throes Of Whiskey War."[37] The Chief, as would be expected, soon gained his freedom, but neither of the battling factions were ready to surrender.

Not in the least intimidated by untiring labors of Roswell's municipal gendarmes was thirty-six year old James O. Lynch, an ex-cowboy with "bad habits" from Lockhart, Texas, but now an illicit supplier of spirituous liquors.[38] On the morning of May 26, 1911, thirsty customers C.S. Wolgamott and G.W. Nations went to Lynch's dwelling and purchased bottled beer, and while there engaged the steely blue-eyed Lynch in a heated conversation, during which the belligerent bootlegger, displaying a lever-action Winchester, crowed, "The first prohibition son of a bitch of an officer that crosses my walk will get it."[39] Cocksure and without the slightest clue, little did Lynch realize that he was already the object of police surveillance.

On the afternoon of May 26th, before the local Police Judge, Marcellus W. Witt, Chief Roy Woofter filed an affidavit against Jim Lynch, charging violations of Roswell City Ordinance #213, possession of intoxicating liquors. An arrest warrant and a search warrant were placed in the hands of Roswell's devout and assertive Chief of Police.[40]

Gathering up two of his most dependable police officers, the Carmichael brothers, Ed and Henry, Chief Woofter began hunting for the slimly-built and prematurely balding Lynch. They found him in an alleyway talking with one of his pals, Fred Higgins. James O. "Jim" Lynch was arrested, and the officer's intention to search his home was made known. The three determined lawmen, their troubled prisoner, and Higgins all set off for the Lynch residence and, along the way, were joined by another of Lynch's friends, "Red Tom" Preston. Continually Lynch protested service of the search warrant on the grounds that his wife was not at home and would not be for several days, whatever difference that was supposed to make.

The rationale behind his remonstrations fell on deaf ears. They proceeded toward Lynch's abode.[41]

Arriving at their destination, the intrepid investigators, prisoner in tow, bounded up the few steps, alighting on the porch that skirted three sides of the house, and then made entry. Inside, standing in the living room, Roy Woofter and the Carmichaels, again reiterated their purpose was to search for liquid evidence. Lynch understood his dire predicament. To no avail he admonished the sleuths not to search his bedroom, it was private—off limits—so he furiously harangued. Naturally the three lawmen knew better, it was to be an all-inclusive search, come hell or high water. In an instant, without signaling his intentions, Lynch bolted from the officers and dashed into the adjoining bedroom, slamming, then locking the heavy wooden door behind him. Chief Woofter kicked at the door twice, ineffectively. The passageway remained sealed tight. Officers on one side, an owl-hoot on the other. A standoff![42]

James O. Lynch, a cowboy with "bad habits" from Lockhart, Texas. However, at the time this photograph was made he was an inmate in the New Mexico Territorial Prison at Santa Fe, charged with the murder of Roswell Chief of Police Roy Woofter. Courtesy, New Mexico Commission of Public Records, State Records Center and Archives.

Don't Give Up The Fight

Leaving Ed Carmichael on guard in the living room, and not knowing the house's floor plan, Roy and Henry raced outside to thwart Lynch's escape through a window or another door, one perhaps opening to the exterior. Chief Roy Woofter was on the west side porch, near a kitchen window. He heard a curse, then a horrendous boom and breaking glass. The 405 grain bullet punched through his stomach and intestines, knocking out hip bone fragments and guts as it spiraled out his back, off center. Amazingly, Roy Woofter didn't fall, but stumbled, doubled over, into the arms of Henry Carmichael who had hotfooted it to the Chief's position at the first, and only indication of alarm. Roy declared to Henry that he was "killed" and made the request of his subordinate to please, please, fetch his beloved wife Margaret. Disregarding their one-time prisoner, Jim Lynch, and their personal safety, the Carmichael brothers hustled Woofter to a nearby residence, making known their need for urgent medical attention.[43] Responding to the call for help, Doctor D.H. Galloway zipped to the bloody location, and began administering first-aid to stabilize the critically wounded, but still conscious and coherent patient. Roy Woofter was removed to St. Mary's Hospital.[44]

The news quickly spread. Many distraught citizens rushed to the hospital, others sought information at the crime scene. Arriving at the latter were Chaves County Sheriff Charles L. Ballard's deputies, Jim Johnson and Clarence R. Young. Johnson and Young stormed through Lynch's front door and found the suspect standing in the middle of the room, Winchester in hand. Lynch surrendered, and whined something about a "man having the right to defend his home."[45] Sympathy, needless to say, was in short supply!

From divergent perspectives at St. Mary's Hospital the challenge was twofold, one medical, the other legal. Feverishly physicians Galloway, Howard Cruthcer, W.W. Phillips and O.R. Haymaker, anesthetized Chief Woofter and began their surgery. Sadly, they discovered, although not surprisingly, that "internal bleeding was very free, especially at the wound in the stomach...and...a large amount of the intestines had passed out at the hole at the back..."[46] After his wounds were closed Woofter was given strong doses of morphine and adrenaline, as well as an enema of strong black coffee, and a saline solution "under the skin."[47]

After recovering from the effects of anesthesia, Roy Woofter was questioned by Chaves County District Attorney L.O. Fullen, the statement carefully recorded by an Official Court Reporter, Earl Iden. Secrecy shrouded Woofter's words.[48] Hush-hush testimony was not going to leak to wily newspapermen and spoil the criminal proceedings against Lynch, not if lawyer Fullen could implement a prosecutor's proper power.

Back at Jim Lynch's house the investigation was pressed. Chief Roy Woofter's leather-covered truncheon was found, destroyed, "except for the wire center" and the murderous bullet was recovered, a "U.S. A. ball, which weighs 405 grains and is made of soft lead."[49] Inside the residence, officers seized a sizable quantity of beer, "iced down in a barrel" and more cold brew from an ice-box.[50] The evidence against Lynch was compelling—well beyond a reasonable doubt.

In his austere surroundings at St. Mary's Hospital, Roy Woofter, suffering severe pain, despite doses of morphine, sustained a semblance of rationality, and to a close friend maintaining watch by his bedside whispered, "Pray for the man who shot me; I am praying for him."[51] Never once did he cry out with vindictiveness, always living up to the "high ideals of his life."[52] Struggling throughout the night Roy Woofter fought for energy, but just at dawn, at 5 o'clock, thirty-one year old Roy Woofter uttered his last words, "Don't give up the fight," and died.

Roy Woofter's casket at the Roswell, New Mexico memorial service. Courtesy, Sarah Hindman.

Devastated by the loss of a husband of just three years, Margaret, almost immediately, left for Albia, and the liberal consolation of family, knowing Roy's brother, Homer, had already departed for Roswell and was to accompany the casket back to Iowa.[53]

Mayor Veal proclaimed May 30th a city holiday in remembrance of Chief Woofter, and a somber memorial service was held in his honor, attended by a throng of saddened and heartsick Roswell citizens. The City Clerk, George M. Williams, remarked that Roy Woofter had been "a manly man, a faithful, kind and devoted husband, a fearless yet tender hearted officer, a noble and upright citizen…and was such as this to die, a noble martyr for the cause of right…"[54] Indisputably, that same unambiguous sentiment accompanied Roy Woofter's earthly remains back to Albia, his headstone reads, "Asleep in Jesus…He Died a Martyr to the Cause of Temperance and Christian Citizenship."[55]

At Jim Lynch's murder trial the whole sordid story was replayed, and even Margaret Woofter was required to return and testify that her husband was never without his badge of office and always wore it where it could readily be seen.[56] After the chain of prosecution witnesses and the able closing arguments, during which part of Woofter's *Dying Declaration* was recapped, "I know I'm dying with no hope of recovery…Jim Lynch yelled keep off my back porch and then fired," the District Attorney rested the Territory's criminal case.[57] Valiantly, Lynch's lawyer tried, but in the end the jury returned its verdict—guilty! Judge G.A. Richardson sentenced Lynch to serve not less than 99 years in the state penitentiary nor more than 100 years, which a local scribe not very cleverly noted, "This, of course, is a life sentence."[58]

Meanwhile, at Roswell, Mayor Veal had turned to one of the premier Southwestern lawmen, William Davis "Dave" Allison, an ex-West Texas sheriff, ex-Texas Ranger and an ex-Arizona Ranger, who was known far and wide as having a "reputation as a brave and efficient officer," to replace Roy Woofter and make unremitting war on criminals. In but short order, the thorny law enforcement task was achieved, and once more public relations promoters and brainy newspaper editors could offer creditable enticements for shuffling down to sunny and pleasant Roswell, New Mexico Territory, a good place to be.[59] Statehood was at hand, hopefully.

So, in a final analysis, Roy Woofter, like most of his contemporary law enforcement brothers, never earned his rightful place in a stirring string of legit Old West histories – not until now! He was a temperance tiger, giving his life in the fight against demon rum.

Lawmen, Outlaws and S.O.Bs.

ENDNOTES CHAPTER 4

"DON'T GIVE UP THE FIGHT"

[1] *Monroe County News*, July 25, 1995. And, correspondence between Woofter relative Sarah Hindman, Albia, Iowa, and author, May 13, 2002. George Marion Woofter, born near Alum Bridge, West Virginia, on November 7, 1843, served as a Union soldier under General Grant. After the war, G. M. Woofter returned to his birthplace and began raising crops—and children. Roy Woofter had one sister, Amelia, and four brothers, Homer, Lloyd, Will and Emery.
[2] *Ibid.* Albia, Monroe County, Iowa is located in the mid-southern portion of the state, approximately 21 miles west of Ottumwa, southeast of Des Monies.
[3] *Ibid.*
[4] Havlorson, John. Typescript. "Roswell's First Police Officer Killed In The Line of Duty." Courtesy, Commander Richard Lucero, Roswell Police Department Archives, Roswell, New Mexico.
[5] *Monroe County News*, August 1, 1995. And see, *Roswell Daily Record*, May 27, 1911. "He (Woofter) came to this country for his health." And, unidentified newspaper clip. Woofter's obituary.
[6] *Ibid.*
[7] Larson, Carol. *Forgotten Frontier—The Story of Southeast New Mexico.* P. 81. "The U.S. Census of 1880 listed Fort Stanton's population as 118; Lincoln's as 638; and White Oak's as 268; but did not show Roswell, as it was too small for inclusion. In June of 1885 there were but nine houses there."
[8] *Ibid.*, P. 82. And see, Julyan, Robert. *The Place Names Of New Mexico.* P. 303-304.
[9] *Roswell Daily Record*, October 1, 1909.
[10] Julyan. P. 304.
[11] *Monroe County News*, July 25, 1995. And interviews with Roy Woofter relative, Carol Marlin.
[12] Hindman. And see, *Roswell Daily Record*, May 27, 1911.
[13] *Monroe County News*, August 1, 1995. "After Roy Woofter got a job on the Roswell police force, he and Margaret moved into Roswell."
[14] *Ibid.*
[15] Halvorson. P. 1. And, *Roswell Daily Record*, May 27, 1911. And, *Monroe County News*, July 18, 1995.
[16] Larson. P. 82. For a biographical sketch of Charles C. Perry see, Ball, Larry D., "Lawman in Disgrace: Sheriff Charles C. Perry of Chaves County, New Mexico," *New Mexico Historical Review*, Vol. 61, No. 2 (April 1986). P. 125-36. For Perry's participation in the capture of noted Oklahoma bandit Bill Cook, see, Alexander, Bob, "an outlaw tripped up by Love," National Association For Outlaw And Lawman History, Inc. (NOLA), *Quarterly*. Vol. XXVI, No. 3. (July-September 2002) P. 7-16
[17] *Roswell Daily Record*, October 1, 1909.
[18] *Ibid.*
[19] *Ibid.* The names were not given in the paper because at the time of the arrests the *complaints* had not been prepared or legally served.
[20] *Ibid.*

Don't Give Up The Fight

[21] Undated newspaper clip, Roswell *Register-Tribune*. Roy Woofter's promotion was not unanimous, the Roswell City Council was divided, six to two. Other news reports referred to Roy Woofter as being a "nervy" young officer.

[22] Unidentified newspaper clip, "He (Bell) referred chiefly to Uncle Jesse Rascoe, whom he said was wanted by ninety per cent of the people."

[23] DeArment, Robert K., "The Long Arm of the Law," *True West*. January 2003. The author's thumbnail sketch of this intriguing frontier personality is first-rate. Jesse J. Rascoe, while he lived, was well-known and feared throughout the Southwest, for truly he had been a good man turned bad, and then good again. Sadly, for history's sake, others, some quite well-known in modern Old West writings have had their reputations speciously puffed up while Jesse has somewhat been overlooked. J. J. Rascoe was the "real McCoy." P. 68-70.

[24] Bonney, Cecil. *Looking Over My Shoulder, Seventy-five Years in the Pecos Valley*. P. 24.

[25] Undated newsclip, *Roswell Daily Record*.

[26] Bonney, P. 157.

[27] Numerous are the mentions in local newspaper editions referring to the city election of 1910 and the resultant reform movement.

[28] *Roswell Daily Record*, September 1, 1910. Arrested, according to the newspaper, were: John Purviance, George Yeager, Charles Montgomery, T. L. Durnam, Frank Blair, and Will Armstead.

[29] Unidentified newspaper clips. Courtesy Carol Marlin, Albia, Iowa.

[30] *Ibid.*

[31] *Ibid.*

[32] *Ibid.*

[33] *Ibid.*

[34] *Roswell Register-Tribune*, undated citation.

[35] Unidentified news clip. Courtesy, Carol Marlin.

[36] *Ibid.* And, for a biography of C.C. Slaughter, one of Texas's leading developers of a viable cattle industry, see Murrah, David J., *C.C. Slaughter, Rancher, Banker, Baptist*.

[37] *Ibid.*

[38] New Mexico State Penitentiary Records, Description of Convict. Courtesy, New Mexico Commission of Public Records, State Records Center and Archives. Santa Fe.

[39] *Roswell Daily Record*, October 14, 1913.

[40] Police Judge's Docket, Cause Number 64, May 26, 1911. P. 487. *The City Of Roswell vs. Intoxicating Liquor and J.O. Lynch*. Courtesy, Richard Lucero.

[41] *Roswell Daily Record*, May 27, 1911. Mrs. Lynch, and a sister, Mrs. A. L. Schneider, were in Arkansas. And see, Bullis, Don. *New Mexico's Finest: Peace Officers Killed in the Line of Duty, 1847-1999*. P. 307.

[42] *Ibid.* And, Halvorson, P. 1.

[43] *Ibid.*

[44] *Ibid.*

[45] *Ibid.* By other accounts, Lynch who had the screen door latched, unlocked the door and meekly surrendered to Ballard's deputies, Young and Johnson. Chaves County Sheriff Charles L. Ballard was a multi-term sheriff and is sometimes credited among those transitional frontier lawmen as being one of the first to employ an automobile for law enforcement work, in a day when most prisoner transportation was accomplished horseback, by wagon, or by rail. See, Ball, Larry

Lawmen, Outlaws and S.O.Bs.

D., Desert Lawmen, *The High Sheriffs of New Mexico and Arizona, 1846-1912*. P. 294 & 355.

[46] *Ibid.* The bullet was recovered near the crime scene by Deputy Johnson and was described as a "U.S. A. ball, which weighs 405 grains and is made of soft lead." Base on this information the murder weapon would have been of a .45-70 caliber. From references made to the fact that the weapon was a Winchester, probability would suggest that it was a Model 1886, lever-action rifle.

[47] *Clinical Record*, St. Mary's Hospital, Roy Woofter, May 26, 1911.

[48] *Roswell Daily Record*, May 27, 1911.

[49] *Ibid.*

[50] *Ibid.*

[51] Unidentified news clip, obituary. Courtesy, Carol Marlin.

[52] *Ibid.*

[53] Grace Boellner, Roswell, New Mexico Territory, to Margaret Forsyth Woofter, Albia, Iowa, June 12, 1911. "I was so pleased to read the piece from the Albia paper in the Record. About the funeral there. I have been sorry since you left that you did not see him in the church before the funeral here." Courtesy, Carol Marlin. And see, *Western Union Telegram*, from Home Woofter, Albia, Iowa to Margaret Woofter, Roswell, New Mexico, May 27, 1911, "Wire at once if Roy is not improving and I will leave today noon." Courtesy, Carol Marlin. And, *Roswell Daily Record*, May 27, 1911. "He (Homer Woofter) was wired the news of the death and will probably reach Roswell Monday evening."

[54] Williams, George M., City Clerk, Roswell, New Mexico Territory. Handwritten tribute to the slain Chief of Police, dated June 2nd, 1911, and titled, "Roy Woofter as I knew and Understood Him." Courtesy, Carol Marlin.

[55] Hindman to author, May 13, 2002. And, Headstone, Roy Woofter.

[56] *Roswell Daily Record*, October 14, 1913.

[57] Halvorson. 3

[58] *Roswell Daily Record*, October 14, 1913.

[59] Bonney, P. 157. "Dave Allison, one of the better known peace officers of the Southwest, was chief of police of Roswell from 1910 until 1912, during the administration of Dr. George T. Veal. Dr. Veal was mayor following a heated local option election. He brought Allison to Roswell because of his reputation as a brave and efficient officer." For a biography of this truly fascinating Old West lawmen, one serving on a transitional frontier, see, Alexander, Bob, *Fearless Dave Allison, Border Lawman*.

CHAPTER 5

"HELL PASO"

William Garlick & Scott Russell, Bold Border Lawmen

Amateur aficionados and, yes, even a brigade of scholars with notable academic credentials rightfully acknowledge the importance of violent happenings at old El Paso. When an ex-mayor and pioneer resident, Sol C. Shutz, publicly commented that during early days the neighborhood was "a gathering place for all types of gamblers, common thieves and desperadoes" and, in fact, that the city was devilishly dubbed "Hell Paso," he wasn't wrong.[1] Frequently hailed as the "The Monte Carlo of the West," the burg was haven and Heaven for drinkers, gamblers, and whorehouse hangers' on, and "although carrying a gun was illegal, gunplay was common."[2] Voluminous histories, biographies, studiously penned journal articles and a plethora of popular melodramatic epistles are reasonably easy to come by. Most with legitimacy paint the town richly in blood-red hues.As the twentieth-century *enlightenment* was unerringly ushered in, truthfully, not too much actually changed in "Hell Paso." It was still as it always had been—wild and woolly—a bordertown, and as such "attracted the best and the worst, acting as magnet for ruffians one step ahead of the sheriff."[3] South of town along the border, and in the far eastern reaches of the county, say, at Sierra Blanca where young Army Lieutenant George S. Patton, Jr. was stationed, it was, compared to the rest of the country, as if a time-warp had taken place. Writing to his wife the future "Blood and Guts" general said, "This is the funniest place I have ever been. It is supposed to be very tough and at least half the men wear boots and spurs and carry guns...I would not miss this for the world. I guess there are few places like it left."[4] The purpose then of this brief narrative is simply to highlight a heretofore overlooked gunfighter type story, and in a modest way honor two Lone Star stalwarts of the badge-wearing variety who were keenly honing their law enforcement skills on a frontier yet in transition.

Due to a paucity of primary source materials, determining precisely when William Henry Garlick, an authentic West Texas cowboy, was first commissioned an El Paso County deputy sheriff is not known.[5] It can be reported that by the time he was forty-four years old, Garlick, employed as a county deputy, was patrolling the Rio Grande with case-hardened Texas Rangers engaged in "shadowing" the activities of a network of questionable revolutionaries, some whom were now and again meandering back and forth across the muddy international line. On at least one occasion during early 1913 the surveillance activities abruptly turned violent when deputy Garlick and his two companions, Ranger Sergeant C.R. Moore and Private Charles Webster, were attacked by a decidedly superior force of rebel soldiers intent on breaching the border. Staunchly holding their ground, the three lawmen opened up with Winchesters and simultaneously emptied three Mexican saddles. While the trio of assailants lifelessly floated down-stream, the remaining mishmash Mexican militia hightailed it back to the safety of their home base—on the other side of the Rio Bravo.[6] During their hasty flight, the insurgents abandoned a battle flag. Later the banner was sent to the Texas Adjutant General at Austin, a succinct comment concerning the person bearing the pennant was affixed: "I don't think our rebel would be in shape to again use the Mauser carbine we got off his saddle."[7] Garlick's decisive action, as well as that of the Rangers, did not miss the favorable notice of Texas Governor O.B. Colquitt who advised Texas Ranger Captain John R. Hughes that he "approved" of the officer's tactics and instructed "you and your men keep them (Mexican rebels) off of Texas territory if possible, and if they invade the State let them understand they do so at the risk of their lives."[8] So forceful had Garlick's and the Ranger's response been, thereafter Hughes' "command never again were required to engage the rebels."[9] The revolutionaries, however, were not necessarily a forgetful people, and they had dangerous pals on the American side.

After the shooting scenario down at the river's squishy edge, the inferno of personal revenge smoldered.[10] Deputy W.H. Garlick, by casting his lot with the Texas Rangers had not endeared himself to a population often suspicious of Anglo motives. And too, slithering along both banks, hiding amid the tangles, willows, and cattails were bandits whose aspirations were not political at all, just pecuniary. W.H. Garlick was a lawman, through and through. He was widely known as being totally "fearless," and considered by most to be an "excellent pistol shot" and "quick on the draw," and as such was lauded by local newspapermen.[11] Garlick was not the kind of man to be intimidated by rabble or ruffians—he still had a job to do—but for certain he was aware of the threats being made against his and other officer's lives.[12]

El Paso County Deputy Sheriff William H. Garlick on horseback patrol along the Rio Grande River, an ever troublesome international line. Courtesy, Grady Russell.

One of those fellow West Texas lawmen was Grover Scott Russell, a twenty-four year old Texas Ranger from Stephenville, Erath County, Texas.[13] Scott's daddy, Samuel Nicholas Russell, a local constable and county fire marshal was extraordinarily well thought of, characterized as a "splendid" peace officer, and reportedly carried a six-shooter that once belonged to the notoriously merciless man-killer, William Preston "Bloody Bill" Longley.[14] Growing tired of life on the farm, Sam's first-born son, Scott, the handsome medium-framed lad with a ruggedly dark complexion and pleasing demeanor, opted to maintain family tradition wearing a lawman's star, one crudely chiseled from a silver Mexican coin.[15] He enlisted with the Ranger service on October 1, 1912.[16] During his assignment at Ysleta just south of El Paso, and irregularly at Fort Stockton to the east, it was but a reasonably short time before Russell too was considered a thoroughly competent borderland peace officer and a deceptively quick gunman.[17] These qualities were quickly recognized by prominent Western writer Zane Grey, who was so impressed upon meeting Scott that later he "used Russell's last name for one of the Rangers in a novel, the only real name he used."[18] Speculation and guesswork have little value in a historical context, but surely it is not unfair to presume that Scott Russell looked at William Henry Garlick, who was twenty years his senior, with admiration and respect, and that Garlick envied Russell's youthful strapping physical strength and exuberant enthusiasm for life. Factually though, it can be reported that the middle-aged father of five and his yet to be married partner, made a formidable detective and peace keeping team around "Hell Paso." And for sure, it was so thought by a particular bunch of striking laborers, along with a whole platoon of straightforward and seemingly shameless cow-thieves.

The border country—both sides—had long been a hotbed for fermenting labor union commotion, in several instances spurred on by intransigent revolutionaries intent upon capitalizing on the working man's dissatisfaction and despair, then using the discord as excuse for efforts designed at toppling first one government or another. Such had been the case at Cananea in the Mexican state of Sonora just a few years earlier, and as a dreadful result many had forfeited their lives.[19] Whatever the reasons, the dissension had seemingly blanched through time, but now, the turmoil once again darkened into gloomy shades of racism and hooliganism. There was a strike in progress at the American Smelting and Refining Company, El Paso's major employer.[20] El Paso County Sheriff Peyton J. Edwards, Garlick's boss, and Texas Ranger Captain John R. Hughes, Russell's chief, had collaborated and made the assignments. When their presence was not specifically obligated to more pressing duties, W.H. Garlick and Scott Russell were to patrol the streets and alleys around the smelter.[21] Indeed it was dicey business, dealing with miscreant firebrands. As reported in the *El Paso Herald*, Texas Ranger Scott Russell had to shoot one:

> About a month ago, ranger Russell, during a riot among the striking Mexican smelter hands, shot a Mexican through the leg.

Hell Paso

This act is believed to have engendered ill feeling against the ranger. Both Russell and Garlick had been stationed at the smelter since the Mexicans went out on a strike.[22]

June 8, 1913, Ysleta, Texas. Decked out for the camera. From left to right, Mrs. Herff Alexander Carnes, Will George, Texas Ranger Jefferson Eagle Vaughn, Mrs. George, Texas Ranger Captain John R. "Border Boss" Hughes, Mrs. Phelps, and Texas Ranger Grover Scott Russell. Courtesy, Grady Russell.

Many on the Mexican side of the river, and others from the Hispanic community on the American side, harbored "ill feelings" toward Russell for popping a cap on one of their compadres, and that same assemblage had no sympathy or regard for his partner, an old deputy sheriff who had not too long before unhorsed one of their chums with a well-placed rifle ball.

If dissension at the smelter wasn't enough for El Paso area lawmen, unquestionably the squadron of miscreant mercenaries involved in trafficking stolen livestock were. Had it not been but a short time before that one of their colleagues had been murdered, two others ruthlessly shot down? U.S. Mounted Customs Inspectors Joe Sitter and Jack Howard, along with a Texas and Southwestern Cattle Raisers Association Inspector, Ad Harvick, while transporting to jail a cattle-thieving suspect, Chico Cano, near the tiny Rio Grande River hamlet of Pilares had been ambushed. Sadly, Jack

Howard was killed outright, and both Sitter and Harvick were wounded. The prisoner escaped.[23] Just a short time later and a little further down river, Mexican bandits who a newspaper editor depicted as "...bad men and are armed to the teeth...," splashed on to American soil, attacking the West Texas ranches of Lawrence Haley and Lee Hancock.[24] Deputy William H. Garlick and Ranger Scott Russell were sharply aware, dealing with "Goddamn cow-thieves" was, to be sure, risky business.[25] And they wouldn't have to leave "Hell Paso" to find them.

William Henry Garlick sitting next to his devoted wife, Martha Jane. Garlick. Their children standing, from left to right, Audrey P., Ruth Gober, Alice Laurie, William Fred, and Katie Lois. Courtesy Button Garlick.

Operating under specific instructions from El Paso County Sheriff Edwards, Garlick inspected all cattle brought to the *Eje del Barrio Libre* corrals, a combination grocery and butcher shop, with an appended tavern.[26] Located "in the Mexican settlement near the El Paso smelter," the multifaceted enterprise was operated by the Guadarrama family, and was rumored to be headquarters for a band of local livestock thieves.[27]

Investigative initiative, complimented by a prescription of persistence and patience on the part of energetic peace officers generally produces result. The exacting details are a bit fuzzy, but during the middle of June, 1913, Deputy Garlick and Ranger Russell, aided by Ranger Webster, determined that Sabino (Savino) Guadarrama, L. Dominguez, and an Anglo, Willie Hill, were the parties who had stolen cattle from the Nunn & Latham operations out on the mesa, not too far from town.[28] The lawmen, after filing a *complaint* with a local Justice of the Peace, James J. Murphy, and receiving arrest warrants, placed all three in jail.[29] A local newspaperman reported the officers were "making it warm" for the "gang" of cow-thieves.[30] Reportedly, after the incarcerations an attorney for the cattlemen filed a *writ of sequestration.*[31] There were at least two direct consequences; a pilfered steer, one inexplicably standing in the Guadarrama's slaughter pen was not to be butchered under any circumstances; and, Juan Guadarrama, Sabino's brother, threatened to "get" the responsible officers, particularly Garlick and Russell.[32] Later, the youthful Ranger told one of his friends at the smelter that he was, in fact, afraid one of the Guadarrama clan might very well back-shoot him.[33] After a preliminary hearing before Judge Murphy at which deputy W.H. Garlick testified, the defendants were released on bond pending action of the Grand Jury.[34] Back at the smelter rancorous threats were once again made. This time it was proffered that a Guadarrama would "get" Garlick "at the first opportunity."[35] In spite of the perils W.H. Garlick and Scott Russell continued with their investigations.

By two o'clock in the afternoon, on June 23, 1913, Garlick and Russell had already had dinner, or as city folk say, lunch, and went to the *Eje del Barrio Libre* complex.[36] Whether or not the lawmen advanced toward the locality for the purpose of serving an arrest warrant on one of the Guadarrama family is not known.[37] Plainly though, the gendarmes were a plucky duo, and into the tap-room they stepped.[38]

Inside the saloon portion of the premises, lawmen approached Sergeant J.H. Sirks, C. Troop, Thirteenth Cavalry, USA, who apparently was taking a break from routine patrols throughout the smelter district, and asked the non-commissioned officer if a particular Guadarrama was on site. They were advised he was not.[39] Garlick and Russell then left the store, only a short time later to meet Sgt. Sirks on the sidewalk, informing him they were returning to the grocery part of the building to purchase some tobacco.[40]

Lawmen, Outlaws and S.O.Bs.

Inspection of accessible data dealing with what actually happened next leaves many, as yet, unanswerable questions; however, for sure the proceedings quickly turned "Western!" A local newspaper staff declared, "What actually took place within the adobe walls of that smelter settlement store, saloon and rendezvous of Mexican border men will probably never be known."[41]

From left to right, Mounted Customs Inspector Greigerson, Texas Ranger Scott Russell (taking his turn as camp cook) Customs Inspector Hughes, and Texas Ranger Captain John R. Hughes. Courtesy, Grady Russell.

Forewarned that Garlick and Russell were coming toward his store, Juan Guadarrama reportedly remarked that, "he was going to kill those sheriffs."[42] And allegedly, Juan's mother, Marina, said something to the effect of, "There comes those sons of bitches."[43] Juan rapidly started loading a pistol, and his mother surreptitiously placed an ax handle, or by other renditions a hatchet, in the folds of her floor length skirt.[44] Upon entering the grocery, Scott Russell purchased some tobacco, rolled a cigarette, inhaled deeply and then remarked the fibrous product was inferior, in fact, rotten. The officer's concentration focused on Juan with the dissatisfied customer complaint. The lawmen were not the least inclined to demonstrate weakness in the face of an enemy—one who had previously threatened their lives—and, momentarily they turned their backs on the Guadarrama matriarch. They shouldn't have! As if stuck by an unexpected thunderbolt, the lawmen were sledgehammered to the floor, blood oozing from nasty head wounds. And, as quick as lightening, Juan began milking his pistol dry, some of the bullets hitting the bodies of the prostrate officers before him. During the bloodlust frenzy Juan either had a second pistol, or reloaded, or picked up one of the officers six-shooters and began using it—or had a measure of aid from an *amigo*. Fate, however, threw a curve. During a chaotic melee, at some moment in the pandemonium, Juan let the cocked hammer slip at the wrong time, the slug went terribly astray, and he screamed out, "Oh, God, I've killed my mother!"[45]

On the street, Sergeant Sirks, after counting nine gunshots, rushed to the Guadarrama store. Guardedly, he stepped inside and observed Garlick and Russell lying in pools of blood, dead. Turning to Juan Guadarrama the soldier asked, "Who killed Garlick?" Juan blatantly shrieked, "I did."[46] With haste Sirks spread the alarm, and in but a short time his superior officer, Lieutenant Prince, threw an effectual guard around the premises which prevented all entry or egress, awaiting appearance of the appropriate civil officers.[47] For damn sure, it had been a hell-to-pop day in old "Hell Paso." There was, however, law enforcement yet to be done. Upon medical examination it was determined:

> Both men had been struck on the head with some blunt instrument and one bullet entered each body. Garlick was shot between the fifth and sixth rib on the right side. The bullet ranged across the body and the physician believes pierced the heart. The base of the skull was fractured from two blows. Russell was shot below the right arm. The bullet passed through the shoulder and pierced the brain...There were two ugly wounds on the head...Mrs. Guadarrama was lying in a pool of blood near the door leading from the wareroom. She was bleeding from a bullet wound in the stomach...she died before she could be sent to the hospital...And it was believed the men were struck from behind and dazed. As they started reeling, and reached in all probability, for their guns, they were shot down. This theory is based on the examination. Both men would have probably died from injuries inflicted by the blunt instruments, according to the belief of the physician.[48]

Closer inspection of Garlick's battered skull exposed that another "bullet entered his head back of the left ear and ranged downward, giving the impression he had been shot while lying on the floor."[49] Dr. F.W. Lynch "declared the wounds had been inflicted before the Rangers could draw their firearms."[50] Sheriff Edwards was in California, and in his prolonged absence Chief Deputy Stanley Good assumed the leadership role in what would become an intensive, very public, and due to racial overtones, a bitterly divisive homicide investigation. According to most news accounts the officer's weapons were not to be found anywhere, adding to speculation the Guadarramas' had destroyed or caused the removal of incriminating evidence. *Quien Sabe?* With the crime scene flawlessly cordoned by a platoon of kaki-clad sentinels armed with 1903 model Springfield rifles, Chief Good ordered arrests be made to the number of nine, and so it was. Placed in custody were Juan, Jesus, David, Sabino and Adolfo Guadarrama, along with T. Echeverria, Pablo Ramos, Manuel Ochoa and Levio Dominguez, all charged with murder.[51] Law enforcement officers were falling all over themselves with praise for the military, a sentiment echoed by the *El Paso Morning Times* which extolled, "His (Lt. Prince) quick work in throwing a picket around the Guadarrama house probably prevented those now under arrest escaping across the Rio Grande into Mexico."[52]

No doubt, many in the Hispanic and Mexican communities saw it somewhat differently, but even they were forced to acknowledge the two lawmen were, indeed, graveyard-dead, and, nobody else had suffered even a scratch. El Paso cattlemen were "much excited" about the killings, but even though it was reported some of the arrested men "have been considered desperate characters and have been in trouble on a number of occasions," there was no serious talk of a lynching.[53] Just in case, however, an extra guard of three deputy sheriffs and three El Paso policemen were placed on duty around the county jail. Ranger Captain Hughes hastily made a report to the Texas Adjutant General at Austin:

> I beg leave to report on the killing of Ranger Scott Russell. Deputy Sheriff W.H. Garlick had a warrant for one Manuel Guadarrama for theft of cattle, and he and Russell went to the store of Juan Guadarrama to arrest Manuel, whom they expected to find there. They did not want to ask for Manuel, so they asked the merchant for a dimes worth of tobacco, as an excuse for entering the store. Mrs. Guadarrama, mother of Juan, struck Russell in the back of the head with an axe handle and stunned him, and Juan shot Russell as he fell—then shot Deputy Sheriff Garlick, killing both. Then he pulled the window curtains and beat them both with a hatchet. There was a bullet hole through the warrant in Garlick's pocket. We have plenty of evidence that the killing was planned

Hell Paso

several days ahead, and that they were prepared for the first opportunity…[54]

Martha Jane (Harris) Garlick, as previously mentioned was the mother of five, and when notified of her husband's death rushed from their home at Fabens on the "verge of a nervous breakdown."[55] A condition made all the more heart-rendering because she was once more with child, and her beloved spouse would never know his yet to be born son, little Henry.[56] Sadly she accompanied the coffin to Valentine, a West Texas settlement, where William Henry Garlick was lovingly laid to rest. Back at Stephenville, Sam Russell was devastated when notified of the death of his son, that gallantly handsome and thoroughly gutsy Texas Ranger, but tearfully and dutifully he made requisite arrangements for having the body returned to Erath County for interment. The Adjutant General wired Captain Hughes to have a Texas Ranger accompany Russell's body on the trip home, and added, "All reasonable expenses will be met by the State."[57] Interestingly, the following year Russell's brother, Sam M., enlisted in the Texas Rangers, and likewise, when he reached maturity, so did Garlick's son, William Fred.[58] And too, in vicinity of the El Paso smelter, at the *Eje del Barro Libre* grocery and saloon, black crepe was draped over the door out of respect and love for the deceased Marina Guadarrama.[59]

William Henry Garlick's son, William Fred, as he appeared enlisting in the Texas Rangers as a "rookie" private, after the merciless assassination of his dad. Courtesy, Marvin Garlick.

95

Lawmen, Outlaws and S.O.Bs.

As would be imagined though, there was not much love lost between the local English and Spanish speaking societies, conspicuously evidenced by cursory glances at just a few contemporary commentaries; the *El Paso Herald* revealed, "After the killing Monday afternoon, a number of the strikers expressed themselves as highly satisfied with what had taken place…a strike leader told one of the Americans at the smelter that the Mexicans could shoot as well as the '*gringos*' and they would be able to care for themselves" should the Americans start anything; and in another edition, "Feeling has not yet fully subsided over the affair and threats against the men now in jail are frequently heard on the streets. These threats take no concrete form and go no further than the statement that the Mexicans 'ought to be hanged'; and, with political incorrectness the *Herald* repeated, verbatim, what the "Border Boss" had to say about the lawmen's missing revolvers, "…A third theory which is given by Capt. John R. Hughes of the rangers is that some of the Mexicans who were in the store took the guns from the natural inclination of a Mexican to steal a six-shooter, wherever it could be found."[60] And so on!

To somewhat abbreviate what proved to be an absorbing battle of legalistic wit, suffice to say Juan Guadarrama and four of his cohorts were indicted for murder, others were released from the jailhouse, free men.[61] From a strategic perspective, there was worry on the part of the prosecution team that perhaps the defense would categorically affirm Marina Guadarrama did in fact kill Deputy Garlick and Ranger Russell, and thus pose a tricky legal question for the court to resolve, "Is a man guilty of murder when he shoots a dead man?"[62] During January, 1914, at El Paso, in the 34th Criminal District Court, the trial commenced.[63] Familiarity with the criminal justice system imbues the sideline spectator with truisms; confessions are sometimes ruled inadmissible; witnesses sporadically recant what they said before; testimony can be fabricated or perjured; honest people make legitimate mistakes; and a smidgen of sneaky skullduggery is not necessarily a stranger. The Prosecution team stuck with their story, while the Defense counsel professed Garlick and Russell initiated the ghastly "difficulty," and Juan only acted in self-defense after his mother was killed by a bullet fired from a lawman's lethal six-gun. No doubt opposing contestants thought the other side guilty of unbridled and unfair shenanigans. The jury did:

> We have taken 116 ballots and no change, and are hopelessly apart
> with no possible chance to agree. We have been here a long time

and would be willing to stay longer if we had a chance to reach a verdict. But we think that we should be permitted to go home tonight, when we know that no verdict can be reached. (Signed) J. T. Lindsey, foreman.[64]

A mistrial! The case was re-docketed, and at the conclusion of a second trial during June 1915, Juan Guadarrama was found guilty of murder in the second degree, and given a five year sentence, to be served at Huntsville, the nerve center for the prison system in Texas.[65] His was the solitary conviction for the appalling crime.

From left to right, Will Vaughn; Scott Russell's brother, Texas Ranger Sam Russell; and Texas Ranger Jeff E. Vaughn. Courtesy, Grady Russell.

Lawmen, Outlaws and S.O.Bs.

It would be romantically pleasant to offer rationalization, or relate that there was some laudable purpose served by the deaths of Deputy William Henry Garlick and Texas Ranger Grover Scott Russell; that because they died, the locale was rid of criminality; or with an over-the-top historic abstract, perhaps it could be written they knowingly and nobly sacrificed their lives altruistically to stabilize a transitional frontier; but truthfully, the "difficulty" was wasteful and foolish! As the old-timers say, during those topsy-turvy early days, life was cheap at "Hell Paso."

Hell Paso

ENDNOTES CHAPTER 5

"HELL PASO"

[1] *El Paso Times*, 06-25-1916. Referring to "Hell Paso" is not this author's terminology, but is taken directly from the newspaper account. "At that time it was called 'Hell Paso,' and he (Schutz) says the title was justly earned."

[2] Marohn, Richard C., *The Last Gunfighter, John Wesley Hardin.* P. 214.

[3] Metz, Leon, *John Wesley Hardin, Dark Angel of Texas.* P. 222.

[4] Blumenson, Martin, *The Patton Papers, 1885-1940.* P. 298-299. At the time Patton wrote the letter, October 20, 1915, the town of Sierra Blanca was in a huge El Paso county, later in 1917, Hudspeth County was created and Sierra Blanca became the county seat. See, Awbrey, Betty Dooley and Dooley, Claude, *Why Stop? A Guide to Texas Historical Roadside Markers.* P. 467.

[5] Undocumented family history usually purports that Garlick went to work as an El Paso County Deputy Sheriff in 1910. Courtesy, Button Garlick, Van Horn, Texas.

[6] Martin, Jack, *Border Boss, Captain John R. Hughes—Texas Ranger.* P. 198.

[7] Ranger Sergeant C.R. Moore, Ysleta, Texas to Adjutant General, Austin, Texas. February 5, 1913. Texas State Library and Archives Commission.

[8] Letter from Governor Colquitt, Austin, to Texas Ranger Capt. John Hughes, El Paso, dated February 3, 1913. The Governor mentioned Deputy Garlick by name. Texas State Library and Archives Commission.

[9] Martin, *Border Boss*, P. 199, "It was anticipated that there might be trouble when the United States seized Ver Cruz in 1914, but none developed."

[10] *El Paso Herald*, 06-24-1913. "What is believed to have originated the plot of the Mexicans to exterminate the officers dates back to January 29, when rangers C. H. Webster and Charley Moore, now deputy United States marshal, and deputy sheriff Garlick encountered a band of rebels on the island…The report was that one of the rebels turned up at the smelter later and reported that Garlick and Moore had killed two of the squad, one of whom was a captain. From that time the report is that the Mexicans sympathizing with the rebel cause, and knowing of the activity of the officers, planned to kill 11 of them…"

[11] *El Paso Morning Times*, 06-24-1913.

[12] *El Paso Herald*, 06-24-1913. "The killing of Russell and deputy sheriff Garlick was but carrying out the plot formed by Mexicans some time ago to assassinate 11 El Paso officers, including rangers and deputy sheriffs, according to a report at the sheriff's office declared to be authentic."

[13] *Warrant of Authority and Descriptive List*, for Scott Russell, dated October 1, 1912, and signed by Capt. John R. Hughes. Texas Ranger Hall of Fame and Museum.

[14] Correspondence to author from Grady Russell, nephew of Scott Russell, January 4, 2002. According to Mr. Russell his grandfather was awarded Bill Longley's six-shooter as a result of his victory over an incumbent constable. In the hotly contested Erath County political race the officeholder told the challenging Russell, who was not supposed to have a chance at success, "Hell, Sam if you win this election I'll give you "ole Bill Longley," his pet name for the cherished revolver. Reportedly the owner of the weapon earlier had participated in the hanging of Longley at Giddings, Texas, acquired his six-shooter, later moving to Stephenville, and when he lost the constable's race was forced to fork

Lawmen, Outlaws and S.O.Bs.

over the revolver to Sam Russell. Later, it was stolen. Grady Russell mentions he remembers the handgun and says, "It had a very long barrel, more than six inches I'm sure and seemed to be a large caliber, like a .44. And see, the 06-24-1913 edition of the *El Paso Herald* for characterization of the elder Russell.

[15] Grover Scott Russell was born December 2, 1887 in Erath County, Texas. Much of the information regarding the Russells' was taken from an unpublished family history written by Soctt Russell's sister, Gayle Adell Russell. Courtesy, Patti and Grady Russell, Incirlik, Turkey.

[16] *Warrant of Authority and Descriptive List.*

[17] *El Paso Morning Times*, 06-24-1913. And, Captain John R. Hughes, Ysleta to Adjutant General, Austin, February 6, 1913. Texas State Library and Archives Commission.

[18] Cox, Mike. *Texas Ranger Tales—Stories That Need Telling.* P. 128-129. Writer Zane Grey went to El Paso, 1913, researching material for a Ranger novel. Also see, Stephenville *Empire-Tribune*, 04-01-2001.

[19] Meed, Douglas V., *Bloody Border: Riots, Battles and Adventures Along the Turbulent U.S.—Mexican Borderlands.* P. 1-31. And, for a condensed examination of the bloody spectacle, see, O'Neal, Bill, "The Cananea Riots of 1906," *Real West*, August 1984.

[20] Cox, *Texas Ranger Tales.* P. 123.

[21] There is no concrete primary source material indicating an actual meeting between Sheriff Edwards and Captain Hughes. The supposition that Garlick and Russell were specifically assigned to patrol around the smelter is gleaned from the *El Paso Morning Times*, 06-24-1913. "After eating their dinner yesterday Garlick and Russell who have been on duty around the smelter for some weeks..." Clearly the two officers were trying to keep a lid on the explosive situation around the smelter, as was the U.S. military.

[22] *El Paso Herald*, 06-24-1913.

[23] Bruce, Leona, *Banister Was There.* P. 158. And see, Cox, *Texas Ranger Tales.* P. 136-146. Two years later Joe Sitter was again ambushed, but on this occasion he was killed. Bolling, Robert S., *Death Rides the River, Tales of the El Paso Road* asserts that Cano was arrested for stealing a horse. Frequently in print, Joe Sitter is identified as "Sitters," but an examination of his *Texas Ranger Oath of Office*, and other documents reflect he signed his name "Joseph Sitter." Texas Ranger Hall of Fame & Museum. For a somewhat different perspective concerning the ambush of Joe Sitter, see, Means, Joyce E., *Pancho Villa Days at Pilares.*

[24] Tyler, Ronnie C., *The Big Bend, A History of the Last Texas Frontier.* P. 162.

[25] Clarke, Mary Whatley, *A Century Of Cow Business—The First Hundred Years Of The Texas And Southwestern Cattle Raisers Association.* P. 15. Apologetically, it must be made emphatically clear that the author, in her treatment of the subject simply used the terminology "damn cowthief," however, on the cattle ranges, around the campfires, and at today's livestock sale-barns, away from ladies' hearing, someone guilty of altering a brand or stealing cattle is purely and simply a "Goddamn cow-thief" or a "son-of-a-bitchin' cow-thief." Ms. Clarke went on to say, "From that day to this, Association members still so described the cow thief, refraining from calling him a dignified name like 'rustler', 'mavericker', etc. They leave those names to fiction writers."

[26] *El Paso Herald*, 06-11-1915.

Hell Paso

---

27 *El Paso Morning Times*, 06-24-1913. And see, *El Paso Herald*, 06-26-1913, "The report is that for some time cattle had been missing. These, it is said, were driven from the pastures to the smelter vicinity, where they were slaughtered."

28 *Ibid.*, 06-28-1913.

29 *Ibid.*, Later, after posting a $250 bond, Will Hill was released from jail. Guadarrama and Dominguez remained in custody, but later after a *preliminary hearing* were released on bond pending Grand Jury indictment. According to the 06-24-1913, edition of the *El Paso Herald* it was Texas Ranger C. H. Webster who actually signed the criminal *complaint*.

30 *Ibid.*, 06-24-1913. Later all three were indicted for cattle theft by an El Paso County Grand Jury.

31 *Ibid.*

32 *Ibid.* And see, *El Paso Herald*, 06-24-1913, "At the meeting in the little lodge room on the hill, the night before, one of the Guaderrama brothers—said to have been Jaun—told ranger Russell that he and his gang would "get" him. Russell took the threat seriously as he had been instrumental in working up a cattle theft case..."

33 *El Paso Herald*, 06-24-1913.

34 *Ibid.*

35 *Ibid.* It is alleged that Sabino (Savino) Guaderrama made this threat against Deputy Garlick.

36 On this issue the particular newspaper reports carrying the story vacillate considerably, some indicating the only purpose the officers had for entering the grocery was to purchase tobacco, while other accounts imply the acquisition of smokes was but a ruse intended to identify who was actually in the store at the time. On one point fiction or fact, however, do not collide—Deputy Garlick and Ranger Russell were, indeed, inside the store.

37 *El Paso Herald*, 06-24-1913. "From the pocket of Garlick's coat was taken a warrant for the arrest of M. Guaderrama on a charge of disturbing the peace."

38 *El Paso Morning Times*, 06-24-1913. And, *El Paso Herald*, 06-24-1913.

39 *Ibid.*

40 *Ibid.* Whether or not the purchase of tobacco was just a ruse to determine who was inside the store remains a mystery.

41 *El Paso Herald*, 06-24-1913.

42 *Ibid.*, 01-16-1914. From the testimony of Francisco Alonzo, aged twelve.

43 *Ibid.* In the newspaper account the expletive is reported as ____ ___ _____.

44 *Ibid.* And, interview with Button Garlick, Van Horn, Texas, great grandson of W.H. Garlick who reports that traditional family history asserts the weapon used to incapacitate the deputy was a hatchet. Later newspaper reports do reveal that a bloody hatchet, matted with hair, was located at the crime scene.

45 *El Paso Herald*, 01-16-1914.

46 *El Paso Morning Times*, 06-24-1913. And see *Death Certificate*, William H. Garlick. Cause of Death, "Gunshot Wound, Murder". Texas Department of Health, Bureau of Vital Statistics.

47 *Ibid.*

48 *Ibid.*

49 *Ibid.* 06-25-1913.

50 *Stephenville Empire-Tribune*, 04-01-2001.

51 *El Paso Morning Times*, 06-24-1913.

52 *Ibid.*

[53] *Ibid.*

[54] Report of Captain John R. Hughes, El Paso to Adjutant General, Austin, June 24, 1913. Texas State Library and Archives Commission.

[55] *El Paso Morning Times*, 06-24-1913. And interview with Button Garlick. Van Horn, Texas.

[56] Interview with Marvin Garlick, deputy Garlick's grandson. Van Horn, Texas.

[57] Telegram. Texas Adjutant General, Austin , to Captain J. R. Hughes, Ysleta. June 24, 1913. Texas State Library and Archives Commission.

[58] *Warrant of Authority and Descriptive List*, Sam M. Russell, 05-11-1913. See same, W. F. Garlick, 04-17-1918. Texas Ranger Hall of Fame and Museum. And see, Stephenville *Empire-Tribune*, 04-01-2001.

[59] *El Paso Morning Times*, 06-28-1913.

[60] *El Paso Herald*, 06-25-1913 & 06-26-1913.

[61] *Ibid.*, 06-30-1913.

[62] *Ibid.*, 06-28-1913.

[63] *Ibid.*, 01-13-1914.

[64] *Ibid.*, 01-24-1914.

[65] *Ibid.*, 06-18-1915.

CHAPTER 6

"HE WAS KILLED BY ME"

Charley Small, Southwest Badman

It's a reasonably safe bet most outlaw/lawman aficionados are not familiar with the sometimes wicked escapades of Charley Small. Charley Small is not an icon; others, for whatever reason, have captured the imagination and interests of latter day storytellers. Much of the journalistic focus has been aimed at retelling tales of "Wyatt" or "Doc" or "Wild Bill" or "Butch" or "Sundance" or "Six-Shooter something" or the seemingly inexhaustible supply of "Kids." Charley Small somehow got lost in the shuffle. His case is closer to the rule, rather than the exception. The riveting sagas of innumerable frontier personalities have simply been overlooked. That Charley Small was real there is not question. That he was an authentic owl-hoot there is not room for skepticism. That he died with hand-stitched boots on his feet and a smoking Winchester in his gnarled hands is undisputed. What then is Charley Small's legitimate story?

It would be a dereliction of historic duty to imply, at least now, that Charley Small's biography is whole. Many are the unanswered questions, but should an authentic spine-tingling yarn be placed in suspension for the passing of yet another century? Optimistically not! The purpose then of this investigation is but to bring Charley Small's name to the forefront, to pique genuine interests, provide a smattering of clues and, hopefully, other capable enthusiasts may then proffer their own findings, thus making an absorbing Western story round.

Charley Small was a Texas product, and he made a scandalous name for himself not only in the Lone Star state, but also in New Mexico, Arizona and Old Mexico. Charley's daddy, Lycurgus Small, migrating from Kentucky, was an early day settler at the Alamo City, arriving there on Christmas day 1846, and San Antonio is where he remained for the remainder of his adventuresome life, another sixty-nine years.[1] Lycurgus Small for a while "drove and acted as guard on the stage between San Antonio and El Paso and had many encounters with Indians and stage robbers."[2] And, at another time, "he was engaged fighting Indians on the Pecos River."[3] Regrettably, exactness is elusive, but sometime during 1857, Lycurgus lovingly welcomed his first born son, Charles, the hub of this Old West story, to the Hill Country of the Lone Star state.[4] While Charley was yet a mischievous little boy, his conscientious daddy gallantly pulled a stint with the Confederacy during the bloody Civil War.[5] At conflict's end, Lycurgus returned to San Antonio, eventually becoming a Bexar County jailer and, later in life, the esteemed owner and operator of "a line of hacks and express wagons."[6] By all accounts, Lycurgus Small was counted as sturdy pioneer stock, a rock-solid and thoroughly trustworthy asset to the historic city. Pinpointing with exacting precision young Charley Small's educational undertakings is problematic, nonetheless, it can be rightly reported, at age thirteen he was still a resident of his father's household, and although he may or may not have formally sat in a stuffy classroom, unceremonious biography will make crystal clear he was destined to be a dishonorable graduate from the school of hard knocks.[7]

In addition to his sisters, Charley had two younger brothers who would later play their assigned roles in this border-country chronicle, Fred and Monty.[8] For a while, Charley Small clerked in a store.[9] He knew there must be more to life than stocking shelves and smiling. Charles Small opted for a career change. Like so many young men before him who cut their vocational teeth in the South Texas *brasada*, Charley Small became a *brush-popper*, a cowboy. And too, somewhere along the path to debatable maturity he won a craving for amber-colored whiskey, dubious comrades, and a debauched contempt for the law and its enforcers.

Exactly when, why, or how, Charley Small ended up in beguiling southwestern New Mexico Territory is indeterminate, but by 1885 he was making for himself an iniquitous name in the territory—and with a terrified newspaper editor. From time to time, Charley Small would amble into Silver City, drunkenly pop a few caps with his smoking six-shooters, terrifying the citizens, and then hightail it out of town. The editor of the *Silver City Enterprise* took offense, chastising Small's errant behavior, provoking Charley to make threats against the newspaperman but, in truth, they came of naught.[10] More sinister, however, was Charley's plot to rob a Silver City bank during denizens' preoccupation with an encore performance of a traveling circus show. Public-spirited residents secreted themselves throughout town, confidently armed with shotguns and Winchesters, but alas, Charley Small so it seems was "posted," some say due to the blabbermouth boasting of Charley Wells, and the criminal's plan was prudently abandoned.[11]

By the time he was about thirty, with an earned reputation for skullduggery and recklessness, Charley was in the vicinity of southwest New Mexico Territory, cowboying near the Mimbres River, from time to time working for the San Vicente Cattle Company on the Pipe Line Ranch, north of Deming.[12] Highlighting the whole sum of Charley's shenanigans is difficult. There are, however, a few shadowy clues that may be peeled back for perusal. Particularly enigmatic, is Charley's precise participation in a snappish shooting scrape. Exactly what transpired and, to be sure, the motive remains sketchy, other than it may have been over an "old quarrel," but in any event, on March 3, 1887, a black man named John Hughes was gunned down by Luz Gonzales, "a Mexican of unsavory reputation" and one of Charley Small's thieving pals.[13] While Dr. Guthrie was anxiously attending to Hughes' life-threatening bullet-wound, Luz Gonzales and Charley Small lit out for parts they hoped would forevermore remain unknown, but everyone predicted the duo would aim for the nearby boundary and cross into Mexico, near Palomas, State of Chihuahua. Charley Small may not have actually pulled the six-shooter's trigger, but he tangled himself in the shameful crime when he and Gonzales "…held up Jim McIntosh and took from him his horse and outfit…"[14] The upshot of it all? A gut-shot John Hughes died and Charley Small became a desperado.[15]

Cunningly, in an act of strategic deception, instead of fleeing to Mexico the hard running fugitives slipped through the narrow-ranged Peloncillo Mountains and sneaked into lovely and lively Willcox, Arizona Territory.[16] From an extraordinarily skillful newspaperman's concise account, it seems that once he made a fateful decision to forsake living by the rules, Charles Small went full-bore and hard-core. After partaking of a meal at a local restaurant, both he and Luz Gonzales opted to pay for supper with "blue whistlers," rather than with silver *pesos*. Dexterously, the Chinese owner of the eatery ducked and dodged, evading any serious bodily injury as result of the malicious merriment. Luz Gonzales escaped. Charles Small didn't. He was nabbed by a local Cochise County deputy sheriff and hauled off to the county lockup at Tombstone.[17] And too, unluckily for Charley, the lawman confiscated his jaded horse, the one carrying Jim McIntosh's Grant County brand.[18]

Meanwhile, over at the capitol in Santa Fe, the territorial governor of New Mexico had posted a $300 reward for the arrest of Charles Small and Luz Gonzales "for the murder of John Hughes, on the Rio Mimbres..."[19] Specifically, whoever delivered either of the two fugitives to sheriff Andrew B. Laird at Silver City could collect an immediate $100 cash payment and upon Grand Jury indictment and District Court conviction, the remaining $200 could then be pocketed.[20] It seems, after all, that shooting at a pitiable Chinaman wasn't really any big deal, *especially* since he didn't get killed and, besides, Small was worth spendable dollars in that bustling mining town just over the mountains. Cochise County deputy sheriff Woods delivered Small to Silver City.[21] A month later, during July, 1887, criminal defendant Charles Small was indicted for the New Mexico robbery.[22] Then he somehow bamboozled somebody into posting the requisite bail monies and out of jail he walked, on bond pending further judicial action at the next term of court.[23]

Earlier, during the first few days of August, 1887, masked hijackers had, for the second time within sixty days, robbed the westbound Southern Pacific passenger train as it screeched to a standstill near Pantano Station, eighteen miles west of Benson, Arizona Territory. Eventually the brigands, after dynamiting the heavy express car door, made off with some $3500. Torrential downpours which were not uncommon during summer months—the monsoon season—quickly washed away all horse tracks, boot-heel imprints, or any other meaningful clues. The hastily thrown together posse was forced to disband, and go home. Taking into account a hefty $1000 reward was up for grabs, that it had been the second humiliating robbery within so short a time and, undeniably, that there was a dearth of leads to scrutinize, area lawmen were disagreeably exasperated![24]

Why he zeroed in on Charley Small is not known but, nevertheless, a sleuthing private-eye offered a tough ex-lawman, proven man-killer, and a future Arizona convict, John Gilmo, a substantial sampling of cash to arrest Charley Small for train robbery. At Deming, carrying no law enforcement commission at all, John Gilmo caught up with Charley Small intent on accomplishing his mercenary task and harvesting gold coins. Small, who wasn't about to be hoodwinked by a counterfeit cop, jerked his Colt's six-shooter and placed it directly between Gilmo's terror-stricken eyes. Thankfully for John Gilmo, legitimate lawman Dan

He Was Killed By Me

Tucker arrived on the scene, disarmed Charley Small, and began trying to separate the factual wheat from the speculative chaff. And as a wry corespondent wrote, a "serious difficulty might have occurred...," but for Tucker's no nonsense intervention.[25] Cognizant of Charley Small's gangster reputation, but in this instance forced to admit there was not the slightest shred of evidence, Dan Tucker kicked Charley Small loose, warning him to forthwith get on with his trip. Charley Small hustled aboard the Silver City, Deming and Pacific train headed for Grant County's shire-town. Incredibly, another Pinkerton type tried to do what John Gilmo couldn't, and Charley Small harangued that he "would not surrender to anyone but an officer of the law, and that he was tired of being arrested, and did not propose to surrender, but that if the detective wanted him very bad he could telegraph to the sheriff to make the arrest when the train arrived at Silver City." The man-hunter wilted, Charley Small pressed ahead with his excursion. Unpitying, a newsman editorialized, in part:

> These detectives are fast becoming the laughing stock of the entire country...They should have some evidence in hand before making their arrests, or give the job up and go home.[26]

Despite caustic comments hurled at ineffectual bounty-hunters, the reader should not be fooled; Charley Small maintained undisputed standing as leader of the "very hard gang of desperadoes" haunting ominous looking Big Burro Mountains, south of Silver City.[27] Whether it was his pending court case that prompted the maneuver or, perhaps, ongoing pressure from indefatigable Southwest lawmen, Charles Small, and his boys, Johnny Bell, "Doc" Hines, an ex-soldier, Von Heine, and the noticeably gimpy Charles Hutchinson, decamped sunny southwestern New Mexico and scampered across the Mexican border.[28]

About forty-five miles due south of Chihuahua City the gang stopped, making their headquarters for about two weeks at J.C. Beatty's ranch. After subtly reconnoitering, in late January, 1888, the thugs struck. Near a whistle-stop, Mapula, the siding-switch was shrewdly tinkered with, and the forward momentum of the targeted train was aborted. Charley Hutchinson threw down on the horrified engineer and his frightened fireman, holding them at bay. It seems that Johnny Bell and Von Heine guarded the section-hands, interdicting any heroic stabs at tomfoolery. Explicable, however, are Charles Small's piteous dealings. He and "Doc" Hines breached the

107

express car door, greedily snatching Mexican silver and gold from hither and yon. It might have been adrenaline pumping fun—while it lasted. The details, to be sure, are scant. Real live bandit Charles Small and his conspiratorial crew, somehow, then or later, managed to get themselves caught, on the south side of an international borderline.[29] In Mexico at the time, robbing trains was a capital offense. One newspaperman quipped, "so this settles Charley Small and his villainous gang forever."[30] The pithy pronouncement was premature.

Mexican prison wardens were not afflicted with compassion, not when it came to dealing with train robbing Americans. Perhaps, Charley Small's plight is best explained by himself. The indefatigable cow-country chronicler J. Evetts Haley had numerous remarkable historical informants. Bob Beverly was one, and thankfully for this narrative, he was personally acquainted with the depraved Charles Small. From intimate face to face meetings, as well as from first-hand contemporary hearsay, he learned about Charles Small's dangerous man-killin' reputation [31] Of his brutal incarceration in a Mexican prison, Beverly paraphrased Charley Small's version:

> He told me he was in Old Mexico, and got into some trouble down there to begin with, and they sentenced him for life to dig salt down under ground. They would take him out a lot of mornings and whip him across the back and then rub salt into the lash wounds.[32]

When Bob Beverly's assertions are circumspectly blended with other worthwhile primary source materials, the correctness of his story seems to ring true. Certainly one well-versed writer of old-time Texas installments was being more than benevolent when he portrayed Charley Small as "a well-known border character who had spent time in a Mexican prison."[33] Another author, spotlighting West of the Pecos lore, depicts Small as a "colorful character," more or less having a "Robin Hood" type appeal in some quarters.[34] As his provocative story continues to unfurl, it is abundantly clear that others saw him standing in a somewhat different light—dark and foreboding. Perhaps he was a badman who was good part of the time. *Quien Sabe?*

Charley Small's compulsory tenure as a battered, ill-treated, and undernourished Mexican prison convict was reasonably short lived. Politically and diplomatically the detention of an American citizen by a foreign government was not generally palatable to U.S. citizens at large. Particularly in this case, with the prisoner being a Texan and the gatekeeper a Mexican, sizable indignation was laid at the governor's mansion doorstep in Austin. Incessant urgings from family and friends, notwithstanding Charley's problematic brushes with the law, resulted in Texas Governor Sul Ross bringing to bear pressure on Mexico's bureaucrats, to such degree that Small was in due course released from the dingy foreign calaboose. Reportedly, Mexican *rurales* brought him to the Rio Grande, devilishly looked on as he waded the muddy river, vehemently telling him in broken English, to never comeback! He was banished from their sovereign soil under penalty of death.[35] And, from that time on, if the more or less anecdotal rumors are given any credence, Charley Small preserved a primeval hatred for Mexicans.

Bob Beverly, former Midland County Sheriff, knowledgeable cowman, and renowned Cattle Association Inspector. In his youth he personally knew desperado Charley Small. Courtesy, Nita Stewart Haley Memorial Library and J. Evetts Haley History Center.

Charley Small started hanging out on the Texas side of the river in the Comstock and Langtry country, Judge Roy Bean's bailiwick.

Lawmen, Outlaws and S.O.Bs.

Both primary and secondary source materials mention a flourishing friendship between that local-court scalawag and the outlaw Charley Small.[36] Habitually hatted with a large silver-trimmed sombrero and riding the "finest Mexican saddle, on as good a horse as I ever saw in the Rio Grande country at that time...," Charley Small was undeniably a colorful border area ne'er-do-well.[37] And of his visceral mania, if the reports are exacting, several border area ranchers thought he was doing just great—a bang up job! For it was to Charley Small and his six-shooter they turned when retribution for wrongs committed on one side of the Texas/Mexican borderline needed to be righted—on the other.

Bob Beverly simply says, "I learned that if a Mex. killed a man on this side of the border, the ranchers along there would give Charlie Small his number, and sooner or later he would come along and tell the ranchers how it happened..."[38] Supposedly, he killed "some Mexicans" who sneaked across the border and robbed the Ames & Jennings store at Comstock, and cold-bloodedly murdered a well-liked desert denizen, Scar Faced Charlie.[39] On another dreadful occasion, Mexican "herders" killed John Otto, "a sheepman working for Igner west of Comstock, at the mouth of Cow Creek, and fled across the Rio Grande." Again, it was but short time before Charley Small exacted revenge and did the deadly work.[40]

Political correctness aside, purportedly, during one conversation Small queried, "Jim, did you ever shoot a Mex.?" When the reply was, "No Charlie, I never had that to do yet," Small unflappably resounded with, "Well, I shot one today, and they always jump right straight up and squall like a cat when you shoot them. I never let one get away when I find them alone."[41]

Even the youthful and impressionable Bob Beverly said Charley Small's fanatical passions were getting him "in bad on this side of the river, after he went over and back to the other side on so many missions of death..."[42] Additionally, not everyone was enamored with Charley Small and his tendency to continuously opt for unmerciful six-shooter justice, and the lad from San Antonio town was never too far removed from trouble or publicity:

> A few weeks ago he entered the town of Del Rio about noon. He was on horseback and with a six-shooter in each hand proceeded to depopulate the streets in short order. He took a shot at every man who dared show his head and kept the town in a reign of terror until a few brave citizens began taking shots at him with Winchesters. He then rode off and crossed the river into Mexico. He returned to Texas a few days ago and was taken in custody at

He Was Killed By Me

Nueces Station by a deputy sheriff who got the drop on him. Small is also charged with horse theft.[43]

Another photograph of the scandalous "Law West of the Pecos", Judge Roy Bean. The judge and Charley Small, an outlaw and all around ne'er-do-well, were more than passing acquaintances. Courtesy, Robert G. McCubbin.

Lawmen, Outlaws and S.O.Bs.

Once more after posting bail, Small was free and, by many, thought to be the leader of a "gang of rustlers" and there were even unverified reports he was fashioning evil plans for a lightening-strike raid on the Simmons and McCormich ranches, at least so thought T.A. Cunningham, Deputy Collector of Customs at Langtry.[44] Texas Ranger Captain J.A. Brooks, from headquarters at Cotulla, in South Texas, dispatched men to the area.[45]

Almost with cyclone speed, the small ranger contingent commanded by Sergeant Daniel Lynch "D. L." Musgrave arrived in the troublesome area, and according to the July, 1893, *Monthly Returns* for Company F, Frontier Battalion, Charles Small on the 11th day of the month was arrested and charged with "smuggling."[46] At Del Rio, Val Verde County, Charles Small was hurriedly locked behind bars once again, just for a little while though—he posted bond.[47] Charles Small was not a happy man in the first place. In the second, "because he had become reckless some years ago," and due to the fact he was running with "bad company and (had) too great an affection for the whiskey bottle," an always gritty hooligan was primed for madness and mischief.[48] Charley Small didn't have to wait too long, nor go too far.

At the legendary Jersey Lilly Saloon, on the night of July 21st, the notorious Judge Roy Bean sponsored a Friday night dance.[49] From miles around celebrants arrived, imbibed, and gaily promenaded to coarse tunes emanating from the squeaky fiddles and rhythmic thumps on battered guitars. For sure it was a shindig, and undeniably Charley Small was there. There is a divergence of opinion, however, on just how well he behaved or, perchance, misbehaved. Some few, his brothers, purport Charley Small "did not drink anything," others seemingly more in line with precedent, infer that he "began drinking to excess."[50] Apart from discrepancies, there is universal consensus, the party lasted into the wee hours—and beyond.

According to T.A. Cunningham, the U.S. Customs man, Charley Small got drunk and tried to "procure" arms. Texas Ranger Sergeant D. L. Musgrave assigned private Tom Lewis to watch Small closely. Charley Small's "malediction and vengeance was so blood-curdling that Sergeant Musgrave stayed awake. Small pounced on Lewis to disarm him and probably would have succeeded but for the timely interference of Sergeant Musgrave."[51] Small promised Musgrave that he would go home and "sleep it off." He didn't go home and he didn't get a *siesta*. Deviously he went to "where the rangers had their Winchesters" and instead of grabbing forty winks he snatched a rifle and began shooting as he "hallooed" a challenge, "Come on.

Come on. You have had your day, now we will have ours."
Predictably, the keyed up rangers shot back with their Colt's six-
shooters, but as of yet, during the ferocious mêlée nobody was
hitting the mark. When his first Winchester was milked dry, Small
threw it down, ran back into the house and hysterically seized
another, but by now, Sergeant Musgrave too, had hurriedly
appropriated a lever-gun. During a real deal hell-to-pop Western
shoot-out, Charley Small was lettin' it rip at his closest target of
opportunity, Texas Ranger Lewis and, simultaneously, Sergeant
Musgrave was firing away at the man run amuck. One of the
sergeant's bullets grazed Small's arm. Small and Musgrave icily-
glared at each other, and then in sync, touched the hair-triggers. The
ranger's bullet inflicted a slight flesh wound on Small's inner thigh.
Small's shot missed, and feverishly he levered another round, "as he
had thrown his gun to his face to fire, Sergeant Musgrave gave him
a dead shot in the left side through the heart, and Small dropped
down with his gun cocked and loaded. He had fired eight times at
the rangers."[52] Thirty-six year old Charley Small was dead!

Sobering up rather emphatically after all the scorching
hullabaloo, a dogged Roy Bean straightened his suspenders, donned
his Justice of the Peace hat, and quickly officiated at a legally rooted
inquest—there was a five-dollar fee to be had.[53] Sergeant Musgrave
was required to enter into a bail-bond arrangement with the judge,
not because there was anticipation of sticky formal criminal charges
actually being filed, but rather, Texas law mandated such in capital
cases when the proceedings were handled at lower courts' level.
Sergeant Musgrave promptly forked over the paltry $100, and was
free to go.[54]

Texas Ranger Sergeant D. L. Musgrave may have just lived to
tell the tale of a dicey early morning shoot-out with a bona fide *mal
hombre*, and he may have deferentially stood before an illustrious
Justice of the Peace for a coroner's inquest, but he still owed his
bosses, Captain Brooks and Texas Adjutant General Mabry, an
official report as to what had happened at Langtry, on July 22nd at 6:
20 A. M. Sergeant Musgrave dutifully the following telegraph
message:

> This morning we were fired on by Chas Small a noted
> desperate character and he was killed by me.[55]

Upon receipt of the tersely worded telegram, Ranger Captain
Brooks immediately transmitted a letter to General Mabry,
unequivocally declaring that Charley Small was "a very bad man."[56]

In a second dispatch, calculating the likelihood that bloody strife at the hands of Charley Small's malevolent buddies might be stirred, Captain Brooks volunteered to "go with one man if necessary" and nip any problem in the bud.[57] Customs Collector Cunningham was thinking their forces should be "augmented by at least two or three others (and) it would doubtless have a tendency to overawe these outlaws."[58] Realistically, on the chipped caliche ground in that far off West of the Pecos country, nothing much happened. And, as with any touchy episode where there were two divergent camps, it wasn't too very long before gossipy partisans and conspiracy theorists were trying to somehow sell the idea that desperado Charley Small had been ruthlessly gunned down in a sinister scheme, shot in the back.[59] Specious claims were more or less muted after a personal interview with Charley's daddy, Lycurgus, who was distressed by the sudden and violent death of one of his sons but, nevertheless, he owned up to reality and publicly whispered that; "Charley was not naturally a bad boy, but was led astray by wild companions and drink. He was generous to a fault and was his own and only enemy. He was kind to every one but himself, and *when he got on sprees was deprived of reason* (emphasis added). In fact I do not believe that he has been in his right mind for the past three years, and I think this has been the cause of all of Charley's troubles."[60]

Daniel Lynch "D.L." Musgrave, an early day Atascosa County, Texas, sheriff, and later an esteemed Sergeant in the Texas Rangers. During a horrific gunplay, Musgrave killed outlaw Charley Small at Langtry, Texas, and then in a classic Old West understatement, unflappably summarized the deathly confrontation to his boss in a snappishly worded one sentence report. Courtesy, Tommy Williams, Sheriff, Atascosa County.

He Was Killed By Me

Texas Ranger Sergeant D.L. Musgrave's pithy report to the Adjutant General after he killed outlaw Charley Small. "This morning we were fired on by Chas Small a noted desperate character and he was killed by me." Courtesy, Texas State Library and Archives.

Charley' brother Fred, who was the city route agent for the *San Antonio Daily Light*, accompanied by his brother Monty, upon learning of the killing rushed to Langtry. He was appalled at what he found—Charley's body was grotesquely laying underneath a leaky railroad water tank.[61] Peculiar, indeed, it was for the heartbroken brothers to comprehend the callousness of West Texas ways. Fred bellyached to a newspaperman, but then later another side of the poignant story was proffered: "Immediately after (the inquest) his body was thoroughly washed and given nice linen underwear, also other apparel was furnished by Roy Bean and other citizens of Langtry. We could procure no ice, so he was laid out under the tank on account of the favorable conditions there for preserving his body for his friends, and a vigil kept with it until it was removed by six men and placed in his coffin."[62] Maybe West of the Pecos people and hard-edged Texas Rangers weren't nearly so bad after all. And, as he stood before a shallow unmarked grave, reverently watching the last spade full of gritty sand haphazardly splashed across Charley Small's pine box, no doubt Sergeant Musgrave pragmatically mused, perhaps it was best "he was killed by me."

ENDNOTES CHAPTER 6

"HE WAS KILLED BY ME"

[1] Correspondence to author from Deborah Countess, Librarian, Texana/Genealogy Department, San Antonio Public Library, San Antonio, Texas, May 6, 2002. Also see, *The San Antonio Light*, August 6, 1911. "When Lycurgus Small came to this city in 1846 the old house stood as it stands today." And, August 5, 1915. "Resident of city for 69 years dies."

[2] *San Antonio Light*, August 5, 1915.

[3] *Ibid.*

[4] United States Census, 1860, Bexar County, Texas. P. 297, L. 5.

[5] *San Antonio Light*, August 5, 1915.

[6] *Ibid.*

[7] United States Census, 1870, Bexar County, Texas. 4th Ward. P. 20. L. 22.

[8] *San Antonio Daily Express*, July 26, 1893. And see, *San Antonio Light*, July 22, 1893.

[9] United States Census, 1880, Bexar County, Texas, P. 178, L. 9.

[10] *Silver City Enterprise*, March 31, 1893.

[11] *Ibid.*

[12] *Ibid.* March 4, 1887 and September 16, 1887.

[13] *Ibid.* The victim, John Hughes, was working for Thomas B. Pheby near the Mimbres mill.

[14] *Ibid.*

[15] *Ibid.* March 11, 1887. "The negro Hughes who was shot last week by Luz Gonzales has since died."

[16] *Ibid.* March 18, 1887.

[17] *Ibid.* In the newspaper account the arresting officer is described simply as "Deputy Sheriff Woods."

[18] *Ibid.* "If he escapes punishment (for shooting at the Chinese cook) there he (Small) will be tried for having stolen a horse from a man whom he held up on the Mimbres."

[19] *Ibid.* April 29, 1887.

[20] *Ibid.* In this edition the date of the killing of Hughes is reported as February 28th, a conflict with most other accounts which indicate the murder occurred in March. An insignificant discrepancy in the telling of Charles Small's idiosyncratic story.

[21] *Ibid.* June 10, 1887. "Small was arrested, and being recognized was brought here because of the reward offered by the governor."

[22] *Ibid.* July 8, 1887.

[23] *Ibid.* September 16, 1887.

[24] Alexander, Bob. *Dangerous Dan Tucker, New Mexico's Deadly Lawman.* P. 150.

[25] *Silver City Enterprise*, September 16, 1887.

[26] *Ibid.*

[27] Mullane, William H. *This is Silver City New Mexico, Volume III, 1888-1889-1890.* P. 2. Quoting an excerpt from the January 20, 1888 edition of the *Silver City Enterprise.*

[28] *Ibid.*

[29] *Ibid.* Scanty details are taken from the letter written by "Doc" Hines to Grant County jailer Buck Galbraith, as reported in the *Silver City Enterprise.*

[30] *Ibid.* A review of an actual newspaper story eludes to the fact that Charley Small, "single-handed" robbed a train on the Mexican Central and received a five-year prison sentence. See, *Silver City Enterprise*, March 31, 1893. By another account in the *Enterprise*, more contemporary with the time (1888) of the robbery, it was reported that Small received a prison sentence of 14 years. Regardless, Charley Small was imprisoned in a Mexican penitentiary for robbing a train, and by most versions was not the lone bandit. The significance of the story is not improved by reconciling differences in the time of his prison sentence, but can be bound in acknowledgment that Charley Small was locked up for train robbery and was no innocent and naïve Angel, then, earlier—or later.

[31] Beverly, Bob. "Who Remembers Charlie Small?," *Frontier Times*, February, 1945. P. 122-124. "At times Charlie Small would come by and visit Uncle Mack and Uncle Jim, who I was staying in camp with…And at other times when Charlie would come by the camp I would be alone and he would talk to me, and I would, kid like, sit with my mouth open and drink in every word he would tell me."

[32] *Ibid.*, P. 124.

[33] Cox, Mike. *Texas Ranger Tales, Stories That Need Telling.* P. 118.

[34] Skiles, Jack. *Judge Roy Bean Country.* P. 178.

[35] Beverly, P. 124.

[36] *San Antonio Light*, July 25, 1893. "Roy Bean gave a dance there Friday night, and Charlie went, and enjoyed himself hugely…" And see, *San Antonio Express*, July 29, 1893. "After the dance at Roy Bean's …Charles Small began drinking to excess, and tried to procure arms." And see, Beverly, "Charlie was a close friend to Roy Bean…" P. 123. Also see, Skiles, "As well as being a friend of Roy Bean's and of other folks at Langtry…" P. 181.

[37] Beverly, P. 123.

[38] *Ibid.*, P. 124.

[39] *Ibid.*

[40] *Ibid.*

[41] *Ibid.*

[42] *Ibid.*

[43] *Silver City Enterprise*, March 31, 1893.

[44] T.A. Cunningham, Deputy Collector of Customs, Langtry, Texas, to W.H. Mabry, Adjutant General, Austin, Texas. July 24, 1893. Courtesy, Texas State Library and Archives Commission. Austin.

[45] Wilkins, Frederick. *The Law Comes To Texas, The Texas Rangers, 1870-1901.* P. 314.

[46] *Monthly Returns*, Company F., J.A. Brooks, Captain, Texas Rangers. July 1893. Courtesy, Texas State Library and Archives Commission. Daniel Lynch "D. L." Musgrave, an uncle of outlaw George Musgrave, was born on December 4, 1840, in Caldwell County, Texas. Before service as a Texas Ranger, D. L. Musgrave served as sheriff for Atascosa County, Texas, for the years 1869-1870. Musgrave died at Marathon, Texas on February 22, 1910. Correspondence to the author, July 29, 2002, from John D. Tanner, Jr., co-author, *Last Of The Old-Time Outlaws, The George West Musgrave Story.* And, correspondence with Tommy Williams, Sheriff Atascosa County, Texas.

[47] *Ibid.* And see, Wilkins. P. 314.

[48] *San Antonio Light*, July 24, 1893. And see, *San Antonio Express*, July 23, 1893. Also see, Beverly, "John (Thomas, Sheriff of Crockett County) told me that no man with eyes like Small ever gave up to any one." P. 124.

[49] *Ibid.* July 25, 1893.

[50] *Ibid.* Remarks of Charles Small's brother, Fred. And, *San Antonio Express*, July 29, 1893, remarks of Deputy Collector of Customs, T.A. Cunningham.

[51] *San Antonio Express*, July 29, 1893.

[52] *Ibid.* Letter to the newspaper from T.A. Cunningham. And see, Beverly, "He (John Thomas) said the Rangers killed Small under the water tank at Langtry." P. 124.

[53] Sonnichsen, C.L. *Roy Bean, Law West of the Pecos*. "Judge Bean's favorite judicial chore was officiating as coroner. Not that he was as fond as all that of dead bodies. He just liked the five dollars he collected every time he served. Stray corpses were always turning up out west of the Pecos and they did much to stabilize Roy's income." P. 124. And see, McDaniel, Ruel. *Vinegarroon, The Saga of Judge Roy Bean, "Law West of the Pecos"*. "He had set himself up as law and order west of the Pecos; and he found no little pride in pointing out that no dispensing job, either legal or liquid, within his jurisdiction had stumped him. Inquests seemed to him rather needless things, especially if there were no fees in sight; but if the ranchers wanted them, why, he was the judge who could hold 'em." P. 75.

[54] *San Antonio Express*, July 26, 1893.

[55] Telegraph Message to Texas Adjutant General Mabry from Texas Ranger Sergeant D. L. Musgrave, Company F., Frontier Battalion. July 22, 1893. Courtesy, Texas State Library and Archives Commission. And the Texas Ranger Hall of Fame and Museum. Waco.

[56] Letter to Adjutant General Mabry, Austin, from Texas Ranger Captain Brooks, Cotulla. July 22, 1893. Courtesy, Texas State Library and Archives Commission.

[57] Telegram to Adjutant General Mabry, Austin, from Texas Ranger Captain Brooks, Cotulla. July 22, 1893. Courtesy, Texas State Library and Archives Commission.

[58] Letter to Adjutant General Mabry, Austin, from Deputy Collector of Customs T.A. Cunningham, Langtry. July 24, 1893. Courtesy, Texas State Library and Archives.

[59] Skiles. "Small walked with the young lady down the hill toward the center of town. Just after the couple walked past the water tank, Small was shot in the back and killed. It was believed generally that a ranger, who Langtry folks later said wanted to make a name for himself, had been hiding near the water tank and ambushed Small as he walked by." P. 181.

[60] Undated press clipping from *San Antonio Daily Express*.

[61] *San Antonio Light*, July 25, 1893.

[62] *San Antonio Express*, July 29, 1893.

CHAPTER 7

"THEY HAVE GUNS...WE OUGHT TO SEARCH THEM"

Robert Lee Burdett, Texas Ranger

One skillful modern-day writer in snagging a title for compilation of Texas Ranger lore succinctly commented the upshot of his research resulted in "stories that need telling."[1] His assessment was right on the money. Indeed, there are many exhilarating Texas Ranger yarns worthy of detection and subsequent printed permanency but, sadly, sometimes legitimate first-rate stories are repetitively rehashed, while others, surely just as good, get short-shrift. The spotlight of this narrative will be focused on a Lone Star stalwart whose career was all too fleeting and all too tragic—almost forgotten.

From the best evidence at hand it can be reported the subject of this short saga, Robert Lee Burdett, usually called "Lee," was born on June 9, 1883, on the family farm at the little community of Sprinkle, not too far from Walnut Creek, Travis County, just a trace northeast of Austin, Texas.[2] Although exactness is hard to pin down, at some point he and his mother Lizzie and a sister, Mary, moved into town and took up residence at 209 West Eighth Street. A brother, Frank, somehow managed a trip across the muddy Rio Grande river, became a provisional Mexico resident, and thereafter engaged in indeterminate employment. Interestingly, for an outlaw/lawman commentary, Robert Lee Burdett's first cousin was the Austin Chief of Police, W.J. Morris.[3] Regretfully, at least for now, little is known about Burdett's early childhood. It is known that the handsome brown-headed and blue-eyed boy topped out at an even six-feet, and somewhat atypically for the men he would later share the sobriquet "Texas Ranger" with, Robert Lee Burdett had more than an rudimentary education.[4] On an enchanting hill south of the capitol city stands St. Edward's College, a Catholic institution founded in 1885 by Edward Sorin.[5] The charming campus with delightful examples of architectural excellence was, at the time, one of Austin's gemstones. Robert Lee Burdett, for a while, was a student. Just how much studious emphasis the strapping youth was placing on furthering his formal education is not known; for sure though, he was an athlete, a center-fielder on one of the college baseball teams, the *Excelsiors*.[6] Whether or not he attended the college on a part-time basis is only speculative, and exactly how he earned his keep is unspecified, other than an entry in the *Austin Daily Statesman* which indifferently mentions a youthful Lee Burdett "worked for several local firms."[7] At some point, Robert Lee Burdett opted for the law enforcement profession. While yet in his twenties he became a Texas Ranger, a member of forty-four year old Captain James Monroe Fox's Company C, stationed at Austin.[8] Missouri born, J.M. Fox previously had served as an Austin city detective and a Travis County deputy constable.[9] On October 5, 1911, Fox was officially sworn in as a Company Captain in the Texas Rangers, and possibly indicative of favorable familiarity, on the very next day he enlisted Robert Lee Burdett as a ranger private.[10]

The meat of Texas Ranger R.L. "Lee" Burdett's life story reposes west of Austin, out on the transitional frontier, that country between the lonesome Pecos river and that Monte Carlo of the Old West, El Paso, which, by some, was aptly tagged as "Hell Paso."[11] Modern civilization had unavoidably encroached on Central Texas; it, by then, was relatively tame—compared to the border country. All along the troublesome international line southeast of El Paso and on down past the river's sweeping turn in the Big Bend country, it was still, out away from the scattered settlements, a raw and untamed land—wild and woolly.

Complementing the already tumultuous lawlessness were the conspiracies, intrigues, and machinations of insurgents busily engaged in the topsy-turvy Mexican Revolution. Many of the rebels saw themselves as foraging for freedom, but on the American side of the boundary line their trans-border thievery and their sometimes lethal incursions were measured as simple hooliganism and homicide.[12] Because of the incessant border country violence, "the constant raiding and cattle rustling, the deaths in American border towns...long ago wiped the sheen off the romance of the Mexican revolution."[13]

Joseph Sitter, a former Texas Ranger, but at the time a United States Mounted Customs Inspector, and his compadre, John Simpson "Jack" Howard, along with a range detective for the Texas and Southwestern Cattle Raisers Association, J.W. "Ad" Harvick, during a long overdue 1913 cow-thieving investigation had been viciously bushwacked near Pilares, one of the "havens for bandits and local thieves" and the trio of lawmen, one and all, were battlefield casualties.[14] Sadly, Howard's wounds proved mortal.[15] Joe Sitter and "Ad" Harvick survived their nasty injuries and lived to tell the gloomy tale. Hard-bitten Texas Rangers listened closely.

The "Excelsiors" junior baseball team at Austin's St. Edward's College. Robert Lee Burdett, the center-fielder, is thought to be the youth seated second from left, first row. Courtesy, St. Edward's College Archives.

Further south in the Big Bend country, and just a month later (February), the ranches of Lee Hancock and Lawrence Haley were raided.[16] The unsmiling Mexican bandits made off with horses, ammunition, saddles and an undisclosed sum of the intractable rancher's uncomplicated personal pride. A local newspaperman reported the merciless raiders were "bad men and armed to the teeth."[17]

Back to the north, along the Rio Grande, Texas Ranger Sergeant C.R. Moore and Private Charles Webster, assisted by a gutsy El

Lawmen, Outlaws and S.O.Bs.

Paso County deputy sheriff, William H. Garlick, had a horrendous gunbattle with mutinous intruders amid the tangled cattails and weeping willows. Several Mexicans fell from their ornately trimmed flat-horn saddles.[18] Texas Governor, O.B. Colquitt, unambiguously backed the lawmen's bold and deadly play.[19] Just a short time later, Garlick and a Texas Ranger private, Grover Scott Russell, were fatally gunned down during a ferocious mêlée with Juan Guadarrama's clan at their *Eje del Barrio Libre* grocery store and taproom, a dubious family business operating in El Paso's smelter district.[20] Seemingly throughout the whole cacti-clad landscape, for hundreds of tortuous miles, the border country was suffering an epidemic of violence.

Unarguably, remote West Texas, from the forlorn and unforgiving tableland simply called the *Llano Estacado*, to the mysterious mountain country further south, was simply ungovernable—at least so thought perplexed state lawmakers at Austin and befuddled U.S. Congressmen at Washington, D. C. Inaction was plainly intolerable. A workable solution was mandatory. At the Bluebonnet State level, when he re-upped as a Texas Ranger Captain, James Monroe Fox's tough contingent was commissioned as Company B, and re-deployed to new headquarters at Marfa, county seat of the harsh Presidio County in faraway West Texas.[21] R.L. "Lee" Burdett moved with the command also.[22] Lee Burdett took up station near the predominately Spanish speaking hamlet of Fabens, down river, not too far south of the *Pass of the North*, El Paso. Recurrently, Lee Burdett hooked up with thirty-two year old Charley P. Beall, a Texas Ranger who like Burdett, could trace his beginnings to the Lone Star State's much more domesticated interior, a birthplace at Oakville, Live Oak County.[23] Charley Beall, for the most part, operated out of the cattle ranching village of Valentine, Jeff Davis County, just south of Robert Lee Burdett's customary bailiwick.[24] Choice of career, circumstance, and cordiality frequently forced the strong-willed pair of crime-fighters to work together. By most all accounts they were a dynamic and formidable peace-keeping team.[25] In spite of the fact the two were authentic tough-as-nails lawmen, even they were aghast at the next turn in border country meanness and mayhem.

On the 23rd of May, 1915, in the company of Texas Ranger Eugene Hulen, and other possemen, Charlie Craighead, Sug Cummings, and H.C. Trollinger, that indefatigable man-hunter, Joe Sitter, who reportedly had "killed several Mexican outlaws on the border," was prowling around the Rio Grande, not too far from Pilares, where, two years before, he had been cowardly ambushed by murderous owl-hoots. Cutting for fresh sign of Mexican bandidos on the U.S. side of the line, Sitter and Hulen separated themselves from the others—they shouldn't have! Both paid for the miscalculation with their lives. Hulen first, then after a blistering battle, during which Sitter fired more than sixty rounds, he too, was killed, eleven bullet holes in his body, his head battered to a bloody pulp, savagely plummeted by ruthless blows from handy and heavy rocks while he lay in puddles of his own blood.[26] Mixed up in the chronological jumble of border country chaos, too, and not unnoticed, was the murder of Pablo Jimenez, who during the same month of May had been wantonly killed by vicious visitors from south of the Rio Grande.[27] Some, those back east of the Pecos, may have religiously proffered that, in the end, the meek shall inherit the earth, but in the Big Bend country the timid had failed to get there.

Second from the left, horseback, Texas Ranger Robert Lee Burdett. Company C. Captain James Monroe Fox standing in the foreground. Courtesy, Texas Ranger Hall of Fame and Museum.

Lee Burdett, pondered his future. Cognizant of the daily dangers he habitually was subjected to, Robert Lee Burdett penned a letter to his adored sister, Mary, vowing that soon he would "take out an accident policy," as he wanted to "make especial provision" for her and his dearly loved mother.[28] On May 26th, with an ominous premonition, Texas Ranger Lee Burdett paid the premium on policy No. 983363 with the North American Accident Insurance Company, and pocketed the Post Office receipt.[29]

On June 8, 1915, Robert Lee Burdett and Charley P. Beall, working together, were on duty at Fabens. Five unruly "Mexicans," their brains reasonably well-pickled, were recklessly and repeatedly driving a hack up and down Faben's solitary grimy thoroughfare, all the while "creating considerable excitement by yelling and cursing."[30] Several times, Rangers Lee Burdett and Charley Beall admonished the belligerent quintet to settle down; if not, they said they would be compelled to arrest them.[31] For whatever the reason, the men departed.

Robert Lee Burdett pulled out his gold pocket-watch and glanced at the time—it was 7:30 P.M.[32] Although the late afternoon had been relatively peaceful, as if appearing from nowhere, the five loud-mouthed Mexicans were back on the street, this time as wobbling pedestrians, but observably looking for trouble. In harmony the rabble-rousers began hallooing insults at lawmen Burdett and Beall, before all of a sudden, they, as if by pre-arrangement, vanished into a forbiddingly dark alleyway.[33] One of the rangers was overheard to remark, "I think they have guns, and, I think we ought to go and search them."[34] Both lawmen agreed upon but one course of action – they stepped into the alley.[35]

They didn't have to look too long, or go too far, before the devilish targets of their investigative query were jammed up—run to ground. Three of the misbehaving Mexican ne'er-do-wells were neatly accosted and searched. It was dark, it was dangerous, it was damn well-obligatory and, not surprisingly, Texas Ranger R.L. "Lee" Burdett, doing the hands-on searching and ranger Charley P. Beall watchfully furnishing a modicum of protective cover, did what the State of Texas was paying them $40 a month to do.[36] For an exceptionally short moment the stop and frisk mission seemed to be running as would be likely imagined. Deferentially, the cantankerous hellions were complying with the officer's no nonsense commands. Shadowy for sure was the alley as Lee Burdett continued his pat-down of a squirmy hoodlum and, in a jiffy, the state of affairs spiraled out of control and abruptly turned "Western." Robert Lee Burdett's wily adversary began to resist and the fight was on. Unbeknownst to the officers, when they entered the poorly lit alleyway, accosting the three hooligans, one of the ruffian's cronies had already hidden himself behind a convenient woodpile. When the fisticuffs erupted he stood up and fired. "The shot was evidently the signal for the commencing of the battle that occurred between the two rangers on the one side and the Mexicans on the other."[37] A lively newspaperman for the *El Paso Morning Times* enlightened his salty readership by reporting "something like thirty or forty shots were fired," but charitably, the wary *Alpine Avalanche* reduced the number to but "twenty shots," the same number as printed in pages of the *El Paso Herald*.[38] All accounts, however, are more or less in agreement, the firing ceased due to a depletion of six-shooter ammunition, rather than by capitulation of any combatants.[39] It was root hog or die. The good-guys milked their six-shooters dry; thankfully, in a way, their Mexican antagonists did too. Thunderbolt quick it was over; the bandidos accomplished their panicky break out at the far end of the alleyway.

Charley P. Beall, no doubt, realizing he felt no excruciating pain, no numbness, was cheerfully reassured. Somehow, and sheer luck is the only levelheaded explanation, he had escaped unscathed. Turning toward Lee Burdett, Beall was sickened by what he saw, his prostrate partner crumpled on the ground, lifeless. Sadly, nearer inspection revealed the patently unthinkable, thirty-two year old Texas Ranger Robert Lee Burdett was dead, a gaping bullet wound in his throat, an exit wound in his back.[40] From the nasty wound's critical anatomical placement, according to most of the news reports, it is suggested Burdett died instantly, various sources saying he fell at the first volley, others asserting that in the "pistol battle," before succumbing to injury and losing consciousness he nimbly "wounded two Mexicans."[41] Reportedly, although a newspaper report is the only source, Burdett emptied his six-shooter. For certain, he went down fightin'.

The alarm was sounded and El Paso County Sheriff Peyton J. Edwards, after rounding up DR.L.G. Witherspoon, and accompanied by his deputies J.B. Kilpatrick and Jim Fulgham, made a mad-dash for Fabens.[42] Dr. Witherspoon's "flying trip," of course, was in vain. Throwing up a protective screen of U.S. Army Fifteenth Cavalry enlisted sentinels, all armed with 1903 model bolt-action Springfield rifles, effectively sealed off all ingress or egress to the little town.[43] It was, however, too late. The buzzards had flown the coop. An easy to read blood-trail offered a scrap of hope, and it was meticulously followed to a local resident's house where it was learned the owner had refused admittance to the bleeding renegade due to the fact, the gunshot victim was still angrily clutching a six-shooter.[44] The wounded man moved on, but his blood trail petered out out.

Unfailingly then, as today, a funeral home ambassador rushed to the battlefield also, this one from the undertaking firm of Nagley & Kaster, El Paso, Texas.[45] Expectedly, the death of a Texas Ranger was big news, more than ever since just a scarce three weeks earlier U.S. Mounted Customs Inspector Joe Sitter and Ranger Eugene B. Hulen had been bushwacked and mutilated. Adjutant General Henry Hutchings notified Governor James E. Ferguson.

> I regret to advise of the death of Ranger Robert Lee Burdett, Company B, Ranger Force. This man was killed in action in line of duty, on 8 June, 1915, at Fabens, Texas. A more detailed report will be submitted on receipt of additional information.[46]

Regrettably the "more detailed report" if indeed it did follow, has been innocently misplaced or otherwise gone astray, but most likely, never formalized other than mentions in the *Monthly Returns* of Company B, Ranger Force, closing June 30th, 1915 and the *Biennial Report of The Adjutant General of Texas*, for 1915-1916.[47]

Captain James Monroe Fox, who had been away on business elsewhere when the tragedy transpired, remarked to a newspaperman, "the Texas border is infested with Mexicans of a desperate character" and "the situation along the Texas-Mexican border in the Big Bend country is out of hand…thieves and bandits are operating in large numbers."[48] Robert Lee Burdett's body was reverently returned by train to Austin, at a cost of $20.95; Nagley & Kaster were sent the bureaucratic State Form necessary for setting out their undertaking bill, which had to be sworn to and returned. On behalf of the deceased ranger, Austin Chief of Police W.J. Morris accepted Burdett's personal property from Lone Star officials, duly recipting for same; and, a few days later, he obediently acknowledged poignant delivery of the personal property to Robert Lee Burdett's mother.[49]

Fascinatingly, the drama, if tribute is granted for unsubstantiated folklore and the makings for a gloriously good tale, has another chapter. Allegedly, Robert Lee Burdett's murderers fled across the Rio Grande to avoid the Texas criminal justice system and a date with an unsympathetic executioner. Consistent with border country legend, one lawman who had a "friendship" with the notoriously colorful Pancho Villa, sought the rebel leader's help in hemming up the killers of ranger Lee Burdett and exacting the requisite revenge. Bigheartedly Villa latched on to the fugitives, stood them before a bullet-chipped adobe wall and "saved the State of Texas the cost of a trial" as thrilled Texas Rangers approvingly looked on.[50] Thereafter, the two Texas lawmen hightailed it back to the Rio Grande, splashed across, and tersely declared, case closed!

They Have Guns...We Ought To Search Them

A quartet of typical Texas Rangers. Youthful, steely-eyed, rarin' to go, not the least camera shy, and armed to the teeth. Standing, from left to right, J. Walter Durbin, with two six-shooters, and Jim King. Seated, from left to right, George Parker and Robert McNamar. From Texas Ranger Sketches, *courtesy the author, Robert W. Stephens.*

Lawmen, Outlaws and S.O.Bs.

It makes one heck of a story, but, in some ways falls short of meshing with several contemporary newspaper assertions. For instance, in dealing with the tragic tale the *El Paso Herald* remarked, "Three men were arrested by the rangers and United States officers."[51] The *Austin Daily Statesman*, of the Burdett and Beall shoot-out reported, "Both the wounded Mexicans are expected to die."[52] And the *El Paso Morning Times* explicitly held, "Three Mexicans arrested in connection with the murder of the ranger were brought to the city and lodged in the county jail early this morning..."[53] Noticeably, not all the culprits were in custody, as gleaned from the comment in another edition of the *El Paso Herald*, "No more arrest have been made..."[54] And then, under the headline, "Two Arrested In The Lee Burdett Killing Case," an adept newspaper reporter for the *El Paso Morning Times* explicitly identified Luz Gandera and Isidoro Cadena as the arrested parties.[55]

Separating the legalize wheat from the chaff, and highlighting border country truisms is, at times, a maddening exercise in ambiguity. Were legitimate arrests made for the cold-blooded murder of Robert Lee Burdett? Did Pancho Villa order the executions of the Texas Ranger's pitiless assassins, and if so, did he oversee the extermination of the guilty, or just two who were convenient? Is there room, in the final chary analysis, for both versions to ring somewhat true—somewhat embellished—somewhat askew? *Quien Sabe*?

Robert Lee Burdett's name has not been commemorated by historical writings about Old West law enforcement or law enforcers, but honestly, seldom do good men take delivery of just reward, so this then, was just a story that needed tellin'.

They Have Guns...We Ought To Search Them

ENDNOTES CHAPTER 7

"THEY HAVE GUNS...WE OUGHT TO SEARCH THEM"

1   Cox, Mike. *Texas Ranger Tales—Stories That Need Telling.*
2   *Austin Daily Statesman*, June 9, 1915. And see, *Enlistment, Oath of Service, And Description—Ranger Force*, signed by Burdett on February 1, 1915 and endorsed by Captain James Monroe Fox. Courtesy, Texas State Library and Archives Commission (TSLAC), Austin, Texas. For the location of the Sprinkle community see *The Roads of Texas.* Page 118.
3   *Ibid.* And see letter, W.J. Morris, Chief of Police, Austin, Texas, to Henry Hutchings, Adjutant General, State of Texas, Austin, Texas, June 15, 1915. Courtesy, TSLAC.
4   Physical Description from *Enlistment, Oath of Service, And Description—Ranger Force*, Texas Ranger Hall of Fame and Museum (TRHF&M), Waco, Texas. Concerning Burdett's advanced education see, *Austin Daily Statesman*, June 9, 1915, "He (Burdett) attended St. Edward's College as a boy..."
5   St. Edward's College was founded in 1885 by Edward Sorin and the institution attained university status in 1925. Courtesy, Ingrid Karklins, University Archivist, St. Edward's University, Austin, Texas.
6   *Twelfth Annual Catalogue, St. Edward's College, 1895-1896.* P. 32. Courtesy, St. Edward's College Archives. Also note, Robert Lee Burdett's brother, Frank, was also a student at the college.
7   *Austin Daily Statesman*, June 9, 1915.
8   *Enlistment, Oath of Service, And Description—Ranger Force*, signed by Robert Lee Burdett on October 6, 1911, endorsed by Captain J.M. Fox, Co. C. Courtesy, TSLAC. Interestingly at the time of this enlistment, for the blank space for "occupation" the words "Peace officer" were written in, an indication that in some form or fashion Burdett saw some type of law enforcement service prior to becoming a Texas Ranger, perhaps a policeman, deputy sheriff, or deputy constable. If so, as of this writing, the specific employment has not been conclusively identified.
9   Davis, Chick & Ritter, Al. "Captain Monroe Fox and the Incident at Pourvenir," *Oklahoma State Trooper*. Winter 1996. P. 36. In their article the authors report that Fox assumed command of Company B, however, from the state archives on Robert Lee Burdett's enlistment papers Fox signs the document as "Captain Co. C, Ranger Force." For his own enlistment, on October 5, 1911, Fox's oath of service papers read "Company C". Courtesy, TRHF&M. Later, after a transfer to far West Texas he was in command of Co. B, as reflected in the *Biennial Report of The Adjutant General of Texas, From January 1, 1915 to December 16, 1916.* P. 11. "Company B—Home station, Marfa; Captain J.M. Fox, one sergeant, twelve privates." Courtesy, TSLAC.
10 Burdett's *Enlistment, Oath of Service, and Description—Ranger Force.* Courtesy, TRHF&M. And see, Davis & Ritter. P. 36.
11 *El Paso Times*, June 25, 1916. "At that time it was called 'Hell Paso' and he (Schutz) says the title was justly earned."
12 Tyler, Ronnie C. *The Big Bend, A History Of The Last Texas Frontier.* For a discussion of border-country bandit conflicts see Chapter 6, "Bandits Along the Border." P. 157-187.

Lawmen, Outlaws and S.O.Bs.

[13] Meed, Douglas V. *Bloody Border—Riots, Battles and Adventures Along the Turbulent U.S.—Mexican Borderlands.* P. 48. Familiarity with this well-researched and adeptly written volume will give the reader an accurate snapshot of early twentieth-century borderland life—and, death.

[14] Ritter, Al. "Death on the Rio Grande," *Texas Department of Public Safety Officers Association Magazine* (DPSOA) March/April 1996. P. 55. Also see, Bolling , Robert S. *Tales of the El Paso Road—Death Rides The River.* P. 8. The author seems to justify waylaying the officers, "It was a rarity at the time if a Mexican prisoner ever made it to jail, usually being shot while 'attempting to escape.' Fearing that Chico Cano would be killed by the lawmen, his brother, Manuel, and two others set up an ambush on the mountain trail to rescue him."

[15] Bruce, Leona. *Banister Was There.* P. 158. And see Tyler, P. 162. Oftentimes Joe Sitter's name is mentioned as being "Sitters," but in fact, examination of his Oath of Office, and other documents, reveals he signed his name, "Joseph Sitter". Courtesy, TRHF&M.

[16] Tyler. P. 162-163. The author identifies Harvick as "J.W. Harwick," but, nonetheless, his Harwick and Harvick were one and the same person. Also see, Cox. P. 139.

[17] *Ibid.* Quoting the *Alpine Avalanche.* P. 163.

[18] Governor O.B. Collquitt, Austin, Texas, to Ranger Captain John R. Hughes, El Paso, Texas. February 3, 1913. Courtesy, TSLAC. And see, Martin, Jack. *Border Boss: Captain John R. Hughes—Texas Ranger.* P. 198.

[19] *Ibid.*

[20] Alexander, Bob. "Hell Paso," *Quarterly* of the National Association For Outlaw And Lawman History, Inc. (NOLA). Vol. XXVI, No. 2 (April-June 2002). P. 5-14.

[21] *Biennial Report of the Adjutant General of Texas, From January 1, 1915 to December 16, 1916.* Courtesy, TSLAC. And see, *Enlistment, Oath Of Service, and Description, Ranger Force*, dated February 1, 1915, signed, "J.M. Fox". Courtesy, TRHF&M, Also see, Gournay, Luke. *Texas Boundaries, Evolution of the State's Counties.* Although created in 1850, Presidio County wasn't organized until 1875, with Fort Davis as the county seat, but later, 1885, Marfa garnered the shire town honors. P. 61.

[22] *Enlistment, Oath Of Service, and Description, Ranger Force*, dated February 1, 1915, signed, "Robt. L. Burdett" endorsed by J.M. Fox. Courtesy, TSLAC and TRHF&M.

[23] *Enlistment, Oath of Service, and Description, Ranger Force*, dated March 1, 1915, signed "C. P. Beall," and endorsed by J.M. Fox. Courtesy, TRHF&M.

[24] *Ibid.*

[25] Several of Ranger Charley P. Beall's arrests can be identified in *Monthly Returns,* Company B, Ranger Force. Month ending June 30th, 1915, Captain J.M. Fox, commanding. Courtesy, TSLAC.

[26] *El Paso Herald*, May 25, 1915. And see, Cox, P. 142. Also see, Webb, Walter Prescott. *The Texas Rangers—A Century of Frontier Defense.* P. 498. This account is off by one year, the ambush of Sitter occurred in 1915 instead of 1916 as reported by Webb. For a slightly different take on the killings, see, Means, Joyce E. *Pancho Villa Days at Pilares.* P. 169.

[27] Tyler. P. 163.

[28] *Austin Daily Statesman*, June 9, 1915.

They Have Guns...We Ought To Search Them

[29] Adjutant General, State of Texas, Austin, Texas, to Will J. Morris, Chief of Police, Austin, Texas. June 12, 1915. Courtesy, TSLAC.

[30] *El Paso Morning Times*, June 9, 1915.

[31] *Alpine Avalanche*, June 17, 1915. "...a gang of Fort Hancock Mexicans went to Fabens. They were said to have been drinking and disturbing the peace. They were warned by Burdett and Ranger Charles Bell (Beall) to cease the disturbance..."

[32] The time is taken from the *El Paso Herald*, June 8, 1915. The fact that Burdett had a gold pocket-watch was determined by an inventory of his personal effects, as listed in correspondence from Adjutant General, State of Texas, Austin, Texas, to Will J. Morris, Chief of Police, Austin, Texas. June 14, 1915. Courtesy, TSLAC.

[33] *Alpine Avalanche*, June 10, 1915. And see, *El Paso Herald*, June 8, 1915.

[34] *El Paso Morning Times*, June 9, 1915.

[35] *Ibid.*

[36] *Ibid.* And see, *Biennial Report of The Adjutant General of Texas, From January 1, 1915, To December 31, 1916.* P. 11. Courtesy, TSLAC. "The pay of the captain is $100 per month, the sergeants $50 per month and the privates $40 per month. The men are required to furnish their horse and arms. The State furnishes subsistence, forage, and ammunition."

[37] *Ibid.* And see, *Austin Daily Statesman*, June 9, 1915. Also see, *El Paso Herald*, June 8, 1915.

[38] *El Paso Herald*, June 8, 1915, and *Alpine Avalanche*, June 17, 1915, and, *El Paso Morning Times*, June 9, 1915.

[39] *El Paso Morning Times*, June 9, 1915. "...it is believed that the supply of ammunition ran out. The Mexicans then beat a hasty retreat."

[40] *Ibid.* The *Alpine Avalanche*, June 10, 1915, says that Burdett was "struck in the breast and killed instantly."

[41] *Austin Daily Statesman*, June 9, 1915.

[42] *El Paso Morning Times*, June 9, 1915. The *El Paso Herald* of June 8, 1915, adds, Texas Ranger O. D. Goodwin, and "special deputies Claude Smith and Miller" to the law enforcement contingent responding to Fabens.

[43] *Ibid.*

[44] *Ibid.*

[45] Letter from Nagley & Kaster, El Paso, Texas, to Adjutant General Henry Hutchings, Austin, Texas. June 9, 1915. Courtesy, TSLAC. And see, *El Paso Morning Times*, June 8, 1915. "Nagley & Kaster's undertaking establishment was notified of the tragedy by wire and at once dispatched a man to Fabens..."

[46] Adjutant General, State of Texas, Henry Hutchings, Austin, Texas, to Governor, State of Texas, James E. Ferguson, Austin, Texas. June 8, 1915. Courtesy, TSLAC.

[47] *Monthly Returns*, Company B, Ranger Force, Ending June 30th, 1915 and *Biennial Report of The Adjutant General of Texas, From January 1, 1915, To December 31, 1916.* The first has the notation, "Burdett killed June 8th, 1915," the latter, "Casualties—considering the risk—have been slight in number, but I deeply regret to record the death in action of Eugene B. Hulen, on May 24, 1915, near Candelaria, Texas, and of Lee Burdett on June 8, 1915, near Fabens, Texas. Both of these rangers belonged to Company B and were killed in line of duty by Mexican bandits."

[48] First quotation, *El Paso Herald*, June 11, 1915. Second quotation, Davis & Ritter, P. 37.

[49] Adjutant General, State of Texas to Captain J.M. Fox, Company B, Ranger Force, Marfa, Texas. June 10, 1915. "Transportation remains of Robert Lee Burdett." And, Adjutant General, State of Texas, Austin, Texas to Nagley & Kaster, El Paso, Texas. June 10, 1915. "Funeral expenses, Ranger Burdett." And, Adjutant General, State of Texas, Austin, Texas to Will J. Morris, Chief of Police, Austin, Texas. June 14, 1915. "Effects of Robert Lee Burdett." And, W.J. Morris, Chief of Police, Austin, Texas to Adjutant General, Austin, Texas. June 15, 1915. "Have just delivered to Mrs. Burdett affects of her son Lee." Courtesy, TSLAC.

[50] Cox. P. 127. The author reports the Texas Rangers who witnessed the execution in Mexico were Jefferson Eagle "Jeff" Vaughan and Ivey Findley.

[51] *El Paso Herald*, June 8, 1915.

[52] *Austin Daily Statesman*, June 8, 1915.

[53] *El Paso Morning Times*, June 8, 1915.

[54] *El Paso Herald*, June 9, 1915.

[55] *El Paso Morning Times*, June 13, 1915.

CHAPTER 8

"AN OUTLAW TRIPPED UP BY LOVE"

Tom D. Love, Caprock Cop, Tenacious Trailer

Tom D. Love was cut from sturdy oak. His grandfather, Wade Love, was a fighter, a veteran of the War of 1812, and later after migrating to Texas from Mississippi, a cowman. Tom's father, Leonard R. Love, just like his papa was a warrior, volunteering for service with a Confederate regiment raised in Coryell County.[1] Reportedly his father Wade, at age 66, signed up too.[2] And, it was in Coryell County, at Gatesville, that Thomas D. Love first saw the light of day, November 10, 1862. After closing hostilities of the Civil War, carrying an authentically painful battlefield scar, Leonard reclaimed and reestablished his muddled livestock operations and once again productively ranged undomesticated cattle throughout Coryell and Hamilton counties; he too was a cowman.[3] What ideas Tom's mother, the former Miss Fannie Powell, had about the cow-business is historical mystery.[4] As a dutifully devoted pioneer homemaker she had little time to squander on abstract theory while doting over her herd of seven, a daughter and six mischievous boys.[5]

There is no drought of biographical sketches featuring colorful cowboy characters, and for the most part the yarns are replete with first one or another wandering down from Tennessee or Arkansas, or maybe from even further back east, and inevitably stopping over in the Lone Star state while serving an apprenticeship in the cattle-chasing and bronco-busting business. Tom D. Love, unlike so many who sought adventure as a Texas cowhand, needed no formal introduction to the locale, or the job. From day one he lived in cow-country. By the time he was fourteen he was already a seasoned top-hand with a catch-rope or a red-hot branding iron, and too, he was capable of screwing down tight on a cold-backed cow pony; after all, it was his family's livelihood. In 1876, about the time George Armstrong Custer met his demise at the Little Bighorn, the Leonard

Love folks moved their mushrooming livestock dealings to the proximity of Buffalo Gap, about 15 miles south of present day Abilene.[6] And, for awhile, Tom D. Love went to a Taylor county school, one "rudely constructed, the chinks between the logs furnishing an ample supply of fresh air, and the benches were made of split logs."[7] By the time he was eighteen though, book-learnin' was not on his mind—cowboyin' was. Tom D. Love left the comfort of hearth and home, striking out on his own to work for wages in the yet to be politically organized Borden County, up near the Colorado River headwaters in West Texas.[8]

In 1880 he cowboyed for stockmen John Flood, John Aston, and B.F. White, according to most reports.[9] Unquestionably it was here, Borden County, that Tom D. Love earned his renowned reputation for cow-savvy and personal integrity. It's reasonably safe to suppose that when the Alabama and Texas Cattle Company bought out his boss's cattle holdings in 1883, the young cowhand had already made quite an impression on the new owner, ranching powerhouse A.P. Bush, Jr.[10] On the spot Tom D. Love was assigned foreman responsibilities for 12,000 head of cattle.[11]

Six years earlier at Graham, in answer to cattlemen's desperation at fending off a horde of cow-thieves, the Northwest Texas Cattle Raisers Association was birthed.[12] The state of affairs had become so deplorable that one country editor lamented after an act of vigilantism, if hanging wouldn't put the "kibosh" on criminals, "maybe cremation would."[13] Well thought-out Association procedures were adopted. The ranch country was divided, and, "men will be allotted to each district, whose duty it shall be to gather all cattle in their district, and notify the owners of the same, and hold them until they are called for by their owners." Furthermore, stockmen were cautioned not to for any reason "molest" cattle not their own within division boundaries until the beeves were gathered and inspected by persons designated by the Association.[14] By 1883 the roundup system had been massaged and fine-tuned. Pinpointing the high regard in which the subject of this account was held can be extracted from the remarks of another frontier newspaperman, "The cattlemen throughout western Texas combined and established a series of line camps along the T. & P. railroad. There were three of these camps, in each of which there were about twenty-five men, the first being near Colorado (City), under charge of T. D. Love, the second under Buck Jones was located near Big Springs, and the third under C.A. O'Keefe, was located south of Midland."[15] Cowmen knew they could thoroughly count on Tom D. Love for an honest tally, and too, for sure they knew he was not a man who would tolerate monkey-business or slipshod shenanigans at his cow-camps. Following year? Same job![16]

Borden County, Texas, Sheriff Thomas Decatur Love. Courtesy, Bill and Richard Love.

Lawmen, Outlaws and S.O.Bs.

The country around Buffalo Gap began to "settle up," and in 1885, Leonard Love, anxious for a little more elbowroom, transferred operations further west to enormously endowed Presidio County in the Big Bend region, adjacent to the Rio Grande River and Mexico.[17] Just how and when Tom D. Love met the stunningly attractive Mallie Morrow is subject to debate but somewhere out in that lonesome and unforgiving Trans-Pecos country during Tom's 1885 Christmas visit the couple were married.[18] Tom D. whisked his new bride back to Borden County.[19]

Borden County Sheriff Thomas Decatur Love standing in the doorway of the county jail at Gail, Texas. Courtesy Borden County Museum.

Although created in 1876, Borden County had not been "organized" due to a sizable under-abundance of people, but over time, as the population increased so then did the need for workable county government. By 1891 Borden County met the criteria and public officials were installed in office at Gail, the newly created county seat.[20] It was cow-country, dominated by cowmen and, in turn, the candidate for sheriff too, had to own cow-person

An Outlaw Tripped Up By Love

credentials.[21] Tom D. Love was sworn in as Borden County's first sheriff.[22] In itself, Borden County, rolling and broken by the Cap Rock Escarpment with drainage to the Colorado River, was big enough but, at the time, Lynn, Dawson, and Garza counties were as yet "unorganized" and for judicial purposes much of that work also fell to Sheriff Tom D. Love, a law enforcement headache of migraine proportion.[23] Specifically of Love it was written that his was a "man's job in those days, as the word of a sheriff was supreme."[24]

A cross-section of Borden County personalities; standing left to right, Jim Craig, wolf trapper; Samp Morrow, rancher; seated left to right, Will Clark, deputy sheriff; and Jim Winslow, "a drifter." Courtesy Borden County Museum.

Lawmen, Outlaws and S.O.Bs.

Nurturing an embryonic criminal justice system on what was legitimately recognized as a transitional frontier, was, in truth, a tough task even for the doughty Tom D. Love. In fairness though he wasn't the only lawman whose bailiwick was seemingly swarming with hard-edged characters mounted on jaded horses, many of whom for whatever reasons had already buried their real name and were ridin' and hidin' from something or someone. One of those legendary *mal hombres* set his course for the Land of Enchantment, New Mexico Territory, traveling straightway through the *Llano Estacado*, traversing the legal domain of a determined sheriff. William Tuttle "Bill" Cook was the outlaw's name.

Predominantly confining his criminality to Oklahoma and Indian Territory, in but a very short time Bill Cook and his most notable sidekick, Crawford "Cherokee Bill" Goldsby, during the mid-1890's were the meat for sensational headlines. Of the cunning criminal Bill Cook, a prominent Western biographer penned, "Newspapers from Kansas City to Texas, and east to New York, touted him as the leader of the worst band of cutthroats west of the Mississippi."[25] And, at the tail-end of the nineteenth-century in an epic of Western Americana journalism, Bill Cook was profiled as "the leader of the most desperate and dangerous gang that ever operated in the Indian country."[26] One newspaperman, comparing the brigand to the likes of John Wesley Hardin and Sam Bass, theorized that William Tuttle was "perhaps the most notorious of the three," and unequivocally declared Cook left "his nasty mark on Southwestern history..."[27] In an encyclopedic depiction of frontier biographies, Cook is simply classified a "desperado."[28]

The gang's henchmen carried gaudy names. Such players as, Elmer "Chicken" Lucas, Thurman "Skeeter" Baldwin, Sam "Verdigris Kid" McWilliams, Henry "Texas Jack Starr" Munson, and of course those more typically tagged, like, Curt Dayson, Lon Gordon, George Sanders, Jim French and Jess "Buck" Snyder—and others.[29] None were choirboys.

The tedious chore of enumerating *all* the felonious misdeeds and murderous mayhem credited to the Bill Cook gang will not be tackled in this outlaw/lawman commentary; others have splendidly pulled off the task. Certainly though, this loathsome league of Western misfits was better known then, than now. Simply it can be said the bandits were generating frightful pandemonium in such proportion that government bureaucrats at Washington, D. C. were teetering on the brink of sending federal soldiers to help worn out local lawmen and deputy U.S. Marshals.[30] Bill Cook and the boys were feeling the heat. Several splashed across the Red River into

An Outlaw Tripped Up By Love

Texas, and, it is at that point in time where the absorbing saga of an elusive outlaw and a cowboy-sheriff began to merge.

On November 14, 1894, Texas Ranger Sergeant W.J. L. Sullivan caught up with part of the band on Sid Webb's ranch, Clay County, just southeast of Wichita Falls.[31] During what proved an exhilarating example of an authentic Old West case of the good-guys versus the bad-guys, the confrontation ended—after a blistering shoot-out— with the arrests of "Skeeter" Baldwin, "Buck" Snyder, William Farris, and Charles Turner.[32] The quartet had been armed to the teeth, and in addition to prisoners, lawmen seized "...six Winchesters, four six-shooters, eight belts, one thousand rounds of cartridges...," and assorted other items which later they determined had been pilfered during an earlier crime.[33] One of the Winchesters was Cook's rifle, a weapon he had discretely left behind while he and a crony, Jim French, were away casing the best spot to rob a Fort Worth & Denver train.[34] Sensibly, after hearing the distant gunshots Bill Cook and Jim French deduced the prudent course of action was not rescue and reinforcement, but rather to hightail it for parts they wished would remain unknown.[35]

If Sheriff Tom D. Love was aware of the skirmish between Texas Rangers and Oklahoma outlaws over in that country just south of the Red River near Bellevue, it's unknown. Either way he had a job to do. Sheriff Love traveled to Garza County, picked up a prisoner and started on the return trip, the bothersome wrongdoer in tow. Trail-weary, he arrived at the Square & Compass ranch managed by Jim Mitchell.[36] Mitchell extended congenial West Texas greetings, accompanied by a traditional cow-country invitation to stay the night. Sheriff Love accepted, and while at the ranch was introduced to two cowboys who were doing day work, but who, as the sheriff mentally noted, appeared uneasy upon learning he was the law.[37] Next day, Love left with his manacled prisoner, dropped him off at the Colorado City jail and returned to his headquarters at Gail.[38] During review of his mail, or an urgent telegraph message by other reports, Love was appraised that the notorious renegades Bill Cook and Jim French might very well be wandering about somewhere in his sizable domain.[39] Bingo! Could that pair of itinerant cowhands maybe have other jobs as well, say, robbing trains and things? Although it was by now snowing and miserably cold, Sheriff Tom D. Love bundled up, saddled up, and headed back to the Square & Compass.[40] The physical descriptions seemed to match. Tom D. Love wasn't positively sure, but almost!

In the meantime, Texas Ranger W.J. L. Sullivan too was meandering throughout the area, trying to develop beneficial clues as to the whereabouts of what amounted to early day top-ten fugitives. Likewise, eventually he would make it to the Square & Compass.[41]

On a chance meeting, Sheriff Love crossed frosty paths with 9R cowboy and sometime deputy, Louis Polk, who was apparently out looking for mama cows.[42] After a nippy strategic huddle, the shivering sheriff and his chilly companion faced the raw wind, destined for the Square & Compass bunkhouse.[43] Upon arrival, however, Love learned the nomadic hobos had last night quit the ranch, and were making tracks, possibly headed for Green Igold's place, a rough hundred miles or so further west. That's what foreman Mitchell surmised. Discounting lunatics, the only people crazy enough to trek about in near subzero weather on a West Texas prairie, when they didn't have to, were crooks or cow-country cops. Sheriff Tom D. Love was one; he figured his quarry must be the other. Love and Polk cinched tight, stepped up, tucked their chins and, despite the falling mercury, set out in pursuit.[44] Along the Colorado River banks Bill Cook's overnight camp was located and painstaking sleuthing began.[45]

Sheriff Love promptly deduced the drifting suspects had parted company, one leading an extra horse was still headed in a westerly direction, the other ambling back toward the southeast, obliquely in line with Colorado City. He and Polk opted to follow the westbound tracks. Notwithstanding the weather, the gritty lawmen continued to cut for sign, and in due course belatedly monitored the target of their chase making hasty stops at remote ranches. After warming by a welcome fire and during polite but productive interrogation, Sheriff Love was convinced the man he was following fit a description of the villainous Bill Cook.[46] Somewhere near the vicinity of Lubbock, their horses utterly fagged, the tenacious lawdogs altered stratagem. Sheriff Love traded for a fresh mount, and Polk reversed course back for Borden County, ostensibly to "hold down the fort" in the sheriff's absence, and also to make contact with Ranger Captain Bill McDonald, appraising him of the latest news.[47]

Whether he received a telegram from McDonald, or, whether he developed investigative leads on his own, as he implies in a 1909 autobiography, Ranger Sergeant Sullivan and a small posse made it to the Square & Compass ranch before moving on to Green Igold's place. Finding a man wanted for an apparent Colorado City misdemeanor at the ranch, the ranger sidetracked his manhunt and arrested Jim Dillard. Later, for an undisclosed reason he arrested Joe Elkins, then according to Sullivan, he made a deal with the two prisoners to snitch on Cook and reveal the bandit's hideout. The

An Outlaw Tripped Up By Love

Lone Star lawman was told the infamous outlaw was heading for Roswell, New Mexico Territory, and true to his word, Sullivan turned out his captives.[48]

Sheriff Tom D. Love stubbornly tracked and trailed, and by most accounts he racked up the distance, day after day — between 400 and 500 miles.[49] Single-mindedly Love pressed across the windswept Staked Plains and into New Mexico Territory. At one point near Four Lakes he lost the trail. Disheartened he did a turnabout, meticulously casting for encouraging sign on the backtrack.[50] Remarkably, on the desolate tableland he once again found the hoof-prints hoped for, and after one of Cook's horses threw a shoe knocking a chunk out of the hoof, following the now distinct dint turned into a comparatively easy chore, especially on the public dirt road leading toward Roswell.[51]

At the lively Pecos Valley town's edge, Cook, using the alias John Williams, made arrangements to overnight his three-shoed horse in a small pasture. Discreetly picking up on this tid-bit of intelligence, with Winchester in hand Sheriff Love set up surveillance, but after awhile dejectedly figured out Bill Cook was not coming back to retrieve the steed.[52] Sheriff Love contacted the local Chaves County sheriff, who also sported a deputy U.S. Marshal's badge, Charles C. Perry. The dual commissioned lawman had an earned reputation as being a man who "knew no fear." And too, he also held widespread distinction as being a hard belligerent drinker, chronic gambler, red-light rowdy, unabashed friend of the underworld, and although unknown to Tom D. Love at the time, contemptuously corruptible.[53]

There are two versions of what happened next. Ranger Sergeant Sullivan, in memoirs published a decade and half after the fact, asserted that he too traveled to Roswell, but by train, and that it was he who counseled Sheriff Perry that Bill Cook was in the region, heading for the mining community of White Oaks in Lincoln County.[54] Another account, penned prior to Sullivan's essay, says the outlaw at Roswell, "...passed several of the Texas Rangers who had come on by rail; they failed to recognize him and Cook continued on his western course."[55] Whether or not Perry and Love departed in the middle of the night on Cook's trail, leaving the ranger asleep at the courthouse as Sullivan contends is debatable. Facts, however, do reveal the two sheriffs hunted the desperate fugitive, and because Tom D. Love was by now so very familiar with Cook's horse-tracks, they picked up his trail about thirty-five miles northwest of Roswell.[56] Successful in their pursuit, the manhunters tracked Cook straight through the Capitan Mountains and onto the ranch of Bill Yates, not too far from Nogal.[57] Backing off, the lawmen went to a nearby ranch operated by Minter Gray (Graves). Employing a sick horse ruse, the sheriffs were able to draw an employee away from Yate's ranch, for questioning. It was revealed an unknown cowboy type, using the handle "John Williams," was indeed staying the night at Yate's place and would at next day's first light go out to a barn and feed his horse before departing on travels to—somewhere. During wee-hours of the morning Sheriffs Love and Perry secreted themselves in Yate's horseshed.[58]

The January 12th (1895) morning sun began peeking over the mountains at just about the same time Bill Cook exited Yate's bunkhouse and headed for the oat bin and feed buckets. After a spate of excruciating days in the saddle and hundreds of torturous miles, Sheriff Tom D. Love, at last, was about to bag his prey—one way or the other. Without hesitancy Bill Cook seemingly stumbled into the lawmen's lair. "Throw up your hands" they hoarsely commanded, and he did! The range had been exceedingly close, by one account a mere three feet, and when the unarmed outlaw suddenly peered into the Winchester muzzles and saw the resolute lawmen he, as well as they, knew the freewheeling days of Bill Cook were over.[59] About his surrender Bill Cook rationalized, "...most any man will give up when he hasn't any show...as they had the drop on me and could have killed me before I drew a gun, if I had had forty."[60]

Hustled back to the warmth of the bunkhouse the officers discovered Cook's six-shooter on his bed, and the handcuffed outlaw regretfully lamented that this; "...was the first time he had been without his pistol. He said that he glanced at the gun...and thought to himself that he should take it with him. But he then decided that there was no need to carry it."[61] Remarking that he didn't think he would need it any longer, Bill Cook made a present of the short-barreled Colt .45 to Sheriff Love, and explained the initials cut into the bone-handled grips were those of his, and his past partner in crime, Crawford "Cherokee Bill" Goldsby.[62]

Traveling back to Roswell on January 13th, the lawmen were met with substantial public praise, and were joined by another noted West Texas peace officer, Sheriff Y.D. McMurray from Colorado City, the county seat of Mitchell County, Texas, who likewise had been scouring the frozen and broken countryside in search of Cook.[63] At the Territorial Capitol one newspaperman proclaimed, "No criminal arrest in the southwest since the days of Billy the Kid and Kit Joy has stirred up as much interest as the capture of Bill Cook..."[64] By order of the United States Marshal for New Mexico

An Outlaw Tripped Up By Love

Territory, Edward L. Hall, the prisoner was brought to Santa Fe for requisition of extradition papers by Perry, acting in his capacity as a deputy marshal, assisted by sheriffs Love and McMurray.[65] Then by rail the infamous outlaw was to be delivered by the trio of officers to federal Judge Parker's court at Fort Smith, Arkansas.[66] And, if it is to be believed, according to Sullivan, who in this particular manhunt always seems to come up a "a day late and a dollar short," the Texas Ranger purposefully met the train at an El Paso stop, and severely chastised C.C. Perry for running off and leaving him snoozing at the Chaves County courthouse.[67] There is, however, room for a degree of doubt, especially in light of Perry's sour disposition and his no nonsense propensity for violence. If C.C. Perry heard any vitriolic remarks uttered by the failed ranger he flatly and, aberrantly, ignored them. Historically, the only source for the words being spoken must be credited to Sullivan himself.[68]

On the right, Texas Ranger Sergeant W. John L. Sullivan. On the left, possibly, G.V. Resci. Sullivan, during his overly hyped version of the chase after the notorious Oklahoma outlaw Bill Cook always seemed to come up "a day late and a dollar short." Courtesy, Texas Ranger Hall of Fame and Museum.

Sullivan goes on to say while in El Paso he boarded the train, and in an affable, but very confidential conversation with Bill Cook, the outlaw allegedly whispered an ominous warning, "Those men

(Perry, Love, McMurray) have gone back there to 'make medicine' against you; for they have all said they intended to beat you out of the reward and honor of my capture, which I think you justly deserve, for you have simply lived on my trail."[69] How Bill Cook surmised Sullivan had "lived on" his trail and therefore he should be afforded the "honor" of his detention will be left to the particular reader, but it should be noted, this was their very first face to face meeting, and even by his own previous remarks, Sullivan admitted he had temporarily abandoned the chase. Intractable Sheriff Thomas D. Love had not! And, in fact, Bill Cook recalled earlier encountering Love at the Square & Compass ranch.[70] Plainly, Cook knew which manhunter had been camping on his trail. From the historical perspective we know what Texas Ranger W. John L. Sullivan later wrote, and too, we unconditionally know that Sheriff Love arrested Bill Cook, and was personally gifted with the celebrated desperado's bone-handled six-shooter. Sheriff Thomas D. Love wasn't a braggadocios man, nor a writer.

The infamous Oklahoma hellion and fugitive William Tuttle "Bill" Cook. Courtesy, Bill and Richard Love.

Complying with their assignment, the three officers and one outlaw continued their trip. At Fort Worth the train was met by 1,500 gawking denizens literally stumbling all over themselves just to get a glance at America's public enemy number one.[71] While in Cowtown the legendary Bill Cook posed for a photographer, Sheriffs Love, Perry, and McMurray vigilantly standing behind him.[72] By the time the locomotive chugged into Fort Smith, another 1000 plus citizens were waiting at the depot. Many were in fact,

An Outlaw Tripped Up By Love

flabbergasted! They had expected to see a grizzled and cocksure badman from "bitter creek," instead what they got was a boyishly looking lad with a pleasing and agreeable demeanor.[73] But, indeed he was an outlaw, and rightfully so he was deposited at the jail. Sheriff Tom D. Love returned to Borden County. Adulation and appreciation awaited his arrival.

Pleased lawmen. Standing from left to right, Mitchell County, Texas, Sheriff Young Douglas "Y.D." McMurry; Chaves County, New Mexico Territory, Sheriff Charles C. Perry; and Borden County, Texas, Sheriff Thomas Decatur Love. Seated, the nationally notorious baby-faced Oklahoma owl-hoot Bill Cook. Courtesy, Richard Love, a photograph from the El Paso Herald.

Sheriffs Perry and Love, and ranger Sullivan all claimed a portion of the reward posted for William Tuttle Cook's arrest and conviction. None received a penny.[74] Bill Cook pled guilty before Judge Isaac Parker, receiving a forty-five year prison sentence. Later he died in prison at Albany, New York.[75] Charles C. Perry, as it turns out, should have been Cook's cell-mate. He absconded with Chaves County funds, to the tune of $7,639.02, and fled the country. Reportedly he was killed in South Africa.[76] Sheriff Thomas D. Love staunchly guarded his good name!

After all the hullabaloo regarding the sheriff's remarkable chase across an inhospitable transitional frontier in search of the owl-hoot had died down, Thomas D. Love's life returned to West Texas normalcy. Love gradually intertwined the cow-business with his law enforcement duties, but upon completion of three terms as Borden County sheriff, he devoted his full attention to the burgeoning livestock industry. Admiringly, Borden County citizens included Tom Love's name on the bronze dedication plaque for a brand new bridge, the inscription read: "T. D. Love, Sheriff, Capturer of the Noted Outlaw, Bill Cook."[77] In 1902, Tom Love moved further west to Sierra Blanca and became even more heavily invested in large-scale cattle ranches along the Texas/Mexican border with other family members who, too, had made a westerly migration to the Big Bend country. Never shirking from public service, Thomas D. Love served as a county commissioner and as a member of the local school board.[78] Later he became President of the Sierra State Bank.[79]

William Tuttle "Bill" Cook's Peacemaker, a Colt's .45 caliber, Serial Number 155728. The six-shooter was given to West Texas Sheriff Tom D. Love by Bill Cook at the time of his capture in New Mexico Territory. Courtesy, Tommie Kimsey, Daphne Hamilton, Richard and Bill Love.

But above all else, and through all; even the fledgling hardscrabble cowboy days; or the perilous man-hunting days; or the financially risky ranch building days; Thomas Decatur Love was a husband and father. He and his beloved Mallie were blessed with four children, two boys, Baylus N. and Tom Prince, and two girls, Luna and Maude, and these were his wealth—even though it was reported he was a millionaire.[80] Cognizant of the colorfully rich period through which he had lived, and the significance of legitimate historical artifacts, Tom Love cherished the six-shooter once given him by America's top crook, and before he died was assured by son Tom Prince that the revolver would forevermore remain a family treasure, which it has.[81]

On October 20, 1934, Thomas Decatur Love, age 72, after a lingering illness sadly passed away.[82] The Fort Worth *Star-Telegram* in a front page headline respectfully remembered, "West Texas Mourns Thomas D. Love, Man Who Caught Bill Cook."[83] We should too!

An Outlaw Tripped Up By Love

ENDNOTES CHAPTER 8

"AN OUTLAW TRIPPED UP BY LOVE"

[1]   Leonard R. Love served as an officer with the 30th Texas Cavalry, Company F. See, *Texas Confederate Soldiers, 1861-1865.* (Hewett, Janet & Lawrence, Joyce, ed.), P. 318. Also see, *Supplement to the Official Records of Union And Confederate Armies,* (Hewett, Janet, ed.) P. 248. And see, Leonard R. Love, Service Records, 30th Texas Cavalry, Harold B. Simpson History Complex, Confederate Research Center. Hillsboro, Texas. Also, Wharton, Clarence, *Texas Under Many Flags.* P. 139. And see, *Early Ranching in West Texas*, "Tom Love—Rancher and Sheriff," by Aline Parks. P. 67-69.

[2]   Unidentified and undated typescript, "The Love Brothers," courtesy Patricia Love, El Paso. If the elder Wade Love signed up for service, it was not with a regular Confederate Army unit, but more likely with a contingent of home-guard militia.

[3]   Wharton, *Texas Under Many Flags*, P. 139.

[4]   *Ibid.* Miss Powell, born in 1841, had come with her parents from Mississippi. The family settled near Fort Gates in Central Texas. Fort Gates, located near Gatesville, Texas, was established in 1849, along with a string of military installations constructed to quell settlers' demands for protection from raiding Comanche and Kiowa Indians. See, *Soldier and Brave*, Ferris, Robert G., Series Editor. P. 315. Also see, Robinson, III, Charles M., *Frontier Forts of Texas* who places establishment of the fort one year earlier, but accurately reports its closure in 1852, as the line of frontier expanded to the west. P. 80.

[5]   *Ibid.* Mrs. Leonard Love lost two children in infancy. Reaching maturity were, Thomas Decatur (Tom D.), George W., Richard C. (Dick), John R., Wirth (Wert), Robert (Rowdy), and Mary Elizabeth (Lizzie).

[6]   Parks, P. 67. And see, Love, Patricia, P. 15. Also see, Holden, William Curry, *Alkali Trails.* P. 60. "Buffalo Gap in Taylor County felt a quickening of life in 1878. The town had grown from a buffalo camp established in 1876. When the county was organized, in 1877, it became the county seat. From 1877 to 1881 the town was an important supply center for the cattle range."

[7]   Wharton, *Texas Under Many Flags*, P. 139.

[8]   *Ibid.*

[9]   *Ibid.*

[10]   Johnson, Frank W., *A History of Texas and Texans*, Vol. V. P. 2392. Also see, Parks, P. 67. And see, Nordyke, Lewis, *Great Roundup—The Story of Texas and Southwestern Cowmen.* P. 100. The author says of Bush, "…a tenderfoot who was to become a power in the cattle industry."

[11]   *Ibid.*

[12]   Murrah, David J., *C.C. Slaughter, Rancher, Banker, Baptist.* P. 39-53. And see, *The New Handbook of Texas*, Volume VI. P. 417. This formative alliance was the genesis for the Texas and Southwestern Cattle Raisers Association of today.

[13]   Robinson, III, Charles. *The Frontier World of Fort Griffin.* P. 109.

[14]   Clarke, Mary Whatley, *A Century of Cow Business, The First Hundred Years Of The Texas and Southwestern Cattle Raisers Association.* P. 16. Also see, Perkins, Doug and Ward, Nancy, *Brave Men & Cold Steel, A History of Range Detectives and Their Peacemakers.* P. 9-22.

[15]   Biggers, Don Hampton. *Buffalo Guns & Barbed Wire, Two Frontier Accounts by Don Hampton Biggers*. Introduction by Greene, A. C.—Biography by Connor, Seymour V. P. 121.

[16]   *Ibid.*, P. 123. "...T. D. Love having charge of the Colorado camp again." And see, *The Cattleman*, Vol. XXI, No. 6 (1934), P. 18. "As wagon boss he (Love) operated roundup crews in many West Texas counties."

[17]   Wharton, *Texas Under Many Flags*, P. 139.

[18]   Presidio County *Marriage License*, T. D. Love and M. Morrow. December 24, 1885. The license was obtained on December 22, 1885, and the ceremony was performed on Christmas Eve.

[19]   Parks, P. 67.

[20]   *Texas Almanac, 1988-1989*. P. 141.

[21]   Johnson, *Texas & Texans*, Vol. V. P. 2392. The author says that Love, "...learned all there was to know about stock raising."

[22]   Tise, Sammy, *Texas County Sheriffs*. P. 47.

[23]   Parks, P. 67.

[24]   Wharton, *Texas Under Many Flags*, P. 139.

[25]   Shirley, Glenn. *Marauders of the Indian Nations—The Bill Cook Gang and Cherokee Bill*. P. ix.

[26]   Harman, S. W., *Hell On The Border, He Hanged Eighty-Eight Men*. P. 643.

[27]   *El Paso Times*, 01-27-1963. *Sundial* article by Noel Johnson.

[28]   Thrapp, Dan L., *Encyclopedia of Frontier Biography*. Volume I, P. 313.

[29]   Shirley, *Marauders of the Indian Nation*, P. ix.

[30]   *Ibid.*, P. x. Shirley's dual biography, in which he characterizes the Cook/Goldsby gang as being "perhaps the most vicious band of criminals that scourged the West" is the most revealing and well-documented account of the disreputable duo. And see, Taylor, Walter, "The Last Marshal," *True West*, April 1962. P. 63. "The Cook gang started to come apart at the seams."

[31]   Sullivan, W.J. L., *Twelve Years In The Saddle For Law And Order on the Frontiers of Texas*. Sullivan authored his volume in 1909. The most recent (2001—Bison Books) edition has been re-titled, *Twelve Years in the Saddle with the Texas Rangers*. Interestingly, under the promotional heading, "Rare $125.00 Book, Reprinted In This Issue!," the Spring 1967 edition of *Old West* offered Sullivan's work to a general public unable to obtain the hard to find volume. For this story, unless otherwise noted, page numbers cited will be from *Old West*. And too, although many writers have totally relied on Sullivan's first person narrative in their recounting of certain anecdotal events, it is highly recommended interested readers must remain cognizant that Sullivan was offering *his* story from *his* perspective. In his narrative Sullivan is off by one year, the fight occurred in 1894 rather than 1895.

[32]   Shirley, *Marauders of the Indiana Nations*, P. 77-78. And see, Sullivan, *Twelve Years*, P. 74-75. Also see, Turpin, Robert F. "Saga of the Deadly Cook Gang," *True Frontier*, November 1969, P. 54. Also see, Paine, Albert Bigelow, *Captain Bill McDonald—Texas Ranger*. P. 121-124.

[33]   *Ibid.*

[34]   Sullivan, *Twelve Years*, P. 75.

[35]   *Ibid.* The author reports Cook and French but half a mile away when the shoot-out commenced. However, Bill Cook later told reporters that he was "...about eight or ten miles from the fight. When we heard of it we left, separated,

and were to meet at Roswell, as we both knew the country." See, *Eufaula Indian Journal*, 01-18-1895.

[36] *Sundial*, 01-27-1963. Square & Compass was owned by Nave-McCord Cattle Co., St. Joseph, Mo.

[37] *San Angelo Standard-Times*, 06-14-1943. Paul I. Wellman interview with W. S. Moore.

[38] Parks, P. 67. & *Sundial,* 01-27-1963,

[39] According to T. P. Love, the sheriff's son, in a *Sundial* interview it was reported the letter was from Texas Ranger Captain Bill McDonald. Shirley, *Marauders of the Indian Nations*, P. 87 suggests that Sheriff Love was telegraphed by Dickens County Sheriff Jeff Harkey. Harman, *Hell On The Border*, P. 650, says, "Two days later, he (Love) received a dispatch from Capt. McDonald, of the Texas Rangers, giving a description of Bill Cook and telling him to look out for him, as he was headed in the direction of Burden (Borden) County." Love in a press interview referenced a message from Harkey, see, *Daily Oklahoman*, 01-26-1895. Either way, he got the message.

[40] Parks, P. 67.

[41] Sullivan, *Twelve Years*, P. 76.

[42] Parks, P. 68.

[43] *San Angelo Standard-Times*, 06-14-1943.

[44] *Sundial*, 02-03-1963. "…and with his deputy, Louis Polk, an old ranch hand, began his pursuit of the outlaws."

[45] Shirley, *Marauders of the Indian Nations*, P. 87.

[46] *Ibid.* "The description was always the same…" And see, Harman, *Hell On The Border*, P. 650. "In the first 400 miles Cook had stopped at but two ranches and a few small camps."

[47] *Sundial*, 02-03-1963. And see, Harman, *Hell On The Border*, P. 650. "Sending a deputy back to Capt. McDonald to notify him of the course taken by the bandits…" Also see, *San Angelo Standard-Times*, 06-14-1943. "…Love borrowed a horse west of Lubbock and continued his hunt alone…"

[48] Sullivan, *Twelve Years*, P. 76. The author mistakenly has the chase and capture happening in 1896, one year too late.

[49] Shirley, *Marauders of the Indian Nations*, P. 87. And, Harman, *Hell On The Border*, P. 650.

[50] *Ibid.* The Four Lakes region is in present day Lea County, New Mexico, northwest of Tatum. See, Julyan, Robert, *The Place Names of New Mexico*. P. 138.

[51] *Ibid.*

[52] *Ibid.*

[53] Ball, Larry D., "Lawman in Disgrace: Sheriff Charles C. Perry of Chaves County, New Mexico," *New Mexico Historical Review*, 61:2 (April 1986) P. 125-136.

[54] Sullivan, *Twelve Years*, P. 76.

[55] Harman, *Hell On The Border*, P. 651.

[56] *Daily Oklahoman*, 01-26-1895.

[57] Shirley, *Marauders of the Indian Nations*, P. 88. Nogal is located 12 miles southwest of Carrizozo, at foothills of the Sacramento Mountains, Lincoln County, New Mexico. See, Julyan, *Place Names*. P. 243.

[58] *Ibid.* And see, Harman, *Hell On The Border*, P. 652.

Lawmen, Outlaws and S.O.Bs.

[59] *Ibid.* And see, *Eufaula Indian Journal*, 01-18-1895. "Cook came in and walked within three feet of the officers, and the first time he saw them he was looking over the two Winchesters."

[60] *Eufaula Indian Journal*, 01-18-1895.

[61] *Sundial*, 02-03-1963.

[62] Shirley, *Marauders of the Indian Nations.* P. 89. And see, *Eufaula Indian Journal*, 01-18-1895. "The gun was given to me by Cherokee Bill."

[63] Harman, *Hell On The Border*, P. 652. Interestingly, Y.D. McMurray in a blisteringly hot political race for sheriff had defeated a multi-term incumbent, the ever popular and well-respected Dick Ware, by a solitary vote. See, Colorado City *Record*, 03-11-90, "Chief Lone Wolf" by Jim Baum, news columnists and local Mitchell County historian. There is the possibility, although it is usually not written, that McMurray was actually in on the arrest also. See, *Daily Oklahoman*, 01-16-1895. "I walked out of the house on a ranch near Nogales, (sic) N. M., and these three men got the drop on me. I did not have my pistols..." Repeated in the *Oklahoma Times-Journal*, 01-15-1895.

[64] *The Daily New Mexican*, 01-14-1895.

[65] Shirley *Marauders of the Indian Nations*, P. 88. Some newspaper accounts add a fourth officer to the prisoner transport detail. See *Eufaula Indian Journal*, 01-25-1895 & *Daily Oklahoman State Capital*, 01-22-1895. Both papers add the name H. S. Sysk, "an ex-sheriff of the same state (Texas)." And see, the *Daily New Mexican*, 01-14-1895, "...(Cook) is expected to reach Santa Fe tomorrow."

[66] *Ibid.*, P. 89.

[67] Sullivan, *Twelve Years*, P. 77.

[68] To the author's knowledge, as of yet, no one corroborates Sullivan's verbal punishment of Perry independent of the Ranger's own remarks. An account devoted to Sullivan's rift with Perry can be found in Harrison, Fred, "A Slight Case Of Double-Cross," *Western Frontier*, May 1989, but it appears, absent other documentation, that the article is wholly based on Sullivan's 1909 autobiography. Additionally, it should be noted that when Sullivan proffered his version of the affair, Perry who had before the turn of the century already absconded with Chaves County coffers, taken leave of the United States, and throughout the Southwest was rumored to have been killed in South Africa. Certainly, over a decade later, there was no possibility of Perry affirming or denying Sullivan's alleged cross-words.

[69] Sullivan, *Twelve Years*, P. 77.

[70] *San Angelo Standard-Times*, 06-14-1943. "When Cook saw Love's face he recognized him as the sheriff he had met at the Square and Compass..."

[71] Harman, *Hell On The Border*, P. 652.

[72] *El Paso Herald-Post*, 05-12-1934. And, photos courtesy Bill and Don Love.

[73] Harman, *Hell On The Border*, P. 652. And see, *Indian Chieftain*, 01-24-1895. "...a great crowd..."

[74] Shirley, *Marauders of the Indian Nations*, P. 92. And see, *Sundial*, 01-27-1963 & 02-03-1963. Also see, *San Angelo Standard-Times*, 06-14-1943. "Cook's captors never received one cent of reward."

[75] *Ibid.*, P. 150. Cook died of natural causes on February 7, 1900.

[76] Ball, "Lawman in Disgrace," P. 135.

[77] *Sundial*, 02-03-1963. And, conversations with Kenneth Bennett, Borden County Treasurer, Gail, Texas, January 2002.

[78] Wharton, *Texas Under Many Flags*, P. 140.

79 *Ibid.*
80 Interviews with Thomas D. Love descendants. And see, Blumenson, Martin, *The Patton Papers, 1885-1940.* In a 1915 letter to his wife, Lieutenant Patton who was stationed at Sierra Blanca, said of the Love brothers, "…who own the whole country and are supposed to be worth millions. They own the town and all work either in their ranches or in the store. To look at them they would appear like laborers. But all seem very nice…I think I will get on with them well as I usually do with that sort of people." P. 299.
81 Bill Cook's Colt .45 six-shooter, with initials carved in the bone handles is still in the possession of the Love family and safely locked away.   Shirley, *Marauders of the Indian Nations*, P. 91 mentions that Love had to give up the revolver as contraband, however, this seems not to be the case. The firearm is pictured in *Sundial*, 01-27-1963, as is Tom Prince Love.
82 *El Paso Times*, 10-21-1934. And see, *The Cattleman*, Nov. 1934. P. 18.
83 Parks, P. 69.

CHAPTER 9

"A SERIOUS DIFFICULTY MIGHT HAVE OCCURRED"

John Gilmo: Town Tamer—Troublemaker—Territorial Prisoner

John W. Gilmo was another one of those mysteriously baffling Old West scalawags whose life story has been overshadowed by better-publicized but arguably less interesting characters. Many of the six-shooter stalwarts, given the chance, were quick to whore themselves—thirsting for profit or prominence—or both. Others, conversely, coolly held their own counsel; it is from this knotty and stoic lot that history has lost so much. On balance they were a fascinating and complex set, even though some were pretenders. This biographical sketch, however, is bona fide, and John W. Gilmo wasn't then a counterfeit cop, mock man-killer, bogus bounty-hunter, fake felon, or an imitation inmate; no, he was authentically and provably many-sided.

Not much is known of John W. Gilmo's early days in Maryland, but by 1880 the twenty-nine year old lad had negotiated a tiresome trip part-way across the United States, alighting at New Mexico Territory's booming and showcase mining town, a mini-metropolis that was "built to last"—Silver City.[1]

The fair complexioned young man, a miner, had been magnetically pulled to the busy and buzzing mineral camp in search of fame and fortune, mainly fortune. Surveying the distinctly picturesque mountain community from icy blue eyes, John Gilmo, not an illiterate man, soon thereafter opted for employment less strenuous than single-jacking in some hard-scrabble hole in the ground.[2] John Gilmo, on February 28, 1880, did a nifty piquet on the Silver City stage and transformed himself into a New Mexico Territory lawman.[3] He went to work as a deputy for the well-known and generally well-regarded Grant County Sheriff, Harvey Howard Whitehill, a genuine southwest New Mexico pioneer and the man who is classically credited with effecting the very first arrest of a legendary juvenile delinquent, Henry Antrim, aka "Billy the Kid."[4]

John W. Gilmo, Grant County, New Mexico Territory deputy sheriff, Silver City town marshal, bona fide mankiller, triumphant and failed bounty hunter, sometimes scalawag, less than clever criminal, and in the end, a sorrowfully imprisoned convict. Courtesy, Yuma Territorial Prison State Historic Park.

Although in the end she could well boast of permanence, in contrast to some other highly touted mining burgs, Silver City, in the beginnings, was not atypical. She was a wild and woolly headquarters town for southwestern New Mexico's burgeoning mining and livestock industries. And as such, she summoned more than her fair share of pimps, prostitutes, poker players, palate-poison patrons, and pistoleros. There were somewhere in the neighborhood of twelve to fifteen saloons and at least three dance halls, "scattered from 'hell to breakfast' all over town."[5] Incontestably, "if the nights were wild and boisterous the days were none the less so…for all was bustle and confusion, with the drunken brawls and crowds singing in and out of the saloons…and yells of half-crazed 'critters' as they drank and fought."[6]

Harvey Howard Whitehill, Grant County New Mexico Territory Sheriff and reportedly the first lawman to arrest William "Billy the Kid" Antrim. Whitehill deputized, then arrested, and afterward hunted murderous train robbers with John W. Gilmo. Courtesy, Silver City Museum.

Earlier, recognizing the critical need for at least a minimal smidgen of peace and tranquillity on rowdy city streets, Silver City's movers and shakers had created the position of Town Marshal.[7] The first man to hold the taxing job was the dangerous frontier lawman, Dan Tucker, but bureaucratic bungling, plus the failure of City Father's to pay adequately or timely gave way to turnover and the job-title was passed about as first one candidate or another gave it a try.[8]

On May 13, 1880, John Gilmo answered the call, stepped up, pinned on the badge, and became Silver City's laid-back answer to solving the municipal crime problem.[9] Yet still he maintained a part-time deputy sheriff's commission, collecting fees for actual work performed, making arrests and serving civil process. John Gilmo, as

A Serious Difficulty Might Have Occurred

Town Marshal, lasted, for whatever reason, but until December 10th, when he tendered his resignation and was replaced by James K. Ferrell, who in turn lasted just two months, and on February 7th, 1881, John Gilmo was back in the police-harness wearing a six-shooter as Silver City's top watch-dog.[10] That he was a no nonsense frontier gendarme can be extrapolated from a *Silver City Enterprise* newspaperman's pithy characterization of another legit Southwest badman, Joel Fowler, reporting that he "was a dare-devil fellow, and the only man that bluffed John Gilmo while marshal of this city."[11] Taking into account Joel Fowler's extremely mean and nasty disposition, and his wicked fondness for gratuitous violence, especially when in his cups, John Gilmo must have, too, been considered a pretty tough customer. Real trouble though was not far away.

Just when Walter M. Harvey, "a poor old inoffensive Scotsman," made it to Silver City is unknown, but via wanderings through old San Francisco, where he purportedly lost a small fortune, and later at Tombstone where he survived the devastating fire of June 22, 1881, the man "who had seen many reverses" was specifically recruited by proprietors of the commodious Southern Hotel to fill the position of head-cook.[12] Walter Harvey accepted the employment offer and relocated, no doubt pleased to have a job.[13] And so, on the night of July 18th, 1881, Walter Harvey was industriously engaged, a butcher knife in one hand and a bloody slab of fatback pork on the greasy cutting-table before him.[14] The justifications, or lack thereof, for Walter Harvey's outburst is veiled by more horrendous events, but for whatever the reason the very much perturbed cook slapped "the face of an imprudent and habitually quarrelsome Chinaman."[15] From the jam-packed hostelry the Oriental man ran, seeking revenge or redress, and—John Law.

Shortly thereafter, Marshal John Gilmo, accompanied by the red-faced complainant, returned to the scene of the reported assault and snappishly accosted a bystander, Albert H. Wisner, who, at the time was loitering in the hotel kitchen. Gilmo roughly grabbed him by the arm, and inquired of the victim if this was not the man who had presented him with the reverberating whack along side the head. Negative was the reply, but boss-chef Walter M. Harvey was pointed out as the perpetrator who had. Unblinking, John Gilmo identified himself as the Town Marshal and then declared to Walter Harvey, "Consider yourself under arrest." Harvey parried back, "What for?" Supposedly Gilmo retorted, "None of your business," and then reiterated that Harvey should consider himself under arrest and, also, to put down the wicked-looking butcher knife. Walter

Harvey failed to comply—fast enough—John Gilmo jerked out his Colt's revolving six-shooter, cocked it, let the hammer down easy, and at once re-cocked it. Walter Harvey stood still, holding the knife. For the second time he was ordered to drop the knife; he didn't. John Gilmo placed his six-gun's cold-steel muzzle close to Walter Harvey's breast and pressed the hair-trigger. Fire belched from the recoiling barrel and the marshal fired twice more, pistols balls slamming into chef Harvey's head and side, ripping yellowing false teeth from his contorted mouth, and causing him to unconsciously crash to the floor, his bleeding skull crudely jammed between two oak-slatted flour barrels. Town Marshal John W. Gilmo, "…walked to the door and disappeared."[16]

Without delay a coroner's jury was impaneled for an inquest and unequivocally it was determined that "Walter M. Harvey came to his death by pistol shots, the pistol being fired by John W. Gilmo."[17] For the most part the community was outright mad, and by mere happenstance the Grant County Grand Jury was in session. Without delay the facts were presented to the panel by District Attorney S.B. Newcomb.[18] John Gilmo was quickly indicted for what most Grand Jurors considered a "cold-blooded and uncalled for murder."[19] An arrest warrant was immediately issued and Sheriff Harvey Whitehill was "hereby commanded" to present the body of John W. Gilmo, "forthwith," to Judge Warren Bristol.[20] Trouble is, it seems Silver City Town Marshal John Gilmo had skipped—with "several hundred dollars of the city's money—the result of collections made in his official capacity…"[21]

Sheriff Harvey Whitehill deputized J.W. Fleming to track down and arrest Gilmo, and he tried. Fleming followed John Gilmo from the vicinity of Duck Creek west of Silver City to Clifton, Arizona Territory, before he reluctantly abandoned the pursuit.[22] After a few days, however, John Gilmo opted to forgo the life of a hunted man and surrendered, sullenly reconciled to taking his chance with a fledgling Criminal Justice system.[23] The sheriff declared:

> I hereby certify that I have arrested the within named defendant John Gilmo and placed him in the common Jail of the County of Grant and Territory afore said and the within named gave bond in the sum of five thousand which was approved by me this 25th day of SepT.A. D. 1881.[24]

John W. Gilmo was the Town Marshal no more, and was replaced by A.G. Ledbetter.[25] The status of his Grant County deputyship remains unclear, and in light of Sheriff Harvey

A Serious Difficulty Might Have Occurred

Whitehill's sometimes questionable appointments, many for part-time lawmen, the assumption that Gilmo held on to a smidgen of legal authority is not totally irrational and, in fact, is somewhat validated by ensuing events, the sheriff and Gilmo working in tandem. The troublesome legal entanglement involving the killing of Walter Harvey was finally resolved during the first part of August, 1882, when, after a contentious jury trial John Gilmo was found not guilty of murder.[26] John Gilmo was a free man, lawfully, but it seems he couldn't stay out of trouble.

On the night of August 24th, 1882, John Gilmo, along with several notable tough cookies in their own right, such as proven man-killer Dan Tucker, and renowned frontier gambler Frank Thurmond, husband of the former Miss Carlotta Thompkins, aka Lottie Deno, were all enjoyably dealin' and drinkin' at Silver City's posh Centennial Saloon. James D. Burns, one of the *sometimes* deputies, arrived from his base, Paschal, a mining settlement fifteen miles southwest of Silver City, and zealously joined in the festivities—maybe too passionately. He got roaring drunk and went on a tear. During a scatterbrained and ominous argument with Grant County deputies William J. "Billy" McClellan and Dan Tucker, aided by the then Town Marshall, Glaudius W. Moore, John Gilmo successfully bargained a shaky truce and, diplomatically, took actual possession of James Burns six-shooter and all was well, so it seemed. Shortly thereafter, however, exercising dim-witted judgment, John Gilmo returned the Colt's six-shooter to the still belligerent James Burns. Aficionados of Old West history, logically, should not be too surprised; bullets and booze is not a peaceful recipe. Somewhat surprising, however, is a scenario during which three real peace officers shoot it out with a third. Dan Tucker, Billy McClellan, and G.W. Moore in a barroom brawl fatally gunned down Burns, pure and simple.[27] Prudently, Gilmo looked west.

According to several newspaper reports John W. Gilmo went to tough Clifton, Arizona Territory, and in partnership with George Chapman opened a saloon, but soon thereafter returned to the vicinity of Silver City and was trying to scratch out a living, mining or otherwise in the Burro Mountains south of town.[28] Soon, however, he returned to law enforcement, or a semblance thereof.

Near Gage station, about fifteen miles west of Deming, New Mexico Territory, during the late afternoon of November 24, 1883, four reckless robbers choked a Southern Pacific locomotive to a stop, boarded the train, and then callously plundered both the express car and terrified passengers alike, looking for loot. The brigands gathered up their booty and lit out for parts they hoped

157

would forever remain unknown, little realizing their crime would go into the record book as New Mexico's very first train robbery. Nor did they comprehend the public's resentful reaction, for in a deliberate act of cold-hearted skullduggery the hellions had gunned down the train's inoffensive and hard-working engineer, Theophelus C. Webster.[29]

The Centennial Saloon at Silver City, New Mexico Territory. It was here that John Gilmo frequently gambled and where his lack of good judgment contributed to the killing of Grant County deputy James Burns by three other area lawmen, Billy McClellan, Dan Tucker, and G.W. Moore. Courtesy, Silver City Museum.

Grant County Deputy Dan Tucker, who at this time was stationed at Deming, put together an eager posse but in the final analysis was just too late and too far behind the fleeing felons.[30] With few clues, the heartless crime fell into the puzzling category of a "whodunit." Both the Southern Pacific Railroad and Wells, Fargo and Company posted substantial rewards for the outlaw's capture, and quickly self-employed bounty-hunter John W. Gilmo, among more than a few others, started smelling the money.[31]

In earnest the good detective work began. The train had been stopped and the engineer murdered by a racially integrated gang of Gila river cowboys, identified as; Christopher "Kit" Joy, an ex-cowboy for Harvey Whitehill; an ever smiling Frank Taggart; ill-tempered ranch-hand Mitch Lee; and George Washington Cleveland, a black man.[32]

The blue-eyed twenty-six year old Frank Taggart, at five foot, eight inches, and sporting a flowing mustache, decked out in his typical "regulation cowboy" costume, didn't stand out too much, except for "a large mouth, which, while in conversation, is always wreathed in smiles."[33] Suspecting that Frank Taggart might be furtively poking about over near St. Johns, Arizona Territory, where he had previously been employed on an Apache County ranch, John Gilmo, Harvey Whitehill, who was not now sheriff, but was Silver City's Town Marshal, and the ex-sheriff's son, Harry, who knew Taggart by sight, set their due course.[34] Arriving at St. Johns they learned Frank Taggart had, before their appearance, somehow acquired 200 head of cattle and was in process of gathering and culling the herd for a drive back to huge Socorro County, New Mexico Territory.[35] Temporarily, John Gilmo and Harvey Whitehill divided investigative forces, Gilmo hiring a "Mexican" as a guide to pilot him across the mountains and onto an interdicting course with Taggart's herd. Cleverly, when he caught up with Frank Taggart, John Gilmo niftily used a ruse, implying Frank was wanted for questioning regarding misappropriated livestock, rather than the capital crime of murder, and the felonious Gage train robbery. Frank Taggart, thinking he still had a secret, surrendered. John Gilmo, although the arrest had actually taken place in New Mexico Territory, transported Frank Taggart back to St. Johns; it was nearest the closest railroad connections, and too, for the purposing of reuniting with Harvey and Harry Whitehill.[36] When Frank Taggart arrived as a prisoner, there was a gnarly confrontation with a platoon of Frank's disconcerted cowboy buddies, who by wily legal shenanigans and brutish intimidation were threatening to liberate their compadre—one way or the other. Their stratagem didn't work as "Harvey (Whitehill) was on to their little racket," forestalling any attempt at legalistic tom-foolery and, too, he was backed-up by John W. Gilmo, who had a reputation. The mouthy crowd, in the end, wilted. In shackles, Frank Taggart was returned to Silver City and lodged in the cold and dank county jail.[37] Under Frank Taggart's entry in Grant County's *Register of Prisoners* logbook is the handwritten notation "captured by John Gilmo," seemingly insignificant information; however, later the point proved pertinent.[38] Harvey Howard Whitehill and John W. Gilmo started counting, at least mentally, railroad and express company monies; it looked like a surefire trade—scrappy Frank Taggart for a sack full of gold. Elsewhere, "Kit" Joy and Mitch Lee had been taken into custody by deputy Andrew J. Best and the notorious, but sometimes corruptible Charles C. Perry, over near Horse Springs on the Plains of San Agustin.[39]

A reward settlement was in the offing and, somewhat curiously, John Gilmo for whatever reason traveled to San Francisco "on business connected with the Gage train robbery," and conferred with Railroad Detective Len Harris of the Southern Pacific and Wells, Fargo and Company's investigator Jim Hume.[40] Of the four resourceful man-hunters, Harvey Whitehill was most ecstatic, for earlier, before the later three arrests, he had tracked and tricked George Washington Cleveland and made him a prisoner. He would be, however, somewhat thunderstruck by the next twist in the saga.

First, not wanting to turn their back on well-worn Silver City tradition, municipal leadership fired Harvey Whitehill from his position as Town Marshal; he had been absent from the city for just too long.[41] Secondly, circumstances beyond his power were soon to divvy the paycheck into lesser portions.

On the morning of the 10th of March, 1884, winds blew ill. The four train robbers and two other prisoners, convicted murderer Carlos Chavez and a suspected horse-thief, Charles Spencer, trounced their jail-keepers, armed themselves rather handily, and made a daring "break for liberty."[42] The fugitives ran, and so too did a posse of hard-charging Grant County residents, steadily reinforced as they finally hemmed up the outlaws in the broken country northeast of town, out along the road to Fort Bayard.[43] During an ensuing and thoroughly emblematic Western gunbattle, George Cleveland, Carlos Chaves and, sadly, standup Silver City citizen Joe Lafferr were all killed. "Kit" Joy temporarily got away, while Charles Spencer, Frank Taggart and Mitch Lee were snagged, although the latter was suffering terribly from nauseating gunshot wounds. Sometimes in rough frontier communities talk was cheap, overblown rhetoric boastful and, in the end, farcically impotent. Such was not to be the case this day, not on the outskirts of town, not by an angry Silver City mob. The gut-shot Mitch Lee and Frank Taggart were summarily hanged on the spot. Sardonically, the mandated coroner's jury lumped all the outlaw's demises into one sorting, finding they had "come to their death by gun-shot wounds and other injuries..."[44] And, keeping in the spirit of the sarcastic revelry, a newspaperman tersely penned that Frank Taggart had "died hard of strangulation—a throat disease that is becoming extremely common among their ilk in this section."[45] At the Grant County sheriff's office the disastrously unlucky "stiffs" were "arrayed" for public display.[46] A cowering Charles Spencer, the youthful and thoroughly tormented accused horse-thief, was shortly reacquainted with the county jail.

Shorty, practical reality dawned on possemen. If the escapees had made good they wouldn't have been in custody, at all, and nobody would have been entitled to rewards, and since heroic efforts on their part had thwarted the evil-doers plans, they too were each entitled to a reward. The clawing and scratching for loot was a first-rate sideshow, a Western story within itself, but for the purpose of this chronicle, John W. Gilmo for his arrest of Frank Taggart ended up with $888.88.[47] Big money at the time!

For the short-go, however, there were no more owl-hoots to chase and once more in the looming Burro Mountains south of town, John Gilmo devoted himself to mineral interests and fussy assessment work.[48] But John W. Gilmo couldn't stay away from trouble for long. During January 1885, and the details are sketchy, he characteristically interjected himself into a mining-camp mêlée with an "intoxicated companion," and not too unexpectedly, a six-shooter went "off prematurely," slightly wounding John W. Gilmo.[49]

Subsequently, John Gilmo went into and out of the saloon business again, unsuccessfully tried to recapture the Town Marshal's slot at Silver City, had an up and down marital liaison with Alice Vega, fathered a son, and minimally served a stint as city marshal at Kingston, over in New Mexico Territory's shadowy Black Range.[50] Bounty-hunting money was toothsome, though, and John W. Gilmo wanted another spoonful. It was easy work.

Near Pantano, Arizona Territory, during the summer of 1887, a horde of *mal hombres* robbed another train and, true to form, a comical opera opened. Ambitious and greedy man-chasers from far and near converged on southwestern New Mexico, feverishly anticipating big bucks for catching crooks.[51] Once more John W. Gilmo was on the make. At Deming, he was buttonholed by a shadowy Pinkerton-type private-eye and promised a cut of the reward, should any be paid, if he would only cause the arrest of desperado Charles Small. The neat little scenario can precisely be dissected into two halves, one speculatively, the other factually. It seems John Gilmo's employer of the moment shrewdly neglected to mention he had not the slightest smidgen of exploitable evidence, and, too, the newly commissioned employee failed to divulge he was no longer an officer of the law, and that his real legal authority was zip![52] Maybe neither of the would-be man-catchers knew about Charles Small's dubious and daring reputation or, perhaps, they did. Either way, it is certain that when John Gilmo braced Charley Small and declared "you're under arrest," he was mistaken! Charles Small didn't want to be, nor was he going to be, John Gilmo's prisoner, and he jerked his Colt's .45, shoved it under John's meddlesome nose, and eared back the hammer. An astute and adroit newspaperman rightly scribbled "that a serious difficulty might have occurred," had it not been for the intervention of a legitimate peace officer, Dan Tucker.[53] The upshot? John Gilmo assumed the role of a chameleon, changed colors and disappeared, some say he forgot something over in Mexico, just thirty miles to the south, and of Charles Small, well, Dan Tucker may have known he was guilty of something or everything, but in this instance there was no valid proof—therefore, rightly, he was unceremoniously "cut loose."[54]

After scrambling out of Dan Tucker's way, at least for awhile, not too much is known regarding John Gilmo's whereabouts. An item in the *Silver City Enterprise* is considerate to the former City Marshal and generally pinpoints that Gilmo had removed himself from New Mexico Territory, but only for a while: "John Gilmo has returned to Silver (City) after an absence of several years. He hails from Arizona, and looks healthy and prosperous."[55] It wasn't too long before he was back in the news—big time. Breaking in the new year, 1891, was simple for John Gilmo and Jesus Esquival, literally ringing it in with a thunderous bang. They, or at least one of them, shot forty-year-old Augustine Jorquez during an apparent robbery gone awry, near Solomonville, Arizona Territory.[56] The gut shot Augustine, who also suffered a second shot to the shoulder, reported two masked men had come into his house and straight away opened fire on him and another man. The two victims grappled with the two attackers, and somewhat inexplicably the gangsters opted for flight, inadvertently dropped a colorful blanket, and fled. Jorquez survived the belly wound, and although he couldn't identify the shooters, he knew they were "Americans."[57]

Graham County Sheriff George A. Olney was not fooled, and after thoughtful and painstaking detective work, secured indictments for Gilmo and Esquival.[58] During October, 1891, at Phoenix, John W. Gilmo was snagged, returned to Graham County and placed in the local jail. At arraignment he entered a plea of *not guilty* and the case was docketed for the next term of District Court. From the county calaboose John Gilmo filed an affidavit for a postponement of his trials in Cause No. 277 (Robbery) and Cause No. 278 (Assault with Intent to Murder).[59] Unable to post bond, Gilmo stayed locked up.[60] During February of the following year, Sheriff Olney arrested Jesus Esquival in New Mexico Territory, and "placed him behind the bars with his cantankerous co-defendant, John Gilmo."[61] After

A Serious Difficulty Might Have Occurred

languishing away in the county jail for nearly six-months, on April 18, 1892, a jury found John W. Gilmo guilty of a reduced charge of Assault With a Deadly Weapon and sentenced him to four years in the territorial penitentiary at Yuma.[62] The next day, anguished owl-hoot Jesus Esquival received an identical dose.[63] On April 25, 1892, after a pleasant springtime train trip, John W. Gilmo became prison inmate No. 817.[64]

The strap-iron entrance to the Arizona Territorial Penitentiary at Yuma. Renowned prison guard B.F. Hartlee outside, horizontally striped inmates inside. It was here that John W. Gilmo spent his last days before a Governor's Pardon, and a subsequent disappearance from the pages of Old West history. Courtesy, Yuma Territorial Prison Historic State Park.

Apparently John W. Gilmo was an exemplary prisoner and a top-notch hand on the prison farm, at least so says his *Proclamation of Pardon*, which was granted on the 22nd day of February, 1895.[65] Where John Gilmo went, or what he did—or didn't do—after getting out of the poky, at least to this writer, is undetermined.

This tidy little Western true story opened with a straightforward acknowledgment that John W. Gilmo's rousing biography is only partially told, yet he was certainly an authentic Old West scalawag. Neither remark is wrong.

Lawmen, Outlaws and S.O.Bs.

ENDNOTES CHAPTER 9

"A SERIOUS DIFFICULTY MIGHT HAVE OCCURRED"

[1] Gilmo's personal history data is basically gleaned from four sources; the 1880 census, New Mexico Territory, Silver City; prison records as maintained by the Yuma Arizona Territorial Prison State Historical Park, Yuma, Arizona, and graciously furnished by that institution; prison records contained in the files of the Arizona Department of Library, Archives, & Public Records, History and Archives Division, Phoenix, and for this story, courteously provided to the author from the collection of Author, Historian and Genealogist, Rita Ackerman, Phoenix, Arizona; and to a lesser extent, old Silver City newspaper archives. The assertion that Silver City was "built to last" is directly attributed to the excellent volume of Berry, Susan and Russell, Sharman Apt, *Built to Last, An Architectural History of Silver City, New Mexico*. "...Silver City strove mightily to become more than a boom-and-bust mining camp." P. 18.

[2] See above citation. Gilmo's prison records reveal that he measured in at five feet, nine inches; had blue eyes; a fair complexion; a head of brown hair; his occupation was that of a miner; and that he could both read and write.

[3] *Grant County Herald*, February 28, 1880.

[4] *Silver City Enterprise*, January 3, 1902. Also see, Nolan, Frederick. *The Lincoln County War—A Documentary History*. P. 57.

[5] Nelson, Susan. *Silver City—Book One—Wild and Woolly Days*. P. 17.

[6] *Ibid.*, P. 18.

[7] Naegle, Conrad Keeler. *The History of Silver City, New Mexico, 1870-1886*. Master of Arts Thesis, University of New Mexico, Albuquerque, 1943. P. 170.

[8] *Ibid.* "During the early years of its history this office (Silver City Marshal) was in a constant state of flux, which made for anything but efficiency in the administration of it." From 1880 to 1884, when the title was made an elective office, "...the position of marshal changed hands nine times." P. 181. For an article length glimpse at a fearless and formidable frontier man-killer and peace officer (Dan Tucker) see, DeArment, R. K., "Deadly Deputy," *True West*, November 1991. For a full-length biography see, Alexander, Bob., *Dangerous Dan Tucker, New Mexico's Deadly Lawman*.

[9] *Ibid.*, P. 181.

[10] *Ibid.*,

[11] Bryan, Howard., *Robbers, Rogues and Ruffians*. P. 94. Quoting an 1883 edition of the *Silver City Enterprise*.

[12] *The New Southwest*, July 23, 1881.

[13] *Ibid.* "...A man (Harvey) who leaves a family..." That Harvey suffered the June 22, 1881 fire at Tombstone is an assumption. The newspaper merely says, "A man (Harvey) followed by misfortune—burnt out in Tombstone...," however, chronologically the significant dates logically mesh. Interestingly Tombstone's indefatigable journal keeper George Parsons makes several mentions of a Walter Harvey, however, it would appear from the calendar dates that it is not the same Walter Harvey, perhaps a son. See, Bailey, Lynn R. (editor), *The Devil Has Foreclosed, The Private Journal of George Whitwell Parsons: The Concluding Arizona Years, 1882-87*.

A Serious Difficulty Might Have Occurred

---

[14] *Ibid.* And see, *Indictment, The Territory of New Mexico vs. John W. Gilmo,* Cause Number 854, District Court, July 1881 Term, Grant County. Courtesy, New Mexico State Records Center and Archives, Santa Fe, New Mexico.

[15] *Ibid.*

[16] *Ibid.*

[17] *Ibid.* Also see, *Indictment, The Territory of New Mexico vs. John W. Gilmo,* Cause Number 854.

[18] *Ibid.*

[19] *Ibid.* And see, *Indictment.*

[20] *Warrant* (handwritten) and *Warrant* (printed form) On July 19, 1881, the day after Gilmo shot Harvey, Judge Warren Bristol, on a *complainant,* issued a murder warrant for the arrest of John Gilmo. After the indictment, on July 20, 1881, the judge formalized the action by issuing an *after-indictment warrant,* which was prepared on a pre-printed warrant form and was also presented to Sheriff Whitehill. At the time, Judge Warren Bristol at Mesilla was serving as Judge of the Third Judicial District and as an Associate Justice of the Supreme Court of the Territory of New Mexico. Courtesy, New Mexico State Library and Archives. Santa Fe.

[21] *The New Southwest,* July 23, 1881.

[22] Warrant Return, Cause Number 854, *Territory of New Mexico vs. John W. Gilmo.* Courtesy, New Mexico State Library and Archives. Santa Fe.

[23] *The New Southwest,* August 6, 1881.

[24] *Ibid.* And see, *Appearance Bond* signed by John W. Gilmo and sureties. Courtesy, New Mexico State Library and Archives. Santa Fe.

[25] Naegle. P. 181.

[26] District Court Grant County, Criminal Docket, Record and Cost Book. *Territory of New Mexico vs. John W. Gilmo,* Number 854. Murder. "Subp. issued, Deft. Aug. 4th (1882) Tried and acquitted...Judgment $.50...Entry in R & C Book $1.50." Courtesy New Mexico State Library and Archives. Santa Fe.

[27] DeArment, P. 17-19. And see, Alexander, P. 98-107. Also see, *New Southwest & Grant County Herald,* September 2, 1882. Dan Tucker, William McClellan, and G.W. Moore were all arrested for the killing of James Burns. None, however, were convicted. Also see, *The Territory of New Mexico vs. Glaudius W. Moore & William McClellan.* District Court Grant County, Criminal Docket, Record and Cost Book. Cause Number 1175. The charges against Tucker were dismissed, and McClellan and Moore eventually came clear at trial. Courtesy, New Mexico State Library and Archives. Santa Fe.

[28] *The New Southwest,* September 23, 1882 and *The Silver City Enterprise,* November 30, 1882. For a highly informative and well-researched glimpse at the iniquitous frontier town of Clifton, Arizona, the home base for a not inconsiderable number of Southwest badmen, see, DeArment, R. K., "The Outlaws of Clifton, Arizona Territory," National Outlaw and Lawman History Association, Inc., *Quarterly.* XXVII, No. 1. (January-March 2003)

[29] *Southwest Sentinel,* November 28, 1883 and *Silver City Enterprise,* November 30, 1883. Accounts of this train robbery are legion. The reader interested in a closer inspection might review, DeArment, R. K., "Sheriff Whitehill & the Kit Joy Gang," *Old West,* Winter 1994; Caldwell, George A., "New Mexico's First Train Robbery," *Quarterly* of the National Association for Outlaw and Lawman History (NOLA), Volume XIII, Number 3 (Winter 1989); Bryan, Howard, *Robbers, Rogues, and Ruffians*; and Cline, Don, "Kit Joy—the One-Legged—Half Blind—

Lawmen, Outlaws and S.O.Bs.

Toothless Outlaw," NOLA *Quarterly*, Volume XXVI, Number 2. (April-June 2002).

[30] Alexander, P. 124. Quoting the *Silver City Enterprise*, "...but it is thought that the desperadoes had too far a start and were too well mounted to be overtaken."

[31] *Ibid.* Rewards for the arrests and convictions of the murderous train robbers were offered, a $1000 per head from Wells, Fargo and Company and $1,000 per head from the Southern Pacific Railroad. Local supplements brought the total per-man bounty up to $2200, a not insignificant amount for the time period.

[32] As with most significant and well-reported Old West episodes there are discrepancies between various renditions and they can range from minor to monumental. For the most part, the investigative techniques used by the officers in identifying the culprits involved in the murder of Webster and the Gage train robbery are reasonably consistent from one report to the other. For a serious analysis, all of the sources cited should be consulted and then a balanced composite of legitimate evidence can be examined and opinions thereafter formulated.

[33] *Silver City Enterprise*, January 4, 1884. Taggart's physical description is taken from the edition of the newspaper and the *Register Of Prisoners Confined In The County Jail Of Grant County, New Mexico*. Courtesy, New Mexico State Library and Archives, Santa Fe. Author Don Cline adds that Taggart "had dark tobacco stains about his mouth and teeth when he smiled." P. 16. In the jail book, under the heading for "Special Marks or Peculiarities," Taggart's atypical mouth "when laughing" was specifically noted.

[34] *Ibid.* And see, Bryan, P. 128. "For his companions on what promised to be a long journey, Whitehill selected his seventeen-year-old son, Harry Whitehill, who knew Taggart by sight, and John Gilmo, a deputy sheriff. The trio boarded a train in Silver City, and rode a series of trains southeast to Deming, north to Albuquerque, and west to Holbrook, Arizona, where they left the railroad and hired horses. They rode sixty miles southeast to St. Johns...It had been a seven-hundred-mile journey from Silver City..."

[35] *Ibid.*

[36] Taggart's actual place of arrest is variously identified; Caldwell mentions Porte Canon de Agua Frio near St. Thomas, Arizona; DeArment reports it was at La Parte el Frio in Socorro County, New Mexico; Cline places the arrest at Socorro, New Mexico; and the *Southwest Sentinel*, January 19, 1884 reported, "Ex-Sheriff Whitehill, accompanied by John Gilmore (Gilmo), brought in the second of the Gage train robbers last Monday. His name is Frank Taggart, and after much difficulty, Whitehill and his companion succeeded in capturing in the western part of Socorro county near the Arizona line."

[37] *Ibid.* And see, *Register of Prisoners*. Taggart placed in jail on January 14, 1884.

[38] *Register of Prisoners*.

[39] Alexander, P. 127. And see, Ball, Larry D., "Lawman in Disgrace: Sheriff Charles C. Perry of Chaves County, New Mexico," *New Mexico Historical Review*, 61:2 (April 1986), P. 126. "Perry and Deputy Sheriff Jack Best trailed the outlaw to near Horse Springs and surprised and captured the outlaws.".

[40] *Silver City Enterprise*, March 7, 1884.

[41] DeArment, P. 16 And see, *Silver City Enterprise*, January 11, 1884. Also see, Naegle, P. 183. "It was very evident that by this time the citizens of Silver City had become disgusted with the handling of the affairs of the marshal's office."

A Serious Difficulty Might Have Occurred

[42] *Silver City Enterprise*, March 14, 1884.

[43] As with the Gage train robbery, this escape, one of many, from the Grant County Jail has been journalistically re-captured in numerous primary and secondary accounts. For two of the best summaries see, DeArment or Bryan. Other rundowns include Cline, Caldwell, Nelson, in addition to various newspaper reports.

[44] Caldwell, P. 15. Quoting the inquest report.

[45] *Silver City Enterprise*, March 14, 1884. And see, Wayne Whitehill to Lou Blachly, Tape Number 503, Page 12. Pioneer Foundation Interviews. "But, anyhow, they put the topes (sic) around their necks and stoed (sic) 'em up in this wagon and then drove the team our from under 'em." Courtesy, Zimmerman Library—Center for Southwest Research, University of New Mexico, Albuquerque.

[46] *Ibid.* Interestingly, in the *Register of Prisoners* is the succinct notation, "escaped, killed on same day."

[47] DeArment. P. 19. The author's coverage of the entire reward dispute is insightful.

[48] *Silver City Enterprise*, December 19, 1884.

[49] *Ibid.*, January 23, 1885.

[50] *Ibid.*, February 6 & 27, 1885; March 20, 1885; April 24, 1885; May 21, 1886; July 30, 1886; December 10, 1886.

[51] Alexander, P. 150.

[52] *Ibid.* Quoting the *Silver City Enterprise*, September 16, 1887.

[53] *Ibid.*

[54] *Ibid.* Charles Small, indeed, was a dubious frontier character and locally noted criminal throughout southern Arizona, New Mexico and Texas. Later, 1892, he was killed by Texas Ranger D. L. Musgrave at Langtry, Texas, during a horrific Old West shootout. See Chapter 6, "He Was Killed By Me."

[55] *Silver City Enterprise*, February 21, 1890.

[56] *Graham County Bulletin*, January 9, 1891.

[57] *Ibid.*

[58] *Ibid.*, February 26, 1892. And, correspondence to the author from historian Scott Nelson, St. Paul, Minnesota, July 22, 2002.

[59] Affidavit for Postponement of Trail, District Court, Graham County, Arizona Territory. *Territory of Arizona vs. John Gilmo.* Cause Numbers 277 (Robbery) and 278 (Assault to Murder), filed October 19, 1891. Courtesy, Kevin and Bev Mulkins, Tucson, Arizona.

[60] *Ibid.*

[61] *Graham County Bulletin*, February 26, 1892.

[62] *Ibid.*, undated news-clipping. And see, *Description of Convict*, Arizona Territorial Prison. Courtesy, Yuma Territorial Prison State Historical Park, Yuma.

[63] *Ibid.*

[64] *Description of Convict*, Arizona Territorial Prison. Gilmo's name, under initial entry at the penitentiary was listed as "John W. Gilmore," and in another log book examined by well-regarded researcher and writer Scott Nelson, he was listed as "John W. Gilman," which historically has caused no little confusion, however, by the time of his release from prison the correction had been made, and he was discharged as John W. Gilmo.

[65] *Pardon For Restoration to Citizenship* for John W. Gilmo, dated February 22, 1895, signed "Thomas Gates" Prison Superintendent. And see, *Proclamation of*

Lawmen, Outlaws and S.O.Bs.

Pardon, John W. Gilmo, signed by Louis C. Hughes, Governor, Territory of Arizona, Executive Department. Courtesy, Rita Ackerman, Phoenix.

CHAPTER 10

"THE MULE PUKED"

Joe Sitter, A Legit Lawman & West Texas Borderliner

Hardly any accomplished aficionados of authentic Outlaw/Lawman tales or Old West nonfiction literature would not know the name Joe Sitter. Many historical writers have made mention of him, typically in a solitary and lonely paragraph buried deep within the broader context of a much larger chronicle and, most of the time, his name is innocently misspelled. Joseph Sitter was his real name, and his biography is worthy of more than the passing casual notice commonly afforded him.[1] Joe Sitter found his professional calling from behind the badges he proudly wore for nearly a quarter-century. He was a lawman through and through. Dissimilar to the likes of an overrated and self-promoting Wyatt Earp or the speciously puffed up exploits of Texas Ranger Sergeant W. John L. Sullivan, Joe Sitter didn't advertise. Favorably complementing Joe Sitter's career choice was an extraordinary development of out-of-doors skills, practicable aptitudes quickly well-recognized. Indisputably, his hard-seasoned Texas border country contemporaries smartly appreciated Joe Sitter's man hunting talents and dogged devotion to duty, and, yes, so did the literary champion of splendid Western sagas, Zane Grey, when, after interviewing real rangers, he penned the classic *Lone Star Ranger*.[2] Perhaps, like a cadre of others, Joe Sitter has been somewhat overlooked simply because the West Texas frontier he functioned on was in speedy transition, shedding one century's old clothes, dressing in more modern formality for the next. Still, the land and the time were wild and woolly, and so too was Joe Sitter. This then is his story.

To the west and southwest of San Antonio, Texas, lays Medina County. The county was carved, in 1848, from the colossal Bexar

Lawmen, Outlaws and S.O.Bs.

Land District, a land mass fully covering, at the time, two-thirds of the whole Lone Star state.[3] Pleasantly portending a gateway to the scenic Hill Country's rolling hills and sparkling streams, the countryside is more than just agreeable, it's downright delightful, a fact not missed by a culturally linked squadron of early day settlers, the Alsatians.[4] From the Old World province of Alsace, on the border between France and Germany, the jaunty immigrants brought with them a mixed and diverse heritage; evidenced by exquisite examples of hand-cut limestone architecture; tantalizing samples that only a master winemaker could concoct; passionate adherence to religious tradition; adroit agricultural acumen; and a zealously entrenched ethic of hard and honest work.[5] Castroville, named after empresario Henri Castro, was the very first site selected for the shire town honors, but later the county seat was moved further west to Hondo.[6]

And it was into this European conclave on the Texas frontier, at Castroville, that Joe Sitter was welcomed into a turbulent nineteenth-century world. On the 13th day of January, 1863, before cessation of Civil War hostilities, the subject of this biographical profile was born, and just a few days later, on the 22nd, his loving parents, Jacques and Virginia Sitter, presented their precious son for Holy Baptism at the picturesque St. Louis Catholic Church.[7]

In fairness to the reader, it must be bluntly acknowledged that concerning Joe Sitter's early childhood and adolescence there is a dearth of primary source data but, thankfully, a wealth of authenticated material detailing his later life is accessible, and the study of his law enforcement life—and death—is the compelling period to zero in on for retelling his spiky story. Simplistically it may be assumed that Joe Sitter, like many other youngsters growing up in the Texas borderlands, acquired those skills so requisite for survival. Undoubtedly he was literate, at least enough to sign his name, albeit with scribbled penmanship, but good sense mandated honing of functional knacks not taught in stuffy one-room schoolhouses. Joe Sitter during those formative years became a proficient marksman, nifty horse rider, skillful steer tripper, legendary sign-cutter and, by anybody's calculated measurement, an all around top-hand. Psychologically, whether it was due to heredity, experience, or stony obstinacy, and it really matters not a whit, Joe Sitter the man had matured into a package of untiring temperament. Once he set his mind to something or on somebody, he was tenacious, perhaps even pigheaded! These character traits would serve him well—for awhile.

The Mule Puked

The notable manhunter, deputy sheriff, Texas Ranger and United States Mounted Customs Inspector, Joe Sitter. Courtesy, Jake Sitters.

Joe Sitter, a twenty-one year old cowboy, on the 4th day of April, 1884, married the strikingly attractive Margaretha "Maggie" Bendele, at Castroville's St. Louis Catholic Church, the very scene of his earlier baptism.[8] They had three children, two daughters, Josephine and Elizabeth, and a son, Joseph Benjamin. Happiness can abruptly come to an end, and it did! Crossing the swollen Medina River, a buckboard Maggie Sitter was traveling in overturned and she nearly drowned. Rushed to nearby Castroville for medical treatment, it seemed that all was well, but alas, unforgiving complications claimed her life on March 8, 1889, just one month after giving birth to her third child.[9] Joe Sitter was devastated.

Leaving the three young children with relatives, Joe Sitter began the grieving process, ridin' and hidin' his pain. Moving south through Kinney County and into Val Verde County (Del Rio) Joe Sitter picked up two things, a deputy sheriff's commission in the border city and a manhuntin' reputation.[10] Joe Sitter, the renowned lawman to be, was reborn, a new chance at life, its pleasures and problems.

Pinpointing all of Joe Sitter's peace officer actions while serving as a deputy sheriff is not compulsory in order to gauge the man. One rousing escapade stands out and will suffice. On September 2, 1891, the Galveston, Harrisburg and San Antonio train was robbed near

Lawmen, Outlaws and S.O.Bs.

Samuel's Siding in the far western reaches of Val Verde County.[11] (See Chapter 1 for the inclusive story). In the overall framework of Old West bandit histories the incident has been the beneficiary of some notice, but not much. Valiantly, a hard-charging posse of Texas Rangers loaded their horses into livestock-cars, rushed to the scene, united with a hastily fashioned platoon of local gendarmes, and gave pursuit.[12] Joe Sitter, although generally credited with membership in the posse, was elsewhere.[13] To maintain exacting truthfulness, the celebrated Texas Rangers, this time, despite their undeniably tough work, after several wearisome days came up short and were forced to dump the pursuit.[14]

During the following month, October 1891, while in Del Rio at the courthouse, Joe Sitter received an informative tip as to a possible location for the wanted train robbers' hideaway. Straight away he set his course for the broken landscape north of Comstock, Texas, and succeeded in flushing out the outlaws' secretive lair—from afar. Prudently, he backed off, notifying Ranger Captain Frank Jones to speedily gather a purposeful posse and rush to his aid.[15] After joining forces with the Lone Star lawmen, Sitter and two citizens ran the odious owl-hoots to ground in the inaccessible and forlorn brush and chaparral country of newly created Crockett County, in the neighborhood of old Fort Lancaster not too terribly far from the county seat, Ozona. After a laboring horseback chase and stereotypical Old West gunplay, the lawdogs at last heeled Tom Stouts, Jack Wellington, and James "Jim" Lansford, but somewhat uncharacteristically, one of the bandits, John Flynt, "suicided," an act a pithy reporter for the *San Antonio Daily Light* chided was wholly fitting, the reprehensible thief "not squealing" when forced to take his "gruel."[16] Afterward, Sitter while describing the dicey capture unceremoniously pointed out that the shooting had been, "promiscuous and lively."[17] For his part in the bold adventure, coming Joe Sitter's way was a cash reward of $750; adulation from an ever appreciative public; self-satisfied wisdom about earning his livelihood as a West Texas law enforcer; and the approving glances from Texas Ranger leadership.[18]

Joe Sitter at the time of the Val Verde County train robbery was a deputy sheriff, afterwards he transferred his financial interests to mountainous Jeff Davis County, establishing a cattle ranch near the sparsely populated community of Valentine, in shadows of the Davis Mountains. Depending on the scribblers' version, Joe Sitter was a Jeff Davis County deputy sheriff, or a constable, or a deputy in nearby Brewster County but, sensibly, the biographical focus can be redirected with accuracy with his next career change.[19] After

172

The Mule Puked

Texas Ranger Captain Frank Jones was killed by Mexican bandits near El Paso County's Pirate Island, on June 30, 1893, the legendary "Border Boss," John R. Hughes was promoted to Captain of Company D, Frontier Battalion. The death of Jones and the ascendancy of Hughes, logically, created a vacancy at the bottom tier of the roster.[20] Underpaid, undermanned and overworked, the indomitable Texas Rangers were in dire need of a new recruit. A good one!

An unusually rare photograph of Company D. Texas Rangers outside their Ysleta, Texas headquarters, circa 1894. George Tucker standing by horses. Seated on the ground, from left to right, Thalis T. Cook, Deputy U.S. Marshal Frank McMahon, Captain John R. "Border Boss" Hughes, William Schmidt, James V. Latham, Carl Kirchner, J.W. "Wood" Saunders, Joe Sitter, and Ed Palmer. Courtesy, Jake Sitters.

Certainly to subsequent Sitter generations the often repeated story is gratifying, for generally it is written that the celebrated Captain Hughes sought out Joe, offered him the position as a ranger private, and was personally elated when the proffer was finally accepted.[21] There is little profit in doubting the tale and, truthfully, it may be categorically confirmed that on the 1st day of August, 1893, a highly regarded Joe Sitter enlisted in the Texas Rangers, drawing $30 per month—paid quarterly.[22]

Twenty-four hours after enlistment with the Frontier Battalion Joe Sitter is, in several stirring accounts, credited with winning "acclaim" during a vicious gunbattle between Texas Rangers and "Mexican border rustlers."[23] Maybe. Undeniably, examination of early Frontier Battalion records proves a treasure-trove for reconstructing historical happenings; however, it must be admitted there are a surplus of inexplicable omissions. Common in the extreme are the entries which mention one ranger by name, supplemented with a remark such as "with one man" or "and three men." The true identities of the unnamed—other Texas Rangers—may be hard to find. Systematic inspection of the August 1893, Company D *Monthly Return* annotates Joe Sitter's recruitment on August 1st, but there is no allusion to any shooting episode twenty-four hours later. Later in the month, though, there was notation of an apprehension mission gone awry:

> Aug. 24. Private J.W. Fulgham in company with Deputy Sheriff George Leakey of Reeves County made scout down Pecos river in search of stolen horses. While out met a man armed with pistol. Attempted to arrest him for carrying pistol. He resisted and drew pistol to shoot when Fulgham shot him twice killing him instantly. Have not found out who he is yet but suppose he is Charles Carroll, out two days, marched 50 miles.[24]

The ever formidable Joe Sitter during his days as a Texas Ranger. Courtesy, Texas Ranger Hall of Fame and Museum.

Whether Joe Sitter was along on this "scout" remains a mystery and, indeed, he very well may have been, or perhaps there was another blistering shoot-out escaping inclusion in the *Monthly Returns*. Realistically, there is not a drought of primary source citations to Joe Sitter, by name, and therefore a reasonably accurate assessment of his overall duties and everyday working assignments as a ranger private may be garnered. For instance, on the 7th of September 1893, Joe Sitter, accompanied by ranger R.E. Bryant, unproductively searched for Presidio County murder suspect Catarino Nieta at San Elizario, Texas. The next month, Joe Sitter and William Schmidt, together with a deputy sheriff from Doña Ana County, New Mexico Territory, made an arduous "scout" in the neighborhood of Hueco Tanks looking for a "band of robbers." After forking well-worn saddles and after four tiresome days, it was regrettably realized that instead of thieving and treacherous owl-hoots, the haggard officers were trailing a "bunch of Pueblo Indians hunting antelope."[25] In November, rangers Sitter and Schmidt arrested Antonio Apadaca for horse stealing at San Elizario.[26] As 1893 gave way to the dawning of a new year, a study of available data clearly reveals that ranger private Joe Sitter was in constant motion along the Texas/Mexican border.

On April 4, 1894, Joe Sitter and ranger Ernest St. Leon splashed through Rio Grande waters and, on Pirate Island, arrested accused killer Juan Reyes, safely locking him away in the El Paso County jail.[27] Five months later Joe Sitter found himself inland, keeping the peace in Pecos County during a cantankerous case of West Texas civil unrest at Fort Stockton.[28] An incumbent sheriff was in a hotly contested political battle. The feuding hullabaloo was anarchic and the ranching community's atmosphere was thick with vitriolic harangues and actual acts of misconduct. Texas Rangers were dispatched to rein in miscreants and maintain order. While on TDY at Fort Stockton, Joe Sitter hauled J.M. Watts to the Pecos County lockup for Drunk & Disorderly, and six days later arrested local Sheriff Andrew Jackson "A.J." Royal for Assault and Battery, turning him over to a local Justice of the Peace for further judicial action.[29] And, interestingly, the next month, October 1894, he and Sheriff Royal made an eleven day "scout" of over 400 miles, but made no arrest.[30]

Soon, however, although not specifically named, Joe Sitter is reasonably alleged to be one of the "two men (Rangers)" present when ranger private J.W. "Jim" Fulgham, again in tandem with Sheriff Royal, on October 11th, 1894, arrested an insurgent newspaper editor and notorious firebrand from New Mexico Territory, who was also a cagey fugitive from United States justice for Neutrality Act violations, Victor L. Ochoa.[31] Legally, Ochoa was an American citizen. Pragmatically, his very heart and soul were rooted in fervently spurring Mexican nationals to free themselves from the paternal bondage and servitude of despotic rule. Ochoa orated, natives listened.

Thinking that Victor Ochoa, who was predictably popular with the Mexican-American denizens of Pecos County, was a commodity worth more to him personally than he would be to a faraway federal government, Sheriff A.J. Royal sneakily entered into an illegal conspiracy with his agitating prisoner. A simple trade was made. If Ochoa would speak favorably to his cultural compatriots, encouraging Hispanic political allegiance in the ever increasingly bitter campaign, assuring Sheriff Royal's reelection, in return the Pecos County jailhouse door's padlock would magically, after midnight, spring open.[32] On the night of October 21st Victor L. Ochoa, at a "grand *baile*," after the crowds' consumption of quantities of distilled spirits, made his pledged speech, in *Spanish*. Slyly, Victor Ochoa, clearly cognizant that Anglos in the teetering and wobbling audience were not at all adept with interpreting words spoken in his native-tongue, blasted into a passionate tirade of revolutionary reasons for overthrowing a south of the border dictator and its tyrannical government. Viva! Blissfully, measuring the crowds' unbridled keenness for his candidacy, and mistakenly believing trustee Ochoa was whipping the crowd into a politically favorable frenzy, Sheriff A.J. Royal smirked cheerfully, now knowing his retention of the Sheriff's office and its perks was a safe bet. The sheriff had been duped. Victor Ochoa may not have kept his snaky word, but Sheriff Royal did, and before dawn the devious inmate was allowed his dubious freedom, slithering into anonymity and the West Texas night's raw chill, an elusive fugitive once more.[33]

Next day, discovering realities of the jailbird's flight, and suspecting Sheriff Royal's complicity, trustworthy lawmen gave pursuit sans local authorities' assistance. Texas Rangers Jim Fulgham and William Schmidt, tracking toward the northwest and New Mexico Territory, while ranger private Joe Sitter and the formidable United States Deputy Marshal, George A. Scarborough, cut for meaningful sign to the southwest and into mammoth Brewster County.[34] After several days, Sitter and Scarborough returned to Fort Stockton, empty handed. Ranger Fulgham and his partner had better luck, nabbing Victor Ochoa near Toyah in nearby Reeves County, then forthrightly depositing him in jail at the county seat, Pecos City.[35] Shortly thereafter Joe Sitter returned to the Company D headquarters camp at Ysleta, on the Rio Grande below

The Mule Puked

that Monte Carlo of the West, old El Paso, or as some preferred, "Hell Paso." Lawman Joseph Sitter had something weighty on his mind. Meantime, Deputy U.S. Marshal Scarborough stayed behind at Fort Stockton, and on November 1st accepted custody of a no nonsense mankiller, Barney K. Riggs, who had been arrested by Texas Rangers for "asst. Prisoner to escape," and on the next day Sheriff Royal himself was taken into custody on an identical charge, as was Camilio Terrazas and John P. Meadows the following day.[36] To make a long story short, Andrew Jackson Royal's good luck, if he ever had any, simply ran out, his reelection attempt a dismal flop—and too, he was foully or fittingly, depending on perspective, murdered![37]

Joe Sitter's second wife, the stunningly beautiful Margarita Hinckley of Mesilla, New Mexico Territory. Courtesy, Jake Sitters.

Events seemed spiraling out of control at tumultuous Fort Stockton town, but back at friendly Ysleta village, Joe Sitter probably paid little notice. Three days before Christmas, on the 22nd, Joe Sitter again tied the matrimonial knot, this time with a stunningly beautiful daughter of John and Mariana Hinckley, the twenty-six year old Margarita, formerly from the historically quaint township of La Mesilla, New Mexico Territory.[38] From this marriage six children were born: Walter Quintin, October 31, 1895; Jacob Dennis, October 9, 1897; Marie Virginia, January 11, 1901;

Henrietta S., June 18, 1903; Mary Berta, June 6, 1905; and Mattie Antonia, June 13, 1907.[39]

W.L. "Lod" Calohan, an intrepid Field Inspector for the Texas & Southwestern Cattle Raisers Association, and an officer "who knew all the men that was stealing cows and all the men who weren't." On occasion he "scouted" with Joe Sitter. Courtesy, Nita Stewart Hale Memorial Library and J. Evetts Haley History Center.

Inspection of existent Texas Ranger records, even after his marriage to Margarita, continue to amplify private Joe Sitter's seemingly perpetual perambulations. During March 1895, in the company of ranger George H. Tucker, and one of the best known Texas & Southwestern Cattle Raisers Association Inspectors, "a man who knew all the men who was stealing and all the men who wasn't," W.L. "Lod" Calohan, the lawmen made a physically taxing 220 mile horseback "scout" into the Land of Enchantment, New Mexico Territory.[40] Shortly thereafter, Joe Sitter made another trip across the state-line and into New Mexico Territory, this time absent from his post of duty for thirteen days and covering some 400 miles, but on this "scout" taking into custody one W.T. Patterson, wanted for Murder at Fort Davis, Texas.[41] Then during the next month he recovered two stolen horses, and assisted by ranger R.E. Bryant briskly arrested Vicanor Chavez for Assault to Murder.[42] Whether or not he was with Sergeant Carl Kirchner on the night of June 11th,

The Mule Puked

1895, cannot be conclusively proven; two rangers were, and Joe Sitter was in close proximity but, in any event, their search for Southwest ne'er-do-wells Vic Queen and Martin Mrose tuned up naught.[43] Just after Independence Day, 1895, Joe Sitter was quickly dispatched to the Devil River's country looking for a gang of would-be train robbers, who it was reported, were plotting their impending stab at high crime.[44] He was out 23 days, traveled 1078 miles, and made three arrests.[45]

During September, 1895, private Joe Sitter accompanied Captain John R. "Border Boss" Hughes to Sonora in Sutton County, Texas, and arrested two of the Holland brothers, S.L. and Tom, wanted in connection with a vicious robbery and murder at Sitter's hometown, Valentine. By rail and by horse, the feisty officers had, when it was all said and done, covered a grueling 1008 miles.[46] Joe Sitter didn't seem to tarry, during January 1896, he was on a "scout" ending up in Lincoln County, New Mexico Territory, before he and the other officers reversed course and headed for home, spending 21 days on the trip and covering 440 miles.[47] He had no sooner returned to base camp when his gutsy presence was again in demand. On the 19th of March, Captain Hughes accompanied by privates Thalis T. Cook, R.E. Braynt, J.C. Yeates, and Joe Sitter hightailed it to a secluded cattle ranch sprawled along Rio Grande River banks, surrounded the diminutive adobe house and next morning without resorting to gunplay effectively arrested Felipe Garcia and Salome Martinez, two of El Paso County's most wanted murder suspects.[48]

Without doubt Joe Sitter was quickly gaining fame and a well-deserved reputation as an indomitable border country law enforcer. Federal Customs' officials were starting to take note, Joe Sitter was frequently working with them hand-in-glove, making more than a favorable and lasting impression. During one investigation in conjunction with U.S. Mounted Customs Inspector E.E. Townsend, the dynamic duo captured thirty-two head of stolen cattle, returning them to the rightful owner. Two days later, with Customs Inspector Greenwood and Deputy U.S. Marshal A.B. Cline, Joe Sitter arrested the notorious cow-thief Pablo Munoz.[49] Soon, he handily arrested Pablo Morales on a murder charge stemming from a thorny El Paso killing and parked the unruly owl-hoot in the Brewster County jail at Alpine, awaiting delivery to Pass of the North officers.[50] Joe Sitter rested not, so it seemed. Thrilled government bureaucrats once again looked Joe Sitter's way, particularly after he arrested an artful arms smuggler, Tomas Burges, for Neutrality Act violations.[51]

On the 25th day of October 1896, Joe Sitter resigned from the Frontier Battalion surrendering his commission as a Texas Ranger.[52]

Lawmen, Outlaws and S.O.Bs.

To the student raptly following the spotty careers of early day lawmen, especially those employed by the Lone Star state, the resignation should not come as a surprise. From its inception the Frontier Battalion had ambitiously authorized many more manpower slots than could ever be rationally paid for, and therefore an economic vacuum justifiably existed between feasibility and foolishness.[53] Into this manmade void stepped financial power-brokers representing special interest groups, the Texas & Southwestern Cattle Raisers Association is but one superlative example. With a legislatively authorized strength and private rather than public funding, a new dimension to legitimate Texas law enforcement was birthed, "Special Rangers." Officially commissioned by the state, but working for private industry, and usually earning much higher salaries than government funded officers, many veteran lawmen made financially smart career changes. It seems, from the best evidence, that Joe Sitter was one of those seeking a better payday and more leisure time. On December 7th, 1896, he submitted his application, requesting appointment as a Special Ranger, "to serve the State without pay," certifying that he was sober and temperate in habits and that he had never been convicted of any crime.[54] For some reason the intrepid blue-eyed applicant did not declared his previous ranger service on the questionnaire, but mentioned his occupation as that of a "cowboy," an indication that cow-work was a prerequisite for the cop-work he would be doing for a private, not public, employer.[55] Naturally, as a Special Ranger, whether paid a recurring stipend or on a commission basis from an Association or individual ranch owners, Joe Sitter could now devote the majority of his time to improving his own livestock holdings at remote Valentine, raising mindful and honorable children, and enforcing the law as realistic circumstances demanded, rather than incessantly toiling in a seemingly inexhaustible and infrequently valued routine. For the moment, life was good for Joe Sitter.

Conjecture in valid historical writings is best left alone, therefore the rationale for the following must simply speak for itself:

> In compliance with Telegraphic instructions received April 9th, 98, from A.G. O. State of Texas, Joe Sitter was enlisted a member of this Company, May 1st, 98.[56]

Joe Sitter, whatever the explanation, soon opted to forsake his Special Ranger commission, and once again was sworn in as a "regular" private in Company D, Frontier Battalion, the ranch at

Valentine his new headquarters.[57] Post haste he was dispatched on numerous "scouts" along the Rio Grande River, usually out several days and covering considerable territory in the recurring quest to retrieve stolen livestock, cattle and horses.[58] Of course, nearer the settlements he was also required to keep the peace and make arrests; Canuto Acosta, Disturbing the Peace; Nestor Garcia, Carrying A Pistol; George Lloyd, Disturbing the Peace; Felix Cullen and George Martin, Fighting; Mequie Apodaca and Gabino Marquez, Theft of Cattle; and so on.[59] And too, the more mundane assignments necessitated attention, such as a five day trip to lonesome Eagle Pass to keep the peace during local elections, or assisting the deputy sheriff at Comstock for a twenty day hunt after flighty train robbers, Bill Taylor and John Keating.[60] And, as always, Joe Sitter was maintaining a close working relationship with U.S. Mounted Customs Inspectors, such as the February 1899, case where they recovered 92 head of smuggled cattle and traveled some 300 miles horseback.[61] Supervisory people at Customs were watching, and they liked what they saw.

In answer to their cry for competent help—men with old fashioned horse-sense—Joe Sitter resigned from the paltry paid Texas Rangers and began on May 1, 1899, his new job as an Inspector, U.S. Mounted Customs Service.[62] His salary doubled.[63]

Many noted Joe Sitter's talents as a tracker, such as, "he could track a jackrabbit through a rock quarry," or "he could read a cold trail like a book," or "he was trained to track like a wolf," or "he knew how to read sign like an Indian."[64] And there is even an anecdotal story in which bossman John Hughe's six-shooter falls out of its scabbard, for awhile unbeknownst to the Captain, and later, the unconquerable Joe Sitter is tasked with doing what his chief couldn't or wouldn't do, finding the darn gun. Joe Sitter, according to Texas folklore, then deftly follows near indistinguishable dints made by dilapidated sandals traipsing ever so lightly across soft sand, right to an apparently unconcerned Tiqua Indian, who, as it turns out, had picked up the sixgun and was hiding it under the gaudy blanket spread before him, attempting an act of clear-cut misappropriation, that is, until the ill-conceived misdeed was shrewdly uncovered by the Southwest's premier tracker.[65] Possibly the story is true, perhaps not. *Quien Sabe?*

There is, however, a truth to be highlighted. The Texas/Mexican borderland in that far-flung Big Bend country was rough country. Long before Joe Sitter's debut in the area, marauding Apache and Comanche warriors, who once used the Trans-Pecos as corridor for searing raids into old Mexico, had been subjugated. Ruffians, rustlers, reprobates and revolutionaries, on the other hand, were still around. The thinly inhabited topography, tortuous and tough, was Heaven, haven, and home for merciless Mexican bandits and American outlaws. It was about to get even rougher.

Around 1910 the southwestern Texas borderline exploded—and imploded. The Mexican Revolution, or more rightly a Mexican Civil War, kicked off and the callous blood letting and the litany of lame excuses commenced. Undeniably there were true patriots to be found, but for Joe Sitter's story they are in short supply. Certain double-crossing desperadoes took advantage of the pandemonium. Francisco "Chico" Cano was one. A desert chameleon could easily change colors at will, and so too could the border bandido Chico Cano.[66]

The notorious Mexican bandit Chico Cano during a temporary truce with United State's soldiers along the border in the lonesome Texas Big Bend county. Courtesy, The University of Texas at Austin, Harry Ransom Humanities Research Center.

The Mule Puked

Chico Cano, the ever treacherous Mexican bandit from the state of Chihuahua, a thief who it was reported would "steal the canteen from a man dying of thirst...",[67] and the interminably intractable Joe Sitter, the U.S. Mounted Customs Inspector from Texas, were by geographical juxtaposition and vocational proclivity poised for war. Machismo and happenstance underpinned outlaw Chico Cano. Mulish pride and circumstance zipped up Joe Sitter. There was no duty for either to retreat, and they didn't!

Well aware of the existence of a cow-stealing warrant commanding Chico Cano's forthwith arrest, and developing critical intelligence as to his whereabouts, Joe Sitter sought the help of a fellow U.S. Mounted Customs Inspector, John Simpson "Jack" Howard. And like Joe Sitter, Jack Howard was an inveterate lawman. A quick glance at his U.S. Custom's application highlights the lawman's biography:

> I have been a cowboy, Wagon boss, trail boss and have worked at the cow business since I was 12 years old. At home on our ranch, also for Red Ergton –V Ranch three years, Charles Schreiner, Kerrville, about nine years. I naturally had to read brands readily in the above situations and can classify and read them as well as anyone...I can ride anything I ever tried to, broken or unbroken horses, having been raised on a ranch. I am perfectly familiar with all the work of same. Can ride an ordinary cow-pony on the round up, encircle and cutting out work around the herd...I have handled firearms all my life and am considered a fine shot, both at moving objects and targets, can shoot horseback as well as upon ground. I use a .30-30 rifle and Colt's .45. I used a Krag-Jorgeson going up San Juan Hill.[68]

Sitter and Howard were accompanied by a third comrade, an intrepid Inspector employed by the Texas & Southwestern Cattle Raisers Association, J.A. "Ad" Harvick. The trio developed a dicey plan for the apprehension operation.[69] In retrospect, they bit off more than they could trimly chew.

The pockmarked mountain country just across the Sierra Vieja Rim in the Texas Big Bend Country was technically United States soil; practically though, the tiny villages of Pilares and Porvenir and their identically named twin-sister hamlets across the shallow Rio Grande River on the Mexican side breathed as but one isolated and collective community—culturally and by time-worn tradition, an appendage of Old Mexico, not America.[70]

Lawmen, Outlaws and S.O.Bs.

Jack Howard at San Antonio preparing for service in the Spanish American War. Later, as a United States Mounted Customs Inspector he and Joe Sitter worked closely as border law enforcers. Courtesy, Sul Ross University, Archives of the Big Bend, Bryan Wildenthal Memorial Library.

Reportedly, at least by one account, Chico Cano was in attendance at the mournful wake for Alvino Bejar's baby in the adobe abode of Nicomedes Martinez, sorrowfully punching out wailing tunes on an accordion.[71] An informant's tip, whether an act of vile treachery or simply splendid public service, was not wide of the mark. Three determined lawmen surrounded the sad little domicile, which wasn't too much of a complicated chore, and outspokenly demanded Cano's surrender, right now! From within a foolishly inept and perceptibly melancholic plea was tendered by Chico's father, Catarino, that the brazen bandido was elsewhere. The alibi fell on deaf ears. As with most Old West stories, there is dispute as to what happened next. By certain accounts the chivalrous officers had gallantly offered to let women and children absent themselves before the fireworks started.[72] Others, however, claim Joe Sitter and his cold-hearted colleagues threatened to burn the house down and make toast of the whole damn bunch, and only after pathetic petitions from some of the hemmed-in men, did the lawmen acquiesce and allow the terrified womenfolk and their brood to quit the premises.[73] And, depending on which *bona fide* variation a reader wishes to choose, Chico Cano ingeniously donned female attire and departed with the frightened females, only to be detected and captured; or, Chico's youngest brother Robelardo dressed up like a little girl and made good a getaway, ostensibly to sound the alarm and recruit help; or, after the forlorn departure of ladies and children, Chico Cano virtuously did the honorable thing, and surrendered.[74] Regardless, Joe Sitter had his man.

Joe Sitter, mounted, second from right, while a United States Mounted Customs Inspector in West Texas. Courtesy, Texas State Library and Archives.

On the night of February 9, 1913, the three doughty law-dogs, "...camped for the night at a little store conducted at Pilares, Texas by one Sabino Hernandez...," each taking a sleepless shift guarding their manacled prisoner.[75] Along that international borderline, however, not everyone rested. Manuel Cano, another of the bold captive's brothers, had painstaking plans of his very own, and he was furtively busy—gathering cohorts and snooping about—tactically studying the terrain. As the morning sun popped up, so too did the lawmen, anxious to dump Chico at the Presidio County jail in Marfa, and go home. Quickly, after sucking down boiled coffee,

Chico Cano was mounted on a sure-footed mule, his ankles tethered together under the animal's belly.[76] To deftly transverse the Sierra Vieja Rim through narrow canyons necessitated careful and conscientious riding—single file. Jack Howard, riding his favorite horse, Brownie, took the lead, followed by a dejected but slyly confident Chico Cano, then tall "Ad" Harvick, and lastly, Joe Sitter.[77]

Following the tight trail, a "high bluff" on the left and a "higher mountain" on the right, the diminutive squadron had traveled but a scant "mile and a quarter" from the back-country store when from behind sizeable boulders some one hundred and fifty feet to the front, a withering rifle fire exploded.[78] At the first shots a wounded Jack Howard tumbled from his horse, and then the mount too, dropped, doorknob dead. Other gutless bushwackers had set their rifles' front beads on Sitter and Harvick, and in an instant they too were knocked out of their saddles, struck by the pelting hellfire. Chico Cano screamed at the seemingly thunderstruck mule, frantically encouraging the beast to take flight, and in but short order was spirited on a wild ride—away from the fight.[79] Fortunately, Howard's horse fell dead with his scuffed saddle scabbard on the topside, and somehow the desperately injured Jack Howard managed to jerk his Winchester free but weakened by the loss of blood was unable to use it. Joe Sitter and "Ad" Harvick, although both were wounded, maintained possession of their lever-guns and unleashed a blistering fire on the shielding boulders. The guttersnipes, their premeditated task finished merely melted away. Joe Sitter staggered toward the crest of the "bluff" on the left side of the canyon, and upon reaching the topside successfully signaled Sabino Hernandez, the aforementioned shopkeeper, and then crumpled to the ground, unconscious. Through the anxious merchant's speedy efforts a rickety wagon was procured and with the help of "other Mexicans," all three bleeding lawmen were removed to the security of the little general store.[80] Upon closer physical examination it was determined that:

> The shot which struck Howard entered the right breast high up and emerged on the left lower than the point of entrance. The bullet appears to have stripped and a portion of it entered his lungs and did not emerge…The shot which struck Sitter entered high up on the left temple and emerged above and behind the ear. (It was feared) the wound will produce serious results as Sitter has been delirious almost constantly since being shot…The shot which struck Harvick entered to the inside of the left thigh and emerged through the outside of the heavy muscle tearing a large hole where

it came out. Unless blood poisoning should result I do not anticipate serious results, although the man will be disabled for quite a long time.[81]

Joe Sitter, kneeling, and Jack Howard, second from left, while employed as United States Mounted Customs Inspectors. The other two individuals at right are unidentified. After this photograph was made, Howard, Sitter, and Ad Harvick, an Inspector for the Texas and Southwestern Cattle Raisers Association, were callously ambushed by the Chico Cano gang. Jack Howard died in the exchange of gunfire, while Sitter and Harvick were wounded. Courtesy, Charles Wright, U.S. Customs Service.

At once a messenger was sent sounding the alarm and in double quick time Texas Rangers, khaki-clad Army men, and U.S. Mounted Customs Inspectors Herff Alexander Carnes and C.R. Moore, both ex-rangers, hastened to the scene. And too, frantically racing to her husband's side, Mary Howard, after unluckily experiencing four successive "blowouts" and suffering an excruciating "little buggy" ride, at last, was lovingly greeted by her steadfast spouse, "Hello, old girlie, how are you?[82] For awhile, Jack Howard sipped mouthfuls of nourishing hot soup and sometimes called out for a drink of water, but mostly he rested, intermittently lamenting that "he never had any chance."[83] Which he didn't, and sorrowfully at 7:15 P.M., February 12, 1913—he died. Dolefully, his devoted Mary penned the closing entry into her deceased husband's daily journal, "FINIS."[84]

Chico Cano on the panicky mule had safely scampered into the clutches of his sniping comrades, had his shackles hacked through, and once more picked up his chosen career of a borderland bandit and wily fugitive, but with payback on his mind. The remaining two wounded lawmen were removed to El Paso for medical attention, Sitter to a Catholic Hospital, the Hotel Dieu.[85] Both, reasonably soon, recovered from their wounds and several months later reported for duty. While recuperating, his head still bandaged, Joe Sitter was visited by the prolific Western writer of the times, Zane Grey, who was putting in order background material for his soon to be published novel, *Lone Star Ranger*. Although at the time not a Texas Ranger, but because he had just recently survived a desperate gunplay, Custom's man Joe Sitter could furnish first-hand insight into the state of affairs along the troublesome borderline, as least so thought Grey. How much literary license was engaged in is not necessarily all that germane but, reportedly, and it was written, Joe Sitter posted Zane Grey that at present along the Rio Grande, "Shore is 'most as bad an' wild as ever!"[86] He wasn't wrong!

On March 29th, 1914, scarcely a year after the deadly battle with Chico Cano's gang, Joe Sitter would do battle with one of its allies, twice convicted cow-thief, Lino Baiza.[87] "Scouting" down the Rio Grande from Valentine, Texas were the Presidio County Sheriff, M.B. Chastain, Joe Sitter and two additional U.S. Mounted Customs Inspectors, Charley Craighead and Sam Neal (Neill), and the Chief Field Inspector for the Texas & Southwestern Cattle Raisers Association, John R. Banister.[88] Halting about four miles below Pilares, the posse camped, facing, across the Rio Grande, a herd of beeves being held by Mexicans, awaiting delivery to American purchasers. There were by estimates, whether exaggerated or not, about 40 to 60 heavily armed *vaqueros* loose herding the cattle, idly killing time in anticipation of U.S. greenbacks arriving. Warily suspicious that the herd would be seized as soon as it crossed the line, the Mexicans were demanding payment be made on their side of the river, which in the end, was the way the transaction was managed. Proceeding toward the village of Candelaria, about 15 or 20 miles below Pilares, the lawmen came upon a tiny settlement of three or four houses.[89] Range detective Banister tells what happened next:

> All at once a man ran out of one of the houses and mounted a saddled horse that was tied there, and made a dash down the bank

of the river, some 50 yards away. Joe Sitters (sic) spurred his horse up to the door and asked, "*Quien es*? Who is that?" Lino Baiza, he was told. Sheriff Chastain and Sitters both ordered the man in English and Spanish to halt but he continued his flight, being by that time down the bank and into the water of the river. "Kill his horse! Stop him, boys!," yelled Sitters. By this time we were all dismounted and firing became general. The bandit's horse continued across the shallow water, Baiza leaning forward urging him on. He was seen to reel in the saddle, and when near a small island, the horse fell with a splash. Baiza rose, waded to the island and crawled into a pile of driftwood to hide. "Boys, let's go get him," said Sheriff Chastain, mounting his horse. Another of our party and I mounted, and we three rode across to the island; we dismounted and approached the drift where we had seen him conceal himself. We could not see him until we were within a few feet of the drift, when he was adjusting his position and bringing his gun around to fire on us. We were ready and he was instantly killed....According to Chastain, Baiza has been one of the most troublesome criminals along this part of the Rio Grande in recent years. The fight was an especial satisfaction to Joe Sitters, who was one of a part of officers ambushed on February 10, 1913, by Baiza and his gang...It seemed right that Sitters should have been present when Baiza met his punishment.[90]

It may be questioned whether or not Lino Baiza was, indeed, a participant in the merciless ambush of Joe Sitter, Jack Howard and "Ad" Harvick, particularly in light of primary source data which clearly mentions during the attack lawmen were "unable to see their assailants."[91] Journalistically justifying borderland killings is an dubious exercise. Specifically of the 1913 assault on Joe Sitter and his comrades it has been written, incredibly, "At that time, Chico had known that Sitters (sic) would make sure he never reached Marfa alive."[92] Conjecture as to what *might* have happened, yet, didn't, is by definition indefinable. In a separate allegation of mysterious mayhem on the murderous side of the Sierra Vieja Rim, it has been written that Joe Sitter, accompanied by his teenage son Walter, and another identified as H. F. Roberston, but who in fact would have been Horace L. Roberson if the story were true, made a midnight raid on sleepy Pilares, Mexico, "burning much of the village and killing one Mexican."[93] Whether the reader accepts the uncorroborated assertion as factual, or, as an example of partisan hearsay, must of course be left up to the particular reader. A judicious study of Joe Sitter's story will not be in want for handy first-rate fundamental material. The next gripping episode in Joe Sitter's adventuresome life's story is steeped richly by word of mouth recitals but, too, backed up by administrative papers and bureaucratic reports, prime examples of governmental red-tape—the historians' treasure-trove.

For Joe Sitter 1915 would prove action-packed. New Year's celebrations were hardly ended, and for a few hangovers barely fading before more serious gunshots permeated the West Texas air. On January 15th Joe's oldest son by his second marriage, nineteen year old Walt, rode into Sierra Blanca horseback behind a herd of bellowing beeves. He had accompanied his boss Horace L. Roberson and another cowhand, Elmer Dumont. By most accounts Roberson was, when provoked, mean as the proverbial junk-yard dog. Before accepting the foreman's job on the gargantuan T O Ranch on the Mexican side of the Rio Grande, H.L. Roberson had been a Sergeant in the Texas Rangers, and was a gunman of regional note, having killed at least two men in the line of duty, and perhaps others outside the law. Whatever factuality would reveal, in this regard and for Joe Sitter's story, it is moot. On the morning of the 16th, Horace Roberson at the Sierra Blanca stockpens got into a serious altercation with Henry Foote Boykin, an area rancher and popular local citizen. During the mêlée Boykin was armed with a "two-bladed" knife and was on the ground, Roberson had a Colt's six-shooter and was atop a panicky and gyrating horse. The long and the short of it is that Horace Roberson killed Foote Boykin as intended, but during the scuffle also killed young Walt Sitter, by mistake.[94]

Joe Sitter scarcely had time to grieve. Chico Cano was still on the loose, creatively dishing out his own brand of acrimonious abuse.

On the morning of May 21, 1915, U.S. Mounted Custom's Inspectors Joe Sitter and Charley Craighead, in the company of Texas Rangers Eugene Hulen, Sug Cummings, and H.C. Trollinger left Valentine and headed across the Sierra Vieja Rim, destination Pilares and exhaustively focused on a particular purpose, recovering a herd of illegally imported horses."[95] On the night of the 22nd the bandit hunters camped near Pilares, and next morning picked up what they considered a readable trail. They proceeded with their "scout." Late in the afternoon the lawmen "…came upon part of the horses in the foothills near the mountains and they were guarded by three men. We had a running fight with them, but it being near dusk, they made their getaway into the mountains."[96] The fatigued and famished officers, as night fell, made camp near an isolated windmill, the nearest source for drinkable water.

The Mule Puked

Bright and early the next morning, May 24th, the squadron of crime fighters, hobbled their pack outfit, leaving the footsore animals behind, and headed out on their saddle-horses seeking the horses and their illegal owners. With rightful knowledge, at last, that they had some of the stolen horses cut off, more or less corralled in a box canyon, "up against a bluff," Joe Sitter divided his workforce, sending Craighead, Cummings and Trollinger up the canyon to gather the four-footed contraband, while he and ranger Hulen sought a "crow's nest," a high point "to get a view of the surrounding country" and to keep "a lookout for the Mexicans."[97] Events unexpectedly spiraled out of control and in a heartbeat turned "Western."

The three man party rode into the canyon, and the "Mexicans" began firing from all sides," forcing the lawmen to dismount, and run for cover, taking their guns (rifles) and cartridges with them.[98] Their brutal adversaries were but forty short yards away.[99]

The landscape was littered with rocks, big ones, and the sprinting officers gained natural fortification. From comforting concealment they could observe Sitter and Hulen, horseback, "on a very small hill," motioning them to get back down the canyon and away from the shooting. With their horses wild-eyed and hopelessly hotfooting it away from the fight, the uneasy officers made a mad-dash back down the canyon, their retreat covered by a withering fire from Sitter's and Hulen's Winchesters.[100] Promptly the "Mexicans" redirected their deadly rifle fire in the direction of Sitter and Hulen. Reality set in. Joe Sitter and Eugene Hulen were trapped, cut off. Five times, the other three attempted repositioning and rescue, only to be driven back by a galling peppering of "blue whistlers" and common sense self-preservation.[101] It must have been maddening:

> We could see them (Sitter and Hulen), but were unable to see the Mexicans. After four hours of slowly working our way back over the mountain, under heavy fire, we gained a position back of where Sitters (sic) and Hulin (sic) had last been seen, but they had changed their position. We decided to try to get out. As we were so badly outnumbered and were famished for water. When we had finally worked our way out of range of the Mexicans' guns the firing ceased and we knew Sitters and Hulin were either dead or had made their escape.[102]

Opting to hike out to the previous night's camp, where they had parked their pack train, Sug Cummings, H.C. Trolliner and Charley Craighead kicked off an eight mile walk over tortuous topography.[103] After an exhausting traipse, finally, the trio negotiated the tiresome trip, secured their pack-horses, and managed it another five miles to the McGee Ranch where the alarm was sounded and the plea for help initiated, by "a Mexican" carrying a note five miles further, to the ranch of John Pool were there was rural telephone service. At Marfa, 40 miles distant, a posse was fashioned post haste and after a roaring open-air automobile trip, and the acquisition of saddle-horses at the Pool Ranch, and then a galloping ride to the McGee Ranch, the lawmen were updated.[104]

By three o'clock in the afternoon on the 25th the posse reached the bushwacking site. Their discovery was sickening. Joe Sitter, as expected was dead, "shot about ten times." Ranger Hulen "had been shot about eight times," but adding to the repulsion, both had been mutilated. Inspector R.M. Wadsworth, who was there, elaborates:

> He (Sitter) was in a very bad condition....I was right there. I helped to put him on a pack-mule myself. He was lying on his back in sort of a cramped position; looked like he died in great agony, his knees drawed up, cramped up, his hands and fingers like that, drawed up over his face; you could see where his flesh had been knocked off his knuckles with rocks; his left eye in his head had been caved in. The rock was lying a little bit to one side; I judge it weighted about 20 pounds. He had eleven bullet holes in his body.[105]

Crime-scene reconstruction revealed that Joe Sitter, after having moved from his first location, had fought like a demon possessed, sixty spent cartridge cases littered the rocky ground around him. Whether any of his shots connected with one of the estimated 30 to 35 assassins remains a mystery.[106] Texas Ranger Eugene Hulen, it was determined, was killed early on—he'd fired but one round after the terrifying move to reposition. The arms and accouterments of the dead had been stolen, clothing too, they lay buck-naked bleaching and bloating in the baking sun.[107] *Perhaps* it is folklore, *maybe* not, but it was reported as true and oft repeated. The deteriorating and decomposing condition of the dead bodies was ghastly and, according to the story, when Joe Sitter was strapped to a pack-mule for removal to Valentine, the horrified animal became nauseated and puked.[108]

At the McGee Ranch it was decided that the best course of action was to bury Joe Sitter and Eugene Hulen, so into the same grave they were interred. Later, however, their bodies were respectfully exhumed by undertakers from Marfa, W.G. Young and C.W. Livingston, Sitter reburied at Valentine, Hulen at his birthplace, Gainesville, Texas.[109]

The Mule Puked

Joe Sitter's rededicated headstone at Valentine, Texas. Coutesy, Jake Sitters.

There in most minds was never any question as to who held sway over the bandits who gunned down Sitter and Hulen; Chico Cano. Although argument may be found, even the bandido's biographers adroitly acknowledge, "Chico had succeeded in baiting them into the canyon."[110] Government authorities secured sufficient evidence, or applied enough pressure, or both—regardless—a federal Grand Jury indicted Cano for the deliberate murders of law enforcers engaged in apprehending a violator in breach of United State's Penal Code statutes. Chico Cano, the well-known outlaw, maintained his lawful status as a wanted Department of Justice fugitive.[111] The issuance of another piece of paper demanding his handcuffed appearance before a U.S. Magistrate on the American side of the Rio Grande dividing line bothered Chico Cano not a whit. His story of borderland banditry continued for years but for this, Joe Sitter's' story, Chico Cano's narrative must close.

In the final historical analysis, Joe Sitter wasn't a Wyatt or Wild Bill or a Wanna-be. No, Joe Sitter was legit, and from the very get-go back at Castroville town, until that 1915 day in May when he was gunned down, Joe Sitter was firmly tethered on the honorable side of the law. Others may have grabbed for the headlines and attention; Joseph Sitter had a River to Ride.

ENDNOTES CHAPTER 10

"THE MULE PUKED"

[1] In most instances Joe Sitter is identified as Joe Sitters and, indeed, the addition of the "s" has understandably led many Western writers and honest historians astray. Examples of Joe Sitter's signature on primary source materials clearly reveal he signed his name sans the "s," and during an interview with his grandson, Jacob D. "Jake" Sitters, the mystery was solved. The addition of the "s" was an appellation of subsequent generations, which is the accepted usage today, however, at the time he was born the subject of this biographical sketch was formally tagged with the name Joe Sitter, and so it was the day he died. Means, Joyce, *Pancho Villa Days at Pilares*, citing Sitter's death certificate reveals that it reads, "Joseph Russell Sitter." P. 180.

[2] Cox, Mike *Texas Ranger Tales—Stories That Need Telling.* "Had the *Lone Star Ranger* been published in the second half of 1915 rather than January, Zane Grey undoubtedly would have wanted to rewrite his introduction so he could let the world know about what had happened to Sitters (sic), the Ranger who told him in 1913 that the Texas-Mexican border was 'most as bad an' wild as ever." A statement that was, in fact, prophetic. P. 136.

[3] Gournay, Luke. *Texas Boundaries, Evolution of the State's Counties.* P. 56.

[4] Awbrey, Betty Dooley & Dooley, Claude. *Why Stop? A Guide To Texas Historical Roadside Markers.* P. 88.

[5] *Ibid.*

[6] Gournay. P. 56. Later, 1892, the county seat was moved from Castroville to Hondo.

[7] *Certificate of Baptism*, St. Louis Church, Castroville, Texas, for Josephus (Joe) Sitter, dated January 22, 1863. St. Louis Church Archives. Castroville, Texas.

[8] *Certificate of Marriage*, St. Louis Church, Castroville, Texas, for Joseph Sitter and Maggie Bendele, dated April 4, 1884. St. Louis Church Archives, Castroville, Texas. That Joe Sitter was, in fact, a cowboy is drawn from one of his *Application to the Texas Adjutant General* forms requesting to serve as a Special Ranger, without pay. Courtesy, Texas State Library and Archives Commission. (TSLAC) Austin. And see, Sitter family genealogical history as prepared by Joe Sitter's grandson, Jake Sitters.

[9] Interview by author with Jake Sitters, October 26, 2002, Castroville, Texas.

[10] *San Antonio Daily Express*, October 23, 1891. "…by a posse of rangers under Captain Jones and citizens under Deputy Sheriff Joe Sitter." And, "Deputy Sheriff Joe Sitter has hunted this gang like a bloodhound and has hung on their trail with bulldog tenacity for more than a week."

[11] *El Paso Daily Times*, September 3, 1891. And see, *Monthly Returns*, Company D, Frontier Battalion, September, 1891. (TSLAC)

[12] *Ibid.*

[13] Handwritten statement, "Joe Sitter's Account of the Trailing and Capture of the Train Robbers," Harry Warren Collection, Sul Ross University, Bryan Wildenthal Memorial Library, Archives of the Big Bend (ABB). Alpine, Texas. This first-person account of his participation in chasing after the train robbers was dictated by Joe Sitter to local educator and historian Harry Warren, and is extraordinarily well-detailed and, somewhat surprisingly, underused and often neglected. Hereafter cited as Sitter to Warren. The data furnished by Joe Sitter, when

compared with official Frontier Battalion *Monthly Returns*, correspondence to the Texas Adjutant General, contemporary newspaper reports, and a marvelous letter from Ranger Captain Frank Jones, as repeated in the January 1929 edition of *Frontier Times*, meshes straightforwardly, providing the fascinated researcher with a significant primary source document.

[14] Texas Ranger Captain Frank Jones to Texas Adjutant General W.H. Mabry, September 11, 1891. (TSLAC)

[15] Sitter to Warren.

[16] *San Antonio Daily Light*, October 24, 1891.

[17] Sitter to Warren.

[18] *Ibid.* For the amount of the reward; *San Antonio Daily Express*, October 23, 1891, for public adulation; and an assortment of *Monthly Returns*, Frontier Battalion, for enlistment of, and investigative activities for, Joe Sitter, private, Company D, Frontier Battalion.

[19] Walker, Wayne T., "Joe Sitters: The Best Damn Tracker In Texas," *Oldtimers Wild West*. December 1978. "Not long afterward (the train robbery) he was appointed deputy sheriff of Jeff Davis county and became a full-fledged member of the lawing fraternity." P. 31. And see, Means, P. 171. "Prior to joining the Texas Rangers, in 1893, Sitter served as a constable and deputy sheriff for several years in Val Verde County, Texas." And see, Michaels, Kevin, "Tracker," *Great West*. September 1974. P. 23, "...he was appointed a deputy sheriff of Jeff Davis County..." Martin, Jack, *Border Boss, Captain John R. Hughes—Texas Ranger*, confirms the overall assertion, but falls short of specificity, adding to the confusion. P. 182. "Sitters' career began when he was appointed a deputy sheriff in his home (?) county." One of Joe Sitter's daughters, Mattie Sitters Baca, merely said, "Father was a rancher before he became a Ranger," page 20, "Marked For Death," *Frontier Times*, March 1965, by Fox, Dorothea Magdalene.

[20] Stephens, Robert W., *Texas Ranger Sketches*. P. 69.

[21] Means, P. 171, "John R. Hughes was sergeant of the company. When Jones was killed and Hughes took command, he recommended Sitter for a vacancy based on his actions in trailing and capturing the train robbers." And see, Walker, P. 31, "Since Captain Hughes had a strong admiration for the courage and abilities of Sitters (sic), he immediately rode to his ranch near Valentine to persuade him to join the Texas Rangers..."

[22] *Monthly Return*, Company D, Frontier Battalion, August 1893. "Joe Sitter enlisted at Comstock, Val Verde County, August 1st." Signed, "John R. Hughes." (TSLAC) The fact that his initial enlistment took place at Comstock, Texas, possibly indicates he had not as of yet relocated to Jeff Davis County, a fact, which for this narrative, is insignificant. And see, *Memorandum* from Robert L. Roberston, Adjutant General, Austin, to Commissioner of Pensions, Washington, D. C., "In compliance with your form letter, January twenty-fourth (1928), it is found that Joseph Sitter enlisted in Co. "D" Frontier Battalion on August 1, 1893..." (TSLAC) Also see, *Names of Applicants for Enlistment*, Texas Ranger Hall of Fame and Museum. (TRHF&M) Waco. Joe Sitter applied for a position as ranger private on July 8, 1893, and was enlisted on August 1, 1893. Also see, State of Texas, *Certification and Request for Payment*, "I hereby Certify that Joseph Sitter a Member of Captain JnO.R. Hughes, Company "D" of the Frontier Battalion, was mustered into the State Service on the 1st day of August, 1893. The said Joseph Sitter has pay due him from August 1st to the present date. There is

due said Joseph Sitter, Thirty Dollars…," signed, "John R. Hughes, Captain," dated, August 31, 1893. (TRHF&M)

[23] Martin, P. 182. "…won acclaim in a fight with outlaws less than twenty-four hours after his name was entered on the Ranger roster." And see, Michaels, P. 23. "Less than 24 hours after becoming Private Joe Sitters (sic), had added to his reputation with an outstanding performance during a fierce gun battle…" A check was also made of the Adjutant General's Correspondence Files and no record mentioning Joe Sitter being involved in a gunbattle during the month of August could be located. Donaly Brice, Texas State Library and Archives, Austin, to author, April 18, 2003.

[24] *Monthly Return*, August 31, 1893, Company D, Frontier Battalion, signed, "John R. Hughes." (TSLAC)

[25] *Ibid.* September, 1893 & October, 1893.

[26] *Ibid.* November, 1893.

[27] *Ibid.* April, 1894.

[28] *Ibid.* August, 1894.

[29] *Ibid.* September, 1894.

[30] *Ibid.* October, 1894.

[31] *Ibid.* Joe Sitter was on temporary assignment at Fort Stockton when Ochoa was arrested. And see, DeArment, Robert K., *George Scarborough, The Life And Death Of A Lawman On The Closing Frontier.* P. 54-59.

[32] DeArment, P. 54-59. And see, Williams, Clayton W., *Texas' Last Frontier, Fort Stockton and the Trans-Pecos, 1861-1895.* P. 368-388. "…Royal had Ochoa make a speech in the courthouse advocating his reelection, and at the same time he promised the fifteen or twenty Mexicans on hand to get Ochoa out of jail in return for their support and votes for reelection. Several Mexicans later stated that such an agreement was made."

[33] *Ibid.* And see, *Monthly Return*, Company D, Frontier Battalion. October, 1894. "Victor Ochoa broke Jail…" (TSLAC)

[34] *Monthly Return*, October, 1894.

[35] DeArment, P. 56. The *Monthly Return* for October asserts that prisoner Ochoa was jailed at El Paso. Likely he was first placed in jail at Pecos, and ultimately delivered to the calaboose at El Paso a few days afterward.

[36] *Monthly Return*, November, 1894. And see Williams, P. 373. For an interesting glance at Barney Riggs, see, Lindsey, Ellis & Riggs, Gene, *Barney K. Riggs, The Yuma And Pecos Avenger.* Although the Fort Stockton saga continued, for the purpose of this biographical sketch of Joe Sitter, it must end. Suffice to say, Royal was not reelected as the Pecos County Sheriff and shortly thereafter, November 1894, Andrew Jackson Royal was fatally and mysteriously gunned down. The historical Old West murder, to this day, remains a "whodunit?"

[37] Williams, P. 378-388.

[38] Interview with Jake D. Sitters, October 26, 2002, Castroville, Texas. Also see, Means, P. 171-172.

[39] *Ibid.*

[40] *Monthly Return*, March, 1895. For a biographical sketch of W.L. "Lod" Calohan, a celebrated range detective for the politically powerful Texas & Southwestern Cattle Raisers Association, see, *The Cattleman*, August 1932, P. 28. And see, *Transcript*, Bob Beverly to J. Evetts Haley, September 13, 1945. Courtesy, The Nita Stewart Haley Memorial Library and J. Evetts Haley History Center. Midland.

[41] *Ibid.* April, 1895.

[42] *Ibid.* May, 1895.

[43] *Ibid.* June, 1895. It should be noted that on June 30, 1895, the fugitive Martin Mrose was killed by officers during a midnight crossing from Mexico into Texas.

[44] *Ibid.* July, 1895.

[45] *Ibid.* Whether or not the arrested subjects were planning to commit a train robbery is problematic, but the three arrested were listed on the *Monthly Return* as Valdez, Yargonio, and Solis, no first names. Sitter locked all three in the Val Verde County Jail at Del Rio, Texas.

[46] *Ibid.* September, 1895.

[47] *Ibid.* January, 1896.

[48] *Ibid.* March, 1896.

[49] *Ibid.* July, 1896.

[50] *Ibid.* October, 1896.

[51] *Ibid.*

[52] *Ibid.* Texas Rangers R.E. Bryant and George H. Tucker were also discharged during the month of October, 1896.

[53] Utley, Robert M., *Lone Star Justice—The First Century of the Texas Rangers.* P. 229. At the time of its inception in 1874 the authorized strength of the Frontier Battalion was 450 men, a figure in every respect too ambitious to actually fund from public coffers. An innovative, although controversial, approach was rationalized to fill the gap between wishful thinking and real dollars. The solution was creation of a category of "Special Rangers," not financed by the state, but paid for from monies furnished by various special interest groups, such as the Texas & Southwestern Cattle Raisers Association, the Railroads, Oil companies, or in certain cases simply as political favoritism. Today, in the twenty-first century, although the specific allocations have been significantly reduced to a more manageable number, there are still "Special Rangers" performing law enforcement tasks in Texas, answering to and paid wholly by private employers.

[54] *Application for Special Ranger Appointment*, dated December 7, 1896, signed, "Joe Sitter." (TRHF&M)

[55] *Ibid.* And see, Means, P. 171. "At that time his (Sitter) civilian occupation was listed as a cowboy. Thus, with the special ranger commission and authority, he was able to arrest any rustler he caught."

[56] *Monthly Return*, Company D, Frontier Battalion, May 31, 1898. (TSLAC)

[57] *Ibid.*

[58] *Ibid.* June, 1898.

[59] *Ibid.* July, 1898; August, 1898; September, 1898;

[60] *Ibid.* November, 1898; December, 1898; January, 1899.

[61] *Ibid.* February, 1899. The actual investigation began with Joe Sitter's departure on January 28th.

[62] *Ibid.* May, 1899. "Joe Sitter was discharged May 13th." Means, P. 171, reports that Joe Sitter joined the U.S. Customs Service on May 1, 1899. The author is most likely correct, the entry on the *Monthly Return* being the date Joe Sitter was dropped from the Frontier Battalion payroll, although he had earlier made the commitment to Customs.

[63] Fox, P. 20. "When a chance came to go into the Customs Inspection work, Dad chose that because the salary was more, twice as large, I believe."

[64] Michaels, P. 22; Cox, P. 137; Fox, P. 20.

[65] Cox, P. 138.

[66] Cano, Tony & Sochat, Ann, *Bndido, The True Story of Chico Cano, the Last Western Bandit.* "Chico was able to outsmart his adversaries most of the time, crossing the Rio Grande at will, and crossing political barriers as well, to join different revolutionary groups in fighting—depending upon who was in power at any give time. Chico was a bandit, not a patriot, and had no qualms about jumping sides, having done so various times." P. 16. And see, Tyler, Ronnie C., *The Big Bend, A History Of The Last Texas Frontier.* "Chico Cano had been terrorizing the Big Bend for years." P. 162. Also see, Martin, P. 184. "The Chico Cano gang of smugglers, whose stronghold lay in the mountains across the river from El Porvenir..." And, Smithers, W.D., *Chronicles of the Big Bend—A Photographic Memoir Of Life On The Border,* "...Chico Cano and his band of bandits..." P. 36. Also see, Cox. "Though revolution was raging in Mexico, the Cano brothers adroitly sided themselves with whomever happened to be prevailing at the time. They were outlaws, not patriots." P. 138.

[67] Cox, P. 139.

[68] *Application For Employment* as a United States Mounted Customs Inspector, for Jack Howard, dated December 21, 1901. Courtesy, Charles L. Wright, U.S. Customs, Presidio, Texas.

[69] Narratives mentioning these three officers apprehension of Chico Cano are legion and a reasonable cross-section are cited in this, the chapter endnotes. For a remarkable and less often cited source refer to, Kieffe, Glenna D. "Finis: The Final Entry," *Customs Today,* Fall 1990. This first-rate piece regarding the death of Jack Howard is in large part based on the story of Howard's wife, who made the final entries in Howard's daily journal so that their two daughters would have the story preserved. Interestingly, the journals are contained in the Archives of the Big Bend collections, Sul Ross University, Alpine, Texas. Copy in author's possession. Also see, Wright, Charles L., "A Western Tragedy," *Customs Today,* Fall 1992, for another excellently penned perspective, written by a Custom's Inspector. For more precise data regarding J.A. "Ad" Harvick, see, *The Cattleman,* July 1953. P. 66.

[70] Keil, Robert, *Bosque Bonito, Violent Times Along the Borderland During the Mexican Revolution.* Map following page 34. Other accounts sometimes place Porvenir on the Texas side of the Rio Grande and Pilares on the Mexican side. See, Smithers, W.D., *Chronicles of the Big Bend.* Map frontpiece. Means identifies both villages with counterparts on each side of the Rio Grande. P. xxiv & xxv. For the purpose of this story any geographical argument is outstandingly moot, in light of the larger calamity of Joe Sitter's captivating story.

[71] Means, P. 35. Also, Cox. P. 139. And see, Cano & Sochat, P. 56.

[72] Cox, P. 140.

[73] Cano & Sochat, P. 56-57. And see, Means, P. 35.

[74] *Ibid.* Generally those writing from base material supplied by old-timers' anecdotal stories—predominately Mexicans and Mexican-Americans—tend to be more critical of Joe Sitter than do journalists highlighting early day Texas Ranger tales, which is where much of the *published* foundation data is to be found. Martin, offers a completely different version of Cano's capture, "...when they flushed a half dozen horsemen in the mountains near the river. They gave chase and captured one of the six when his pony fell. He proved to be Chico Cano." P. 184. Jacobson, Lucy Miller & Nored, Mildred Bloys, *Jeff Davis County, Texas,* credit Sitter with the arrest of others besides Chico Cano, "They succeeded in capturing Chico Cano and two of his henchmen, however the rest of his band

escaped." The "other two" are not named. P. 206. One primary source document
adds, besides Cano, another to the list. "…these officers had arrested two
Mexican smugglers and were taking them to Marfa to Jail…," *Letter*, J.A. Harvin,
Collector of Customs, Eagle Pass, Texas to Secretary of the Treasury,
Washington, D. C. February 14, 1913. National Archives, Washington, D. C.
Seemingly not written elsewhere, this report states that during the attempt to free
Cano, the secreted riflemen, who fired from twenty to twenty-five rounds, killed
the other prisoner during the volley. Fox opts for Martin's version, "They saw six
riders dash toward the mountains. The Americans lashed their horses and chased
the Mexicans. One horse fell and sprawled his rider, Chico Cano. Sitters (sic)
grabbed the Mexican and pulled away his firearms…" P. 69. Thankfully, for the
objective historian, there is a plethora of heretofore untapped primary source
material available, and the interested reader may draw his/her own conclusions
after thorough examination of all readily available data.

[75] Luke Dow, Deputy Collector of Customs to Collector of Customs, Eagle Pass,
Texas. February 15, 1913. Courtesy, National Archives, Washington. D. C.
[76] Cano & Sochat, P. 57.
[77] Deputy Collector of Customs Luke Dow to Collector of Customs, Eagle Pass,
Texas. The creditable weight awarded to Luke Dow's statement is somewhat
amplified by the fact he rushed to the scene of the shooting, arriving at 1:00
o'clock A. M on the 13th and interviewed Harvick and Sitter while the matter was
still fresh. For the name of Jack Howard's horse refer to Kieff, P. 20.
[78] *Ibid.*
[79] *Ibid.* Cano & Sochat report, "Sitters (sic) was the first target of the resecuers,
because they knew that he would shoot to kill Chico if he got the slightest
chance." P. 58. The primary source document seems less imbued with a lopsided
tilt, simply stating, "Simultaneously with the firing on Howard, Sitter and Harvick
were fired on and both shot from their horses.."
[80] *Ibid.* Some secondary reports indicate Howard was killed outright, an honest
but, nevertheless, error.
[81] *Ibid.* And see, *Telegram*, Collector of Customs (J.A. Harvin), Eagle Pass,
Texas, to Secretary of the Treasury, Washington, D. C. February 12, 1913.
"Deputy collector Dowe reports from Valentine Howard shot through above heart
probably fatal. Sitter shot in head chance for recovery. Harvick cattle inspector
shot both legs not dangerous. Unable to get details Large posse have gone to
scene of trouble." National Archives, Justice Department Records. Washington,
D. C.
[82] U.S. Mounted Customs Inspector John Simpson "Jack" Howard's journals.
Courtesy, Archives of the Big Bend, Sul Ross University. Alpine, Texas.
[83] *Ibid.*
[84] *Ibid.* And see, Kieffe, P. 20. Also see, Wright, P. 6-9.
[85] Cox, P. 140.
[86] *Ibid.* P. 136.
[87] Bruce, Leona, *Banister Was There*, P. 155.
[88] Bruce, citing in entirety the report of John R. Banister, Chief Field Inspector,
Texas & Southwestern Cattle Raisers Association, from Candelaria, Texas, to
Association Secretary E. B. Spiller, Fort Worth, Texas. March 31, 1914. P. 156-
160.
[89] *Ibid.*
[90] *Ibid.*

[91] Luke Dow to The Collector of Customs, February 15, 1913.

[92] Cano & Sochat, P. 81.

[93] Jacobson & Nored, P. 208. The authors rightly cite source material, which in this case, was based solely on anecdotal remembrances of old-timers, many quite naturally repeating borderland stories as they had heard them passed by word of mouth, oral history. An out of hand discounting of the material is wholly inappropriate, likewise taking them strictly at face value, totally uncorroborated is equally perilous if, indeed, the goal remains a search for truth.

[94] See Chapter 12 for complete analysis of the Roberson/Boykin/Sitter shootings and citations to sources contained in endnotes. Also see, Alexander, Bob, *Fearless Dave Allison—Border Lawman.* P. 166-169.

[95] Captain James Monroe Fox, Company B, Ranger Force, Marfa, Texas to Texas Adjutant General, Austin, Texas, May 27, 1915. Courtesy, Texas State Library and Archives. Austin. Charles A. Craighead was born August 26, 1879, near Sutherland Springs, Wilson County, Texas. He served not only as a U.S. Mounted Customs Inspector, but also as a Texas Ranger, United States Deputy Marshal and an Inspector with the Texas & Southwestern Cattle Raisers Association. See, Gilliand, Maude T, *Wilson County Texas Rangers.* P. 121. Texas Ranger E. B. Hulen, born at Gainesville, Cooke County, Texas, with no prior law enforcement experience enlisted in the Texas Rangers at Austin, Texas on March 29, 1915. Courtesy, Texas Ranger Hall of Fame and Museum. (TRHF&M). Waco. H.C. Trollinger was born during 1878 at Bedford County, Tennessee. He first enlisted in the Texas Rangers in 1915 and was promoted to Sergeant of December 15, 1917. (TRHF&M)

[96] Jacobson & Nored, P. 209. Quoting an account made by the surviving members of the posse, cited to source, "The Killing of Ranger Hulen and Inspector Sitters," *Voice of the Mexican Border Centennial Edition,* 1936.

[97] *Ibid.* And see, United States Marshal John H. Rogers, Western District of Texas, Austin to Attorney General, Washington, D. C., May 29, 1915, places the site of the ambush as, "about 8 miles east of Pilares, near the Rio Grande in Presidio County, and about 40 miles in a southerly direction from Valentine and about 60 miles in a westerly direction from Marfa:" Courtesy, National Archives. Washington, D. C. For a biography of John R. Rogers, a former Texas Ranger Captain, see, Spellman, Paul N., *Captain John H. Rogers, Texas Ranger.*

[98] *Ibid.*

[99] Fox to Adjutant General, May 27, 1915. (TSL&A)

[100] *Ibid.*

[101] Cox, P. 141. Most all accounts, secondary and primary, indicate that Craighead, Cummings and Trollinger tried five times to reunite with Sitter and Hulen.

[102] Jacobson & Nored, P. 209. And see, Cox, P. 14l. "The officers had no way of knowing if the silence meant their colleagues had escaped, or been captured or killed."

[103] Fox to Adjutant General, May 27, 1915. (TSL&A)

[104] *Ibid.* "After walking all day, Craighead, Trollinger and Cummings, found a Mexican who carried a note to Pool's Ranch asking for help." And see, Webb, Walter Prescott, *The Texas Rangers, A Century of Frontier Defense.* P. 498.

[105] Webb, P. 499. Quoting Wadsworth's testimony.

[106] Jacobson & Nored, P. 209. "There were between 30 and 35 men in the band of Mexicans." And see, Webb, P. 499. Also see, Cox, P. 142.

The Mule Puked

Fox, P. 70. "The men carefully lifted the naked bodies on Pack mules and carried them out of bleak Pilares Canyon." Also see, Webb. P. 499.

[108] Webb, P. 499. "The men recall that the pack-mule on which the custom inspector's body was carried became sick and vomited." Also see, Fox. P. 70. "This stark tragedy affected not only the Rangers, but even the pack mules, especially the one on which Sitter's body was carried, for the poor animal became sick along the trail." And see, Cox, P. 143. "On the way back to the Pool Ranch, the mule burdened with Sitter's body became sick and vomited." *Quien Sabe?*

[109] Cano & Sochat. P. 81. And interview with Jake Sitters, the grandson of Joe Sitter.

[110] *Ibid.* Also see, J. L. Camp, United States Attorney, Western District of Texas, San Antonio, Texas to The Attorney General, Washington, D. C. June 5, 1915. "It is the general impression that this is the same band that killed Inspector Jack Howard about two years ago. " And, United States Marshal John H. Rogers, Austin, Texas to The Attorney General, Washington, D. C. May 29, 1915. "It is the general opinion that this crime was committed by what is known as the Cano gang of outlaws." Courtesy, National Archives, Washington, D. C.

[111] *Ibid.*

CHAPTER 11

"I SHOT AT THEM TWICE WITH A SIX-SHOOTER"

William D. "Keechi" Johnson, Extraordinary Manhunter

Not many Old West aficionados are geographically familiar with Keechi Creek. Likewise, few Old West readers have heard of Southwest lawman, William D. "Keechi" Johnson. While lesser lawmen, and less interesting Western characters, had books written about them, Keechi Johnson was largely forgotten. His compelling story needs telling, at least in abbreviated form.

William D. "Keechi" Johnson, Grant County, New Mexico Territory, deputy sheriff and noted man-tracker. Courtesy, Roy B. Sinclair.

I Shot At Them Twice With A Six-Shooter

Keechi Creek is in Texas. Its headwaters leach to the surface in that rough and broken country south of Jacksboro, Jack County, not too far from the picket-post shadows of old Fort Richardson.[1] The region was home to Comanche raiders, buffalo hunters, and later cowboys and homesteaders, but just how Keechi Johnson got his nickname from a watercourse is not known..[2]

William D. "Keechi" Johnson was born sometime during December, 1855, in the Yellowhammer State, Alabama.[3] Keechi Johnson, at some point along life's journey learned his reading, writing, and arithmetic, at least so a United States census enumerator was advised and, when chronologically proper, an examination of Keechi's writing skills and overall business acumen offers undisputed confirmation.[4] And too, it seems Keechi Johnson had a little more on his youthful mind than book learnin' and career choices, for while yet a strapping young stalwart he married a girl from North Carolina, his beloved Carolyn, though she was better known to family and friends simply as, Carrie.[5] For whatever reason, the young couple left the southeastern United States, fortuitously chancing their way to the Lone Star State, sometime prior to the birth of their first born son, Don, in 1880. Interestingly, Jack County, organized in 1857, was named after William H. and Patrick C. Jack, who had managed the migration from North Carolina by way of Alabama, the very birthplaces of Keechi and his wife.[6] Coincidence? The two spent at lest some time settled in the area of Jack County, where Keechi Creek meandered, and that's where young Johnson was likely saddled with the sobriquet, "Keechi." Factually, however, it can be rightly reported the Johnson's handled a trip to Taylor County, Texas, and it was at agreeable Abilene that they made their most enduring home. By the time she was thirty-seven years old Carrie Johnson had given birth to three sons, the aforementioned Don, then Tyra in 1883, followed seven years later by Hollis. In between the younger boys precious daughter Zora was born and, after the last of the lads, baby sister Ora arrived in West Texas during late Spring of 1892.[7]

At this juncture Keechi Johnson wasn't leading an awe-inspiring life. Emphatically, Keechi was no six-shooter man; he didn't even carry one. Alas, he was simply a house painter and wall-paper hanger—a damn good one too.[8] So good in fact, he adroitly attracted an opportunistic business partner and the two entrepreneurs, sometime around the Spring of 1891, expanded operations over to New Mexico Territory at what was then thriving Eddy, but now it's called Carlsbad. Eddy, a flourishing transitional village, was "building up rapidly" and to the casual observer she was economically outgrowing her municipal britches. In theory a perfect location for selling colorful paint products, skillfully sub-contracting, and nimbly plastering designed wallpaper.[9] Stir a little hardware business into the capitalistic mix and the recipe for success was assured.[10] While it lasted! Unfortunately, "times became less lively" and Keechi Johnson moved further west, to old Grant County and the booming burg of Silver City, where once more he engaged in the business of painting and hanging paper. There is no evidence of marital disharmony, but for whatever the reason, Carrie and most of the children maintained residence on Abilene's pleasant Walnut Street, while Keechi was industrially engaged in New Mexico Territory; for much of his time away from home he was accompanied by his oldest son, Don.[11]

While working at nearby Pinos Altos, Keechi Johnson built an intimate friendship which, in the end, amended his life. At the turn of the century James K. Blair was elected sheriff.[12] He was considered an exemplary officer.[13] However, when he turned to his inexperienced and untested personal friend, Keechi Johnson, commissioning him as his "principal" or "riding" deputy, several predicted Sheriff Blair had made a poor choice. Many a man had been recklessly gunned down at Silver City or at one of her fractious mountain suburbs; it was dangerous for a veteran, let alone a rookie deputy sheriff. Within but a short time though, the newly appointed lawman exposed the fiber he was rightly made from and earned a straightforward reputation as being "safe, faithful and efficient."[14] If truth be told, Keechi Johnson apparently had an innate knack for detective work and owned striking fugitive hunting talents, and before too very long it was correctly reported that once it "became known that Deputy Sheriff Johnson started after a man, his arrest would surely follow."[15] An old-timer who personally knew Keechi extolled his finesse at the man-huntin' craft, "You could depend on (Keechi)... If there was anything you (were) wanted (for)…you were liable to see old Keechi…Because he'd just come up…He was just as slouchy as an old tramp but when he came along…*he arrived.* Now, that was all there was to it!…He usually went by himself too."[16] Keechi Johnson didn't have a crystal ball; had he, most likely he wouldn't have had time to glimpse into the future. But 1900 was shaping up to be one heck of a year for man-tracking.

Throughout the frontier west, sheriffs and deputies had been forced to suffer dreadful headaches as unfortunate consequence for assuming roles as keepers of their respective county jails.[17] The Grant County jail at Silver City, although there is yet to be published an exacting tally, may very well have earned the dubious distinction as being the Wild West's most porous calaboose. "Jail deliveries" from this particular lockup border on the epidemic, but rightfully, it must be made clear that no one sheriff was forced to undergo the discomfiture and humiliation alone; the professional misery was evenly disbursed.[18]

Grant County Sheriff James K. "Jim" Blair, William D. "Keechi" Johnson's personal friend and professional employer. Courtesy, Frank Blair.

On Wednesday, February 21st, 1900, five prisoners, *unbelievably* still maintaining personal possession of their pocketknives, sawed, cut, or hacked their way through and enlarged a wooden window sill and promptly jumped out of the Grant County lockup. Riding, racing, or running off toward a setting sun were horse and cattle stealers Willie Jobe and Frank Woods. Three others, Pedro Aragas, James Godfrey and John Ray were in point of fact just plain thieves.[19] Sheriff James K. Blair hastily fashioned a posse, including Keechi Johnson, and the manhunt was pressed.[20] The *Silver City Enterprise* says the scalawags were, at last, jammed up and deputy sheriff William D. "Keechi" Johnson was credited with the daring apprehension.[21] Rounding up this flock of particular jailbirds was, for the most part, relatively easy work.

Perhaps it had been a preliminary heat, a warm-up and portentous forewarning of things to come. Keechi Johnson's next manhunt would prove to be a grueling monument to tenacity, a tormenting test of pure physical resilience, an example of unflinching personal audacity and, ultimately, the state of affairs would call for delicate international diplomacy.

Whether or not Keechi Johnson and Sheriff Blair took in the sights at Santa Fe is indeterminate; certainly the seven prisoners they were hauling didn't. They, instead, were delivered to Holm O. Bursum, Superintendent, Territorial Penitentiary.[22] Abruptly, any pleasantness linked to the officer's excursion was canceled. On March 28, 1900, while at the territorial capitol, lawmen Blair and Johnson received the distressing news, during their absence again prisoners from the Grant County jail were on the loose. At once the law enforcers departed for Silver City.[23] By 12:00 o'clock high, next day, they were back home and flabbergasted at what they learned.[24]

At first it was rumored local prisoners had fashioned a key from a pewter spoon, but the assertion turned out to be mere gossip, as unfussy reality later revealed the "delivery" had been effortlessly pulled off due to uncomplicated negligence. Six wily jailbirds had simply unfastened the cage door and fluttered away.[25] Naturally, Sheriff Blair and Chief Deputy Johnson, too, learned that a hurriedly formed posse was already in the field, including Keechi's twenty year old son, Don.[26] Undoubtedly Keechi had cause for concern. Two of the escapees were considered pretty tough customers.

No one was too bothered about the loss of inmates Frank Harvey and George Brown, in fact, a newspaperman adroitly wrote the two "were tramps, whose absence was more desired than their presence."[27] Two of the other brigands, of course, were not to be haphazardly dealt with, but the search for cow-thief Delbert O'Neal and an ordinary thief, Robert Bisbee, was not thought to be an overly risky task.[28] The two remaining Grant County owl-hoots, well, that was a different story.

George Stevenson had been in lockup as a result of killing an innocuous gambler, Billy Woods, at Santa Rita after a wild night of drinking and general hell-raising.[29] The dead man was well-liked and Stevenson showed no remorse.[30] The other escapee, James Brooks, was lazily whittling away time in jail as result of his stealing a stock-saddle from J. T. Rabb, but he wasn't just a petty thief. During 1898 he had "figured prominently" in a murder at Cook's Peak, but the case had later been dismissed due to insufficient evidence. And too, although his clear-cut role remains clouded, some way he was tangled up in a Las Cruces, New Mexico Territory bank robbery—mired in the mess well-enough to snitch on two boys from San Antonio, Texas—thereby serving as the catalyst for "their detection and arrests."[31] Clearly, George Stevenson and James Brooks were not men to take lightly, and Keechi's fatherly worry for his son's attachment to the hard-ridin' posse is understandable.

Keechi couldn't idly stand by. Accompanied by Grant County deputy Miles Marshall, Keechi Johnson directed his efforts toward tracking and trailing the fugitives. Luckily, Delbert O'Neal had been captured in the vicinity of Cow Springs, south of Silver City, by "one of the deputies working under George Scarborough" representing the Grant County Cattlemen's Association.[32] Keechi and Miles thereafter profitably tracked Robert Bisbee to the Frost Ranch on March 30th, finding him "perched behind a water tank" and, by hook or by crook, somehow he had nimbly armed himself with an "ugly looking Winchester."[33] Upon spying the approaching mounted officers, trifling Bob Bisbee took off on foot, making a witlessly mad-dash, scarily brandishing the pilfered lever-gun and, for a moment, it seemed he might really outdistance the lawmen and make it to nearby foothills, that is, until they each took aim and deftly dropped some rifle balls in front of the breathless *mal hombre*. Robert Bisbee, after vainly begging the no nonsense peace officers to forgo the formality of handcuffing him, unconditionally surrendered.[34] With two of the jailbirds returned to the coop, and nobody up in arms regarding the liberating flight of two others, attention was quickly focused on reclaiming George Stevenson and James Brooks, and perhaps clipping more than just their wings. Plainly, it should have turned out to be a routine manhunt. It didn't. Moreover, it proved to be a problematical and knotty mess.

At the very same time southwestern New Mexico Territory lawmen were fishing about for consequential clues or conclusive tracks left by Stevenson and Brooks, over in Arizona Territory, just across the borderline, a very sad story was playing out. On April 3rd a well-known Southwest lawman, George A. Scarborough, the man who killed the notorious "Uncle" John Selman at El Paso, Texas, four years earlier, was himself gunned down by cleverly concealed bushwackers.[35] After a wretchedly long night, at long last, the suffering George Scarborough was protectively removed to his home at Deming, but sorrowfully on April 5th, he died.[36]

Furious posses from both Arizona and New Mexico territories were ferociously combing the countryside trying to nab the murderers. Deputies Keechi Johnson and Miles Marshall were members of the pack of human bloodhounds. Not just a few cogitating laymen and several bewildered lawmen thought George Stevenson and James Brooks could have been the guilty culprits—

Lawmen, Outlaws and S.O.Bs.

the killers of Scarborough. As it happens, they weren't; nevertheless, they were still very much wanted fugitives. Picking up critical intelligence that Stevenson and Brooks had crossed the Southern Pacific tracks near Separ, a railroad depot between Deming and Lordsburg, Keechi Johnson and Miles Marshall peeled off from the others and spotlighted their notice on the desperate duo, attentively snooping for the "correct trail."[37] The surveyor's precisely sighted line dividing Old Mexico from New Mexico meant little to Keechi Johnson. Both he and Miles were by now exhaustively won over to but one notion; they had cut the "correct trail" and were rightfully stalking the proper prey. They had the scent! Implications of worrisome international politics weren't even measured. George Stevenson and James Brooks were headed south, so too, were Keechi Johnson and Miles Marshall and, if need be, higher authorities could sort it out later. Over tortuous topography, deeper and deeper into a foreign land the two deputies probed, 145 miles or so.[38] Strength of mind and gut wrenching days in the saddle paid off. Keechi Johnson explained in a letter addressed to Sheriff James Blair, who had fretfully been waiting at Silver City for any reliable news from his stanch deputies. The succinct epistle was unfalteringly hand-carried over the wearisome hundred-plus mile back-trail to the international borderline by a haggard but pleased Miles Marshall, and mailed from the U.S. Post Office nearest the worn-down lawdog's Mexican base camp, Naco, Arizona Territory:

> Dear Jim—I got a Mexican officer here and followed Brooks to Oputo, arrested him and started back with him. I found Stevenson on the road back here. I cannot place fugitive warrant before this judge here, so he says, but he has turned them over to me to hold until he can find out from the president of this district. So you hurry up some authority to hold them until you can secure the papers to extradite them. I will have to remain here to hold them on my own responsibility until I get further authority from the United States, so don't delay. Marshall will remain at San Bernardino until he gets news and instructions from you. You might telegraph Gov. Otero to get permission from the governor of Sonora State to hold for papers. It would reach me in two and one-half days from Montezuma, the governor's home. Yours Truly, W.D. Johnson.

> P. S.—They take the men from me and send them to Montezuma next week; the judge here has written to the President to know what to do with them. They may send them to Oputo the head of the district. W.D. J.[39]

I Shot At Them Twice With A Six-Shooter

From the best evidence at hand, certainly it seems the Mexican civil authorities were sympathetic of Keechi Johnson's somewhat flimsy law enforcement predicament. On the one hand he had effectively executed a bold strategy and ensnared a pair of highly hunted two-legged predators. On the other, however, he was stuck in the quagmire of a bureaucratic bog. At the time, if done legally, an international extradition was not commonplace and, in this instance, a brand new agreement between Mexico and the United States was to be tested.[40] Waltzing across the border was out of the question. Politicos were now intertwined in the machinations. While Keechi Johnson frustratingly killed time, waiting for the governmental pen pushers to give him the soothing clearance to go north, and after Miles Marshall had returned to help guard the prisoners, he offered an insight into the regimen of their dull days.

Initially, he held prisoners Stevenson and Brooks in a clammy underground tunnel while his notification to Sonora's Governor was proffered. Upon receipt of an official go-ahead to indefinitely detain the captives, they were then moved to a two-room adobe house, badguys in one room, good guys in the other. An added touch of security was tapped out when leg irons were riveted around the desperado's ankles. Fortunately, since guard duty was an around the clock chore, Keechi was able to hire a "Mexican police" for one watch at $3.00 per day. And too, because he and Miles had a "frying pan and two lard buckets" to cook with twice a day, Keechi proclaimed they were faring better than having to eat "frijoles y menudo" at a local no menu café. Disappointingly, since he was nearly a hundred miles from the American border, communication was a major hurdle, one that could not be remedied by recurrent trips to the international line;"our horses would not justify the trip." Clearly he blamed the intransigent George Stevenson for the dreary delay:"Stevenson don't think he can be touched. Brooks would have gone through without papers if Stevenson had not influenced him to stay." And, nonchalantly he mentioned the prisoners were whining about their detention and the subsequent holdup, bemoaning that the whole affair was "very monotonous," a sentiment Keechi may have very well shared. Other than an anticipated humdrum complaint about hot weather, Keechi and Miles appeared to be doing okay, remarking that financially they were "pretty well fixed," but did want to get clear of sweltering Mexico sometime before they went "defunct," but characteristically Keechi determinedly guaranteed, "We are here to stay until we get the fellows out."[41]

Somewhat atypically for border country matters, on this diplomatic occasion splendid cooperation was offered, and Mexican authorities showed "every disposition to assist the Grant County Deputies."[42] At long last it was over. Keechi Johnson and Miles Marshall, armed with six-shooters and Winchesters, but more importantly, with lawful extradition documents, duly chained their prisoners and set out for the arduous trip home.[43] Surprisingly, on the return journey over "rough country" no one knew the whereabouts of the party for three weeks, and because they were well overdue a distraught Sheriff Blair and other courthouse officials were "feeling uneasy."[44] Unbeknownst to fretful friends and worried citizens, Keechi and Miles had traveled almost "day and night until they reached Lordsburg" on June 19, 1900, and then obtained the services of J.M. Harper to drive them to Deming in a wagon, so they could make link with the Silver City, Deming and Pacific train. Upon arrival at Deming, the careworn cops determined that the "connections were unfavorable" and they "concluded to finish the trip overland."[45] After their eventual arrival at Silver City the troublesome prisoners were slammed in the jail under tight guard and the two deputies were awarded their long unpaid adulation from a truthfully thankful public, who took note that it had been "one of the longest pursuits ever made by a local officer."[46] Another newspaperman plainly declared, "no greater task has ever been undertaken by any officer of the County and none was ever more faithfully performed."[47] Keechi Johnson and Miles Marshall had been gone just short of three months. Indisputably the prickly chase had been a rousing law enforcement assignment and a personally punishing ordeal, yet, as previously pointed out, 1900 was to be one hell-of-a man-tracking year. It was still summertime!

Silver City more or less sprawled out from *La Cienega De San Vicente*, a low, marshy spot and by nature delightfully charming.[48] The brash mountain country just to her north however is rough country, a seemingly endless expanse of mountain and canyon that would one day become the nation's first designated wilderness area.

Predictably though, lurking in mountain shadows were just a few tough frontier spirits stubbornly preoccupied with eking out a living in that forlorn Mogollon country, either chasing riches underground, chipping away in a chancy mine or running after wild cow-creatures on the topside, above ground. Into the upper Gila headwaters one clan arrived with a plan.[49] "The Jenks boys had acquired a few cattle and ranged them in that area. In the summer of 1900 some cattle had been stolen from northern Grant County and there was much suspicion that these boys were implicated."[50] Their nefarious cow-stealing and brand-defacing schemes in due course hurdled any legalistic qualms, and officially authorized papers were placed in the hands of deputy sheriff William D. "Keechi" Johnson.[51]

Gathering up his camp gear, mounting his best saddle-horse, and good-naturedly hallooing for his tough-as-nails partner, Miles Marshall, to "hustle up," deputy sheriff Keechi Johnson straightaway made tracks, north, into the ominous looking Mogollons. It was August 16, 1900. The vigorous duo worked their way through craggy canyons, over mountain hogbacks, and about sharply defined precipices, seventy-five miles or so, all the while neatly poking around, cutting for meaningful sign. For four trying days and four bone-chilling nights—it was cold in the high country after dark— they hunted. In that incredibly lonesome Upper Gila section, the unbendable officers finally picked up what they each thought were the cow-thieving gangster's trace, but all too quickly, it split. Temporarily fine-tuning strategy the deputies doubled back a short way and rightfully sought help. Upon returning to the fork in the trail, Keechi Johnson and rancher W.Z. Redding went one way, Miles Marshall and cowman P.M. Shelly, the other.[52] Providentially for Miles Marshall and his neophyte deputy, the once promising looking brand-blotcher's tracks fizzled out, and the pair grudgingly negotiated their way back to Silver City.[53]

William Zachary "Zack" Redding, a Gila River country New Mexico rancher and an ally of "Keechi" Johnson in the hunt for cattle rustling suspect Ralph Jenks. Courtesy Dave Johnson.

Lawmen, Outlaws and S.O.Bs.

In some ways explicit details are sketchy, but not surprisingly Keechi Johnson at a point along the Gila's West Fork faithfully executed court-papers and arrested twenty-five year old Ralph Jenks, "one of the principals leaders of the gang of rustlers" which were infecting the region.[54] With Jenks in tow, Redding returned to his ranch, and Keechi Johnson, depending on which version is chosen, either headed out looking for some more of Jenk's clan, or, started for Silver City and dinner at the dungeon. A smidgen of historical haziness is acknowledged, but by each and every account there is accord—deputy Keechi Johnson and defendant to be Ralph Jenks were a long way from anywhere.

Alongside an invigorating mountain tributary, White Creek, deputy Keechi Johnson on the morning of August 27th, went to the front, taking the lead, leaving an annoyed Ralph Jenks in the rear, delegated to prodding along the troublesome packhorse.[55] Approaching the head of Raw Meat Creek, Keechi saw two riders, one riding a gray, the other forking a roan, angling in his direction, that is, until they espied him. Right away the furtive horsebackers spun and hightailed it over a shielding ridge. Keechi gave an immediate galloping chase, gruffly demanding three times, "Hold up." Purportedly, crying out one time, "Hold on, John!" While skirting on the side of a hill, shots rang out and bullets knocked Keechi Johnson to the ground. One bullet had shattered his left leg below the knee, another had wickedly punched through his left arm and "ranged upward, coming out the left side of his neck." During the touchy life or death mêlée Keechi had managed to pop two caps, and later proclaimed, "I shot at them twice with a six shooter but I do not know whether I hit them or not." Ralph Jenks, who may have wisely hesitated during the gunbattle, after a few minutes rushed to Keechi's side. Following the lawman's whispered commands, Ralph Jenks extracted two spent hulls from Keechi's Colt's revolver, refilling the cylinder with fresh loads, and allegedly returned the Peacemaker to the severely injured deputy. Unable to travel a forty mile mountain trail to the mining settlement of Mogollon, and suffering terribly, Keechi told Ralph Jenks to catch his horse, remove his battered Winchester from the saddle scabbard, and place it beside him. Keechi then directed Jenks to speedily make tracks for the nearest ranch, send back someone to remain with him, and continue on until he could secure the services of a back-country physician. Compassionately, accused cow-thief Ralph Jenks pulled out a goatskin water-bag and tendered it to Keechi, and then from the packs retrieved some old clothes and kindheartedly placed them beneath Keechi's head before audaciously departing on his mission of mercy. This is how Ralph Jenks, the only eyewitness, told the story.[56]

Promptly Jenks hazarded an agonizing journey to the Ross Ranch five miles above the previously mentioned Redding Ranch. At the former, he obediently detailed Keechi Johnson's dire dilemma, reporting he was headed for Mogollon to prudently notify lawful authorities, Socorro County Deputy Sheriff Foster and local Justice of the Peace, James Kerr. Apparently, on the way Ralph Jenks made a detour, contacted his brother Roy, and it was he, who actually carried news of the tragedy to Mogollon. Simultaneously, with due speed after his hearing the appalling news, cowman W.Z. Redding was soon riding for Silver City, via Pinos Altos, to echo the heartrending alarm. [57]

Psychoanalyzing Keechi Johnson's thought processes while his head rested on that pile of smelly and rumpled clothes is futile. By the time Mogollons' resident county officials were "piloted" to the crime scene by Ralph Jenks, William D. "Keechi" Johnson was mournfully dead. After the mandated inquest, the coroner's jury on the 29th day of August, 1900, buried Keechi beneath an enchanting clump of trees on the north side of the trail, in what was thereafter deferentially christened, Johnson Canyon.[58]

Jenk's cabin, deep in the mysterious Mogollon Mountains north of Silver City. The mounted rider left of the abode is undetermined. Courtesy, Silver City Public Library.

The news of two Grant County area lawmen both being mercilessly waylaid within such a short time period had the surrounding community incensed:

Lawmen, Outlaws and S.O.Bs.

His (Keechi) loss, as was the killing of Ranger Scarborough, only a few weeks ago and in similar manner, is a cause for universal regret and sorrow throughout the County and Territory; for no better, no braver and not truer officers in the faithful performances of dangerous duties ever held a commission to look after the protection of property, the preservation of life and the bringing to justice of outlaws and evil doers in this or any other county, than George Scarborough and Deputy Sheriff Johnson, whose deaths have occurred so closely together and in each instance by ambush and shots from the hands of outlaws and desperadoes who are already a menace to thieves and property of all honest citizens in this and adjoining country.[59]

Ralph Jenk's story didn't set well. Not when it was repeated to Sheriff Jim Blair, to Keechi's number one son, Don Johnson, and to Ed Scarborough, son of the deceased George A. Scarborough. And too, not just a few were surmising they knew the truth and "...disbelieve the story entirely, thinking the matter a hoax pure and simple, and that Jenks taking advantage of the deputy's being alone, overpowered him, when off his guard in watching for the other outlaws, and managed to make his escape."[60] Others speculated that when Keechi latched on to Ralph, his brother Roy "took a roundabout trail to a point where he knew they would have to pass and, by fast riding, was there upon their arrival (and) he shot and killed the deputy."[61] Gumming up the works was the fact that but a short time earlier hijackers had robbed the Helen Mining Company's store at nearby Graham, New Mexico Territory, just down Whitewater Creek from Mogollon.[62] The three owl-hoots, J.C. Gibson, Jack Davis, and John Ward, all from Globe, Arizona Territory, just west of New Mexico Territory's Mule Creek, neglected in their foolish scheming, however, to take note that besides foodstuffs and bolts of calico, the store housed a U.S. Post Office, elevating the callous offense to a federal court level.[63] Unquestionably outlaws were scorching about throughout the isolated and sparsely inhabited region. So too, were peace officers and overwrought mountain country denizens, many afraid for their very lives. Rumors were fallaciously flying. A local newshound working for the *Silver City Independent* went so far as to suppose that Keechi's calling out the name "John" was because it rightly belonged on one of the suspected robbers from Arizona Territory, John Ward.[64] *Quien Sabe*? Grant County's top lawman, Sheriff Jim Blair, didn't need his sights adjusted, he was locked on target, zeroing in on Ralph Jenks.

I Shot At Them Twice With A Six-Shooter

Blair sent a surreptitious message to Deputy Foster at Mogollon to please arrest Ralph and Henry (Harry) Reinheart, one of the Jenks brothers' pals. He did.[65] Ralph Jenks tried to cry foul. Droning out a plea for sympathy in a handy letter to a Silver City newspaper editor, Ralph Jenks denied being in Keechi Johnson's custody, "...Mr. Johnson had taken all my cartridges. I was not under arrest as some suppose, but was going with him to show him my cattle for which he had a search warrant to inspect. He told me some cattle had been stolen from the upper part of Grant County and that he was looking for them. When he was shot he was fully 600 or 800 feet from where I was holding the packhorse...I had no gun and could do nothing but take a strong hint not to go further. If I had done so I am sure the next shot would have done me, as the man who was shooting was a dead shot. I was simply an accidental witness to the affair..."[66] Not too many folks believed him.[67]

William D. "Keechi" Johnson's grave, near Raw Meat Creek in the Gila Wilderness, fortified and protected from encroaching animals. Johnson Canyon in named in honor of "Keechi." Courtesy, Silver City Public Library.

The next chapter in the Old West narrative rightfully belongs to Ed Scarborough and his biographer, but a laid-back blurb is obligatory for putting Keechi Johnson's gripping story in the wraps. At Mogollon, Sheriff Blair divided his posse, one bunch taking off in search of Ralph's brother, Roy, the other squadron transporting Ralph Jenks and Harry Reinhart back for a visit with the Blind

Lawmen, Outlaws and S.O.Bs.

Mistress of Justice at Silver City. On the trip back, riding along Duck Creek at 9 o'clock P.M., Ralph Jenks irrationally grabbed Ed Scarborough's shotgun from its leather scabbard, and frantically fumbled as he tried to chamber a round. Unflappably, Ed told him to drop the scattergun, he didn't, and Scarborough unlimbered his six-shooter and shot him three times, "twice in the breast and once in the head..."[68] Ralph Jenks, needless to say, fell over—doornail dead.[69]

Not unexpectedly, as was the case with nearly all thorny Western killings, public sentiment was to some extent divided, one partisan side categorically justifying the shooting of Ralph Jenks, the other equating it with an act of vengeful murder. Routinely, Ed Scarborough was forced to tilt with the criminal justice system, but, in the end, Judge Parker "instructed the jury to bring in a verdict of not guilty, which they did without leaving their seats."[70] Ironically the two revered lawmens' sons, Don Johnson and Ed Scarborough, continued their constabulary type careers. Both men were enthusiastically enlisted as charter members (1901) when the territory of Arizona shaped a peace keeping force of rangers. Shortly thereafter the two young men parted professional company, physically and philosophically. Don Johnson, after Luna County was carved from Grant County in March, 1901, later became its sheriff and, yet still after that, was the kingpin police officer for El Paso, and finally, ended his lengthy law enforcement career by distinguished service as Chief of Police at Monterey Park, California. Ed Scarborough, well, he went to prison, escaped, and idled away his misspent life—somewhere.[71]

Following cautioned, but reasonably impartial historical analysis there could still be room for friendly disagreement as to the strict gory details about Keechi's last manhunt and untimely demise. Many a secret remains in the mute Mogollons. There are, however, in this instance two historic truisms. William D. Johnson wasn't a braggadocios man, and as that venerable old-timer recalled, "...if you were wanted...you were liable to see old Keechi...when he came along...*he arrived.* Now, that was all there was to it!"

I Shot At Them Twice With A Six-Shooter

ENDNOTES CHAPTER 11

"I SHOT AT THEM TWICE WITH A SIX-SHOOTER"

[1] *Handbook of Texas Online*, a joint project of The General Libraries at the University of Texas at Austin and the Texas State Historical Association. And see, *The Roads of Texas*, Jack County, P. 50. Also see, *Texas Almanac, 1994-1995.* P. 223. Keechi Creek in West Texas should not be confused with Upper and Lower Keechi Branch in Central Texas. That the subject of this narrative was a West Texas product is confirmed through family history interviews with descendants.

[2] *Silver City Enterprise*, August 31, 1900. "...familiarly known and called 'Keechi', which name originated from his having lived many years on the Keechi river in Texas..."

[3] Twelfth Census of the United States, 1900, Abilene, Taylor County, Texas.

[4] *Ibid.*

[5] *Ibid.* In actuality Keechi's wife Carrie was several months older than her husband. And, interview with Louise Hearn Sinclair, granddaughter of William D. "Keechi" Johnson. May 24, 2002.

[6] Gournay, Luke. *Texas Boundaries, Evolution of the State's Counties.* P. 70.

[7] Twelfth Census of the United States, 1900, Abilene, Taylor County, Texas.

[8] *Ibid.* And see, *Silver City Enterprise*, August 31, 1900. "...engaged in selling paints, wall paper, etc, and doing painting."

[9] *Silver City Enterprise*, August 31, 1900. Also see, Julyan, Robert. *The Place Names of New Mexico.* P. 63-64. "Carlsbad originally had the same name as the county for which it is the seat—*Eddy.*"

[10] Interview with Roy B. Sinclair, Jr., May, 23, 2002. Mr. Sinclair is a great grandson of William D. "Keechi" Johnson and reports family tradition maintains the paint and wall paper business at Abilene was supplemented by a general hardware store. Predictably, if the assertion is accurate, the same would be the case for Johnson's merchandising efforts at Eddy.

[11] DeArment, Robert K. *George Scarborough, The Life and Death of a Lawman on the Closing Frontier.* P. 247.

[12] Ball, Larry D. *Desert Lawmen, The High Sheriffs of New Mexico and Arizona, 1846-1912.* P. 52 & 359.

[13] *Ibid.* "Siringo applauded Sheriff Arthur Goodell and James K. Blair of Grant County. They were 'model officers.'" P. 52.

[14] *Abilene Reporter*, September 14, 1900. "W.D. Johnson, chief deputy sheriff of Grant county..." And see, *Silver City Enterprise*, August 31, 1900. "...he (Blair) selected Mr. Johnson as his principal deputy."

[15] *Ibid.* Citation to *Silver City Enterprise.*

[16] Henry Brock and John Cox to Lou Blachly. Tape Number 95. Courtesy, Terrence M. Humble, Bayard, New Mexico.

[17] See Ball's chapter, "Keeper of the Keys: The Sheriff as Jailer," *Desert Lawmen.* P. 108-27.

[18] Escapes from the Grant County jail at Silver City are legion. An all inclusive list will not even be attempted but, just to name a few; there was the September 6, 1879 incident where three murder suspects, assaulted a jailer, stole a six-shooter and fled; or the time in 1884 when train robbing murders, "Kit" Joy, George Washington Cleveland, Frank Taggart, Mitch Lee, accompanied by prisoners

Lawmen, Outlaws and S.O.Bs.

Carlos Chaves and Charles Spencer, raced for illegal liberation, resulting in the death of a posseman, the shooting death of an inmate, and the lynching of two others; or there was the time a notorious "Bronco" Bill Walters and Mike McGinnis busted out in 1891; or the time a youthful murderer, Howard Chenowth, was "delivered" by his friends/relatives on Christmas Day, 1905; not counting two escapes, totaling ten prisoners, highlighted in this narrative of Keechi Johnson's interesting story.

[19] *Silver City Enterprise*, February 23, 1900.

[20] *Ibid.* August 31, 1900. "During the term of office of Sheriff Blair, two jail escapes have been accomplished, and in each instance Deputy Johnson had returned the jailbirds to their places in the county jail."

[21] *Ibid.* August, 31, 1900. The *Silver City Independent* of February 27, 1900, reports two of the escaped prisoners were re-captured near the Shelly Ranch.

[22] *Santa Fe New Mexican*, April 30, 1900. Also see, *Silver City Independent*, April 3, 1900. "Sheriff Blair and Deputy Johnson were absent in Santa Fe, where they had gone with the prisoners sentenced at the recent term of court..." And see, *The National Cyclopedia of American Biography*. P. 524. "(Bursum)...superintendent of the territorial penitentiary, 1899-1906." Also see, Owen, Gordon R. *The Two Alberts—Fountain and Fall*. P. 360. "...when territorial penitentiary warden Holm Bursum..."

[23] *Silver City Enterprise*, March 30, 1900.

[24] *Silver City Independent*, April 3, 1900.

[25] *Ibid.* April 6, 1900. "It appears now that guard Rose left his bunch of keys lying on his desk and they (prisoners) simply extracted the key...This sort of carelessness led Sheriff Blair to make a clean sweep of his employees..."

[26] *Silver City Enterprise*, March 30, 1900.

[27] *Silver City Independent*, May 29, 1900.

[28] *Silver City Enterprise*, March 30, 1900.

[29] Humble, Terrence M. "The Pinder-Slip Mining Claim Dispute of Santa Rita, New Mexico, 1881-1912," *Mining History Journal*. 1996. P. 92.

[30] *Silver City Independent*, May 23, 1899. "He laughed and joked after the verdict had been rendered..."

[31] *Silver City Enterprise*, March 30, 1900. And see, *Silver City Independent*, May 29, 1900. "...(Brooks) is also thought to be implicated in the Bowman bank robbery at Las Cruces..." Also see, Riley George to Lou Blachly, transcript No. 506, Wayne Whitehill interviews. Courtesy, Zimmerman Library—Center for Southwest Research, University of New Mexico. Albuquerque. And see, Rasch, Philip, "The Las Cruces Bank Robbery," *True West*. January 1981. P. 48-50. For a more recent analysis see the first-rate article by Harold Edwards, "Sheriff Pat Garrett's Puzzle: A Blow-by-Blow Account of Solving a New Mexico Bank Robbery," *The National Tombstone Epitaph*. January 2003.

[32] *Silver City Independent*, April 3, 1900.

[33] *Ibid.*

[34] *Silver City Enterprise*, April 6, 1900.

[35] DeArment. P. 224.

[36] *Ibid.*, P. 229. And see, *Silver City Enterprise*, April 6, 1900. "Deputy Sheriff George Scarborough, who for the past two years has been the terror of cattle and horse thieves along this border, died Thursday morning at 2 o'clock, from the result of a wound received Tuesday morning in the Chiracahua Mountains." Also see, DeArment, R. K. "True West Legends: George A. Scarborough," *True West*,

I Shot At Them Twice With A Six-Shooter

June 1999. P. 31-34. "The wounded officer is taken by train to Deming where doctors amputate his leg…Scarborough dies in his home with his wife and children at the bedside."
[37] *Silver City Enterprise*, April, 27, 1900. And see, *Santa Fe New Mexican*, April 30, 1900. Also see, Hunter, Sr., J. Marvin. "George Scarborough, Peace Officer," *Frontier Times*, June 1947. P. 439. "That day Sheriff Jim Blair and a posse from Silver City arrived."
[38] *Ibid.*, June 22, 1900.
[39] *Ibid.*, May 4, 1900. And see, Thrapp, Dan L. *Encyclopedia of Frontier Biography*, Vol. III, P. 1273. The author correctly credits Keechi Johnson and Miles Marshall with the arrests of Stevenson and Brooks in Mexico but erroneously criss-crosses the chronology of events.
[40] *Ibid.*, April, 27, 1900. "It will be an extremely difficult matter to extradite the captured criminals from old Mexico. It was so under the old treaty and will be equally as difficult under the recent treaty between the United States and Mexico." And see, *Silver City Independent*, May 29, 1900. "These (Stevenson and Brooks) are the first extradition to New Mexico from Mexico under the new treaty."
[41] *Ibid.* May 25, 1900.
[42] *Silver City Independent*, May 29, 1900.
[43] *Ibid.*
[44] *Ibid.* June 19, 1900.
[45] *Silver City Enterprise*, June 22, 1900.
[46] *Silver City Independent*, April 23, 1901.
[47] *Silver City Enterprise*, August 31, 1900.
[48] Nelson, Susan & Ed. *The Silver City Book I, "Wild and Woolly Days."* P. 5. "The Mexicans named the marshes *La Cienega de San Vicente* (the marshes of St. Vicente). Here, for years and years, the Apaches, under Mangas Colorado and his forefathers, gathered to celebrate their victories over the enemy and to hold their councils of war."
[49] McFarland, Elizabeth Fleming. *Wilderness of the Gila*. "A man named Jenks and his two sons had settled at the site of the McKenzie cabin on White Creek. They brought in a small bunch of cattle, built a log cabin, and cleared out a small piece of land to farm. After they got settled, during the latter part of the 1890s they started in to stealing other people's cattle to build up their herds. They kept this up until 1900 when the officers got to trying to catch them." P. 57.
[50] Hoover, H.A. *Tales From The Bloated Goat, Early Days in Mogollon.* P. 53.
[51] *Silver City Enterprise*, August 31, 1900. "Jenks, Reinhart and others have been watched by the cattle association officers for some months…a few days ago, charges were sworn out against them."
[52] *Silver City Independent*, September 4, 1900.
[53] *Ibid.* P.M. Shelly dropped off at his ranch before getting all the way back to Silver City.
[54] *Silver City Enterprise*, August 31, 1900. And see, DeArment. P. 247. "Johnson, meanwhile, had apprehended a suspect named Ralph Jenks and started back." Also see, Hoover. P. 53-56. According to Hoover's account, it is possible that Jenks had not been *formally* placed under arrest but, instead, was accompanying deputy Keechi Johnson on the trail, headed for the grazing range to inspect brands on suspected stolen cattle. And see, Hunter, J. Marvin. *The Story of Lottie Deno, Her Life and Times.* P. 168. "Jenks was a young, unmarried man, about 25 years of age."

219

Lawmen, Outlaws and S.O.Bs.

[55] *Ibid.* September 7, 1900.

[56] *Ibid.* And see, *Silver City Independent*, September 4, 1900. Also see, *Abilene Reporter*, September 21, 1900. "The full particulars of the killing have not yet been learned, and some doubt seems to be thrown on the story of the only man with him..."

[57] *Ibid.* The scene of the shooting, as described below, actually occurred in what was then colossal Socorro County but now, after organization in 1921, Catron County.

[58] *Ibid.* And see, Murray, John A. *The Gila Wilderness.* P. 200. "This canyon is named for law officer Keecheye (sic) Johnson, killed there after arresting one of the Jenks family, who resided at the confluence of White Creek and the West Fork, for stealing cattle." Also see, Julyan. P. 179. "...Johnson was sent to White Creek to arrest one Ralph Jenks, suspected of rustling, but when he got to this canyon Johnson was killed—hence the name." Johnson Canyon can be located on United States Forest Service Map, *Gila National Forest, New Mexico*, South Half, just below R. 16 W. Grant County researcher and authoritative local historian, Terrence M. Humble, reports the killing of Keechi Johnson took place near the junction of Raw Meat Creek and what is now Johnson Canyon, near the West Fork of the Gila.

[59] *Ibid.*

[60] *Ibid.*

[61] Hoover. P. 55.

[62] *Silver City Enterprise*, October 5, 1900. Also see, *Silver City Independent*, September 4, 1900. And see, Sherman, James E. and Barbara H. *Ghost Towns and Mining Camps of New Mexico.* P. 104.

[63] *Ibid.*

[64] *Silver City Independent*, September 4, 1900.

[65] *Silver City Enterprise*, September 7, 1900.

[66] Hunter, P. 169-170. Quoting a letter from Ralph Jenks to the *Silver City Independent*.

[67] *Abilene Reporter*, September 21, 1900.

[68] DeArment, P. 247-250. And see, Hunter, P. 170-171. Also see, *Silver City Enterprise*, September 7, 1900. And see, *Silver City Independent*, September 4, 1900.

[69] *Ibid.*

[70] *Silver City Enterprise*, September 14, 1900. And see, McFarland, P. 8. "Scarborough said Jenks made a play for his gun. However, people say Jenks was disarmed and was supposed to have had on a pair of gloves. Anyway, Jenks was killed." Also see, Jack Stockbridge to Lou Blachly, Tape Number, 405.4. Courtesy, Terrence M. Humble, Bayard, New Mexico.

[71] O'Neal, Bill. *The Arizona Rangers.* P. 9. At twenty-two years of age, Don Johnson was the youngest Arizona Ranger enlisted. Don Johnson served as sheriff of Luna County during the 1907-08 time period. See, Ball. P. 360. Reference to service with the El Paso Police Department is from Keechi Johnson's great grandson, Roy Sinclair, Jr., supplemented by a letter from the Chief of Police for Monterey Park, California. To date, the most inclusive biographical information regarding the life of Ed Scarborough is contained in DeArment's chapter "Ed," P. 247-261. *Gorge Scarborough, The Life And Death Of A Lawman On The Closing Frontier.*

CHAPTER 12

"THE HORSE REARED, I SHOT OVER MY SHOULDER"

Horace L. Roberson, Determined, Dangerous and Deadly

Horace Lorenzo Roberson was tough as nails, some even say downright mean. Authenticated facts confirm his reservoir of raw nerve, and whether or not he had a gnarly and nasty disposition, well, realistically that assessment depended on whether you were friend or foe. To fall into the category of the former was smart, to imprudently summon his wrath could be fatal. And too, being on his good side was sometimes the prudent place to be, because for most of his adult life, Horace L. Roberson was firmly anchored on the right side of the law, a badge pinned to his scuffed leather vest and a six-shooter appended to his left hip.[1] Most commonly referred to by his initials, but sometimes called "Hod," H.L. Roberson, truly, was fashioned from the old school.[2]

Like so many of his stalwart Old West contemporary comrades, the thrilling saga of H.L. Roberson has for the most part been innocently overlooked, not because he was not functioning on an authentic frontier but, perhaps, because it was a *transitional* frontier, and his life story spanned the time-line separating overworked tradition from encroaching technology. Twentieth-century movie producers and script-writers, rightly, reached back in time with their efforts to corral with celluloid the rambunctious Western tales of white-hatted marshals chasing outlaw S. O. Bs. Most of the players were in fact wearing gray hats. And in that far-flung border country south of El Paso, even after the turn of the century, it was just as wild and just as woolly as in days gone by. In fact, George S. Patton, Jr. who was stationed at Sierra Blanca, Texas, while a shave-tail lieutenant wrote, "This is the funniest place I have ever been. It is supposed to be very tough and at least half the men wear boots and spurs and carry guns…There are not over twenty houses in the town and one saloon. Yesterday a ranger jokingly threatened to shoot me for not taking a drink with him so after I refused I bought him a bottle of beer and drank one myself…I would not miss this for the world. I guess there are few places like it left."[3] George Patton wasn't wrong! There were few places like it left, and that forlorn and lonesome Sierra Blanca country is where the focus of this Old West story unfurls.

Two of the toughest and most feared early twentieth-century Southwestern lawmen, William Davis "Dave" Allison and Horace Lorenzo "H.L." Roberson. This photograph was made at a time when both were Field Inspectors for the Texas & Southwestern Cattle Raisers Association. Courtesy, The Cattleman.

H.L. Roberson was a Texas product. He was born in Guadalupe County, November 30, 1874.[4] Resembling so many lads before him, H.L. Roberson decked out in the usual outfit. Wandering the South Texas *brasada* with seemingly natural inclinations, and by deftly honing the requisite skills he became a *brush-popper*, a cowboy.[5] And like so many youthful Westerners, when the vexing Spanish American War captivated patriotic spirits, Horace L. Roberson enlisted as a United States soldier, and for about a year saw service in the Philippines.[6] Dissimilar to most of like ilk, however, the brown-headed six-foot H.L. Roberson, with haunting brown eyes, opted not to drink, nor did he partake of the customary snuff dips or chaws, or smokes from craftily rolled hand-made cigarettes, or their more convenient but appreciably more costly counterparts, those new-era "tailor-mades."[7] Coffee too, was taboo.[8]

Well past early youth, H.L. Roberson chose to become a Lone Star lawman. On October 11, 1911, at San Antonio, Texas, Roberson took the oath as a Texas Ranger private under command of the legendary Captain John R. "Border Boss" Hughes, who posted the new recruit at Ysleta, on the Rio Grande, just a tad south of that haughty Queen of the border cities, old El Paso.[9] Gathering up the required regalia, a bed-roll, rifle and six-shooter, plus a horse and saddle, the rookie ranger reported for duty.[10] Horace L. Roberson didn't have to wait too long, nor go too far, before his mettle was tested. A scant two months after he signed on H.L. Roberson killed a "Mexican," Alejandro Melendez, who reportedly came at him with a knife. Although routinely indicted for the shooting, Roberson came clear on the criminal charges upon proffering an understandable plea of self-defense.[11] On another occasion, although exacting details are sketchy, Roberson and another Texas Ranger, Ira Cline, killed another "Mexican" at Marfa.[12] H.L. Roberson later, under oath, testified that at the time he was acting as a legitimate posse member.[13] Evidently pleasantly impressed with Roberson's no nonsense attitude, devotion to duty, and unflinching audaciousness, John R. Hughes, on April 11, 1914, promoted H.L. Roberson to Sergeant, raising his paycheck $10—to $50 per month.[14] Admittedly there is a paucity of primary source material; however, examination of correspondence between Captain Hughes and the Adjutant General of Texas indicate that Horace L. Roberson was favorably recognized for his cow-business expertise and, on occasions, was particularly assigned to investigate the theft of livestock.[15] And undeniably it has been written, "Only those men who had stolen cattle saw the dark side of him."[16] Was there a mean streak shrouded deep within his psyche? Adding to the lawman's workload and untiring reputation was the constant border patrols resultant from the Mexican Revolution and the bloodshed and carnage then well underway.[17] Despite relentless tragedy and turmoil associated with that conflict, Texas Ranger Sergeant H.L. Roberson caught an approving eye from a private interest group, the Chicago based Nelson Morris Cattle Company which was responsible for operating the gargantuan T O Ranch, with its fourteen thousand head of cattle, scattered over a million inhospitable acres, across the boundary line in "Old Mexico."[18] It was that country where prosperity was oft measured by the number of smokeless-powder cartridges filling criss-crossed bandoleers. It was bandit country and, too, it was that sweltering and bleakly harsh country where it seemed that both poor persons and poor cows had found their last home.

A management decision resulted in Brown Pascal from Sierra Blanca losing the foreman's job on the Mexico ranch. The position was offered to Roberson, and upon consultation with Captain Hughes, because it was a much higher paying job, H.L. Roberson resigned from the Texas Rangers and accepted new employment on September 1, 1914.[19] As expected, some of the folks at Sierra Blanca weren't too happy. Brown Pascal was well thought of. One author postulates, and probably correctly, that Horace L. Roberson had been specifically hired "to seek out the toughest men he could find to help him run the ranch..." and "The Nelson Morris Cattle Company went out and hired the toughest men they could find."[20] Horace L. Roberson nonchalantly summarized his job description, stating his duties as foreman were "...to take charge of the branding of calves and other cattle..." and "...there had been cattle thefts and raids."[21]

In one instance, H.L. Roberson and his feisty crew of T O Ranch buccaneers were apparently captured by one of Pancho Villa's captains. Untangling the knot of reasons for the T O Ranch cowboys' release is romantic but problematic.[22] Whatever the cause, the prisoners were freed, scampered back north across the border, and according to legend therein engaged in a spate of vicious retribution and the murder of innocent sleeping Mexicans, although, in fact, the allegations are uncorroborated. Nevertheless, and whether or not it was or was not mere folklore, the reputation of H.L. Roberson as being an unforgiving enemy was ratcheted up a notch or two.[23]

It appears H.L. Roberson was simply devoid of personal trepidation and fear from his near death engagement with some south of the border Villista firing-squad. He went back across the volatile international line and began shaping a herd of cattle for delivery at Sierra Blanca. And too, it seems he paid little attention to the rancorous rumors and the wafting tid-bits of malevolent gossip. Unquestionably, H.L. Roberson knew many of Sierra Blanca's denizens were utterly furious over his replacing Brown Pascal as foreman down on the T O Ranch. Remarks that they were "going to fix" Roberson and that "they were going to get rid of him" were making it to the ex-Texas Ranger's ear.[24] One chap, at least according to U.S. Mounted Customs Inspector J.E. Vaughn, Henry Foote Boykin, a robust 6'3" cattle rancher, who by most accounts was considered to be "all man—all the time" and was particularly

The Horse Reared, I Shot Over My Shoulder

esteemed in faraway West Texas, vowed that he "was going to kill him (Roberson) and he (Vaughn) told H.L. "to look out for that Sierra Blanca bunch." H.L. Roberson replied "that he had his eyes open."[25]

The poisonously dangerous Horace L. Roberson, back row, second from left. Celebrated Texas Ranger Captain Frank A. Hamer is in second row, fourth from left, and the utterly fearless William D. "Dave" Allison is front and center. Courtesy, Pat Treadwell.

Gathering an ample herd of cattle, on or about January 11th, 1915, the intrepid ranch foreman Horace L. Roberson, cowboy Elmer Dumont, and nineteen year old Walt Sitter, the son of Customs Inspector and a noted man-hunter, Joe Sitter, obliquely angled away from the Rio Grande river with the beeves, headed north.[26] Fundamentally, for three days they trailed the cattle along the rutted public road, through the Love brother's pastures south of town, and finally, near dark on January 15th, and after a nonchalant show of cowboy choreography, neatly penned the bellowing bovines in the Sierra Blanca railroad's stockyard pens. After watering, feeding, and alleviating the pack-mule's burdens, the worn-out trio unsaddled their jaded personal mounts and went into the local Brown News café for an overdue supper.[27] Warily, Roberson noticed that their arrival in town seemed to be eliciting quite some

225

commotion, outside—in the dark.[28] After supper, and moving over to the Palace Hotel, ironically owned by Mrs. Brown Pascal, Roberson retired for the night, but he "had on his mind the talks that he had heard made against him."[29] Sitter and Dumont camped out near town.

Henry Foote Boykin, West Texas cattleman wittingly gunned down by ex-Texas Ranger and a future Texas & Southwestern Cattle Raisers Association Inspector, H.L. Roberson, during an argument spiraled out of control in the Sierra Blanca stock-pens. Courtesy, Henry Foote Boykin, Jr.

On the morning of the16[th], Horace L. Roberson ate again at the Brown News Café.. He then went in search of Dumont and Sitter, but not surprisingly, they had already been up, packed the mules and had gone to a handy bunkhouse to bite a biscuit. Roberson saddled his horse, mounted up, and led the pack-mules to Sierra Blanca's public watering tank. The animals needed no coaxing. From the saddle H.L. Roberson saw that something was stirring up choking dirt clouds and bothering T O cattle. Horace L. Roberson loped toward the pens to investigate.[30]

At the enclosure he found Tom Cross and Foote Boykin on the ground, inside the pen with T O cows. As with nearly all Old West tales, especially where six-shooter violence all of a sudden erupts, there is invariably a divergence of opinion. This then, is that point in the story. According to Roberson, he asked, "What are you-all doing to those cattle?" Foote Boykin, again in keeping with Roberson, growled, it's none of your "damn business."[31] Furthermore, Foote Boykin stridently cursed Roberson and called him a "damn cowardly son of a bitch."[32] H.L. Roberson climbed down off his horse and jerked his Winchester from the saddle-scabbard, thinking

The Horse Reared, I Shot Over My Shoulder

Foote Boykin had a six-shooter and was fixin' to put it to use, but upon seeing that his fuming adversary was armed only with an open pocket-knife, he climbed back on his horse and rode away to recover the pack-mules, which, by now were ambling away from the water tank.[33] After securing the mules so that they would not stir up the milling cattle, H.L. Roberson rode around a wing of the stockyard fence and when he came near Foote Boykin, who purportedly still had the knife in his hand, found himself at the stinging end of yet another ferocious cussing. Roberson instantly answered the harangue with a coiled hard-twisted catch-rope, trying to knock the knife out of Boykin's hand. Foote Boykin successfully wrenched the lariat out of Roberson's hand, who had to let go in order to maintain a seat in the saddle, and Foote Boykin then defiantly tossed the rope over the corral fence into the dirt and squishy manure, still with the Barlow knife in his other hanD.H.L. Roberson jerked out his Colt's revolver, but opted to employ it as a club rather than a six-shooter, but this disarming technique failed. Unexplainably Roberson missed hitting Boykin's hand—Boykin reserved use of the knife. The word war stayed fresh. As Horace L. Roberson reined his cow-horse around the corral's guiding wing, and into the pen, Foote Boykin jumped from his top-rail perch, into the corral and grabbed Horace L. Roberson's now filthy rope. The T O Ranch foreman justified:

> I asked him to put up his damn knife and give me my rope, and when my head was turned aside he threw the rope over the fence. He had his knife in his left hand and when I missed the rope and asked him to give it to me he replied that 'he did not have my damn rope.' Cross (Tom) then handed me the rope, and I took it in my right hand and started to coil it up. (Boykin) had been drawing closer and closer to me, and as I started to fold the rope up, he started to rush me. I started to strike him with the rope and threw it at him, threw the whole rope at him. He rushed at me with the knife raised in his right and, and struck my horse, just in front of his ribs, and then he reached up at my body. I pulled my pistol with my right hand, the horse reared and jumped, and I shot back over my right shoulder.[34]

As previously mentioned there are two faces for every coin, at least two sides to every story, in every Old West tale. Most Sierra Blanca people saw the unfolding drama shaded a little differently. Many tendered a slightly different assertion than Roberson's hard-core followers, commenting that a dividing fence within the corral system collapsed and T O cattle intermixed with others, and that Tom Cross and Foote Boykin were, indeed, in the pen but for the purpose of properly sorting the cattle when they were ruthlessly and rudely braced by a quarrelsome and loud-mouthed H.L. Roberson, spoiling for a fight. Some saw a pocket-knife clutched in Foote Boykin's hand—others didn't.[35] One witness observed a "two-bladed" knife, afterwards, on the bloody cow-lot ground.[36] *Quien Sabe*? Many thought but one thing, pure and simple—murder!

Walter Quintin Sitter, nineteen year-old son of U.S. Mounted Customs Inspector Joe Sitter, unwittingly killed by Horace L. Roberson during the spiky gunplay with Henry Foote Boykin at Sierra Blanca. Courtesy, Jake Sitters.

There are, however, facts which are indisputable. No doubt H.L. Roberson's gelding was snorting and rearing. And too, incontestably, Horace L. Roberson was trying to screw himself down tight atop the wildly gyrating brute and unable to shoot straight. The upshot of the first gunshot? A youthful Walt Sitter, who was not actually involved in the quarrel, but who was standing nearby, fell over, mortally wounded by a stray bullet. Thinking he had missed Boykin, and not realizing he had just killed his own cowhand, Roberson kept shooting, milking his Peacemaker dry. The old adage, "never take a knife to a gunfight" was apposite; Foote Boykin was plummeted to the stinky cow-lot floor by Roberson, "one bullet to the right side of the back, another in the left side, and one in the breast."[37] Befuddlement soon returned to reality, and H.L. Roberson, realizing he had just shot down a friend, and fully cognizant that Foote Boykin was one of Sierra Blanca's favorites, and well-aware he wasn't at all popular in the little border-area community, and not wanting to swing at the end of a sneakily knotted lynch-rope, galloped away, making tracks like a scalded greyhound. Depending upon the version, Horace L. Roberson either surrendered to Texas Rangers at Ysleta, or voluntarily turned himself in to a close personal friend and career peace officer, William Davis Allison, who in turn deputized two ranchers to travel by train and deliver Horace L. Roberson to the Texas Rangers at Ysleta.[38] The latter version seems the most likely, but either way, Horace L. Roberson was a prisoner.

Well-known or not, well-liked or not, the sometimes heroic and the sometimes despised Horace L. Roberson was quickly indicted by an El Paso County Grand Jury, charged with "murder with malice aforethought" in the killings of H.F. Boykin and Walter Sitter—with a pistol.[39] Leaving Bertie Violla (Morton) Boykin, the doting mother of five children, a grieving and heart-broken widow didn't set too well with hard-boiled West Texas cow-country folks.[40] Twice before H.L. Roberson had effectively dodged actual full-blown murder trials for the men he had killed, rightly or wrongly. This time though, it was different. Sierra Blanca town folk were livid. Foote Boykin had been one of their own, H.L. Roberson wasn't. Many believed Foote Boykin was unarmed and was mercilessly gunned down. If Roberson wasn't just too damn quick on the trigger, how come wholly blameless Walt Sitter was killed? Shortly after the shooting, nearly "every one in town had contributed (money) to the prosecution of the case."[41] Out West Texas way, this time, Horace L. Roberson's fat was in the fire!

Horace L. Roberson had high-powered and highly-placed backers of his own, primarily from the law enforcement community and from the Texas and Southwestern Cattle Raisers Association, an organization adroitly able at exercising its political muscle.[42] And, in fact, the renowned Texas Ranger Captain John R. Hughes would later become one of his bondsmen.[43] The case, however, was not open and shut, and although he was at large from jailhouse custody on bail, this fussy tilt with the criminal justice system was going to be a lingering and dicey affair.[44]

At El Paso, on November 29th, 1915, before Judge Dan M. Jackson's 34th Judicial District Court, the defendant, Horace L. Roberson, formally entered his plea of not guilty.[45] Jury selection began immediately, and out of a special gathering of 100 men, and after the formal *voir dire* questioning of forty-six men, only ten could be seated. Many confirmed they had already formed an opinion and were summarily excused. The sheriff was ordered to issue additional summons, he did, and the twelve man trial jury was, at last, impaneled.[46] Representing the State of Texas were the El Paso County District Attorney, W.W. Bridgers, former judge L.A. Dale, and the law firm of Lea, Grady and Thomasen. On the defendant's team were lawyers Victor Moore, W.B. Ware, John Dyer and J.M. Harris.[47]

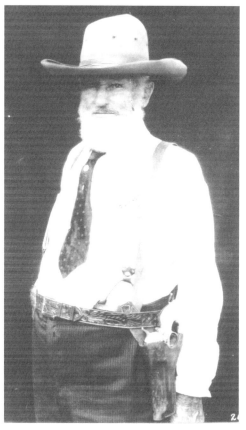

Legendary Texas Ranger Captain John R. "Border Boss" Hughes. Both Horace Roberson and Dave Allison were Sergeants under his command in Company D. He testified to their fearlessness at the murder trials of Hiliary U. Loftis (Tom Ross) and Milton Paul "Milt" Good. Courtesy, Texas Ranger Hall of Fame and Museum.

The Horse Reared, I Shot Over My Shoulder

Upon finally receiving the case for consideration the jury was out but two hours. The verdict, when they returned, was, *guilty as charged*, and the same jury assessed Horace L. Roberson's punishment at twenty years in the State of Texas penitentiary at Huntsville.[48] A newspaperman covering the trial for the *El Paso Morning Times* was in fact flabbergasted by the defendant's imperturbable courtroom demeanor, "If the verdict of the jury was in the nature of a crisis, Roberson met it squarely and without flinching. His face was sphinx like. No emotion of any character betrayed his real feelings."[49] Almost immediately, December 18th, the attorneys for H.L. Roberson, not unsurprisingly, filed a motion for a new trial, it was granted, and the original guilty verdict was set aside.[50]

Nearly a year later, and again at El Paso, a trial jury determined that H.L. Roberson's killing of Foote Boykin was, for sure, a criminal offense, but this time they found a lesser charge, Manslaughter, and issued him a ticket to the penitentiary—five years. Imbued with the astounding success of the first appeal, another was forthrightly formalized, and the prison sentence was, again, temporarily suspended.[51]

The Texas Court of Criminal Appeals, on October 17, 1917, ruled there was no reversible error in the lower court's decision and Horace L. Roberson's El Paso County conviction for Manslaughter and the five year prison confinement was affirmed.[52] Once again, with the fortitude of a tenacious bulldog, Roberson's lawyers cried for one more chance with the Texas Court of Criminal Appeals. Incredibly their legalistic stratagem paid big dividends. In a stunning, and almost unheard of shift, the higher court reversed its earlier position, finding the original trial judge had failed to instruct the jury that, since at the time of the shooting the defendant was moving the cattle to Sierra Blanca, and the fact the he was in process of moving the T O herd from Sierra Blanca, Roberson could be characterized as a *traveler* and as such, at the time under Texas statutes, had the legal right to carry a sidearm, a signal fact the jury should have been appraised of, and weren't. Once more, a new trial.[53]

By now, 1918, Hudspeth County (Sierra Blanca), Texas, had been organized and the criminal case was transferred there as that would be the court of competent jurisdiction. Not implausibly a motion for a change of venue was filed, and, indeed, it was rightly determined that Horace L. Roberson could not expect an unbiased and fair trial at Sierra Blanca, and the action was reassigned back to the El Paso County District Court docket for a new trial.[54]

And so be it! Back at El Paso County, Texas, in Cause Number 9082, Horace L. Roberson, once more went on trial for the killing of Foote Boykin at Sierra Blanca in 1915—it was now November, 1919. Yet once again, twelve honest and true men found him guilty of Manslaughter, and this time he was awarded a sentence of two years with the Texas Department of Corrections. Huntsville, Texas. Well, not just yet, his steadfast and utterly tireless lawyers submitted a motion for another trial and another change of venue. Certainly, at this point the reader will find little surprise. The motion for a new trial was granted, the change of venue was approved. The new trial was scheduled to take place at Austin, Travis County, Texas.[55]

For the fourth trying time, and possibly setting some type of record, on June 21st, 1920, Horace L. Roberson in Cause Number 18,002, Travis County, Texas, went on trial before a jury of his peers for the killing of Foote Boykin, five years earlier.[56] This time in Central Texas, nearer the seat of state government, and in closer proximity to power brokers from private interest groups, and decidedly distant from that "Sierra Blanca bunch," the odds would be, ultimately, stacked in Roberson's favor. After several days of scrappy testimony, on the 26th, the following formatted message was presented to the Criminal District Court:

State of Texas
County of Travis

Hon. Jas. R. Hamilton, Judge Criminal Court: We the jury find the defendant, H.L. Roberson, not guilty.
W.M. Graham, foreman.

In conclusion of the seemingly never ending account of H.L. Roberson's legal skirmishes, he, at long last, was lawfully a free man, and the judge unambiguously ordered, "he is hereby adjudged not guilty of the offense for which he has just been tried, and that he go hence without delay, fully discharged from all further liability hereunder."[57] With precious Fifth Amendment protections under the United States Constitution relating to what is generally labeled, *Double Jeopardy*, Horace L. Roberson had, depending on personal perspective, either "beat the rap" or had been cleared of any wrongdoing. From the get-go, prosecutors and even those diametrically at odds with Horace L. Roberson, were sorrowfully aware there was no profit to be had in pursuing any legal actions against him concerning the untimely death of Walt Sitter.

The Horse Reared, I Shot Over My Shoulder

Unquestionably, as earlier mentioned, H.L. Roberson, through the entire convoluted legal battle, did not suffer scorn as would be expected of an emblematic murder defendant. Shortly after the Foote Boykin killing, Roberson, on the May 8, 1916, had been commissioned a Special Texas Ranger, his salary paid by the Texas & Southwestern Cattle Raisers Association.[58]

And in their employ he stayed until a fateful day in 1923, Easter Sunday, and by mere chance, too, it was April Fool's Day. H.L. Roberson and Dave Allison, who was also a fellow Inspector for the Association, were at Seminole, Texas, in anticipation of giving testimony to a Gaines County Grand Jury the next day. The Southwestern ranch-country lawmen had been checking up on the dubious and nefarious activities of two well-known cattle thieving suspects, Milton P. Good and his cohort, a man going by the alias Tom Ross, but who in fact had come into the world as Hillary U. Loftis.[59]

The Roberson family plot and Horace L. Roberson's grave site, City Cemetery No. 6, San Antonio, Texas. Courtesy, Jan Devereaux.

Around eight o'clock that night, Roberson, Allison, the Gaines County Sheriff, a smattering of local lawyers, and two ranchers were idly passing time in the tiny lobby at the Gaines Hotel. Abruptly peacefulness was aborted by the deafening crescendo from shotgun and pistol blasts. Milt Good and Tom Ross, unsmilingly and cowardly, had poked their weapons through a slightly open door and remorselessly cut loose. Their actions were a dimwitted attempt at thwarting the law—killing the witnesses. However, their aim was true, and both Dave Allison and Horace L. Roberson were instantly killed. Then what happened? Although the next chapter in the rousing saga is quite Western, involves an illustrious act of genuine feminine heroism, four more colorful murder trials, and reams of national press coverage, well, it's another story.

Horace L. Roberson was dead. He had been tough as nails, some even say downright mean.

ENDNOTES CHAPTER 12

"THE HORSE REARED, I SHOT OVER MY SHOULDER"

[1] *St. Louis Post-Dispatch*, July 22, 1923. "She stooped, felt for the six-shooter which she knew Horace Roberson wore in a holster at his left side..." And see, *Seminole Sentinel*, April 5, 1923. "...had been a peace officer practically all of his life..."

[2] Fenton, James Irving. *Tom Ross: Outlaw and Stockman*. Master of Arts Thesis, University of Texas at El Paso. El Paso, Texas. 1979. P. 85. "Roberson, too, boasted impressive credentials as a peace officer." Although author Fenton mentions Roberson was sometimes referred to as "Hod," throughout West Texas he was more commonly known as "H.L." Roberson, and, in fact, this author in examining *Enlistment, Oath of Service, and Descriptive Lists* for his various stints of service with the Texas Rangers, has failed to find the subject identified other than "H.L. Roberson."

[3] Blumenson, Martin. *The Patton Papers, 1885-1940*. P. 298-299.

[4] Examination of several *Enlistment, Oath of Service, and Description, Ranger Force* are generally in agreement as to Roberson's date and place of birth, although from document to document there are historically insignificant differences. Courtesy, Texas Ranger Hall of Fame and Museum. Waco, Texas. Also see, Means, Joyce. *Pancho Villa Days at Pilares*. P. 66. The headstone birth date is used in text.

[5] Means reports that Roberson, "...had lots of experience at ranching: as a cowboy at Val Verde, at the Matador ranch, perhaps as a gunman, in Dickens County, at a ranch for Ben Borroum of Del Rio, and for Dave McCormick in San Antonio....had been an inspector for the Cattleraiser's (sic) Association in Texas." Also see, *The Cattleman*, Volume IX, Number 11 (May 1923), P. 14. Roberson's subsequent employment with the Texas and Southwestern Cattle Raisers Association confirms his earned reputation among cattlemen and cowboys. It is true, however, for awhile Roberson served as a train conductor.

[6] *The Cattleman*, (Spiller, E. B., editor) Vol. IX, No. 11. (May 1923). P. 14. And see, *St. Louis Post-Dispatch*, July 22, 1923.

[7] Fenton, P. 86.

[8] *St. Louis Post-Dispatch*, July 22, 1923. "He (Roberson) always kept himself perfectly groomed. He used neither liquor, tobacco, nor coffee."

[9] *Enlistment, Oath of Service, and Description, Ranger Force*. H.L. Roberson dated October 11, 1911, signed by Captain John R. Hughes. Courtesy, Texas State Library and Archives Commission. Austin.

[10] Smithers, W.D. "The Long Rio Grande," *True West*, August 1963. P. 40. "...and supply his own food and feed for his horse!...The State did allow him (Rangers) $1.50 a day to help pay for the grub and feed. Rangers had no uniform but wore western boots and clothes bought from their own funds."

[11] *Indictment*, El Paso County, *State of Texas vs. H.L. Roberson*, December 2, 1911.

[12] Means, P. 77.

[13] *El Paso Morning Times*, December 3, 1915. "You testified on direct examination that you killed two Mexicans, didn't you?" "Yes sir." That was qualified by the statement that the witness was a member of a posse when the Mexicans were killed. "Who was the first man?" "He was a Mexican. The house

had been surrounded. They wanted to arrest him." "Who was the other?" "A Mexican. Two were shooting at him. I don't know who hit him."

[14] *Enlistment, Oath of Service, and Description, Ranger Force.* H.L. Roberson, dated April 11, 1914, signed by Captain John R. Hughes. Courtesy, Texas Ranger Hall of Fame and Museum. Waco. On this paper work the word "private" is crossed through, and the word "sergeant" is handwritten above. Later reports refer to H.L. Roberson as a Ranger Sergeant. At the time Captain Hughes was drawing $100 per month, the sergeants $50, and the privates $40. List of Texas Ranger *Salary Warrants* from Asst. Adjutant General State of Texas to Captain Jr. R. Hughes, Ysleta, Texas, February 5, 1913. Courtesy, Texas State Library and Archives Commission. Austin.

[15] Captain John R. Hughes to Adjutant General Henry Hutchings, June 24, 1913. "I will send Sergt. Roberson and Private Cline back to Valentine to take up some important work after cattle thieves." And, Captain John R. Hughes, Ysleta, Texas to Adjutant General, Austin, Texas, February 6, 1913. "H.L. Roberson is at Dickens (Texas)". Courtesy, Texas State Library and Archives Commission. Austin.

[16] Perkins, Doug & Ward, Nancy. *Brave Men & Cold Steel—A History of Range Detectives and Their Peacemakers.* P. 22.

[17] Captain John R. Hughes, Ysleta, Texas, to Adjutant General, Austin, Texas, June 30, 1913. "I returned to El Paso this morning with horses. Have five men here with me, Sergt. Roberson and Privates Cline, Knight, Webster & Vaughn…The El Paso people have finally got excited about the battle of Juarez and every one I meet wants to talk about it…" Courtesy, Texas State Library and Archives Commission. Austin.

[18] Means, P. 66. And see, *Death Rides The River, Tales of the El Paso Road,* Robert S. Bolling. P. 7. Also see, *El Paso Times,* December 3, 1915. The letters T O are an abbreviation for Texas & Old Mexico, see, *The Cattleman,* May 1923. P. 14.

[19] *Ibid.* And see, *Oath Of Members Ranger Force,* H.L. Roberson, Sergeant, Company A, Ysleta, Texas. With notation, "Resigned 4 September 1914." Courtesy, Texas Ranger Hall of Fame and Museum. Waco.

[20] *Ibid.* & P. 74.

[21] *El Paso Morning Times,* December 3, 1915.

[22] Means, P. 70. And see, Bolling, P. 9. That Roberson and his cowboys were temporarily detained at Ojinaga, Chihuahua, Mexico, is usually not disputed, the reasons for their ultimate release, however, are. Among the litany of explanations are that Roberson was released because of his cool and defiant attitude, or that the U.S. State Department diplomatically pressured Pancho Villa, or that a cleverly worded telegram was deceptively sent over Pancho Villa's forged signature, just to enumerate three.

[23] *Ibid.* The author lists by name several "Mexicans" that Roberson reportedly killed, but the proof cannot rise past the level of word of mouth hearsay passed from one generation to the next. In due fairness to the author, however, the border area, particularly for the time period under examination, was an extraordinarily violent piece of real-estate, and unquestionably many deaths, especially if their were no opposing witnesses, went unreported and unrecorded. Roberson, under oath, admitted killing four men in the United States. Whether or not he was responsible for killing "Mexicans" on the other side of the border will forevermore be dependent on personal perspective and the weight awarded speculation. Also

see, *El Paso Morning Times*, December 3, 1915. "Didn't you kill four Mexicans in one bunch when you started working for the T. & O.?" Roberson, "No, sir." "Isn't it a fact that all told you have killed ten men?" Roberson, "No, sir." Isn't it a fact that you have got ten notches on your stick?" Roberson, "No, sir." "That isn't true?" Roberson, "No, sir."

[24] *El Paso Morning Times*, December 3, 1915.

[25] *Ibid.* And see, *203 Southwestern Reporter, Roberson v State of Texas.* P. 349. "There was evidence that appellant had been informed that the people in the vicinity of Sierra Blanca were hostile to him and would probably do him harm, and that deceased had threatened to kill him." The Customs man who made Roberson aware of the threats was Jefferson Eagle Vaughn, ex-deputy sheriff, ex-Texas Ranger, U.S. Mounted Customs Inspector, and later sheriff of Presidio County, Texas. For a brief, but informative thumbnail sketch of this attention-grabbing border country lawman see, Cox, Mike. *Texas Ranger Tales—Stories That Need Telling.* P. 126-128. And interview by author on September 12, 2002, with Henry Foote Boykin, Jr., the son of the deceased Boykin characterized in this chronicle. At the time his father was killed H. F. Boykin, Jr., was but three years old. Quite naturally, he has no first-hand remembrance of his father's death, but does recall occasions he, along with other children, were placed in a building for protection while "Mexican" bandits either rode through, or were reported near, Sierra Blanca. Henry Foote Boykin, Jr., says his father, at the time of his death, owned 48 sections (30,720 acres) north of the community of Sierra Blanca. Additionally, Mr. Boykin advised that, although it is sometimes written his father's name was "Foot," the proper spelling is "Foote."

[26] Bolling, P. 10.

[27] *El Paso Morning Times*, December, 3, 1915. Also see, Means, P. 72. And see, Bolling, P. 10.

[28] *Ibid.* "…he saw Tom Cross looking through the window directly at them. It was dark outside, but in addition to Cross, Roberson could distinguish several 'dark forms'…He (Cross) stood out there looking through this glass…"

[29] *Ibid.* And see, Bolling, P. 7 & 15. "Brown Paschal, whose wife owned the Palace Hotel, Sierra Blanca, was dismissed as foreman of the T O in September, 1914 and replaced by H.L. Roberson." "Roberson, Dumont, and Sitter soon afterward left the Brown News, with Roberson going to the Palace Hotel and the others returning to the Clarence Wood bunkhouse to spend the night."

[30] Bolling, P. 14.

[31] *El Paso Morning Times*, December 3, 1915. And see same, November 17th.

[32] *203 Southwestern Reporter, Roberson v State of Texas.* P. 350.

[33] *Ibid.*

[34] *Ibid.*

[35] *Ibid.* "…except that one or more of them testified that they saw a knife in Boykin's hand at the time he ran at Roberson."

[36] Tape recorded interview of Bill Norton by Henry Foote Boykin, Jr., July 18, 1988, at Truth or Consequences, New Mexico. Mr. Norton was a teenager at the time of the killing of Foote Boykin, Sr., and was an eye-witness to the shooting. Mr. Norton remembers that Roberson shot Joe Sitter in the stomach, shot Foote Boykin, Sr. twice from horseback, and then rode up closer and shot him once more. Courtesy, Henry Foote Boykin, Jr.

[37] *203 Southwestern Reporter, Roberson v State of Texas.* P. 353

[38] Means, P. 72. Bolling, P. 21. Blumenson, P. 298. For an in depth look at a truly remarkable Southwestern peace officer and man-killer, see, Alexander, Bob, *Fearless Dave Allison, Border Lawman.*

[39] *El Paso County Indictment*, Number 6743, H.L. Roberson, deft. Murder (Boykin). January 22, 1915. And, *El Paso County Indictment*, Number 6744, H.L. Roberson, deft, Murder (Sitter). January 22, 1915. Courtesy, Colquitt Warren collection. The legalities of Roberson's murder case would span several years and, therefore, a certain confusion exist concerning court jurisdiction. At the time of the offense, January 16, 1915, the incident occurred in what was then El Paso County, but later, Hudspeth County. In February, 1917, Hudspeth County, the second largest county in Texas was organized. See, Gournay, Luke, *Texas Boundaries—Evolution of the State's Counties.* P. 122. Due to Roberson's trials, appeals, re-trials, and changes of venues, over time, indictments were filed in both El Paso and Hudspeth Counties.

[40] Interview, Henry Foote Boykin, Jr., September 12, 2002.

[41] *El Paso Morning Times*, December 3, 1915. "On cross examination, Mr. (Dick) Love admitted he had contributed $100 to a fund to prosecute the case. He said Boykin was his friend…He did not know who raised the fund. He said he did not help raise it. Just contributed."

[42] Warren, Colquitt. *Beating The Rap.* P. 58. Horace L. Roberson's connections with the Texas & Southwest Cattle Raisers Association is well-documented in numerous primary and secondary source materials. At the time of his death, 1923, he was in their employ as a Field Inspector.

[43] *Ibid.*, P. 62.

[44] *El Paso Morning Times*, November 30, 1915. "Roberson has been on bond since the preliminary hearing and subsequent indictment."

[45] *The State of Texas vs. H.L. Roberson*, Judgment Plea—Not Guilty. Number 6743. Courtesy, Colquitt Warren collection.

[46] *El Paso Morning Times*, November, 30, 1915.

[47] *Ibid.*

[48] *Judgment, The State of Texas vs. H.L. Roberson.* El Paso County, Texas. Case Number 6743. "We the jury in the above styled & numbered suit, find the defendant, H.L. Roberson, guilty of murder as charged in the indictment & assess his punishment at twenty years (20) in the State Penitentiary." Courtesy, Colquitt Warren collection. And see, *El Paso Morning Times*, December 5, 1915.

[49] *El Paso Morning Times*, December 5, 1915.

[50] *Ibid.*

[51] *Judgment, The State of Texas vs. H.L. Robinson* (Roberson), December 8, 1916, El Paso County, Texas. Case Number 6743. "It is further ordered of the court that the execution of the above sentence be and the same is hereby suspended pending appeal notice of which appeal was this day given in open court." Courtesy, Colquitt Warren collection.

[52] Warren, P. 60.

[53] *Ibid.*, P. 62.

[54] *Criminal Docket*, Hudspeth County, Texas. Case Number 7. *The State of Texas vs. H.L. Roberson.* October 12, 1918. "It appearing to the Court that it is impossible to obtain a jury in this case in Hudspeth County and that a like condition exists in Culberson County (Van Horn), the nearest adjoining county, it is ordered that the venue herein be changed…" Courtesy, Colquitt Warren collection.

[55] *Judgment*, El Paso County, Texas. Case Number 9082, *The State of Texas vs. H.L. Roberson.* November 10, 1919. Courtesy, Colquitt Warren collection.

[56] Warren, P. 62.

[57] *Ibid.*, P. 63.

[58] *Enlistment, Oath Of Service, And Description Ranger Force*, H.L. Roberson. May 8, 1916. Special notation, "Cattle Raisers Assn." Courtesy, Texas State Library and Archives Commission. Austin.

[59] See, Fenton for a biography of Tom Ross. See, Alexander for a biography of Dave Allison. See, Good, Milton P., for an autobiography, *Twelve Years in a Texas Prison.* Horace L. Roberson is characterized throughout the first two, and hardly mentioned at all by one of his killers, Milt Good, in the latter. Also see, DeArment, Robert K., "Bloody Easter," *Old West*, Spring, 1994. The author's succinct biographical sketches of lawmen Dave Allison and Horace Roberson, and outlaws Milt Good and Tom Ross (Loftis) are excellent, especially for a magazine length article.

CHAPTER 13

"AND WE SAY, WELL DONE DAN!"

Dan Coomer, A Cow-Thief's Nightmare

To be sure, the battle of Earpville is still being valiantly waged. But unbridled absorption with one bunch of worthy frontier figures sometimes results in others suffering dismal neglect. Such has been the case with Daniel "Dan" Coomer, a tough-as-nails southwestern New Mexico pioneer, and as an on the scene newspaper reporter commented, a man who was a legitimate "terror to thieves," and was in large part responsible for curbing the "lawless element."[1]

Dan Coomer was not a lawman, not in an official capacity, nor was he a gunfighter as the term is oft applied today but, in his time, woe be it to evil-doers who miscalculated, misappropriating from his or his neighbor's herds, or those who otherwise chose to commit felonious misdeeds in old Grant County, New Mexico. Dan Coomer didn't boastfully carry a notch-stick—but he could have! Dan Coomer had a strong sense of right and wrong, and lived life accordingly.[2]

Although he was born in Washington County, Tennessee, by the time of his eighth birthday on June 18, 1854, Dan, along with his parents and younger brother Jesse were living in razorback country near Van Buren, northwestern Arkansas.[3] After sentiment for the Civil War erupted into hostilities, at the age of sixteen Dan volunteered for service, but because of his youth was offered the blacksnake bullwhip of a teamster rather than the soldier's Spencer and saber.[4] Unquestionably it was with this employ, driving oxen cantankerous Confederate mules, that Dan Coomer fine-tuned his outdoor skills. And too, although it is more speculative than factual, it was during this arduous test of a young man's mettle that Dan made the mindful resolution to become an entrepreneurial freewheeler, rather than a common day-laborer. By Spring of 1867, at the tender age of twenty-one years, along with his brother, Dan

240

had ventured into southwestern New Mexico Territory and located a ranch near the Mimbres River, about 25 miles east of Silver City.[5]

By any stretch of the imagination it was tough country. The geography was simply unsympathetic and unforgiving.[6] The Apache were raiding for reward or revenge.[7] And, outlaws of a fairer complexion were common. Of the area and the *mal hombres*, one prominent Western writer mentioned that southwestern New Mexico was "the blistering cauldron where so many Wild West gunmen made their reputations," and was in fact, "the gunfighter proving ground of the Southwest."[8] Of Silver City specifically, it was logically written that "the town was tough almost to the limit of human endurance."[9] Quickly, Silver City was developing a "reputation that it did not really crave."[10] Dan Coomer, despite the critical challenges had come to stay, hell or high water—redman or rustler!

Before launching into an anticipated series of rousing Western scenarios, it is requisite to report Dan Coomer was twice married, fathered two sons, Johnny and Denzel, and most unfortunately, mourned the loss of an infant daughter, Carolina. Dan Coomer, for want of better terminology "spread himself thin" in the business world, sometimes too "thin," suffering several financial upheavals and reverses, but ultimately meeting with many more successes than failures. Throughout the northern section of old Grant County he was involved in numerous business ventures, ranging from building contractor, butcher shop operator, sawmill owner and lumberyard tycoon, as well as an intermittent mining speculator, and always, a cattle rancher at heart.[11]

And, it wasn't too very long before Dan Coomer found himself immersed in crime fighting. Such as the time (Oct. 1877) he served on a coroner's jury investigating the shooting of a respected Silver City resident, Richard Howlett, who it was determined came to his death by "a pistol ball wound" fired from the six-shooter of a notoriously dangerous Tom Bowe.[12] Soon though, conniving criminality would cast Dan Coomer in the role of an actual "player," rather than a simple sideline spectator.

Trying to carve an equitable living out of frontier New Mexico was in fact a formidable task, made much more troublesome by killers and cow-thieves. In September of 1879 they struck Dan Coomer's herd, making off with sixty-five head.[13] Upon learning a key component of the family's livelihood was furiously being driven from his range, Dan Coomer traveled to Silver City and applied to the sheriff of Grant County, Harvey Howard Whitehill, for help.[14] For whatever reason the sheriff allegedly remarked, "It wouldn't be worth while to follow them, as they would get away with the cattle anyhow" and added, "They will get you, too, if you don't let them alone."[15] Astonished at the lack of interest and display of abject timidity on the part of Grant County's top lawman, the strong-minded Dan Coomer opted to solve his own problem—his own way! When appraised of the sheriff's deplorable absence of zeal, a "prominent" black rancher from the lower Mimbres, George Williams, gamely volunteered to back Dan Coomer's play.[16] The two stalwarts set out in pursuit.

Picking up the rustler's trail near Silver City, Coomer and Williams watchfully tracked. For twenty-four consecutive days, with little sleep, Coomer and Williams cut for sign, following the trail through the Burro Mountains, down the Gila River, through the Carlisle Mountains, down the Gila once again and on to Pueblo Viejo. The outlaws were followed to Fort Grant, Arizona Territory, and then once again, back into the Burros—and it was there—that Dan Coomer caught up with the careworn cow-thieves.[17] Two unidentified outlaws died with their boots on while *resisting* arrest, or by other accounts while *escaping*, but by all reports the pair ended up dead as a result of Dan Coomer's marksmanship. Later, an old-timer would report, "I went and viewed the bodies where they lay, and if they had tried to run, they evidently hadn't gone far, as one lay partly across the other."[18] A third terrified reprobate, finally in possession of a smidgen of common sense, high-heeled it ahead of Coomer's wrath for Lone Mountain, some nine miles east of Silver City.[19] With his cattle scattered in the picturesque Burros, Dan Coomer opted to gather his four-legged property rather than chase after the remaining offender. He sent word to one of the deadliest lawmen to ever serve the Southwestern border country, Dan Tucker, who effectively arrested the third thief, an Army deserter.[20] And reportedly, fearing retribution from Coomer or *maybe* not wanting to test cow-country justice, the disobedient soldier somehow made sure military authorities at Fort Grant knew of his whereabouts, and later, was overjoyed when blue-coated sentinels arrived and placed him in federal custody.[21] Dan Coomer, after rounding up his beeves and returning them to his ranch, rode to Silver City, looked up Dan Tucker and offered to surrender, should there have been any warrants issued for his arrest concerning the killings.[22] Naturally there hadn't been—nor would there ever be. Of the deaths, one thoroughly impressed newspaperman, simply reflecting public opinion, lauded Coomer with the remark, "and we say, well done Dan!"[23]

"And We Say, Well Done Dan!"

Dan Coomer, if the reports are true, was about to have another clash with Sheriff Whitehill. Convicted of first degree murder in District Court were Charles Williams, whose real name was Barney O'Toole, who had killed a man in nearby Georgetown, and Louis Gaines, who had killed a fellow black soldier from Fort Bayard on Christmas Eve the year before, reportedly with a common table knife. They were sentenced to be hanged in Silver City on August 20, 1880.[24] Whether or not he is purposefully hurling a barb at Dan due to bitterness between his father and Coomer, at this late date will never be known, but Wayne Whitehill, the sheriff's son, said:

> One of the toughest jobs was when he (his father) had to hang a negro and a white man together. The negro had killed a lieutenant and another negro. The white man had killed a Mexican. About this time a lot of Southerners had drifted into Silver City. They were led by a fellow named Dan Coomer. They swore that the Sheriff would never hang a white man and a negro together. When the day set for the hanging arrived, it looked like war for sure. Even the women had guns. But Papa went right thru with the hanging just the same.[25]

Factually it can be stated Sheriff Whitehill did deputize approximately sixty well-armed citizens, was accompanied by the deadly Dan Tucker, proceeded with the hanging, and according to *The Southwest*, "Every arrangement was perfect and the men died almost without a struggle, the necks of both being broken by the fall…After the execution all dispersed quietly, and this evening the town is without unusual excitement."[26] Perhaps Dan Coomer was somewhat peeved at seeing a black man and a white man sharing the same scaffold—perhaps not—but assuredly he was not going to exchange gunshots with legally constituted authorities, most especially since one of those lawmen was Dan Tucker, a man he personally held in high regard.[27] Although historical fidelity mandates inclusion of the hanging story in this biographical narrative, before categorically assigning Dan Coomer the role of a racist bigot, it must be remembered he had not too long before returned from an extended manhunt with George Williams, a black rancher from the lower Mimbres, the solitary pair affably camping out together for twenty-four nights. Make no mistake, Dan Coomer and Harvey Whitehill were not chums, and never mincing words, the forceful rancher would later remark the sheriff had surrounded himself with a "gang" which was capable of depreciating the "stock interests of the county…" by as much as "twenty per cent."[28]

Lawmen, Outlaws and S.O.Bs.

Scene of double hanging, 1880, at the outer edge of Silver City, New Mexico Territory, Dan Coomer allegedly argued with Grant County Sheriff Harvey H. Whitehill over the perceived insult of executing a black man and a white man on the same scaffold—at the same time. Courtesy, Silver City Museum.

After the dazzling escapade during which Coomer killed two rustlers, one would think intuitive thieves would have given Dan's cattle ranch the "go-by." Such was not the case. During September, 1880, livestock thieves made off with twenty of Dan's steers. Unbeknownst to Coomer at the time, the animals were sold to an unprincipled civilian butcher at Fort Cummings, in the shadows of the notorious Apache killing ground, Cooke's Peak. Once again Dan Coomer chased after his cattle, doggedly following the trail to the military reservation. Learning the steers had recently been slaughtered, Dan Coomer quite naturally asked the butcher to name the sources for his livestock. The meat-cutter chose not to "snitch," that is, until Dan Coomer audaciously poked a hair-trigger Winchester into his face—he blabbed! With the names of the thieves now known, Dan Coomer went in search of Bud Rice and another named Johnson, possibly "Toppy" Johnson, a well known cow-thief operating out of the Black Range.[29]

Forewarned that Dan Coomer had blood in his eye, the rustlers vehemently spewed death-threats of their own. Coomer wasn't overawed. Dan finally caught up with Bud Rice at Fort Bayard, near Santa Rita. The confrontation was reported:

"And We Say, Well Done Dan!"

He met Bud Rice fact to face, and while Rice was 'drawing' the ranchman 'got there', shooting the thief through the head. To make sure that Rice wouldn't handle any more 'short stock' he gave him two more bullets, and then loafed around the post for a few hours with the hope of 'getting' five or six more of the man's pals.[30]

Learning that a sometimes questionable deputy sheriff, Billy McClellan, who one old-timer characterized "as notorious a horse and cattle thief as ever lived," had somehow been mixed up with the aforementioned desperadoes and, the not so veiled death-threats, Dan Coomer once again had dispute with Grant County Sheriff Whitehill, who refused to dismiss the corrupt deputy.[31] Pointedly, Dan Coomer declared that he "would kill McClellan on sight."[32] He didn't have to. Drunk and racing his horse down Silver City's Bullard Street, "at breakneck speed," Billy McClellan fell, stuck his head—and died![33] Speaking of frontier law enforcement in general, a knowledgeable journalist of the time, noted "it seemed to have an elastic application, and was sometimes stretched to the limit and at other times contracted to its minimum."[34] New Mexico Territory was still part of the western frontier, and for sure, policing in old Grant County sometimes seemed suspiciously inept. Later commenting about his seemingly ongoing friction with Sheriff Whitehill, Coomer remarked, "He had but one good deputy that I know of, and that was Tucker. He may have had others for a short time but I never knew them."[35]

And, on March 10, 1884, one of those courageous deeds would once again catapult Dan Coomer into an arena of violence and onto the stage of public adulation. During midmorning the quartet arrested for the November 24th (1883) murder of Southern Pacific Railroad engineer Theopholus Webster, and robbery of the train near Gage station, "Kit" Joy, Mitch Lee, Frank Taggart and George Washington Cleveland, along with a convicted murder, Carlos Chaves, and an accused horse thief, Charles Spencer, ingeniously orchestrated a foolhardy jailbreak from the Grant County Jail.[36] After overpowering their guards, stealing arms, ammunition, and horses from the Elephant Corral, the guttersnipes fled Sliver City heading east on the Fort Bayard Road.[37] Heroically, citizen J.C. Jackson, armed only with a revolver, grabbed a horse and ridding bareback followed the escaping prisoners at a reasonably safe distance, but close enough to somewhat retard the speed of their flight, as from time to time the escapees were forced to stop and fire

245

a shot or two in his direction.[38] Thankfully, it wasn't too long before Jackson was joined by forefront posse members, T.E. Parks, Frank Andrews, and the always plucky Dan Coomer.[39]

Christopher "Kit" Joy, cowboy, train-robber, killer and fugitive. Dan Coomer engaged him along with his murderous partners in crime during a horrific "Western" gunbattle on the outskirts of Silver City. Courtesy, Silver City Museum.

Dan Coomer, alone, and about a hundred and twenty-five yards behind the hooligans, approached square on their track, while his companions maneuvered to gain the left flank.[40] "The six escapees, spotting Coomer closing in on them, turned and charged him, firing fifteen to twenty shots at him without effect. Coomer dismounted and sought refuge among some tree stumps. From here he shot and killed the horse Carlos Chavez was riding. Chavez climbed up on the back of a horse ridden by one of his companions…The outlaws continued north, with Coomer following them on foot, firing as he went, while Jackson, Parks, and Andrews began firing upon them from the left…"[41] Finally the fugitives took to the brush on foot, and a horrific gunbattle took place during which Chavez and Cleveland were killed outright, and it was reported that Dan Coomer wounded Mitch Lee, the unlucky bandit "being shot from side to side, just above the hips."[42] "Kit" Joy, after brutally ambushing and killing posse member Joseph N. Lafferr, a highly respected Silver City salesman and school-board trustee[43], temporarily made good with his escape, but later, was gravely wounded, had a leg amputated, and after a no nonsense trial at Hillsboro, New Mexico Territory, was delivered to the penitentiary in handcuffs and on a crutch. Out of ammunition and by now badly outnumbered, Frank Taggart and Charles Spencer exercised their only realistic option and surrendered to the possemen.[44] A newspaperman was on site, and continues the tale regarding live criminals who were now in custody of an infuriated posse:

> It was here determined without a dissenting voice that Mitch Lee and Frank Taggart should, by request, attend a neck-tie party and a vote should be taken as to what disposition should be made of Spencer...The crowd, which was increasingly rapidly, was about evenly divided as to Spencer's fate, and it was decided to return him to jail.[45]

Speaking about the murder of the train engineer, the severely injured Mitch Lee, just before he was hanged, viciously blurted out, "Well, by God! I did kill him!"[46] No doubt Dan Coomer felt a rationalizing pang of satisfaction upon hearing those words—clearly the man he had just gut-shot through and through was nothing more than a cowardly murderer—and too, he probably had little sympathy for Frank Taggart who "died hard of strangulation, a throat disease that is becoming extremely common among their ilk in this section."[47]

The brainy newsman may have written with a touch of sardonic wit about the thrilling capture and killing of escaped murderers, horse thieves, and train robbers, but humor was absent the minds of many who were personally involved—one way or the other. Today, however, the legal shenanigans do seem somewhat comical. Making a long story short, without resorting to exacting details, suffice to say after the murderous train robbery near Gage station, both Wells, Fargo & Company and the Southern Pacific Railroad offered rewards amounting to over $8000, a not insignificant sum at the time. Express company detectives James Hume for Wells, Fargo and Len Harris working for the railroad, indeed, were literally besieged with impassioned inquires.[48] Needless to say, nearly everyone mixed up in the original investigation and apprehension, or in re-capturing thugs after the jailbreak, was wanting a slice of the money.[49] Dan Coomer was not an exception. Since there was little agreement as to how the monies should be divvied, the whole matter ended up in court.[50] In the end, his attorney, W. A. Hawkins, was effective in arguing the case and Dan Coomer, as well as fellow posse members, T.E. Parks and Frank Andrews each walked away with a $500 chunk of the reward monies.[51]

Fort Bayard, New Mexico Territory where Dan Coomer finally caught up with and killed cow-thief Bud Rice. Courtesy, Silver City Museum.

As contentious as the September court case had been, Dan Coomer had little time to squander, wondering about spending his cut of the reward money. On Thanksgiving Day, 1884, he received word that a portion of his cattle ranging north of Central City were being stolen, slaughtered, and barbecued over searing coals before disappearing forevermore. Predictably, as everyone anticipated of the intractable Dan Coomer, the very next day, heading a five man posse he pushed forward in a diligent search for clues and cow-thieves.[52] North of Fort Bayard he found the evidence—entrails and hides—and followed sometimes obscure tracks to a wood-camp where he fearlessly threw down on "two Mexicans," one of whom confessed (not surprisingly) he knew the parties responsible for butchering Coomer cattle. Taking the informant with him as a guide, and as a hostage of sorts, Coomer's squad traveled to Central City where Jose Lopez, Albino Fresques, Danacio Gonzales, and Julio Castillo were pointed out. Dan Coomer made a citizen's arrest of all four, and boldly hauled them before local Justice of the Peace Givens. And again, not unsurprisingly, the whole group sang like yellow canaries, readily admitting their guilt. Thereafter, Dan Coomer delivered the prisoners to Silver City, turning them over to the Grant County Jailer where each were held in lieu of a $2000 bond and action of the Grand Jury.[53]

Characteristically, once again when an emergency arose Dan Coomer implicitly was in the vanguard. During May 1885, he was leading a forty man squadron, twenty on horseback and twenty more riding in wagons, in efforts directed toward protecting out-of-the-way settlers and chasing wayward Apaches who had jumped confinement at San Carlos Indian Reservation, embarking on a path of death and destruction.[54] Although on this particular mission Dan Coomer's platoon of citizen volunteers failed to engage the enemy, he fervently pressed the chase between Juniper Springs and the Pinos Altos Mountains, so much so, according to an editor's comments in the *Silver City Enterprise*, the bronco Apache were forced to abandoned seven ponies, which they promptly shot before vanishing into southwestern New Mexico wilderness.[55]

Disgruntled citizens, chagrined with the U.S. Army's sometimes seemingly futile efforts at catching or killing renegade Apache fighters, decided to take matters into their own hands, naturally, with the Governor's blessings. New Mexico denizens, once again, began forming militia companies throughout the territory. And, during one such emotionally charged public meeting in July (1885) at Silver City's Crown Hall, Dan Coomer was elected first lieutenant for "the new territorial regiment of mounted infantry."[56] Scantly two months later, Coomer was publicly extolled for his management of an exceedingly torturous scout, straight into the bowels of sinister Mogollon Mountains, north of Silver City. Of Dan Coomer, and his Captain, John W. Fleming, it was said that they "are always in front on the trail. They seemingly never tire, and certainly are good officers."[57]

Dan Coomer's willingness to interject himself into a fight—as long as he thought the cause was just—was not solely confined to doing battle with rustlers or Apache. Coomer's last gunplay was reasonably well documented, and is indicative of his problem solving and no nonsense mind-set. In early December, 1888, previous Galveston, Texas, resident Frank Heflin, a reputed mankiller, was making Silver City home. Frank Heflin was accomplished at tanking up on numbing doses of liquor, then becoming belligerent. On one such occasion his drunken shenanigans spiraled past any semblance of reasonable control. Frank got drunk, and with a double barreled shotgun went after his wife. As she ran from his threats and vile intimidation, running for her very life, he cut loose. "The entire right side of the unfortunate woman was filled with heavy duck shot, some of which entered the intestine…" making the hopes of her recovery doubtful.[58] Leaving his wounded spouse on the neighbors doorstep where she had fallen, Frank Heflin shamelessly headed back to his house. Quickly, because he was nearby, Dan Coomer was brought up to speed on what had just transpired. He acted decisively and without hesitation, calling on the drunken shooter to surrender. "Heflin replied by throwing a double barreled shotgun down on Dan, who fortunately was near a stone wall, behind which he dodged, and not too soon, as the shot from the gun struck the rocks all around him. Dan then raised and fired, but as Heflin was then inside his house and shooting from the door, no accurate aim could be taken."[59] No doubt much to his relief, Dan Coomer was joined by the local constable and his son, and the pinned down lawmen fired between twenty-five and thirty rounds trying to dislodge Heflin. Finally, after the besotted hellion fired two blasts from his shotgun, the impromptu possemen stormed the house and arrested Frank Heflin. Luckily, they were not injured, but alas, Frank Heflin was found to be wounded and bleeding. Whose shot actually found the mark— lacking modern-day ballistics tests—is indeterminate. Perhaps it was Dan Coomer's, perhaps not. Contemporarily it mattered not a whit. The community was glad Heflin was shot, by somebody. Sardonically a local newspaperman penned, "…but unfortunately it proved to be only a slight flesh wound."[60] The officers carted Frank Heflin off to the calaboose, and Dan Coomer went ahead with his customary business, seemingly unconcerned that he had just survived another gunfight. Once again, as so often was the case, he had lived up to his fearless reputation, doing his civic duty in "curbing the lawless element."

Perhaps outward appearances were somewhat misleading, since within a reasonably short time Dan Coomer's health began to fail. Although the diagnosis is undetermined, it can be factually reported while on a trip to Hot Springs, Arkansas during late Spring of 1890, Dan's health worsened and, sadly, the man who lived life to the fullest, the man who gave no quarter and asked for none—at age forty-three—was forced to surrender his last breath.[61] Dan Coomer's remains were returned to Silver City, and with honor, "before a large number of friends" he was interred in plot N-143-H at the Masonic Cemetery, leaving an estate "which places his family in comfortable circumstances."[62]

Undoubtedly there remain many unanswered questions concerning Dan Coomer's life and oftentimes heroic exploits, and maybe an ardent interest will be stirred, resulting in development of fresh clues and historic evidence worthy of further investigation. And just as surely, it would be tempting, but historically imprudent, to give Dan Coomer unwarranted status as a primary example of the Western gunfighter, especially when some have already earned their place on the roster with bogus credentials or with the naïve help of Hollywood movie-producers. Two accomplished modern-day writers and researchers, acknowledging there is no conclusive proof Wyatt Earp ever killed anyone, recently wrote it is indeed "a lamentable record for America's premier 'gunfighter'."[63] Dan Coomer's record was real! One nervy newspaperman of that period wrote, "In several instances (he) started the thieves on the road to a better life."[64] So, when twenty-first century historians and outlaw/lawmen aficionados are making thoughtful analyses about formidable champions of generations past, it would be reasonable to speak favorably of Dan Coomer and echo the grateful words of a frontier editor, "and we say, well done Dan!"

Daniel Coomer's headstone. Masonic Cemetery, Silver City, New Mexico. Courtesy, Terry Humble.

ENDNOTES CHAPTER 13

"AND WE SAY WELL DONE, DAN!"

[1] *Silver City Enterprise*, 04-04-1890
[2] *Ibid.*
[3] *Ibid.* And see, United States Census, 1880, Grant County, New Mexico Territory.
[4] *Ibid.*
[5] *Ibid.* And see, Julyan, Robert., *The Place Names of New Mexico.*
[6] Ungnade, Herbert E., *Guide to the New Mexico Mountains.*
[7] Thrapp, Dan. *Victorio and the Mimbres Apaches* and *The Conquest of Apacheria.* Also see, Sweeney, Edwin R., *Mangas Coloradas, Chief of the Chiricahua Apaches.*
[8] Alexander, Bob, *Dangerous Dan Tucker, New Mexico's Deadly Lawman.* Leon Metz's comments from the Introduction. P. 4.
[9] Casey, Robert J., *The Texas Border And Some Borderliners.* P. 313.
[10] *Silver City Independent*, 06-05-1917. And see, Ball, Larry D., "Militia Posses: The Territorial Militia In Civil Law Enforcement in New Mexico Territory, 1877-1883," *New Mexico Historical Review*, 55:1 (1980). "...Silver City, Grant County, where lawless men often gathered." P. 60.
[11] The breadth of Dan Coomer's business speculations are far too numerous to enumerate in an article, but suffice to say an examination of early newspaper accounts at Silver City, New Mexico and review of early Grant County courthouse records, clearly reveals the scope of Coomer's financial dealings. Also see, New Mexico Territorial Census, 1885. And see, *Grant County Herald*, 06-03-1876 regarding the death of his infant daughter.
[12] *Grant County Herald*, 10-06-1877. Also see, *Enterprise*, 03-21-1884, "Tom has led a remarkable career as a murderer and fugitive from justice for some time past...It is supposed that he killed his first man in Pueblo some twelve years ago...He next turned up in Arizona in the stage robbing business...Shortly after his arrival in Silver City he killed a man named Jack Clark in Ward's dance-house...In September, 1877, he killed Richard Howlett." And the *El Paso Lone Star* reported, "Tom is a bad one, has killed several persons, and if not brought to justice is liable to cause the death of others," in a story picked up by the *Enterprise* for 05-23-1884.
[13] *Ibid.*, 09-20-1879, and see, *Silver City Enterprise*, 10-01-1886.
[14] *Silver City Enterprise*, 10-01-1886. Harvey Howard Whitehill was the fourth sheriff of Grant County, New Mexico and the first lawman to arrest "Billy the Kid."
[15] *Ibid.*
[16] The *Silver City Enterprise* story does not identify Dan Coomer's partner in this adventure other than "a colored gentlemen," however, the Silver City Museum Director, Susan Berry, has determined the person was George Williams, who for the time period in question ranched on the lower Mimbres. The *Silver City Independent*, in a June 5, 1917 edition, refers to Williams as being among "the men prominent at that time in the development of the district..."
[17] Of the pursuit a 10-10-1879 edition of the *Grant County Herald* reported, "He (Coomer) traveled as far as the Point of Mountains, this side of Tucson, and thence to Hooker's Ranch, Fort Grant, Fort Thomas, San Carlos and Pueblo

"And We Say, Well Done Dan!"

Viejo." The account used in this text was, however, taken from the *Silver City Enterprise*, 10-01-1886.

[18] *Silver City Enterprise*, 12-26-1902.

[19] *Ibid.*, 10-01-1886.

[20] *Ibid.* For more information on a truly formidable and exceedingly dangerous Southwestern lawman see, DeArment, Robert K., "Deadly Deputy," *True West*, November 1991. Also see, this author's biography, *Dangerous Dan Tucker, New Mexico's Deadly Lawman*.

[21] *Ibid.* The *Silver City Enterprise* reports the U.S. Army deserter received a five year sentence.

[22] *Grant County Herald*, 10-10-1879.

[23] *Ibid.*, 09-20-1879.

[24] Alexander, *Dangerous Dan Tucker*. And see, *The Daily Southwest*, 07-27-1880. Also see, *Grant County Herald*, 02-12-1881, "Barney O'Tool was the real name of the man who was executed here last August under the name of Chas. Williams..." And see, *Silver City Enterprise*, 12-12-1902.

[25] *Silver City Enterprise*, 10-27-1949., "I'll Never Forget," by Lou Blachly.

[26] *The Southwest*, 08-20-1880.

[27] *Silver City Enterprise*, 10-01-1886.

[28] *Ibid.*

[29] *Ibid.*, & 12-12-1902.

[30] *Ibid.*

[31] *Ibid.*, 12-12-1902. According to the informant, "the two (McClellan and Bud Rice) used to make periodical trips away to the south, and come back with a goodly supply of stock, and then would go on a weeks spree..." There are several early day newspaper reports reflecting the legal problems of Billy McClellan, such as this in the *Enterprise*, "Wm. McClellan, who in Las Cruces last week was found not guilty in the trial for the killing of Burns, has been indicted for stealing horses and placed under $500 bonds."

[32] *Ibid.*

[33] *Southwest Sentinel*, 05-19-1883. And see, *Silver City Enterprise*, 05-18-1883.

[34] Rye, Edgar, *The Quirt and the Spur*. P. 165.

[35] *Silver City Enterprise*, 10-01-1886.

[36] *Southwest Sentinel*, 11-28-1883. And, *Silver City Enterprise*, 03-14-1884. Also see, official *Register of Prisoners Confined in the Grant County Jail*, New Mexico State Records Center and Archives. And, for a comprehensive article about the crime and its aftermath, see, DeArment, Robert K., "Sheriff Whitehill and the Kit Joy Gang,," *Old West*, 1994 (Winter).

[37] *Ibid.*, 03-15-1884.

[38] *Ibid.*

[39] Bryan, Howard., *Robbers Rogues and Ruffians*. P. 134.

[40] *Southwest Sentinel*, 03-15-1884.

[41] Bryan, P. 134. And see, *Silver City Enterprise*, 03-14-1884, "From here he (Coomer) opened fire on the gang, his second shot bringing Chaves from his horse...". Caldwell, George, "New Mexico's First Train Robbery," *NOLA Quarterly*, Vol. XIII, No. 3 (Winter 1989) reports that Coomer was wounded in the vicious exchange of gunfire, however, most renditions omit such remarks. If in fact, Coomer was wounded during the shoot-out, the paucity of primary source materials suggesting the same indicates any injuries sustained were less than critical.

Lawmen, Outlaws and S.O.Bs.

[42] *Southwest Sentinel*, 03-15-1884. This report also credits Dan Coomer with killing, or at least wounding, Chavez, "In this fight Coomer narrowly escaped being shot and it is almost certain that he wounded Chavez." And see, Nelson, Susan., *The Silver City Book I, "Wild and Woolly Days.,"* P. 44, "Out about three miles the robbers made a stand to fight. The first thing they did was to shoot George Washington between the eyes." This version implies Cleveland was killed by his cohorts for "snitching." Wayne Whitehill, who was a youngster at the time, told historian Lou Blachly that "Kit" Joy shot Cleveland "…right in the forehead." Whitehill to Blachly, Pioneers Foundation Interview, Zimmerman Library—Center for Southwest Research, University of New Mexico. Other versions and the newspaper story credit Ed Mayer with killing George Washington Cleveland.

[43] Ailman, H. B. (Lundwall, Helen, ed.), *Pioneering in Territorial Silver City.*

[44] *Silver City Enterprise*, 03-14-1884.

[45] *Ibid.*

[46] *Ibid.*

[47] *Ibid.* Charles Spencer was returned to the Grant County Jail.

[48] Dillon, Richard, *Wells, Fargo Detective—A Biography of James B. Hume.* P. 218. And see, Ball, Larry, *Desert Lawmen, The High Sheriffs of New Mexico and Arizona, 1846-1912.* P. 93.

[49] *Silver City Enterprise*, 05-16-1884.

[50] *Ibid.*, 09-05-1884. And see, *Southwest Sentinel*, 10-18-1884.

[51] *Ibid.* And see, DeArment, "Sheriff Whitehill & the Kit Joy Gang," *Old West*, P. 19. Also, the paying of cash incentives was not uncommon, "Between December 1873 and February 1885, according to the General Cash Books, Wells Fargo rewarded at least one hundred people: sheriffs, citizens, and guards." See, Chandler, Robert J., "Wells Fargo: 'We Never Forget!'," *NOLA Quarterly*, Vol. XI, No. 4, (Spring 1987), P. 7.

[52] *Southwest Sentinel*, 12-06-1884.

[53] *Ibid.* Also see, *Silver City Enterprise*, 12-05-1884.

[54] *Silver City Enterprise*, 05-29-1885. That our subject was in charge is unequivocally confirmed, "…under the leadership of Dan Coomer…"

[55] *Ibid.*

[56] *Southwest Sentinel*, 07-25-1885. John W. Fleming, a self-made mining mogul, public spirited citizen, and, in the end, a reported millionaire, was made Captain of the militia company. See, Berry, Susan & Russell, Sharman Apt., *Built to Last, An Architectural History of Silver City, New Mexico.* P. 21, 37, & 44.

[57] *Ibid.*, 09-22-1885.

[58] *Silver City Enterprise*, 12-07-1888. Later it will be reported that Mrs. Heflin did not die as a result of the gunshot wounds.

[59] *Ibid.*

[60] *Ibid.*

[61] *Ibid.*, 04-04-1890.

[62] *Ibid.* And, information furnished by local Grant County historian and researcher Terry Humble. Coomer's headstone is inscribed with a date of death as March 26, 1891, but his obituary was carried in an April 4, 1890 edition of the local newspaper, which by implication suggests the marker was mistakenly engraved at a later date, but was placed at the grave site anyway, .

[63] Bailey, Lynn R. and Chaput, Don., *Cochise County Stalwarts.* Volume I, P. 114.

[64] *Silver City Enterprise*, 04-04-1890.

CHAPTER 14

"I JUMPED OFF MY HORSE AND STARTED SHOOTING"

Herff Alexander Carnes—A Babyfaced Texas Terror

Oftentimes when hurling good-natured barbs between each other, one joking lawman will rag another with annoying criticism such as, "Damn, you couldn't track an elephant after a snowstorm." Well, if truth be known, there weren't too many snowstorms in faraway West Texas, but the subject material for this biographical sketch could positively trail a pachyderm, literally. But, more of that story later. Herff Alexander Carnes was no animal catcher. He was a manhunter

To the layman, that brushy country below San Antonio is generically dubbed, South Texas. Indisputably, the region is rich. Rich with history, rich with heralded triumphs, rich with heartbreaking defeats. The area was pathway and homeland for many of the Canary Islanders sallying forth during 1731, led by the indefatigable Juan Leal Goras.[1] A hundred years later, after the stinging Apache raids on Spanish Mission livestock herds pastured nearby had to some extent been curbed, Stephen F. Austin, at the welcoming induction of Spanish Governor Don Drasmo Seguin, drafted his plans for colonization.[2] And, nearly forty years later, out of this massive chunk of South Texas real estate, Wilson County was sharply carved, on February 13, 1860. By the following August the new county was formally organized, a make-do courthouse at Sutherland Springs in John Irwin's mercantile store.[3] As with most squabbling tit for tat battles to gain coveted shire town honors, the county seat was next awarded to the community of Lodi, then back to Sutherland Springs, then back to Lodi, and lastly, after all the comical, but not uncommon commotion, in 1885, to Floresville.[4] From its beginnings Wilson County was bandit country, and after closing hostilities of the Civil War it still was. It was also cow-country.

Herff Alexander Carnes, Texas Ranger, standing, first from left. Captain John R. Hughes is seated, first from right. Courtesy, Texas Ranger Hall of Fame and Museum.

Not terribly far from the courthouse at Floresville in the southwestern reaches of Wilson County is the community of Fairview, and that is where Joseph Milton Carnes, a farmer and farrier, and his wife Mary Catherine, lovingly nicknamed "Mollie," welcomed into the world their third born son, Herff Alexander, on the 23rd day of May, 1879.[5]

Herff A. Carnes was no doubt a typical little boy growing up on the still sometimes wild and woolly South Texas frontier. No doubt Herff, at an early age, learned to fork feisty mounts, cast hand-built loops at lively livestock, and let the hammers drop on Colt's revolving pistols and lever-action Winchesters. And too, based on inspection of primary source documents, it is clear Herff was literate and articulate, a clear indication of at least minimal attendance in a Wilson County schoolroom.[6] Anecdotally there is, indeed, a delightful tale regarding five-year old Herff, who, accompanied by his daddy and older brother Burt, traveled to Floresville for observance of the dedication ceremonies at the freshly completed county courthouse. Later that evening at a toe-tapping dance, William Alexander Anderson "Big Foot" Wallace was chosen to lead the traditional Grand March. Reluctantly the celebrated Indian fighter and ex-Texas Ranger consented, although he was decidedly embarrassed at the shabby condition of his moccasins. So eager were the crowd to have Wallace's participation, John Griffith was persuaded to open up his dry goods store and outfit the hard-as-nails stalwart with a brand-new pair of shoes. Apposite to his nickname, of course, the footwear was too small, and only after the application of an "ample supply of talcum powder" could size twelves' be forced into the shoes. One joyful promenade around the "spacious" courtroom was sufficient suffering. "Big Foot" stepped outside, removed the tight fitting clodhoppers and began rubbing his tender and blistered feet. To youngsters Herff and Burt it was more than kinda funny, a grizzled and fearless frontiersman, whining—and barefooted![7]

It would appear that Herff Carnes grew to manhood honorably, and by the time he turned twenty-one years old (1900) was "operating a ranch in New Mexico."[8] Scarcely three years later, however, the 5'7" blue-eyed lad had turned his back on the life of a farmer and stockman, becoming one of the Lone Star's finest. On February 13, 1903, at Floresville, Texas, Herff A. Carnes, riding a $65 horse, enlisted as a private in Company D., Ranger Force (Texas Rangers), taking his oath of office before the legendary "Border Boss," Captain John R. Hughes.[9] Later, on July 13th, he reaffirmed his oath at Company Headquarters, Alice, Nueces County, Texas.[10]

Texas Ranger Private Herff A. Carnes was on duty just a few days when he was dispatched to Duval County to make an arrest in a murder case. He arrested Teadoro Garza and delivered him to the county jail at San Diego.[11] Shortly thereafter Carnes traveled to San Antonio and "arrested a negro wanted for murder."[12] As Autumn drew near, Herff was assigned to Laredo, acting as "a quarantine guard in a yellow fever scare."[13] Enumerating all of Carne's arrests and "scouts" is an exercise that, for the most part, could be executed by meticulous inspection of Ranger Force Company D., *Monthly Returns;* indeed, the records are accessible. Numerous are the arrests he made for a multitude of criminal violations, misdemeanors and felonies. Illustrative of his workload and steadfast attention to duty can be extrapolated by examination of the *Monthly Returns* for just one time period, December, 1904. Of fourteen entries made by Captain Hughes, eight mention Carnes, and his arrests take in a wide variety of offenses; Disturbing the Peace; Illegal Voting; Smuggling; and Theft of Horses.[14] The next year, in June, according to *Monthly Returns* there were nineteen arrests. Herff Carnes made eight of the apprehensions by himself, and assisted with two more.[15]

Texas Rangers, left to right, H.P. "Red" Brady, J.C. "Doc" White, unknown, Herff A. Carnes, and Milam Wright. Courtesy, Texas Ranger Hall of Fame and Museum.

The youthful ranger was making a name for himself within Lone Star peace officers' circles, catching the approving eye of both state officials and federal authorities. During January, 1906, he stood in the spotlight once again, along with two other Texas Rangers, James Campbell "Doc" White and Milam H. Wright. At the request of Harris County Sheriff Anderson the trio of lawmen were sent to Humble to keep the peace during a volatile oil-field labor dispute.[16] Without a doubt the explosive situation didn't measure up to overstated tradition; one riot, one ranger! Nevertheless, the plucky trio "held off more than three hundred enraged strikers before the controversy was settled."[17] The courageous officers received adulation for their stellar performance.[18]

Later in the year when a vacancy was created by resignation, Herff Alexander Carnes was promoted to Sergeant of Company D., Ranger Force.[19] Ascension to the rank of a non-commissioned officer did not alleviate Herff Carne's everyday work burdens. Forthrightly he arrested W.C. Rice and J. Davenport for fighting, placing both in jail and, shortly thereafter, he and Milam Wright arrested five murder suspects.[20] When Company D. was reassigned to the Trans-Pecos area of West Texas, dutifully, Sergeant Herff Carnes presented himself for duty, and it was the Big Bend and border country that captured his very heart and soul, for the remainder of his life. A review of Company D. *Monthly Returns* clearly reveals the fact Sergeant Carnes was in almost constant motion, roaming all over the gargantuan area making arrests ranging from malicious mischief to murder. And, during November, 1909, when Company D. "changed stations" with Company B. at Amarillo in the Texas Panhandle, once more Herff A. Carnes obediently transferred, but the beguiling border country was calling, irresistibly so.[21] While on duty, riding the scattered rails on the lonesome *Llano Estacado*, Sergeant Carnes was saddened to learn that his brother Quirl Bailey, who too was an unswerving Texas Ranger, had been ambushed and brutally murdered in a South Texas shoot-out with "Mexicans" along the banks of the Rio Grande.[22] No doubt still stricken with heartfelt grief, Sergeant Herff Carnes was somewhat pleased and thankful, when Company D. headquarters was reassigned to Ysleta, just below El Paso, during December of 1910.[23]

Known throughout the ever troublesome region as a "respected and feared" border country peace officer, a lawman "noted for his composure and ability to think fast in emergencies," it wasn't too very long before Texas Ranger Sergeant Carnes was recruited by federal bureaucrats. Herff Carnes was offered, and accepted, the much higher paying job of an Inspector with the United States Mounted Customs Service.[24] And it would be in this employ that Herff Alexander Carnes would have to fight his two most punishing battles.

The Lone Star border country, from a lawman's viewpoint, had never been quiet. Admittedly there were fragments of time when there seemed a relative degree of calm; 1915 wasn't, however, one of them. Across the international line, conspiracy and violence flourished. Some cleanly referred to the ongoing bloody turmoil as the Mexican Revolution, others rightly saw it as a Civil War, but from an American perspective it was plainly just, *trouble*. And, when Basilo Ramos was arrested in South Texas, at McAllen, in wily possession of the *Plan of San Diego*, a detailed insurgent blueprint for the uncomplicated killing of "North American males over 16 years of age" and the retaking of Texas, New Mexico, Arizona and California, a bleeding race war ensued with atrocities legitimately credited to both accounts.[25] Adding to the murder and mayhem were the cross-border raiders who were essentially bandits. Already during 1915, Texas Ranger Robert Lee Burdett had been ruthlessly gunned down at Fabens, and a scant three weeks later, Mounted Customs Inspector Joe Sitter and another ranger, Eugene Hulen, had been fatally bushwacked west of Valentine.

Working out of Sierra Blanca, Texas, Mounted Customs Inspector Herff Carnes, in the company of William Davis "Dave" Allison, an El Paso County Constable by official commission, but paid as a range detective by area cattlemen, and Customs Inspector J.D. White, on the morning of August 27th began a routine horseback patrol, searching for cow-thieves, smugglers, or any other desperadoes haunting the mountainous and sparsely populated ranch country.[26]

There should be little doubt Herff Carnes looked at Dave Allison, his senior by twenty-five years, with awe. Certainly a shave-tail U.S. Army lieutenant, George S. Patton, Jr., did. The future "Blood and Guts" General remarked that Dave Allison was an "old man with a sweet face and white hair…and the most noted gunman here in Texas…"[27] Later, George Patton, would thankfully praise the old-time Southwest lawman for teaching him a priceless thing or two about the practicalities of a genuine gunplay, "I started back when I saw a man on a horse come right in front of me, I started to shoot at him but remembered that Dave Allison had always said to shoot at the horse of an escaping man and I did so and broke the horse's hip, he fell on his rider."[28] During the time he lived, W.D. "Dave" Allison was known far and wide for his unfettered fearlessness. Like Herff A. Carnes, at an earlier time, Dave Allison had been a Texas Ranger Sergeant under command of Captain Hughes. Shortly thereafter, acting as a Special Ranger, Dave Allison neatly, over in North Texas, put the shackles on Bob Brown, a fugitive running from his participation in a 1900 Fairbank, Arizona Territory train robbery gone dreadfully awry, one during which express messenger Jeff Milton had been shamefully sledgehammered to a boxcar floor by the wicked volley fired by the outlaws. But even before that he had been a well-regarded and five times elected West Texas sheriff at Midland. And, after his trusty service to the state of Texas, Dave Allison, for awhile, was a lieutenant with the hard-bitten and daredevil Arizona Rangers. Afterward, for a stint he served as the resolute Chief of Security for Colonel Bill Greene at the mogul's mining operations in Cananea, Sonora, Mexico. Dave Allison is attributed with organizing the dogged and gravely outnumbered defensive forces during a murderous 1906 labor strike and bitter riot. Reportedly, during the

"I Jumped Off My Horse And Started Shooting"

horrific six-shooter scrap Dave Allison fought like a demon possessed! And yet still later, after the one-armed Texas mankiller and poisonously dangerous Jesse J. Rascoe had his crack at the job, and after Roy Woofter was fatally gunned down during the "Whiskey War" while serving as City Marshall at Roswell, New Mexico Territory, Dave Allison stepped in and wrestled the town away from the sway of bootleggers and whore-mongers. During 1915, in the vicinity of Sierra Blanca, Texas, William D. "Dave" Allison was a cow-thief's nastiest horror, maybe even his very last deathly deliberation.[29]

On the 29th of August, somehow Inspector White's horse suffered a wire cut, and owing to the fact his packhorse was working sans iron horseshoes, the federal lawman was forced to reverse course for Sierra Blanca. Herff Carnes and Dave Allison persisted with their arduous scout, arriving, by sundown, at the Tom Yarbro ranch southwest of Van Horn, Texas. There they were informed that R.C. "Dick" Love and his cowboys had engaged five "Mexican bandits" in a running gunbattle south of Sierra Blanca and the "heavily armed" fugitives were now, as night fell, somewhere snaking their way through the jagged and mysterious Eagle Mountains, probably headed east though Frenchman's Canyon.[30] Fervently Dick Love, after scooting back to the ranch in fading light, was fast summoning his brothers, of which there were several, and other alarmed cowmen, nimbly orchestrating the morrow's manhunt. Dick Love telegraphed a warning:

> Look out for five Mexicans in Eagle Mountains, well armed, are going your way.[31]

At first light on the 30th, Herff Carnes and Dave Allison "started for the gap in the Eagle Mountains," the route they hunched the bandits would pass through. They weren't wrong! At 8:00 o'clock in the morning they cut their prey's trail, eastbound through the Taylor Ranch, toward domineering High-Lonesome Mountain in the Van Horn Range. Quickly they rushed back to Taylor Ranch headquarters and saw to notification of the Culberson County Sheriff, John A. Morine, instructing him, right quick, to draw together a tough posse and come to the ranch, "where they would find saddle horses waiting."[32] Hurriedly, Carnes and Allison resumed the chase, once again picking up the desperadoes' trail at nearby Green River Draw, and after a short pursuit, pinpointed the bandits' last breakfast fire. The lawmen's outdoors skills, through years of matter-of-fact know-how, were keen. The Mexican bandits were "not more than an hour and a half or two hours ahead."[33] Common sense dictated Carnes and Allisons' next move—wisely they waited at the smoldering and dying campfire—for about an hour. Eagerly they were joined by two hard-riding posses, Sheriff Morine and three men from Van Horn, and "Rowdy" Love's crew of eight, who had safely navigated the narrow gap through the Eagle Mountains.[34] Assuming command of both posses, Dave Allison directed the "hot pursuit" and, after about five miles, it was clearly deduced that the bandits, wholly unaware they were still the prize at the other end of an unsmiling chase, had ridden into a blind canyon for an overdue siesta, south of High-Lonesome Mountain, about nine miles from the border.[35] Foolishly the bandits loitered. The gritty posse didn't.

West Texas ranchers, the Love family, several of whom were posse members in the torturous chase after and subsequent killing of the well-known Mexican Revolutionary personality Pascual Orozco, Jr., and his four heavily-armed compadres. Standing, from left to right, George Love, Lizzie Love, Tom D. Love (captured outlaw Bill Cook), Wert Love, Bob Love. Sitting, from L. to R., Dick Love, Fanny Love, Leonard Love and J.R. "Rowdy" Love. Courtesy, Richard and Bill Love.

"I Jumped Off My Horse And Started Shooting"

Herff A. Carnes, left, and a border law enforcement comrade, tentatively *identified as Edgar Neal. Courtesy, Texas Ranger Hall of Fame and Museum.*

Adroitly laying plans for the forthcoming battle, Dave Allison strategically divided his forces, sending Sheriff Morine and seven men around the right side of the mountain to "cut them off from escape," while he, "in the lead" and the other possemen charged down the mountain until in "close firing range." Herff Alexander Carnes succinctly, almost casually, comments, "We all dismounted and began firing."[36] And adds, "The Mexicans having first fired at us as we charged off the mountain, Mr. Allison and several others commanded them to halt, but instead, they returned fire. They were so taken by surprise that their fire was unsteady, and for that reason none of our posse were injured. The battle lasted only about fifteen or twenty minutes..."[37]

Culberson County Sheriff John Morine supplements:

Lawmen, Outlaws and S.O.Bs.

The place the Mexicans were in, was hidden from our view in a rincon at the head of a very rough rocky canon and after acting upon a plan to surround them I was to take the right hand swing and appear above them and the other part of the posse to swing to the left but before arriving at my position the Mexicans evidently suspicioned something for they immediately grabbed their arms and fired on the left hand party as soon as they made their appearance. We all closed in about the same time and after a fusillade of shots all the Mexicans were killed. Upon making an examination of the Mexicans' camp we obtained five horses, three of which I am positive were stolen horses, also five saddles, bridles and blankets, five 30-30 Marlin octagon barrel safety rifles, one Smith and Wesson 44 Special Revolver, one 45 Colt's revolver and approximately between 1000 and 1500 rounds of 30-30 cartridges. There was also found in the camp some fresh jerked beef supposed to have been part of a calf butchered by them the evening before on George Love's ranch...[38]

Herff Alexander Carnes, left, and the fortunate survivor of a ghastly Mexican border bushwhacking, Texas Ranger Pat Craighead. Courtesy, Texas Ranger Hall of Fame and Museum.

"I Jumped Off My Horse And Started Shooting"

Pascual Orozco, Jr., topsy-turvy Mexican Revolutionary General. Dubious patriot or Mexican bandit? Killed below High-Lonesome Mountain south of Van Horn, Texas, with four others by a hard-charging posse of lawmen and unfaltering Big Bend Country cattlemen. Herff Carnes was in on the gunplay. Courtesy, El Paso Public Library.

Upon closer inspection of the dead Mexicans and during an inventory of their personal belongings, it was discovered that one of the men had dyed his mustache black and a "packet" of mustache dye was found in his coat pocket.[39] And too, in the saddle pockets of this *mal hombre* were "coded messages" and "reports of American troop movements along the border."[40] As Carnes and Allison mused, perhaps, just perhaps, the dead men grotesquely sprawled before them were a little more than common, run-of-the-mill, Mexican bandits. Herff Carnes even ventured a guess, that the one with the deceptively colored mustache sure looked like the sometimes loved and sometimes despised and always contentious Mexican revolutionary character, Pascual Orozco, Jr., a slippery fugitive from American criminal justice—wanted on the U.S. side for jumping bail and Neutrality Act violations. Indeed, Herff Carnes was so curious, he "wired the Collector of Customs to send some one to identify him."[41] U.S. Mounted Customs Inspector Louis Holzman and an *El Paso Morning Times* reporter, Dave James, traveled to the scene and made an official identification.[42] The dead were, indeed, Pascual Orozco, Jr.; Jose F. Delgado, a former Mexican Army officer; Christoforo Caballero, an ex-Chief of Guards at the Juarez Custom's Port of Entry; Andreas Sandoval, a loyal foot-soldier to Orozco; and Miguel Terrazas, a Big Bend country guide, and some say a purveyor of weapons.[43]

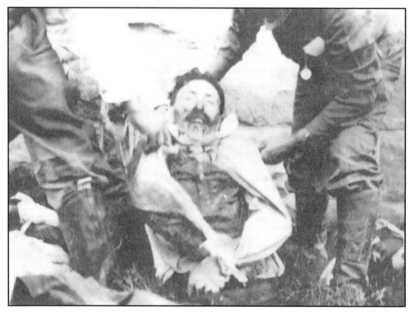

Pascual Orozco, Jr., on display, in death, at the Van Horn, Texas depot. The posse that killed him, and four others, Herff Alexander Carnes included, stood trial for murder in a Culberson County courtroom. Courtesy, El Paso Public Library.

An onsite *Inquest* was held by T.R. Owen, Justice of the Peace, Precinct No. 1, Culberson County, Texas, and the deceased remains were in due course transported to town for embalming, disposition and—display.[44] At the Van Horn depot, the bodies were laid out for all to see, and for a photograph or two. The unanticipated killing of Pascual Orozco, Jr., was, indeed, big-time news, worthy of national press coverage and U.S. State Department inquiry. During his life Pascual Orozco, Jr. had laid his stamp on the sly schemes and intrigues in several of Mexico's recurring revolutions, and depending on personal political perspective, his donation to history was either a wearisome stain or a worthy statement. In certain quarters he was seen as treasonous, a traitor; others thought him a patriot, their liberator; yet there was an exclusive clique that thought him nothing but a pirating opportunist. West Texas cowmen weren't sympathetic or kindhearted; making off with their horses and butchering their beef was not foraging off the land for a laudable cause, it was simply, *theft*!

Culberson County Texas Sheriff John A. Morine stands with the property seized from Pascual Orozco and his associates after the 1915 shoot-out in the Van Horn Mountains. From Apache Days and After *by Thomas Cruse. Courtesy, Caxton Printers, Ltd., Caldwell, Idaho.*

Clearly, a devotee of exhilarating outlaw/lawmen escapades will not be surprised. The melancholic fascination with Pascual Orozco, Jr. was not assuaged with his death. Border country lawmen on the U.S. side saw his overdue demise as fitting payback for banditry, others in the predominately Spanish speaking El Paso County and across the Rio Grande saw Orozco as a victim, murdered. Wild conspiracy theories ran rampant. Wasn't Pascual Orozco in fact carrying $50,000 in gold, and just where was the money now? Why were not Texas possemen killed or wounded during that sizzling showdown just south of an out-of-the-way and secretive High-Lonesome Mountain? Weren't Pascual Orozco, Jr. and his cohorts good shots, too? If truth be really known, Pancho Villa, Orozco's longtime arch-enemy, stage-managed the assassination, an evil architect for the politically calculated and cold-blooded murder, didn't he? Had not the ruthless possemen—to the last man—the Culberson County elected officials, the cowmen, the Judges, and the Van Horn townsmen all taken a blood oath of secrecy? The jabber escalated, unabated. The forever fragile United States/Mexico relationship was strained, perhaps, irrevocably. Was there no way out of the diplomatic quagmire? Well, yes, there was. Seemingly, politicos at Washington, D. C. in the U.S. State Department offered a prescription for silencing protests and a workable exit strategy.[45]

During an October, 1915, term, an *all*-Anglo Culberson County Grand Jury returned indictments regarding the deaths of Pascual Orozco, Jr. and his slain allies. Charged with "murder with malice aforethought" were Sheriff John A. Morine, U.S. Mounted Customs Inspector Herff A. Carnes, William D. "Dave" Allison, George, Bob, "Rowdy," Prince, and B.M. "Judge" Love, along with Joel T. Fenley, A.B. Medley, Pete Wetzel, J.O. English, J.W. Mellard, and an El Paso County Deputy Sheriff, William H. Schrock.[46] Formal criminal charges against three of the shoot-out participants, "Rowdy" Love, J.W. Mellard, and J.O. English, were inexplicably dismissed.[47] On October 5th, the other eleven defendants surrendered on the courthouse steps, were officially placed under arrest, and delivered to the courtroom for a speedy trial and judgment by their peers. And a short trip before the Bar of Justice it would prove to be.[48] The murder case styled *The State of Texas vs. John A. Morine, et als*, Cause No. 35, in the 34th Judicial District of Texas, at Van Horn, was heard in but short order. After careful analytical review of the proffered evidence, and after receipt of *Instructions* from Judge Dan M. Jackson, the twelve man, *all*-Anglo, jury retired for uncomplicated deliberations. From the get-go there had been not doubt, certainly not beyond a standard of reasonableness. The verdict:

> We, the jury in the above entitled and numbered cause, find the defendants not guilty.[49]

"I Jumped Off My Horse And Started Shooting"

The final outcome of the legal shenanigan was perfectly predictable from the very onset of State Department urgings. In far-flung and turbulent West Texas during that shard of time, no *all*-Anglo trial jury was about to convict an *all*-Anglo posse of killing an *all*-Mexican squadron of bandits. The State Department saved face with a trial and diplomatic wiggling, the State of Texas feigned an act of mending border fences, farcically, and the scapegoats, Herff Alexander Carnes included, skated.

Straightforward raconteurs of authentic Old West yarns must candidly admit, that in spite of hoped for melodrama, in reality, a frontier peace officer's workdays were long, sometimes monotonous, and could be terribly nondescript—one tour of duty blandly blending with the last, and the next. Indisputably the Grim Reaper ever presently lurked, maybe around an adobe corral corner, in the shadows at the end of a mahogany bar, or concealed in the willows and canebrakes down by the murky river, but the lawman wasn't perilously challenged face to face, day by day. A case in point.

Texas Rangers on patrol and riding their favorite mounts in the Big Bend country of far West Texas. Charles Brown on "Buckskin" on the left, and on the right J.C. "Doc" White riding "Old Sorrel." Courtesy, Texas Ranger Hall of Fame Museum.

Lawmen, Outlaws and S.O.Bs.

Constantly watchful and always attuned to trickery employed by contraband smugglers, U.S. Mounted Customs Inspector Herff Carnes, once in a while stumbled upon baffling clues and incomprehensible tid-bits of intelligence. While yet working out of Sierra Blanca, Herff Carnes on one such "scout," accompanied by an adept El Paso County Deputy Sheriff, H.A. Moore, gracelessly was forced to admit he was exhaustively stumped. While working horseback southwest of town, in the vicinity of the Quitman Mountains, the dynamic duo cut the trial made by a weird set of tracks, dints neither had ever seen before. Moore expanded, "It looked like somebody had put buckets on the sand at regular intervals."[50] Unsheathing Winchesters from saddle scabbards, Carnes and Moore relentlessly trailed, all the while apprehensive that some industrious smuggler had a new trick up his shrewd sleeve. The wary and rightly diffident pursuit lasted for miles, and miles, and miles. Then it ended, abruptly! The formidable team of Herff Alexander Carnes and H.A. Moore came face to tail with a lumbering elephant unceremoniously tied to a red-painted, but slow-moving circus wagon. Perhaps their tactical mission was a Texas first, perhaps not. It would prove to be years and years before either gutsy gendarme publicly admitted to the folly.[51].

After finishing his tour of duty at Sierra Blanca, Herff Carnes was transferred, reassigned to Ysleta. Herff and Letha, his wife of twenty odd years, joyfully relocated to the lively border town and it was there that they made a permanent home. There is little doubt Herff Carnes, at least from time to time, pondered about his life, the ups and the downs. The callous murder of Quirl, both a blood and law enforcement brother had been exceptionally trying for Herff, but the loss was somewhat tempered with knowledge that his older brother, Burt, was, and had been since 1917, the straightforward and esteemed sheriff at his birthplace, Wilson County.[52] There too, was solace in knowing he had almost finished the fulfilling charge of raising two of his beloved children, nineteen year-old Hughes A. Carnes, a student at North Texas State Teachers College in Denton, and seventeen year-old Mary Elizabeth, about to graduate from the Ysleta high-school. They had been lovingly patterned into courteous, trustworthy, and decent people. Their little brother, David, too had a bright future.[53] After fifty-three years and well-seasoned maturity, Herff Carnes unquestionably recognized that his youngest child, the six-year old, had been absolutely born at the right time. Modern technology was at hand. There were airplanes overhead, automobiles sputtering about, electrifying power at the mere flip of a switch, and no more necessary trips outside in the middle of the night. Life in 1932, undeniably, was good.

To be sure, Herff Carnes, on reflection, was bowled over. Had he not, during his lifetime, witnessed the celebrated "Big Foot" Wallace dance? Had he not ridden horseback many a mile, and made many arrests with legendary "Border Boss" John Hughes, and had he not stood firm during a ghastly gunbattle along side that "quiet looking old man with a sweet face and white hair," Dave Allison? Atypically for the times, when most men hopped from job to job, had he not had but two, Texas Ranger and Mounted Inspector? Times, indeed, were changing, the work, however, was not. The smugglers were still smuggling; on foot; by heavily burdened donkey; by well-guarded pack-trains; in boxcars pulled by chugging locomotives; and even now, by fast speeding Fords. Down along the river it was still wild and woolly, an Old West despairingly trapped in a time warp.

Most of Thursday had already faded away, it was 7 o'clock in the evening, the 1st of December 1932. Herff Carnes, with three other Inspectors, acting on an informant's tip had secreted themselves two miles southeast of Ysleta, down by the Rio Grande amongst the cattails and willowy reeds, fronting a well-worn smugglers' crossing. The contraband was to be illicit liquor, the Mexican smugglers were to be "heavily armed."[54] Lying on the sandy and damp ground the river guards waited, patiently. Not unpredictably, two men, the "advance guard" for the smugglers, began crossing the river, about twenty-five yards apart.[55] The snitch's treachery was reliable, right on the money. The normally feisty Inspectors strained themselves into quietness. Not a whisper. Not even the blink of an itching eye. The two Mexicans, suspiciously paranoid, but not sure, approached. Closer and closer. Foreheads were perspiring, palms were sweating, hearts were pounding, and adrenaline was pulsatingms, but all too quickly truth hit home, their stratagem was fundamentally, in this instance, flawed. Their camouflage techniques had been good, too good. The two advancing lookouts, almost now even with them, were going to pass by, one on either side of the Inspectors, completely unawares. That is until shooting started, if it did, then the Customs officers would be caught in a withering cross-fire, an inescapable deathtrap. Smugglers to the front, smugglers in back of them. It was now or never!

Herff Carnes rose from his position and advanced on the Mexican nearest him, his rifle in hand, but not at the ready. As Carnes hallooed the challenge, with lightening quickness the smuggler fired. "The bullet, striking his (Carne's) pistol, split before entering his abdomen at the right side. The fragments of the steel-jacketed pellet went through his body."[56] Herff was mercilessly battered to the ground, the halved projectile punching and damaging life sustaining organs—two crippling corridors. The other aghast Inspectors, armed with "automatic shotguns" opened fire on the two smugglers, who by now were hotfooting it back across the Rio Grande. Whether or not either was killed or wounded is debatable, but on the American side of the line the owl-hoots were not apprehended, ever.[57]

The severely wounded Herff Carnes was at once removed to the Masonic Hospital at El Paso, thirteen miles away. Herff's medical condition was diagnosed as critical, and the attending physician, Dr. J.H. Gambrell, advised newspapermen, "he is barely holding his own."[58] Blood transfusions were needed, and Herff Carnes received three from Custom's Inspectors, Clay Roberts, L.L. Gemoets, and Albert Bean. El Paso Customs Service, the whole staff, volunteered to without delay donate blood, as did 25 appalled and grief-stricken United States Border Patrolmen.[59] Herff's oldest son rushed home to Ysleta from Denton, Mary Elizabeth fretted, little David cried, and Letha prayed, prayed that her adored husband would live another upbeat fifty-three years, to have at least enough time for knowing and doting over his grandchildren. It was not to be; sadly, on December 4th after valiant efforts to forestall death's grip, Herff Alexander Carnes died. The next day, at Restlawn Cemetery, after funeral services officiated by the Reverend L.L. Evans, the thirty-year veteran of hard-core Texas/Mexico border law enforcing was at last, laid to rest in the country he cherished so very, very much, West Texas.[60]

The peace officer, while he lived, was well known throughout the American Southwest, respected for his work. Unfortunately, in the rush to capitalize on Western theatrics, fictional or otherwise, Herff Carne's good name got mislaid in the twentieth-century journalistic shuffle. Simply said, it shouldn't have. Herff A. Carnes was one heck of an Old West lawman. And, by damn, he could track an elephant, too!

ENDNOTES CHAPTER 14

"I JUMPED OFF MY HORSE AND STARTED SHOOTING"

[1]   Awbrey, Betty Dooley & Dooley, Claude, *Why Stop? A Guide To Texas Historical Roadside Markers.* P. 164-165.

[2]   *Ibid.*

[3]   Gournay, Luke, *Texas Boundaries, Evolution of the State's Counties.* P. 84.

[4]   *Ibid.* The county seat was first moved from Sutherland Springs to Lodi in 1867. Back to Sutherland Springs during March of 1871. In July 1871, six-months later, to Lodi again. Floresville, as reported in the text, victoriously and permanently won out in 1885.

[5]   United States Census, 1880, Wilson County, Texas. And see, Stadler, Louise, *Wilson County History.* P. 43. And, Gilland, Maude T., *Wilson County Texas Rangers, 1837-1977.* And see, *El Paso Times*, December 5, 1932. Herff's oldest brother, Willie D., died at age eleven from an undisclosed cause. Another older brother, Alfred Burton "Burt" Carnes was born on April 1, 1877, and a younger brother Quirl Bailey was born on June 1, 1884, followed by another, Webb McNeill in 1892. Additionally, Herff Carnes had sisters, Atlanta Lee (Attie), Tommie C., Lola, and Vivian. And see, Meyr, Irma M. *Cemeteries of Wilson County, Texas.* In the 1900 United States Census, Wilson County, Texas, Herff Carnes is listed as living with his parents and employed as a "farm laborer." His father, Joseph M. is listed as a farmer in the 1880 Census, and as a farrier in the 1900 Census.

[6]   That Herff A. Carnes had some formalized education can be extrapolated from the fact there are examples of his signature. In most instances he signed documents with his initials, "H.A." Carnes. And later, as an Inspector for the U.S. Mounted Customs Service, there is a first person narrative report, apparently typed on an early day manual typewriter, authored by Carnes. Also, refer to Census Records where it is noted that Herff Carnes could "read, write, and speak English."

[7]   Gilliland, P. 100-101. For a thumbnail sketch of William Alexander Anderson "Big Foot" Wallace, see, Thrapp, Dan, *Encyclopedia of Frontier Biography*, Volume III, P. 1506. For interesting reading, see, Sowell, A.J., *Life of "Big Foot" Wallace.*

[8]   *El Paso Times*, December 5, 1932. Herff Carnes must have traveled to New Mexico for the ranch management job after, June 18, 1900, for on that day a census enumerator listed him as living in his father's household, Wilson County, Texas, Justice Precinct No. 5.

[9]   *Oath of Service, Ranger Force.* "H.A. Carnes," dated February 13, 1903, signed, "John R. Hughes, Capt., Co. 'D' R. F." Courtesy, Texas State Library and Archives Commission, Austin. (TSLAC)

[10]   *Oath of Service, Ranger Force.* "H.A. Carnes," dated July 13, 1903, signed, "Capt. JnO.R. Hughes." And see, *Monthly Returns*, Company D., Ranger Force, February, 1903. (TSLAC)

[11]   *Monthly Return*, February, 1903.

[12]   *Monthly Return*, June, 1903.

[13]   *Monthly Return*, September, 1903.

[14]   *Monthly Return*, December, 1904.

[15]   *Monthly Return*, June, 1905.

Lawmen, Outlaws and S.O.Bs.

16 *Monthly Return*, January, 1906.
17 *Monthly Return*, February, 1906. And see, Martin, Jack, *Border Boss, Captain John R. Hughes—Texas Ranger.* P. 181.
18 Martin. P. 181.
19 *Monthly Return*, September, 1906. And see, *Monthly Return*, October, 1906. Also see, *Enlistment, Oath Of Service, And Description, Ranger Force.* Carne's reenlistment as Ranger Sergeant, dated August 26, 1908. Courtesy, Texas Ranger Hall of Fame and Museum. (TRHF&M) Waco.
20 *Monthly Return*, October, 1906.
21 *Monthly Return*, November, 1909. And subsequent *Monthly Returns* reflecting Herff Carne's arrests and the placement of numerous prisoners in the Potter County Jail at Amarillo.
22 Gilliand, Maude T., *Horsebackers Of The Brush Country, A Story Of The Texas Rangers And Mexican Liquor Smugglers.* For this version of the killing of Quirl B. Carnes the author cites the *Floresville Chronicle.* P. 74-77.
23 *Monthly Return*, December, 1910.
24 The exacting date when Herff Carnes was sworn in with the United States Customs service is, at this time, undetermined. An *El Paso Times*, December 5, 1932, article simply makes reference to Carne's length of service by remarking, "In February 1903, he was made a Texas ranger and, working in that capacity, soon became well known along the entire Texas border from El Paso to Brownsville. Ten years later Mr. Carnes entered the customs service and, with the exception of a few months when he was stationed at Sierra Blanca, he served in Ysleta." Gilliand, *Wilson County Rangers*, says, "After serving with the Texas Rangers for eight years he resigned and joined the U.S. Mounted Customs Service where he served for more than twenty-one years under the El Paso Office." P. 48.
25 Meed, Douglas V., *Bloody Border, Riots, Battles and Adventures Along the Turbulent U.S.—Mexican Borderlands.* Refer to the author's excellent treatment of the turmoil in Chapter V, "Race War in the Lower Rio Grande Valley," P. 115-134.
26 Herff Carnes to Collector of Customs, El Paso, Texas, September 1, 1915. Courtesy, National Archives, Washington, D. C.
27 Blumenson, Martin, *The Patton Papers, 1885-1940.* P. 298.
28 *Ibid.* P. 333.
29 For a complete biography of this truly remarkable Southwest lawman, see, Alexander, Bob, *Fearless Dave Allison, Border Lawman.*
30 Carnes to Collector of Customs, El Paso. September 1, 1915. And see, Statement of W.H. Schrock, *Inquest*, August 31 and September 1, 1915. Culberson County. Courtesy, Culberson County District/County Clerk, Van Horn, Texas. And see, *El Paso Morning Times*, September 1, 1915. "Orozco and his companions mounted hastily, sent a shower of shot at Love and Shock (sic), and made a running fight for liberty."
31 Telegraph message, from R.C. Love to John Morine, Culberson County Sheriff, Van Horn, Texas. August 30, 1915. As contained in *Inquest* documents. Courtesy, Culberson County District/County Clerk, Van Horn, Texas.
32 Carnes to Collector of Customs, El Paso, Texas. September 1, 1915.
33 *Ibid.*
34 *Ibid.*

[35] *Ibid.* And see, Meed. P. 53-54. "Dismounting and creeping up close to the canyon, they saw Orozco and his band in the canyon, sitting around a small campfire."

[36] *Ibid.*

[37] *Ibid.*

[38] Statement of Culberson County Sheriff John Morine, at the *Inquest* into the deaths of Pascual Orozco, Jose F. Delgado, Christoforo (Caballero), Andreas Sandoval and Miguel Terrazas, August 30, 1915. Courtesy, Culberson County/District Clerk, Van Horn, Texas. (The spelling has been corrected in Sheriff Morine's statement.)

[39] Meed. P. 55.

[40] *Ibid.*

[41] Carnes to Collector of Customs, El Paso. September 1, 1915.

[42] *Ibid.* And, *El Paso Morning Times*, August 31, 1915. "...Although the five dead Mexicans had not been fully identified one is believed to be General Pascual Orozco, the 'Colorado' leader." And see, Cano, Tony & Sochat, Ann, *Bandido, The True Story of Chico Cano, the Last Western Bandit.* P. 91. "Only afterwards when the authorities from El Paso arrived on the scene, was Orozco positively identified among the dead."

[43] Meed. P. 47. And see, *Inquest, The State of Texas, County of Culberson,* "In the matter of the death of Pascual Orozco, Jose F. Delgado, Christoforo (Caballero), Andreas Sandoval and Miguel Terrazas."

[44] *Inquest*

[45] *El Paso Herald*, October 7, 1915. "This case will probably he tried this week here and the record of all proceeding will be forwarded to the State Department." And, Meyer, Michael C., *Mexican Rebel: Pascual Orozco and the Mexican Revolution 1910-1915.* P. 133. "likely that the United States was embarrassed about the manner in which Orozco met his death." Also see, Cano & Sochat, P. 97. "It is likely that the American government was embarrassed about the manner in which the Orozco party had met their deaths, and the just wanted to bury the problem." For another of the conspiracy theories see, Bolling, Robert S., *Death Rides the River, Tales of the El Paso Road.* For the most balanced and evenhanded evaluation, Meed is recommended, "As to the other charges and rumors, the best evidence available indicates that: to the charge of Ley Fuga— probably guilty; to the charge of a plot of entrapment and robbery—very doubtful. The posse was too diverse and composed of too many men with reputations for honesty and truthfulness to make this likely. And from a cynical point of view, there were too many men in the posse for any secrets to be kept for long." P. 57. Also see, Alexander for an analysis of Dave Allison's participation and leadership of the posse.

[46] *Indictment*, Culberson County Grand Jury, October Term, 1915. Courtesy, Culberson County/District Clerk. Van Horn, Texas. And see, *El Paso Herald*, October 7, 1915. "Sheriff and 11 Citizens Indicted."

[47] *Instructions* to the Jury, Cause No. 35, *The State of Texas vs. John A. Morine, et al.* 34th Judicial District of Texas. October Term, Culberson County, Van Horn, Texas. Courtesy, Culberson County District/County Clerk, Van Horn, Texas. As cited in the text, the names of "Rowdy" Love, J.W. Mellard, and J.O. English are dropped in all legal documents post the original indictment.

[48] *Capias* Warrant, *The State of Texas vs. J.A. Morine, et al.* Courtesy, Culberson County District/County Clerk, Van Horn, Texas.

[49] *Jury Verdict Form*, Courtesy, Culberson County/District Clerk, Van Horn, Texas.
[50] *El Paso Herald-Post*, December 5, 1932.
[51] *Ibid.*
[52] Gilliland, P. 104. And, *El Paso Times*, December 2, 1932.
[53] *El Paso Herald-Post*, December 2, 1932. And see, Gilliand, *Horsebackers of the Brush Country*. P. 81. The newspaper cites Herff's eldest son as a Jr., however, Gilland who prepared genealogical research identifies him as Hugh A., living at Tacoma, Washington in 1968. The youngest son, David M. Carnes, became a physician.
[54] *El Paso Times*, December 2, 1932.
[55] *El Paso Herald-Post*, December 2, 1932.
[56] *El Paso Times*, December 2, 1932.
[57] *Ibid.* And see, Gilliand, quoting the December 5th edition of the *El Paso Times*. P. 48.
[58] *El Paso Herald-Post*, December 2, 1932.
[59] *Ibid.*
[60] *Ibid.* December 5, 1932.

CHAPTER 15

"A COWBOY RUN AMUCK"

Howard Chenowth, A Good Boy Gone Wrong—Long Gone

"An acorn don't fall too far from the tree." The comment is not an infrequent characterization repeated by those engaging old-timers sitting around courthouse squares, spittin' and whittlin'. Certainly their blunt observations are not grounded with scientific truth, but in many cases they're right. John Augustus "Gus" Chenowth was tough as the proverbial boot, hard-working, hard-boiled, and during a *mano a mano* quarrel, stubborn as a cross-eyed mule. Howard Chenowth, his son, was too!

John Augustus "Gus" Chenowth, genuine Arizona pioneer, grizzled freighter, whiskey maker, fire and brimstone lay preacher, and a no nonsense mankiller of record. Courtesy, Amos and LaDorna Chenowth.

Lawmen, Outlaws and S.O.Bs.

Gus was an early Arizona Territory pioneer and, in fact, a list of Phoenix's forefathers would have to include the elder Chenowth.[1] He made his living by overseeing whip-popping teamsters cajole his "fleet of wagons and eight-horse teams." And too, he was an Indian fighter by some accounts, or a hardhearted Indian murderer by others but, regardless of modern era correctness, his contemporaries sanctioned his Yavapai killing excursion.[2] With the organization of Maricopa County (Phoenix) in 1871, Gus Chenowth, a Democrat, was nominated as the political party's first candidate for the coveted position of sheriff. The heated battle for votes was scorching, and the dark cauldron of mutual contempt boiled over. During a bitter argument as to who said what to who, and amid emphatic denials, Gus Chenowth, in a righteous act of self-defense and just by a whisker escaping the blast from a double barreled shotgun, killed his political adversary, James "Whispering Jim" Favorite.[3] Maintaining his status as a mainline contributor in Maricopa County historical events, Gus married the stunningly attractive and devoutly religious Mary Murray, the fledgling county's very first wedding ceremony.[4]

Later, after relocating to the San Simon Cienega in southeastern Arizona Territory, Gus fathered children, hauled freight, and preached hellfire and brimstone sermons as a lay preacher; that is when he wasn't making a little first-rate whiskey. Pious he may have been, pitiable he was not. Exactly where the truth lays buried is yet to be exhumed but, anecdotally, one Gus Chenowth story is oft repeated, seemingly taking on a life of its own. It seems, so it is said, that a wanna-be badman, John "Cherokee Jack" Rogers, thinking he could relieve Gus of the showy and spirited horse he was riding, tried to hijack Chenowth at a friendless and mysterious canyon in the Chiricahua Mountains. Reportedly with a well-worn bible in one hand and a smoking Colt's six-shooter in the other, Gus Chenowth shot the robber dead. Dutifully, Chenowth struggled with lashing the dead man across his horse, managed the mortuary trip to Galeyville, and the next day reverently preached at the pathetic fellow's meager funeral.[5] *Quien Sabe*? In a totally separate and unrelated story, Gus sent a short and snappily worded message to a notorious Southwest owl-hoot, "Black Jack" Ketchum, warning that he would kill him deader than a cold iron anvil, "sure as hell," if he ever tried to steal a Chenowth horse.[6] Somewhere in the dusty recesses of these yarns reality pokes through. John A. "Gus" Chenowth, a demonstrated mankiller, was not to be trifled with, an inflexible trait he lovingly passed to his heirs.

Howard Pinckney Chenowth was born on May 2, 1881, in newly fashioned Cochise County, Arizona Territory, over near the New

"A Cowboy Run Amuck"

Mexico line, a few miles east of tumultuous Tombstone, and just scant short months before the gunplay at the O. K. Corral.[7] Through inherited bloodlines, fatherly training and nimble adaptation to the harsh environmental in southeastern Arizona and southwestern New Mexico, Howard P. Chenowth quickly journeyed through the maturation process. When he crossed the finish line at twenty-one years of age he was a package of many functional talents; self-reliant; skilled in the use of Peacemakers and Winchesters; a surefire bronc-stomper; a journeyman wild cow catcher; an adept distiller of premium homemade whiskey; and, quite naturally so it seems, a man with "a strong resistance to being pushed around."[8] Unlike many of his generation. Chenowth, much to his credit, could boast of chalking up the equivalency of a high-school education at the New Mexico State Normal School in picturesque Silver City.[9] Somewhat more typically though, after hitting the books and learning to cipher, Howard did what many of his youthful colleagues did. He became, by inclination and circumstance, a cowboy.[10] Reportedly, on his first crack at landing employment at the celebrated Diamond A in southwestern New Mexico, he was flatly rejected because the General Manager thought he might prove a "little wild."[11] On the second try, in 1904, his friend and a Diamond A foreman, Pat Nunn, who himself was described as "reckless and just full of the devil," interceded and successfully secured Howard Chenowth's cowboy job on the gargantuan cattle ranch.[12] Pat Nunn, in retrospect, should have heeded his boss man's portentous premonitions.

After sending the wagons to Cow Springs, a headquarters of sort for one division of the Diamond A, Pat Nunn, on August 27, 1904, at long last gave the anticipated nod, approvingly okaying a trip to Silver City, and a sinful taste of whatever the town had to offer lonesome and thirsty cowboys.[13] At Silver City, as with most burgs wholly dependent on a mining and/or cow-business livelihood, there was no dearth of liquor or ladies. Accompanied by Howard Chenowth, and another Diamond A employee, Martin "Mart" Kennedy, a cowboy from Abilene, Texas, Pat Nunn shifted in the saddle and they all set their tracks for Silver City. Upon arrival Nunn told Chenowth and Kennedy to either leave their six-shooters at the Old Man Corral at the corner of Arizona and Yankee Streets or definitely turn them over to an overworked bartender at Bob Golding's Club House Saloon before they started drinking; he had both personal and Diamond A business in want of tending, and would reunite with them later, sometime during the evening.[14]

279

Howard Pinckney Chenowth, son of "Gus", student, stockman, and shootist. Courtesy, Amos and LaDorna Chenowth.

Day turned to dark. Sobriety gave way to slurred speech. Little did it matter though, Howard Chenowth and Mart Kennedy were having one hell-of-a-good-time. Fully sour-mash sloshed, Chenowth undertook, ineffectively, to ride a Diamond A horse, Bonito, into the Palace Saloon, but was dissuaded.[15] In due course, around two o'clock in the morning, Pat Nunn, after catching up with his "boys," made a levelheaded supervisory decision; it was time to leave town, stop the fun, and head toward the cow-camp. Hangovers were sure to collide with morning's first light. Nunn gave the order, "let's go."

"A Cowboy Run Amuck"

Chenowth complied but Mart Kennedy "demurred."[16] Outside, where the horses were tied, Pat Nunn and Howard Chenowth stepped up into their slick-forked saddles, Mart Kennedy didn't. Clearly by now thoroughly perturbed, Nunn admonished Kennedy to either mount up or strip his personal hull from the Diamond A horse. Mart Kennedy loosened the latigo and belligerently jerked his saddle off, at the same time cursing his foreman for all to hear. Pat Nunn was not inclined to accept the insult. There were few men in the whole world who could berate him and get away with it, and a sassy Mart Kennedy wasn't one.[17] As if in but one motion, Pat Nunn jumped from his horse and almost while in mid-air unfastened his gunbelt and threw it to the ground, just before he landed squarely in the middle of Mart Kennedy's business. It was over, almost before it started, so it seemed. Pat Nunn was "the better man physically" and in but short order had pummeled Kennedy to the grimy street and was straddling him asking the befuddled cowboy if he still wanted a piece of a ranch foreman's ass.[18]

Diamond A foreman Pat Nunn, seated second from left. Howard Chenowth shot at him and missed, shot at him and hit, twice—demolishing his pocket watch with the first shot, shooting off his eyebrows with the second. From, A Hundred Years Of Horse Tracks, *courtesy the author, George Hilliard.*

One version has it that Kennedy cried for help, the other has it that Chenowth angrily declared no man could abuse his friend. There is, however, consensus on the young cowboy's next move. In a heartbeat he bailed off his horse. Catlike he picked up Pat Nunn's cartridge belt and scabbard. It is generally believed Nunn, if he saw the move at all, paid little notice, thinking Howard Chenowth, although totally smashed, was simply retrieving his six-shooter for safekeeping. He erred.[19]

Rushing to the evident commotion was Grant County Deputy Sheriff Elmore Murray. Quickly he began separating the two combatants, jerking Kennedy to his feet and admonishing Nunn to cease and desist, and just as suddenly, Chenowth yanked his foreman's Colt from the holster, slipped the hammer and fired. The deafening roar and illuminating muzzle flash staggered Murray, the "blue whistler" zinging over his shoulder and thudding to rest, somewhere. The opening scuffle continued, deputy Murray doggedly holding on to both fist-fighters while Chenowth eared back the cock for another bite. The second shot was heard as the bullet tore into Pat Nunn's vest, chest high, triggering but a wicked bruise. Fortunately the bullet had collided with a pocket watch and not flesh and bone. Not content with his botched marksmanship, Howard Chenowth once more dropped the pin and busted a cap. The third bullet struck its intended target, more or less, grazing Pat Nunn's forehead and "tearing away his eyebrows."[20] With his suntanned brow now powder-burned, blood flooding down his face, temporarily blinded and bewildered, Pat Nunn stumbled and bumbled into the nearby Club House Saloon—away from Howard Chenowth who had "run amuck."[21]

The twenty-three year-old Chenowth, stewed to the gills and "appearing frantic with passion," tenaciously resisted Murray's efforts to gain possession of Nunn's blue-steeled revolver. Grasping one of Howard's arms, at the same time still frantically tussling with Mart Kennedy, the beleaguered peace officer was anxiously struggling for a cessation to the out of control warfare. The two cowboys, now thoroughly crazed by alcohol and adrenaline fought deputy Murray like tigers, trying to snatch the officer's sixgun from its holster, Kennedy hysterically pleading to Chenowth, "Don't give up the gun, kill the sons-of-bitches."[22] Seeing Elmore Murray's dire predicament, an ex-deputy United States Marshal and ex-Grant County Constable, Perfecto Rodriquez, forty-five years-old and sans a handgun, rushed headlong into the mêlée. His courage cost him his life. With his free hand Chenowth leveled the misappropriated six-shooter and fired. The bullet ripped into Rodriquez's heart and he died on the spot, instantly.[23] The battle royal continued up Texas Street, between the Club House and Palace saloons, Murray fearlessly doing close in work, knowing if he stepped back and let go, he too would be shot. Twirling, spinning, kicking, flaying, biting and gouging the unrestrained madness breathlessly moved up the dimly lit street—targeting further tragedy. The Silver City Town Marshal, William H. Kilburn, raced to the scene, unarmed, determined to aid straight-away an exhausted Murray who by now had a fast-fading hold of Chenowth's gun hand. Just as the marshal was pluckily hurling himself into the fracas, Chenowth managed to wrestle the weapon into a firing position, and fired. The bullet tore a gaping hole in Kilburn's neck. The City Marshal crumpled to the ground, paralyzed.[24]

Near collapse, lawman Elmore Murray had his hands full—literally—ferociously battling for any advantage with two besotted and insanely unmanageable cowhands. Finally, Chenowth and Kennedy broke free and ran.[25]

As would be expected, the street-fight had attracted no little attention, even during the wee morning hour. An assemblage of Silver City's sleepy denizens began gathering. Dr. O.J. Westlake rushed to attend Kilburn's neck wound, the marshal ntly gasping for every mouthful of air. Incredibly, Mart Kennedy, after the passage of but less than an hour, ambled or wobbled back into the Palace Saloon—for one more drink. Immediately he was snatched up by Grant County deputy Charles L. Williams and jailer James L. Gill. The arrestors started for the jail with the staggering prisoner. Sheriff's deputy John L. Burnside, and an on the spot deputized John Collier, covered the officer's backtrail should the loose fugitive Chenowth somehow attempt to liberate their drunken and mouthy freight. Upon passing Samuel Lindauer's mercantile store, Collier espied Chenowth crouching behind some dry goods crates. Collier, for the moment, said naught. Further down the street, and well out of Chenowth's earshot, Collier made his sighting known, acquired a shotgun, and with Burnside returned to the Lindauer store to apprehend their prey. Collier hallooed a challenge to Chenowth, "give up your six-shooter and come out." Howard Chenowth snubbed the proposition. Several times the demand for surrender was tendered. Each time it was rebuffed.[26]

Howard Chenowth, after spurning several proposals to peacefully submit, "jumped from the dry goods box and started towards Collier, holding his six-shooter in plain view."[27] Foolishly, whether purposeful or not, Chenowth raised the threatening Colt from his side. John Collier squeezed the shotgun's hair-trigger.

Lawmen, Outlaws and S.O.Bs.

Chenowth fcll, pole-axed to the ground, suffering a nasty head wound, the charge having been partly deflected by a nearby post. He was lucky the offending pellets were No. 6 birdshot; in the other pipe was lethal 00 buckshot.[28] Immediately Chenowth was taken to the hospital and, after medical treatment, lodged in the Grant County Jail. Under special guard, a newspaperman for the *Silver City Independent* made firsthand observations, "If he has any realization of the crime for which he has to answer he has given no indication of it. His actions seemed to indicate that he did not even know where he was, but this may have been assumed."[29]

Held without bond, Howard Chenowth and Mart Kennedy, after a preliminary hearing before Justice of the Peace William H. Newcomb, awaited action of the Spring Term of a Grant County Grand Jury for the murder of Perfecto Rodriquez.[30] Chenowth's legal troubles doubled. City Marshal William H. Kilburn, on Sunday, September 4, 1904, at Silver City's Ladies Hospital, died.[31]

There was never dispute as to Howard Chenowth's criminal culpability; clearly he, not Mart Kennedy, had fired the fatal shots, and it was he who would have to swallow the payback. Mitigating circumstances? Perhaps there were, at least to some appreciable degree, in some minds. Judge F.W. Parker, after a lengthy and hard-fought trial, and the return of a categorical guilty verdict, sentenced the youthful Diamond A cowboy to fifty years in the Territorial Penitentiary at Santa Fe. A "visit to eternity" at the end of a hangman's knot was thwarted. Hastily, Howard's knowledgeable lawyer, James S. Fielder, appealed. Chenowth remained in jail at Silver City awaiting a January 1906 decision of the Territorial Supreme Court.[32]

On Christmas Day, 1905, Santa Claus may have stopped by and forked over a sack full of delightful holiday presents for Silver City's little children; he didn't, however, stop at the jail—Howard Chenowth's relatives did—the gift they brought was illicit liberty. At seven o'clock in the evening, a masked man appeared at the lockup carrying a seemingly oversized six-shooter and pointedly ordered jailer Frank Watson to open Chenowth's cell, remarking to the not so surprised prisoner, "Howard I have come after you." Chenowth, seizing upon the moment, dramatically replied, "Well if you have come after me, I guess I'll have to go."[33] And he did! After making sure the conspirators had in fact evacuated the premises and were not cleverly lurking somewhere about, Watson, who had been locked in the compartment vacated by Chenowth, frantically sounded the embarrassing alarm. Grant County Sheriff Charles A. Farnsworth, relatively new to the job, soon learned what many of his predecessors were already well aware of; the Grant County Jail was a historically problematic and porous institution. Unable to pick up meaningful sign after dark, the sheriff sent a description of Chenowth throughout New Mexico and Arizona Territories, and Old Mexico as well, offering a reward of $600 for his capture and confinement. Next day's investigation revealed that several accomplices were involved, as they had left footprints in the snow, and it was further disclosed that one of the owl-hoot's horses was shod all around, the other two were not.[34] More than one account asserts that a relay of fast horses had been prearranged for sprinting Chenowth across the international line, seventy-five miles south of Silver City.[35] Howard Chenowth had, for the moment, clearly turned his back on a chancy criminal justice system and an unpredictable ruling from the territory's high court. Howard Pinckney Chenowth's disappearance, as was the case with so many wily Old West fugitives, was headline news only for awhile, all too soon bumped from the newspapers by some other equally exhilarating, but much fresher shame.

Although primarily based on anecdotal reconstruction, Chenowth's post Silver City days can to some extent be inspected, for the most part accurately. After fleeing incarceration, Howard's family hid him in a slyly constructed secret room beneath a nondescript haystack.[36] Reportedly, after the manhunt pressure abated, Howard in the company of one of his brothers, wandered throughout northwest America and even into Canada for a short while. Later, after a sojourn in sweltering Alabama, Howard Chenowth departed the United States and went to work doing what he did best, cowboying, but this time in Brazil.[37]

Taking an assumed name, Charles Martin, Howard Chenowth adroitly turned into a thoroughly reconstituted man, and, apparently, a good one. There is not dispute that in the *Estado de Matto Grosso* the fugitive from frontier New Mexico justice cast aside the foolish conduct of his youth. During his eleven year sojourn in Brazil, Howard married and fathered seven children: Daisy, Amos, Douglas, Ola, Ula, Frances, and Ruby.[38] Contributing his innate cow-sense to the burgeoning South American livestock business then well underway, Howard Chenowth was never without meaningful work.[39] Sadly though, Howard's world, once again, came crashing down. Unpredictably, especially in light of her previous uncomplicated deliveries, his beloved wife died during childbirth. Although his sisters-in-law dutifully submitted their sincere desire to raise the children, Howard, "devastated" by the loss, opted to return his motherless children to the American Southwest, if there was but a way.[40]

Left: Howard Chenowth's South American born wife, Yulé. Courtesy Amos and LaDorna Chenowth.

Right: Don Carlos Butendorp, Howard Chenowth's German born brother-in-law and a Brazilian cattleman. Courtesy Amos and LaDorna Cneowth.

The Chenowth clan back in the United States had been tirelessly and vigorously campaigning for the granting of a Governor's Pardon. On March 5, 1927, the newly inaugurated New Mexico Governor, R.C. Dillion, because the crime had been "the act of an irresponsible youth under the influence of alcohol" and committed at the urgings of "an older, more worldly companion," the pardon was granted. [41] After a nauseating three-week voyage and a seasick docking at the Port of New Orleans, the Chenowth children, who could only speak Portuguese, managed the railroad trip with their father to Lordsburg, New Mexico, and at long-last into the arms of a delighted grandmother's very first hugs.[42] During his absence,

"A Cowboy Run Amuck"

Howard's unflagging pioneer father, Gus, had passed to the other side.

Howard Chenowth's foreign born children, from left to right, Eula, Francis, Amos, Daisy, Ruby, Douglas, and Ola. Courtesy, Amos and LaDorna Chenowth.

With characteristic resilience the Chenowth children assimilated into the Southwestern culture, learning the English language and productively graduating from high school. Howard Chenowth, by heart and bowed-legs had always been a cowboy, and so it was to be for the next twenty years as he honorably drew wages at southwestern New Mexico and southeastern Arizona cattle ranches. Failing physical health, not spirit, however, ever so gradually began taking its inescapable toll. Shortly after retiring his spurs and hanging his well-worn leather leggins on a handy tack-room peg, during his sixty-fifth year, Howard P. Chenowth, died at Tucson in 1947.[43]

A noted Western historian and prolific writer, in summing up Howard Chenowth's fascinating life's story, said that but for a boy's childish sail down "a whiskey river," the grown man had little to be discomfited by.[44] And just as surely, when the pithy newspaperman had penned, "A Cowboy Runs Amuck," he too knew the deadly misbehavior was aberrant, not typical. Out of hand then it can be implicitly understood those old-timers weren't necessarily wrong, "An apple don't fall too far from the tree."

Howard P. Chenowth's tombstone in Cochise County, Arizona. Courtesy, Amos and LaDorna Chenowth.

Amos Chenowth holding his daddy Howard's lever-action Winchester. Photo courtesy, Jan Devereaux.

"A Cowboy Run Amuck"

ENDNOTES CHAPTER 15

"A COWBOY RUN AMUCK"

1 Hayes, Alden, *A Portal To Paradise*. P. 109-110.
2 *Ibid*. During September of 1868, Gus Chenowth, with others, attacked an encampment of sleeping Yavapai Indians near La Paz, Arizona Territory. The Anglos, who had long suffered Indian depredations, thought the Yavapai were preparing for a raid on the town. The U.S. Military, in an after the fact investigation, thought otherwise, describing the violent engagement as "a cold-blooded cowardly murder committed by low-lived, drunken cowardly villains."
3 *Ibid*. And see, Ball, Larry D., *Desert Lawmen, The High Sheriffs Of New Mexico And Arizona, 1846-1912*. P. 66. "As voters looked forward to their first general elections in newly created Maricopa County in 1871, a tragic quarrel erupted between two candidates for the sheriffalty, John A. (Gus) Chenowth and James Favorite. The former shot and killed the latter." Also see, Aleshire, Peter, "Tumultuous Chiricahuas," *Arizona Highways*. November 2002. "...killed his too-critical opponent for sheriff in a controversial case of 'self-defense',..."
4 *Ibid*.
5 *Ibid*.
6 Sinclair, John, "The Magical Peloncillos, The Sugarloaf Mountains," *New Mexico Magazine*. July 1979.
7 Biographical data furnished to the author by Amos and LaDorna Chenowth, Howard Chenowth's son and daughter-in-law.
8 Hayes. P. 228.
9 *Ibid*. And see, Cline, Ellen, "The Story Of A Cowboy," *Cochise County Historical Journal*. Fall/Winter 1997/198.
10 Metz, Leon C., *The Encyclopedia of Lawmen, Outlaws, and Gunfighters*. P. 43.
11 Hayes. P. 229.
12 Hilliard, George, *A Hundred Years Of Horse Tracks, The Story of the Gray Ranch*. P. 90. And see, Hayes, P. 229. Also see, Metz., P. 43. And see, Cline, P. 38. For another characterization of Nunn, see, Marvin Powe to Lou Blachley, Pioneer Foundation interviews, Tape No. 234, Page 5. "...Pat (Nunn), he was awful to drink and carouse around..." Courtesy, Terry Humble, Bayard, New Mexico.
13 Turner, Alton, "New Mexico Shoot-Out," *Frontier Times*. March 1969. Cow Springs is located in the northwest portion of what is now Luna County, New Mexico, but at the time of the Chenowth gunplay was in Grant County, south of Silver City, New Mexico.
14 Turner, P. 36. The author states that one of Pat Nunn's personal business missions was to buy his wife a new watch for Christmas. The assertion *may* be true, although it is not supported by documentation, but in any event Nunn's possession of a pocket-watch plays significantly in the story.
15 *Silver City Independent*, August 30, 1904. The name of Chenowth's horse is drawn from Robert Bell to Lou Blachley, Tape No. 21, Page 16. Courtesy, Terry Humble.
16 *Ibid*. And see, *Silver City Enterprise*, September 2, 1904.
17 Turner, P. 36. "Not many ever crossed Pat, even strangers."

Lawmen, Outlaws and S.O.Bs.

[18] *Silver City Independent*, August 30, 1904. And see, Testimony of Pat Nunn, *Territory of New Mexico vs. Howard Chenowth*, Case No. 1111 (1906), New Mexico Supreme Court Records, New Mexico Records Center and State Archives. Santa Fe. "…I supposed he (Kennedy) was going to get on him (horse), and he turned and says 'I won't go a damn step', I told—pull the saddle off his horse and I would take his horse out; then he pulled his saddle off of him and laid it down and started to take the bridle off of him and I told him not to turn the horse loose to put my rope on him and I taken the rope off my saddle horn and pitched it over to him, one end of it, and then he commenced to curse me…I got down off my horse and started up to him and he made a remark that I had a gun on, he said something about pulling my gun off and I unbuckled my gun and threw it down on the side walk and slapped him and we clenched and I throwed him down and he said that he was not able to fight me any fist fight but he would fight me next morning with a gun. I told him I didn't want to fight him with a gun. About that time the shot was fired, first shot." Interestingly, in the courtroom testimony, Pat Nunn identified his revolver as a "Colt's, .45, Serial Number 221976," and that it had been loaded with five loads, the hammer resting on an empty chamber. Chenowth, during the deathly mêlée fired five shots.

[19] *Silver City Enterprise*, September 2, 1904.

[20] *Ibid.* In some renditions Chenowth's first bullet connected with the pocket watch, and the second completely missed, but in all accounts, the third shot connected with Nunn's forehead, taking him out of the action.

[21] *Silver City Independent*, August 30, 1904. The headline reads, "Cowboy Runs Amuck And Four Men Are Shot," a not unfair analysis. And see, Marvin Powe to Lou Blachley. "…and it hit the watch. I saw the watch and it was just smashed flat, but the bullet bounced off. Then he shot again and that's when he just plowed a furrow through his (Nunn) head, just cut that from there to there and it just flopped down over his eyes…and, up till he died he had this big red mark where it was sewed up there, clear across there."

[22] Testimony of Deputy Sheriff Murray, *Territory of New Mexico vs. Howard Chenowth*.

[23] *Silver City Enterprise*, September 2, 1904.

[24] Bullis, Don, *New Mexico's Finest: Peace Officers Killed In The Line Of Duty, 1847-1999.* P. 156-159. Also see, *Silver City Enterprise* & *Silver City Independent*, as cited. And see, Testimony of Charles Langdon, *Territory of New Mexico vs. Howard Chenowth*. "Kilburn didn't do anything but walked down in rapid gait as I previously stated and as I said after he was shot he fell like a dead weight and never moved, practically paralyzed."

[25] *Ibid.*

[26] *Silver City Independent*, August 30, 1904.

[27] *Ibid.*

[28] *Ibid.* And see, Marvin Powe to Lou Blachley, "He (Collier) thought he had buckshot in it and he just had little birdshot and there was just one or (sic) shots hit his head there and knocked him out."

[29] *Ibid.*

[30] *Silver City Enterprise*, September 2, 1904.

[31] *Silver City Independent*, September 6, 1904. And see, Chesley, Hervey *Trails Traveled—Tales Told.* "He killed a constable there and a marshal. One of them was a Mexican officer." P. 147.

[32] *Silver City Enterprise*, December 29, 1905. And see, Cline. P. 40. "The trial began in April (1905) and ended in May when Chenowth was found guilty of murder in the second degree after the jury had been deadlocked 24 hours."

[33] *Ibid.* Hayes identifies the gun wielding relative, "The various Chenowth family accounts agree that Howard's younger brother, Hale, was the masked man who broke him out of jail, but there is disagreement about who helped." P. 231.

[34] *Ibid.*

[35] Ball. P. 219. The author indicates James K. Blair was Grant County Sheriff at the time of Chenowth's delivery from jail, however, the sheriff holding office at the time was Charles Farnsworth, clearly cited in several newspaper accounts. The well-known and highly regarded Blair had, in fact, been the sheriff at the time of the initial crime in 1904, but had, by the time of the escape in 1905, relinquished the office.

[36] Hayes, P. 232, "He (Gus Chenowth) removed bales from the middle of the pile to make a small bay that could be quickly closed off with a bale of hay. Howard lived there for months, until the hunt cooled and he could quit the country." And see, Cline, P. 42. Howard Chenowth later told his son Amos "…that the family had fixed a room in a haystack that was so well hidden that no one would know it was there. He stayed there for some time, until they thought it was safe to leave the ranch."

[37] Cline. P. 42. According to the author, who obtained her information from Amos Chenowth, Howard's son, the fugitive father went to work for the fabled King Ranch in South America, using an alias, Carl Martin. Unquestionably Howard Chenowth, during a considerable number of years, ranched in South America for cattle empire entrepreneurs, but apparently there is room for understandable, unintentional, and wholly innocent confusion. In a letter to the author from Lisa A. Neely, Archivist for the King Ranch, dated November 20, 2002, the following information was tendered: "In reply to your request for verification of the material on Carl Martin and his employment with the Brazilian property of King Ranch, I'm afraid there has been a lot of misinformation. King Ranch did not begin its ranching operation in Brazil until 1953."

[38] Cline, P. 43. And, conversation by author with one of Howard Chenowth's daughters-in-law, LaDorna Chenowth.

[39] *Ibid.*

[40] *Ibid.*

[41] *Ibid.* "Everyone involved with the case, former jurors, witnesses, lawyers, and even the victims' families had urged the governor to sign the papers." And see, Metz, P. 44. "With the death of his wife in 1927, Chenowth returned to New Mexico, where after considerable effort he received a governor's pardon."

[42] *Ibid.* Mary Chenowth was eighty-five years old at the time her Portuguese speaking grandchildren arrived from South America.

[43] Metz. P. 44. And see, Cline, P. 44.

[44] *Ibid.* The author's actual words are, "Except for that one voyage on a whiskey river many years ago, Chenowth's life had been honorable and productive."

BIBLIOGRAPHY

NON-PUBLISHED SOURCE MATERIAL:

Texas State Library and Archives Commission, Austin, Texas:
   Monthly Returns, Companies B, C and D, Frontier Battalion (Texas Rangers).
   Muster Roll, Company C, Frontier Battalion.
   Adjutant General's Correspondence Files.
   Biennial Report of the Adjutant General of Texas, From January 1, 1915 to December 16, 1916.
   Report of the Adjutant General of Texas, for the Fiscal Year, 1878.
Texas Ranger Hall of Fame and Museum, Waco, Texas:
   Applications for Commissions as Special Rangers.
   Oaths of Office (Texas Rangers).
   Warrants of Authority & Descriptive Lists (Texas Rangers).
   Salary Warrants (Texas Rangers).
National Archives, Washington, D. C.:
   United States Executive Document No. 93, 45th Congress, 2nd Session, 1878.
   Investigative Report of U.S. Mounted Customs Inspector Herff A. Carnes.
   Department of Justice Records, Joe Sitter.
United States Census Records:
New Mexico State Records Center and Archives, Santa Fe, New Mexico:
   Indictment, *Territory of New Mexico vs. John W. Gilmo.*
   Warrants for the Arrest of John W. Gilmo.
   Criminal Docket, *Record and Cost Book*, District Court Grant County, New Mexico.
   Register of Prisoners Confined in the Grant County Jail.
   Supreme Court Records, *Territory of New Mexico vs. Howard Chenowth.*
   Prison Inmate Records.
Arizona Department of Library, Archives & Public Records, Phoenix, Arizona:
   Pardon for Restoration of Citizenship, John W. Gilmo
El Paso County District Court, El Paso, Texas:
   Indictments, *State of Texas vs. Horace L. Roberson*
   Judgments, *State of Texas vs. Horace L. Roberson*
Culberson County District Court, Van Horn, Texas:
   Inquest Statements regarding the death of Pascual Orozco, Jr.
   Indictment, *The State of Texas vs. John A. Morine, et al.*
   Capais Warrant, *The State of Texas vs. John A. Morine, et al.*
   Instructions to the Jury, *The State of Texas vs. John A. Morine, et al*
   Jury Verdict Form.
.Travis County District Court, Austin, Texas:
   Judgment, *State of Texas vs. Horace L. Roberson*
Graham County District Court, Safford, Arizona.
   Affidavit for Postponement of Trial, *Territory of Arizona vs. John Gilmo.*
Yuma Territorial Prison State Historic Park, Yuma, Arizona:
   Inmate intake records.
The Cattleman, and Texas & Southwestern Cattle Raiser's Museum. Fort Worth, Texas:
   Archival Association Reports and biographical data on Inspectors.
Manuscripts, Thesis, Archival Reports, and Miscellaneous:
   "Joe Sitter's Account of the Trailing and Capture of the Train Robbers." Joseph Sitter to Harry Warren. Sul Ross State University, Bryan Wildenthal Memorial Library, Archives of the Big Bend. Alpine, Texas.
   The personal journals of Jack Howard. Sul Ross University, Bryan Wildenthal Memorial Library, Archives of the Big Bend. Alpine, Texas.

292

Bibliography

"The Salt War of San Elizaro (1877), *Master of Arts Thesis*, Charles Francis Ward. 1932. University of Texas, Austin, Texas.

"Roswell's First Police Officer Killed In The Line of Duty." John Havlorson, Typescript. Roswell Police Department Archives, Roswell, New. Mexico.

Police Judge's Docket. *The City of Roswell vs. Intoxicating Liquor and J.O. Lynch.* City of Roswell. Roswell, New Mexico.

Clinical Records. St. Mary's Hospital. Roswell, New Mexico.

Grace Boellner, Roswell, New Mexico, to Margaret Forsyth Woofter, Albia, Iowa.

"Roy Woofter As I Knew Him," by Roswell City Clerk George M. Williams.

Wayne Whitehill and Riley George to Lou Blachly, *Pioneer Foundation Interviews*, University of New Mexico, Zimmerman Library—Center for Southwest Research. Albuquerque, New Mexico.

Henry Brock and John Cox to Lou Blachly, *Southwest Oral Histories*, Southwest Archives. Western New Mexico University Museum. Silver City, New Mexico.

Jack Stockbridge to Lou Blachly, Terry Humble Collection, Bayard, New Mexico.

Marvin Powe to Lou Blachly, Terry Humble Collection, Bayard, New Mexico.

"Tom Ross: Outlaw and Stockman," *Master of Arts Thesis*, James I. Fenton. 1979. University of Texas at El Paso, El Paso, Texas.

"The History of Silver City, New Mexico," *Master of Arts Thesis*, Conrad Keeler Naegle. 1943. University of New Mexico. Albuquerque, New Mexico.

Collection Summary of the Harry Warren Papers, 1885-1932. Sul Ross University, Archives of the Big Bend, Bryan Wildenthal Memorial Library. Alpine, Texas.

CORRESPONDENCE AND INTERVIEWS:

Rita Ackerman. Phoenix, Arizona.

Jim Baum. Colorado City, Texas.

Melleta Bell, Bryan Wildenthal Memorial Library, Sul Ross University, Alpine, Texas.

Kenneth Bennett. Gail, Texas.

Pat Bennett. Glendale, Arizona.

Susan Berry, Director, Silver City Museum. Silver City, New Mexico.

Dean Bohannon, Texas & Southwest Cattle Raisers Association. Lubbock, Texas.

Henry Foote Boykin, Jr. Mansfield, Texas.

Jim Bradshaw, The Haley Memorial Library & History Center. Midland, Texas.

Donaly Brice, Texas State Library and Archives. Austin, Texas.

Nancy Brown, University of New Mexico, Center for Southwest Research. Albuquerque, New Mexico.

Don Bullis, Rio Rancho, New Mexico.

Tami Cantu, Wilson County Library. Floresville, Texas.

Maxine Chance, Culberson County Historical Commission. Van Horn, Texas.

LaDorna Chenowth. McNeal, Arizona.

Ellen Cline. Lake Isabella, California.

Gaylan Corbin, Archives of the Big Bend, Sul Ross University. Alpine, Texas.

Deborah Countess, San Antonio Public Library. San Antonio, Texas.

Pete Crum, Silver City Public Library. Silver City, New Mexico.

Robert K. DeArment. Sylvania, Ohio.

Jan Devereaux. Waxahachie, Texas.

Harold L. Edwards. Bakersfield, California.

Peggy Fox, Harold B. Simpson History Complex, Confederate Research Center. Hillsboro, Texas.

Button Garlick. Van Horn, Texas.

Marvin Garlick. Gazell, California.

Larry Gray, Texas & Southwestern Cattle Raisers Association. Fort Worth, Texas.

Milton Gustafson, National Archives. College Park, Maryland.

Daphne Hamilton. El Paso, Texas.

Lawmen, Outlaws and S.O.Bs.

Sarah Hindman. Albia, Iowa.
Todd Houck. Midland, Texas.
Terry Humble. Bayard, New Mexico.
Dave Johnson. Zionville, Indiana.
Ingrid Karklins, University Archivist, St. Edward's University. Austin, Texas.
Tommie Kimsie. El Paso, Texas
Louise P. Ledoux, Crockett County Library. Ozona, Texas.
Ellis Lindsey. Waco, Texas
Bill Love. Sierra Blanca, Texas.
Richard Love. El Paso, Texas.
Richard Lucero, Roswell Police Department. Roswell, New Mexico.
Felicia Lujan, New Mexico State Records Center & Archives. Santa Fe, New Mexico.
Dennis McCown. Austin, Texas.
Robert G. McCubbin. Santa Fe, New Mexico.
J. P. "Pat" McDaniel, The Haley Memorial Library & History Center. Midland, Texas.
Nancy McKinley, Midland County Historical Museum. Midland, Texas.
Clayton McKinney. Midland, Texas.
Paula Mitchell Marks. Austin, Texas.
Carol Marlin. Albia, Iowa.
Sibel Melik, Archivist, New Mexico State Records Center and Archives. Santa Fe.
Leon Metz. El Paso, Texas.
Kevin Mulkins. Tucson, Arizona.
Linda Briscoe Myers, University of Texas, Harry Ransom Humanities Research
   Center. Austin, Texas.
Scott Nelson. St. Paul, Minnesota.
Valerie Nye, New Mexico State Records Center & Archives. Santa Fe, New Mexico.
Linda Offney, Yuma Territorial Prison State Park. Yuma, Arizona.
Gary Painter, Sheriff Midland County. Midland, Texas.
Aline Parks. Snyder, Texas.
Chuck Parsons. Luling, Texas.
Michael Pilgrim, National Archives. Washington, D. C.
Art Roman, Deming Luna Mimbres Museum. Deming, New Mexico.
Grady Russell. Incrlick, Turkey.
Judy Shofner, Texas Ranger Hall of Fame and Museum. Waco, Texas.
Roy B. Sinclair, Jr. El Paso, Texas.
Jake Sitters. Castroville, Texas.
Dick Staley, El Paso Public Library. El Paso, Texas.
Robert W. Stephens. Dallas, Texas.
Cookie Stolpe, Miller Library, Western New Mexico University. Silver City, New
   Mexico.
Christina Stopka, Texas Ranger Hall of Fame and Museum. Waco, Texas.
John D. Tanner, Jr. Fallbrook, California.
Janis Test, Abilene Public Library. Abilene, Texas.
Mart Tidwell. Sierra Blanca, Texas.
Robert Stuckey, Culberson County Historical Museum. Van Horn, Texas.
Susan Wagner, *The Cattleman*. Fort Worth, Texas.
Tommy Williams, Sheriff, Atascosa County, Jourdanton, Texas.
Charles L. Wright, U.S. Customs. Presidio, Texas.
Mary Beth Wright, Roswell Public Library. Roswell, New Mexico.

BOOKS:

Adams, Clarence S. & Joan N., *Riders of the Pecos and The Seven Rivers Outlaws*. Old-
   time Publications. Roswell. 1990.
Adams, Ramon F., *Six-Guns and Saddle Leather*. Dover Publications, Inc. Mineola, New
   York. 1998.

Bibliography

Ailman, H. B., (Lundwall, Helen, editor) *Pioneering in Territorial Silver City*. University of New Mexico Press. Albuquerque. 1983.

Alexander, Bob, *Dangerous Dan Tucker, New Mexico's Deadly Lawman*. High-Lonesome Books. Silver City. 2001.

_____, *Fearless Dave Allison, Border Lawman*. High-Lonesome Books. Silver City. 2003.

_____, *Sacrificed Sheriff, John H. Behan*. High-Lonesome Books. Silver City. 2002.

Awbrey, Betty Dooley, *Why Stop?—A Guide To Texas Historical Roadside Markers*. Lone Star Books. Houston. 1999.

Bailey, Lynn R., & Chaput, Don, *Cochise County Stalwarts*. Two Volumes. Westernlore Press. Tucson. 2000.

Ball, Larry D., *Desert Lawmen, The High Sheriffs of New Mexico and Arizona, 1846-1912*. University of New Mexico Press. Albuquerque. 1992.

_____, *The United States Marshals of New Mexico & Arizona Territories 1846-1912*. University of New Mexico Press. Albuquerque. 1978.

Berry, Susan & Russell, Sharman A., *Built to Last, An Architectural History of Silver City New Mexico*. Silver City Museum Society. Silver City. 1995.

Biggers, Don Hampton, *Buffalo Guns & Barbed Wire, Two Frontier Accounts by Don Hampton Biggers*. Texas Tech University Press. Lubbock. 1991.

Blumenson, Martin, *The Patton Papers, 1885-1940*. Da Capo Press. New York. 1998.

Bolling, Robert S., *Death Rides the River, Tales of the El Paso Road*. By author. 1993.

Bonney, Cecil, *Looking Over My Shoulder, Seventy-five Years in the Pecos Valley*. Hall-Poorbaugh Press, Inc. Roswell. 1971.

Broaddus, J. Morgan, *The Legal Heritage of El Paso*. Texas Western College Press. El Paso. 1963.

Browning, James A., *Violence Was No Stranger*. Barbed Wire Press. Stillwater. 1993.

Bruce, Leona, *Banister Was There*. Branch-Smith, Inc. Fort Worth. 1968.

Bryan, Howard, *Robbers, Rogues and Ruffians*. Clear Light Publishers. Santa Fe. 1991.

Bullis, Don, *New Mexico's Finest: Peace Officers Killed In The Line Of Duty, 1847-1999*. New Mexico Department of Public Safety. Santa Fe. 2000.

Burton, Jeff, *Dynamite And Six-Shooter*. Palomino Press. Santa Fe. 1970.

Cano, Tony & Sochat, Ann, *Bandido, The True Story of Chico Cano, the Last Western Bandit*. Reata Publishing Company. Canutillo, Texas. 1997.

Caperton, Thomas J. & Cohrs, Timothy. *Fort Selden*. Museum of New Mexico Press. Santa Fe. 1993.

Casey, Robert J., *The Texas Border And Some Borderliners*. The Bobbs-Merrill Company, Inc. New York. 1950.

Chaput, Don & Baily, Lynn R. *Cochise County Stalwarts*. Two Volumes. Westernlore Press. Tucson. 2000.

Chesley, Hervey E. *Trails Traveled—Tales Told*. Nita Stewart Haley Memorial Library. Midland. 1979.

Clarke, Mary Whatley, *John Chisum, Jinglebob King of the Pecos*. Eakin Press. Austin. 1984.

_____, *A Century Of Cow Business—The First Hundred Years Of The Texas And Southwestern Cattle Raisers Association*. Cattle Raisers Association. Fort Worth. 1976.

Cohrs, Timothy & Caperton, Thomas J., *Fort Selden*. Museum of New Mexico Press. Santa Fe. 1993.

Cox, Mike, *Texas Ranger Tales—Stories That Need Telling*. Republic of Texas Press. Plano, Texas. 1997.

Cramer, T. Dudley, *The Pecos Ranchers in the Lincoln County War*. Branding Iron Press. Oakland. 1996.

Curry, George, *George Curry 1861-1947, An Autobiography*. University of New Mexico Press. Albuquerque. 1958.

Davis, Ellis A. & Grobe, Edwin H., *The New Encyclopedia of Texas*. Texas Development Bureau. Dallas, Texas. n. d.

Davis, John L., *The Texas Rangers: Their First 150 Years*. The University of Texas at San Antonio, Institute of Texan Cultures. San Antonio. 1975.

Lawmen, Outlaws and S.O.Bs.

DeArment, Robert K., *George Scarborough, The Life and Death Of A Lawman On The Closing Frontier.* University of Oklahoma Press. Norman. 1992.

_____, *Knights of the Green Cloth—The Saga of Frontier Gamblers.* University of Oklahoma Press. Norman 1982.

_____, *Alias Frank Canton*, University of Oklahoma Press. Norman. 1996.

Dillion, Richard, *Wells, Fargo Detective—A Biography of James B. Hume.* University of Nevada Press. Reno. 1986.

Edwards, Harold L., *Goodbye Billy The Kid.* Creative Publishing. College Station. 1995.

Fallwell, Gene. *The Texas Rangers.* Highlands Historical Press, Inc. Granbury, Texas. 1959.

French, William, *Recollections of a Western Ranchman.* High-Lonesome Books. Silver City. 1990.

Frost, H. Gordon and Jenkins, John H., *"I'm Frank Hamer"—The Life of a Texas Peace Officer.* Pemberton Press. Austin. 1968.

Fulton, Maurcie G., *History of the Lincoln County War.* University of Arizona Press. Tucson. 1968.

Gard, Wayne, *Cattle Brands of Texas.* First National Bank of Dallas. Dallas. n. d.

Garrett, Pat, (Nolan, Frederick, editor) *The Authentic Life of Billy The Kid.* University of Oklahoma. Norman. 2000.

Gilbreath, West, *Death On The Gallows, The Story of Legal Hangings in New Mexico, 1847-1923.* High-Lonesome Books. Silver City 2002.

Gillett, James B., *Six Years With The Texas Rangers.* University of Nebraska. Lincoln. 1976.

Gilliland, Maude T., *Wilson County Texas Rangers, 1837-1977.* By author. Plesanton, Texas. 1977.

_____, *Horsebackers Of The Brush Country, A Story Of The Texas Rangers And Mexican Liquor Smugglers.* By Author. Pleasanton, Texas. 1968.

Gournay, Luke, *Texas Boundaries—Evolution of the State's Counties.* Texas A & M University Press. College Station. 1995.

Harman, S. W., *Hell On The Border, He Hanged Eighty-Eight Men.* University of Nebraska Press. Lincoln. 1992.

Harkey, Dee, *Mean as Hell—The Life Of A New Mexico Lawman.* Ancient City Press. Santa Fe. 1989.

Harvick, Mary L. Dwyer & Graham, Ann (contributors), *A History of Crockett County.* Anchor Publishing Co. San Angelo, Texas 1976.

Hatley, Allen G., *Bringing The Law To Texas.* Centex Press. LaGrange, Texas. 2002.

_____, *Texas Constables, A Frontier Heritage.* Texas Tech University Press. Lubbock. 1999.

Hayes, Alden. *A Portal To Paradise.* University of Arizona Press. Tucson. 1999.

Haynes, David, *Catching Shadows—A Directory of 19th Century Texas Photographers.* Texas State Historical Association. Austin. 1993.

Hertzog, Peter, *Outlaws of New Mexico.* Sunstone Press. Santa Fe. 1984.

Hewett, Janet B. (editor), *Supplement to the Official Records of the Union and Confederate Armies. Part II, Record of Events.* Volume 68. Broadfoot Publishing Company, Wilmington, North Carolina. 1998.

_____, (editor) *Texas Confederate Soldiers, 1861-1865.* Broadfoot Publishing Company, Wilmington, North Carolina. 1997.

Hilliard, George. *A Hundred Years Of Horse Tracks—The Story of the Gray Ranch.* High-Lonesome Books. Silver City. 1996.

Holden, William Curry, *Alkali Trails.* Texas Tech University Press. Lubbock. 1998.

Hoover, H.A., *Tales From The Bloated Goat, Early Days in Mogollon.* High-Lonesome Books. Silver City 1995.

Hunter, J. Marvin., *The Story of Lottie Deno, Her Life and Times.* The Four Hunters. Bandera, Texas. 1959.

Ingmire, Frances T., *Texas Ranger Service Records, 1847-1900.* Six Volumes. 1982. Ingmire Publications. St. Louis.

Bibliography

Jacobson, Lucy Miller and Nored, Mildred Bloys. *Jeff Davis County, Texas*. Fort Davis Historical Society. 1993.

Jenkins, John H., and Frost, H. Gordon, *"I'm Frank Hamer"—The Life of a Texas Peace Officer*. Pemberton Press. Austin. 1968.

Johnson, Frank., *A History of Texas and Texans*. The American History Society. New York. 1916.

Julyan, Robert, *The Place Names of New Mexico*. University of New Mexico Press. Albuquerque. 1998.

Justice, Glenn, *Little Known History of the Texas Big Bend*. Rimrock Press. Odessa, Texas. 2001.

Keil, Robert, *Bosque Bonito—Violent Times Along the Borderland During the Mexican Revolution*. Center For Big Bend Studies. Sul Ross University. Alpine, Texas. 2002.

Keleher, William A., *The Fabulous Frontier, Twelve New Mexico Items*. The Rydal Press. Santa Fe. 1945.

Klasner, Lily, *My Girlhood Among Outlaws*. University of Arizona Press. Tucson. 1988.

Larson, Carol, *Forgotten Frontier—The Story of Southeast New Mexico*. University of New Mexico Press. Albuquerque. 1993.

Lindsey, Ellis, & Riggs, Gene, *Barney K. Riggs—The Yuma And Pecos Avenger*. Xlibris Corp. 2002.

Little, Marianne E. Hall & Parsons, Chuck, *Captain L. H. McNelly, Texas Ranger—The Life And Times Of A Fighting Man*. State House Press. Austin. 2001.

McDaniel, Rule, *Vinegarroon—The Saga of Judge Roy Bean, "Law West Of The Pecos."* Southerners Publishers. Kingsport, Tenn. 1936.

McCright, Grady E. & Powell, James H., *Jessie Evans: Lincoln County Badman*. Creative Publishing. College Station. 1983.

McFarland, Elizabeth Fleming, *Wilderness of the Gila*. The University of New Mexico Press. Albuquerque. 1974.

Madison, Virginia. *The Big Bend Country of Texas*. October House, Inc. New York. 1955.

Marohn, Richard C., *The Last Gunfighter, John Wesley Hardin*. Creative Publishing. College Station. 1995.

Martin, Charles, *A Sketch of Sam Bass The Bandit*. University of Oklahoma Press. Norman. 1997.

Martin, Jack, *Border Boss, Captain John R. Hughes—Texas Ranger*. State House Press. Austin. 1990.

Means, Joyce E., *Pancho Villa Days at Pilares*. By author. Tucson. 1994.

Meed, Douglas V., *Bloody Border: Riots, Battles and Adventures Along the Turbulent U.S.—Mexican Borderlands*. Westernlore Press. Tucson. 1992.

Metz, Leon, *John Wesley Hardin, Dark Angel of Texas*. Mangan Books. El Paso. 1996.

_____, *The Encyclopedia of Lawmen, Outlaws, And Gunfighters*. Facts On File, Inc. New York. 2003.

_____, *Border, The U.S.-Mexican Line*. Mangan Books. El Paso. 1989.

_____, *Turning Points In El Paso Texas*. Mangen Books. El Paso. 1985.

Meyer, Irma M., *Cemeteries of Wilson County, Texas*. By author. Floresville, Texas. n. d.

Meyer, Michael C., *Mexican Rebel: Pascual Orozco and the Mexican Revolution, 1910-1915*. University of Nebraska Press. Lincoln. 1967.

Miller, Rick, *Sam Bass & Gang*. State House Press. Austin. 1999.

Morris, John Miller, *El Llano Estacado*. Texas State Historical Association. Austin. 1997.

Mullane, William H., *This is Silver City New Mexico, Volume III, 1888-1889-1890*. Silver City Enterprise. Silver City. 1965.

Murrah, David J., *C.C. Slaughter, Rancher, Banker, Baptist*. University of Texas Press. Austin. 1981.

Murray, John A., *The Gila Wilderness*. University of New Mexico Press. Albuquerque. 1988.

Nash, Jay Robert, *Encyclopedia of Western Lawmen & Outlaws*. Da Capo Press. New York. 1994.

National Cyclopedia of American Biography. James T. White and Company. New York. 1921.

Lawmen, Outlaws and S.O.Bs.

Nelson, Susan. *Silver City—Book One—Wild and Woolly Days.* Silver Star Publications. Silver City. 1978.

New Handbook of Texas. Six Volumes. Texas State Historical Association. Austin. 1996.

Nolan, Frederick, *The Lincoln County War, A Documentary History.* University of Oklahoma Press. 1992.

Nordyke, Lewis, *Great Roundup—The Story of Texas and Southwestern Cowmen.* William Morrow & Company. New York. 1955.

Nored, Mildred Bloys and Jacobson, Lucy Miller. *Jeff Davis County, Texas.* Fort Davis Historical Society. 1993.

O'Neal, Bill, *The Arizona Rangers.* Eakin Press. Austin. 1987.

_____, *Encyclopedia of Western Gunfighters.* University of Oklahoma Press. Norman. 1979.

Owen, Gordon R., *The Two Alberts—Fountain and Fall.* Yucca Tree Press. Las Cruces. 1996.

Paine, Albert Bigelow, *Captain Bill McDonald—Texas Ranger.* State House Press. Austin. 1986.

Parks, Aline, (contributor) *Early Ranching in West Texas.* Complied by the Snyder, Texas Unit of the Ranching Heritage Association. Snyder, Texas. 1986.

Parsons, Chuck and Little, Marianne E. Hall. *Captain L. H. McNelly, Texas Ranger—The Life and Times* of *A Fighting Man.* State House Press. Austin. 2002.

_____, *Clay Allison—Portrait Of A Shootist.* Pioneer Book Publishers. Seagraves, Texas. 1983.

Parsons, George (Bailey, Lynn R., editor) *The Devil Has Foreclosed, The Private Journal of George Whitwell Parsons: The Concluding Arizona Years, 1882-87.* Westernlore Press. Tucson. 1997.

Patterson, Richard. *Historical Atlas of the Outlaw West.* Johnson Books. Boulder. 1985.

Perkins, Doug & Ward, Nancy, *Brave Men & Cold Steel, A History of Range Detectives and Their Peacemakers.* Texas and Southwestern Cattle Raisers Association. Fort Worth. 1984.

Price, Paxton P., *Pioneers of the Mesilla Valley.* Yucca Tress Press. Las Cruces. 1995.

Raht, Carlysle Graham, *The Romance Of Davis Mountains And Big Bend Country.* The Rathbooks Company. Odessa. 1963.

Rasch, Philip J. (DeArment, Robert K., editor) *Warriors of Lincoln County.* National Association For Outlaw And Lawman History, Inc. Stillwater, Oklahoma 1998.

_____, (DeArment, Robert K., editor) *Gunsmoke in Lincoln County.* National Association For Outlaw And Lawman History, Inc. Stillwater, Oklahoma. 1997.

Riggs, Gene, and Lindsey, Ellis, *Barney K. Riggs—The Yuma And Pecos Avenger.* Xlibris Corp. 2002.

Robinson, III., Charles M., *Frontier Forts of Texas.* Lone Star Books. Houston. 1986.

_____, *The Frontier World of Fort Griffin.* The Arthur Clark Company. Spokane. 1992.

Rosa, Joseph, *The Gunfighter—Man or Myth?* University of Oklahoma Press. Norman. 1969.

Russell, Sharman Apt & Berry Susan. *Built to Last, An Architectural History of Silver City New Mexico.* Silver City Museum Society. Silver City. 1995.

Rye, Edgar, *The Quirt and the Spur.* Texas Tech University Press. Lubbock. 2000.

Sherman, James E. & Barbara H., *Ghost Towns and Mining Camps of New Mexico.* University of Oklahoma Press. Norman. 1975.

Shipman, Mrs. O. L., *Taming the Big Bend: A History of the Extreme Western Portion of Texas from Fort Clark to El Paso.* Privately printed. Marfa, Texas. 1926.

Shirley, Glenn, *Marauders of the Indian Nations—The Bill Cook Gang and Cherokee Bill.* Barbed-Wire Press. Stillwater. 1994.

Sifakis, Stewart, *Compendium of the Confederate Armies—Texas.* Facts on File, New York.

Skiles, Jack, *Judge Roy Bean Country.* Texas Tech University Press. Lubbock. 1996.

Smithers, W.D., *Chronicles of the Big Bend.* Texas State Historical Association. Austin. 1999.

Bibliography

Sochat, Ann, & Cano, Tony, *Bandido—The True Story of Chico Cano, the Last Western Bandit*. Reata Publishing Company. Canutillo, Texas. 1997.
Sonnichsen, C.L., *Roy Bean, Law West Of The Pecos*. The Devin-Adair Company. New York. 1958.
_____, *The El Paso Salt War*. Texas Western Press. El Paso. 1961.
Sowell, J. J., *Life of "Big Foot" Wallace*. State House Press. Austin. 1989.
Spellman, Paul N., *Captain John H. Rogers, Texas Ranger*. University of North Texas Press. Denton. 2003.
Stadler, Louise. *Wilson County History*. Taylor Publish Company. Dallas. 1990.
Stephens, Robert W., *Texas Ranger Sketches*. Privately Printed. Dallas. 1972.
_____, *Walter Durbin, Texas Ranger and Sheriff*. Clarendon Press. Clarendon, Texas. 1970.
_____, *Bullets And Buckshot In Texas*. By Author. Dallas. 2002.
Sullivan, W.J. L., *Twelve Years In The Saddle For Law And Order on the Frontiers of Texas*. University of Nebraska Press. Lincoln. 2001.
Sweeney, Edwin R., *Mangas Coloradas, Chief of the Chiricahua Apaches*. University of Oklahoma Press. Norman. 1998.
Tanner, Karen & John D., Jr., *Last Of The Old-Time Outlaws, The George West Musgrave Story*. University of Oklahoma Press. Norman. 2002.
Thompson, Cecilia, *History of Marfa and Presidio County, Texas, 1535-1946*. Nortex Press. Austin. 1985.
Thompson, Jerry, *A Wild and Vivid Land, An Illustrated History of the South Texas Border*. Texas State Historical Association. Austin. 1997.
Thrapp, Dan., *Encyclopedia of Frontier Biography*. Three Volumes. University of Nebraska Press. Lincoln. 1988.
_____, *Victorio and the Mimbres Apaches*. University of Oklahoma Press. Norman. 1974.
_____, *The Conquest of Apacheria*. University of Oklahoma Press. Norman. 1967.
Tise, Sammy, *Texas County Sheriffs*. Tise Genealogical Research. Hallettsville, Texas. 1989.
Tyler, Ronnie C., *The Big Bend, A History of the Last Texas Frontier*. National Park Service. Washington, D. C. 1975.
Ungnade, Herbert E., *Guide to the New Mexico Mountains*. University of New Mexico Press. Albuquerque. 1972.
Utley, Robert M., *Lone Star Justice*. Oxford University Press. New York. 2002.
Ward, Nancy, & Perkins, Dave, *Brave Men and Cold Steel—A History of Range Detectives and Their Peacemakers*. Texas and Southwestern Cattle Raisers Association. Fort Worth. 1984.
Webb, Walter Prescott, *The Texas Rangers, A Century of Frontier Defense*. University of Texas Press. Austin. 1935.
Wedin, AnneJo P., *The Magnificent Marathon Basin—A History of Marathon, Texas, Its People and Events*. Nortex Press. Austin. 1989.
Wharton, Clarence R., *Texas Under Many Flags*. The American Historical Society, Inc. New York. 1930.
Wilkins, Frederick, *The Law Comes To Texas*. State House Press. 1999. Austin.
Williams, Clayton W., *Texas' Last Frontier, Fort Stockton and the Trans-Pecos, 1861-1895*. Texas A & M University Press. College Station. 1982.
Wylie, Rosa Lee, *History of Van Horn and Culberson County*. Culberson County Historical Survey Committee. Van Horn, Texas. 1973.
Young, Roy B., *Cochise County Cowboy War, "A Cast of Characters"*. Young & Sons Enterprises. Apache, Oklahoma. 1999.

JOURNALS AND PERIODICALS:

Aleshire, Peter, "Tumultuous Chiricahuas," *Arizona Highways*. November 2002.
Alexander, Bob, "Hell Paso," National Association For Outlaw And Lawman History, Inc., *Quarterly* (NOLA). XXVI. No. 2. (April-June 2002)

Lawmen, Outlaws and S.O.Bs.

_____, "an outlaw tripped up by Love," NOLA *Quarterly*. XXVI, No. 3. (July-September 2002)

_____, "and we say, well done Dan," NOLA *Quarterly*. XXVII, No. 1. (January-March 2003)

Ball, Eve, "Headwaters of the Gila," *True West*. August 1978.

Ball, Larry D., "Lawman in Disgrace: Sheriff Charles C. Perry of Chaves County New Mexico," *New Mexico Historical Review*. 61: 2 (April 1986).

_____, "Militia Posses: The Territorial Militia In Civil Law Enforcement in New Mexico Territory, 1877-1883," *New Mexico Historical Review*. 55:1 (1980)

Beverly, Bob, "Who Remembers Charlie Small?," *Frontier Times*. February 1945.

Brand, Peter, "Sherman W. McMaster(s), The El Paso Salt War, Texas Rangers & Tombstone," Western Outlaw-Lawman History Association, (WOLA) *Journal*. (Winter 1999)

Caldwell, George A., "New Mexico's First Train Robbery," NOLA *Quarterly*. Vol. XIII. No. 3. Winter (1989).

Chandler, Robert J., "Wells Fargo: We Never Forget!," NOLA *Quarterly*. Vol. XI. No. 4. (Spring 1987)

Christiansen, Paige W., "Pascual Orozco: Chihuahua Rebel—Episodes in the Mexican Revolution, 1910-1915." *New Mexico Historical Review*, XXVI. (April, 1961).

Cline, Don, "Secret Life of Billy the Kid," *True West*. April 1984.

_____, "Kit Joy—the One-Legged—Half Blind—Toothless Outlaw," NOLA *Quarterly*, Vol. XXVI. No. 2. (April-June 2002)

Cline, Ellen, "Howard Chenowth—The Story of a Cowboy," *Cochise County Historical Journal*. Fall/Winter 1997/1998.

Cool, Paul, "El Paso's Real Lawman, Texas Ranger, Mark Ludwick," NOLA *Quarterly*, Vol. XXV. No. 3. (July-September 2001)

_____, "Salt War Sheriff: El Paso's Charles Kerber," NOLA *Quarterly*, Vol. XXVII. No. 1. (January-March 2003).

_____, "Bob Martin: A Rustler in Paradise," WOLA *Journal*, Vol. XI, No. 4. (Winter 2003)

Cramer, T. Dudley, "The Killing of George Scarborough," The Haley Library *Newsletter*. Summer. 2000.

Cunningham, Eugene. "Bass Outlaw—The Little Wolf," *Old West*. Fall 1965.

Davis, Chick & Ritter, Al, "Captain Monroe Fox and the Incident at Pourvenir," *Oklahoma State Trooper*. Winter 1996.

DeArment, Robert K., "The Long Arm of the Law," *True West*. January 2002.

_____, "Deadly Deputy," *True West*. November 1991.

_____, "Sheriff Whitehill & the Kit Joy Gang," *Old West*. Winter 1994.

_____, "True West Legends: George A Scarborough," *True West*. June 1999.

_____, "The Outlaws of Clifton, Arizona Territory," NOLA *Quarterly*. Vol. XXVII, No. 1. (January-March 2003.)

DeMattos, Jack, "John Kinney," *Real West*. February 1984.

Devereaux, Jan, "Gentle Woman, Tough Medicine," NOLA *Quarterly*. XXVIII, No. 2 (April-June 2003)

Edwards, Harold L., "The Shooting of Bronco Bill," NOLA *Quarterly*. Vol. XXI, No. 2. (April-June 1997)

_____, "Burt Alvord, The Train Robbing Constable," *Wild West*. October 2002.

_____, "Sheriff Pat Garrett's Puzzle—A Blow-by-Blow Account of Solving a New Mexico Bank Robbery," *The National Tombstone Epitaph*, Vol. CXXIV, No. 1. (January 2003)

Fernlund, Kevin J., "Senator Holm O. Bursum and the Mexican Ring, 1921-1924," *New Mexico Historical Review*. October 1991.

James I. Fenton. "Tom Ross: Ranger Nemesis," *NOLA Quarterly*. Vol. XIV, No. 2 (Summer 1990)

Fox, Dorothea Magdalene, "Marked for Death!," *Frontier Times*. March 1965.

Haley, J. Evetts. "The Cowboy Sheriff," *The Shamrock*. Summer 1963.

Harrison, Fred, "A Slight Case of Double-Cross," *Western Frontier*. May 1989.

Bibliography

Hinton, Jr., Harwood , "John Simpson Chisum, 1877-84," *New Mexico Historical Review*, Vol. XVL, No. 3. (July 1956)

Humble, Terrence M., "The Pinder-Slip Mining Claim Dispute of Santa Rita, New Mexico, 1881-1912," *Mining History Journal*. 1996.

Hunter, J. Marvin, "The Killing of Captain Frank Jones," *Frontier Times*. January 1929.

_____, "Early Day Stage Robbers," *Frontier Times*. January 1947.

_____, "George Scarborough, Peace Officer," *Frontier Times*. June 1947.

Kieffe, Glenna D., "Finis: The Final Entry," *Customs Today*. Vol. XXV, No. 4 (Fall 1990).

Majors, Frederick, "Bass Outlaw Was A Texas Riddle," *Golden West*. August 1974.

Metz, Leon, "Nobody Calls Him Henry," *The Roundup*. Vol. XXXII, No. 9 (October 1984)

_____, "Gunslingers And The Art Of Gunfighting," *Wild West*. April. 1998.

Michaels, Kevin, "Tracker," *Great West*. September 1974.

Moorman, Donald R., "Holm O. Bursum, Sheriff 1894," *New Mexico Historical Review*. No. 36. (1964)

Mullin, Robert N., "Here Lies John Kinney," *The Journal Of Arizona History*. No. 14. (Autumn 1973)

Nolan, Frederick, "The Horse Thief War," *Old West*. Summer 1994.

_____, "The Saga of the San Augustine Ranch," *True West*. June 1999.

_____, "Boss Rustler, The Life and Crimes of John Kinney," *True West*. September 1996.

O'Neal, Bill, "The Cananea Riots of 1906," *Real West*. August 1984.

Potter, Jack, "The Jingle-Bob Herd," *New Mexico Magazine*. July 1945.

Rasch, Philip J., "Bass Outlaw, Myth And Man," *Real West*, July 1979.

_____, "The Las Cruces Bank Robbery," *Frontier Times*. January 1981.

_____, "The Rustler War," *New Mexico Historical Review*. Vol. XXXIX, No. 4 (October 1964).

Ritter, Al., "Death on the Rio Grande," *Texas Department of Public Safety Officers Association Magazine*. March/April 1996.

_____, & Davis, Chick, "Captain Monroe Fox and the Incident at Pourveniar" *Oklahoma State Trooper*. Winter 1996.

Rosson, Mary'n, "The Day Bass Outlaw Tried To Drink Up The Town," *Frontier West*. December 1974.

Sinclair, John, "The Sugarloaf Mountains, The Magical Peloncillos," *New Mexico Magazine*. July 1979.

Sinclair, John L., "On the Hoof," *New Mexico Magazine*. October 1939.

Smithers, W.D., "The Long Rio Grande," *True West*. August 1963.

Spangenberger, Phil, "Pistol Packin" In The Old West," *Guns and Ammo*. Annual. 1994.

Taylor, Walter, "The Last Marshal," *True West*. April 1962.

Theisen, Lee Scott (editor), "Frank Warner Angel's Notes On New Mexico Territory, 1878," *Arizona and the West*, Vol. 18, No. 4. (Winter 1976)

Turner, Allen, "New Mexico Shoot-Out," *Frontier Times*. March 1969.

Turpin, Robert F., "Saga of the Deadly Cook Gang," *True Frontier*. November 1969.

Walker, Wayne T., "Joe Sitters: The Best Damn Tracker in Texas," *Oldtimers Wild West*. December 1978.

_____, "Bass Outlaw, Renegade Ranger," *Oldtimers Wild West*. August 1979.

Wright, Charles L., "A Western Tragedy," *Customs Today*, Vol. XXVII, No. 4. (Fall 1992)

NEWSPAPERS:

El Paso Daily Times
Mesilla News
Las Cruces Borderer
Las Cruces Thirty-Four
Mesilla Valley Independent
Silver City Enterprise
San Antonio Daily Express
Grant County Herald (New Mexico)

Lawmen, Outlaws and S.O.Bs.

Rio Grande Republican (New Mexico)
Deming Headlight
Galveston Daily News
The Daily Southwest (New Mexico)
Silver City Independent
Santa Fe New Mexican
Monroe County News (Iowa)
Austin Daily Statesman
Roswell Daily Record
Roswell Register-Tribune
Stephenville Empire-Tribune (Texas)
Alpine Advocate (Texas)
Alpine Avalanche (Texas)
Eufaula Indian Journal (Oklahoma)
San Angelo Standard-Times
Daily Oklahoman
Colorado City Record (Texas)
Oklahoma Times-Journal
El Paso Herald-Post
The New Southwest (New Mexico)
Southwest Sentinel (New Mexico)
Graham County Bulletin (Arizona)
Abilene Reporter (Texas)
Seminole Sentinel (Texas)
St. Louis Post-Dispatch
El Paso Lone Star

INDEX

303

Lawmen, Outlaws and S.O.Bs.

Index

Lawmen, Outlaws and S.O.Bs.

Index

Lawmen, Outlaws and S.O.Bs.

Index

Lawmen, Outlaws and S.O.Bs.